THE REFORMATION
OF THE HERETICS

The Waldenses of the Alps, 1480–1580

Euan Cameron

CLARENDON PRESS · OXFORD

1984

Oxford University Press, Walton Street, Oxford OX2 6DP

London Glasgow New York Toronto
Delhi Bombay Calcutta Madras Karachi
Kuala Lumpur Singapore Hong Kong Tokyo
Nairobi Dar es Salaam Cape Town
Melbourne Auckland

and associated companies in
Beirut Berlin Ibadan Mexico City Nicosia

Oxford is a trade mark of Oxford University Press

Published in the United States
by Oxford University Press, New York

British Library Cataloguing in Publication Data
Cameron, Euan
The reformation of the heretics: the Waldenses of
the Alps, 1480–1580.
1. Waldenses — History
I. Title
273'.6   BX4873
ISBN 0-19-822930-5

Library of Congress Cataloging in Publication Data
Cameron, Euan.
The reformation of the heretics.
(Oxford historical monographs)
Revision of the author's thesis (doctoral — University
of Oxford, 1981)
Bibliography: p.
Includes index.
1. Waldenses — Alps, Western, Region.   2. Waldenses —
Italy, Northern.   3. Alps, Western, Region — Church
history.   4. Italy, Northern — Church history.   I. Title.
BX4881.2.C36 1984   284'.4   83-23660
ISBN 0-19-822930-5 (Oxford University Press)

Typeset by Hope Services, Abingdon
Printed in Great Britain
at the University Press, Oxford

FOR RUTH

who helped me find Chanforan

Preface

This work is a revised version of a doctoral thesis submitted to the University of Oxford in November 1981. The Warden and Fellows of All Souls College have provided the support and many of the facilities which have helped and hastened its completion. For access to materials I am indebted especially to the libraries of Cambridge University and of Trinity College, Dublin; to the Bibliothèque Nationale, Paris; to the Archives Départmentales of the Isère at Grenoble and of the Hautes-Alpes at Gap; and above all to the Bodleian, which has facilitated consultation both of its own stock and of that of other libraries, and to the Codrington Library at All Souls.

Robin Briggs supervised the thesis, read and helpfully criticized numerous inadequate drafts both before and after submission, and steered the work towards a form which might be fit for publication. Jill Lewis and Peter Burke examined the thesis and made suggestions for improvements, which I have tried to incorporate in this version. Keith Thomas as a tutor directed the undergraduate efforts which led me ultimately to this kind of work; since that time he has given unsparingly of his advice and attention to rid this essay of many obscurities and ill-chosen thoughts and phrases with which its earlier forms were disfigured, and to help in many other ways.

I owe a different kind of debt to the many scholars both within and outside the Waldensian Church to whose writings numerous references will be found in the following pages. Although I have been forced to disagree in several ways, some trivial and some more significant, with the historians who have laid the foundations of Waldensian history, I am fully aware that this book could not have been written but for their achievements.

All Souls, April 1983   E. K. C.

Contents

Maps

Abbreviations

ADH-A	Archives départmentales des Hautes-Alpes
ADI	Archives départmentales de l'Isère
ADI A	ADI MS B 4350
ADI B	ADI MS B 4351
BCTHS	Comité des travaux historiques et scientifiques, *Bulletin historique et philologique* (after 1915 *Bulletin philologique et historique*)
Bèze, *Corresp.*	*Correspondance de Théodore de Bèze*, ed. H. Aubert and others (Genève, 1960–)
BN	Bibliothèque Nationale, Paris
BP	BN MS Latin 3375
BSBS	*Bollettino storico-bibliografico subalpino*
BSEHA	*Bulletin de la société d'études . . . des Hautes-Alpes*
BSHPF	*Bulletin de la société d'histoire du protestantisme français*
BSHV/BSSV	*Bulletin de la société d'histoire vaudoise* (1884–1933) *Bollettino della società di storia valdese* (1934–5) *Bollettino della società di studi valdesi* (1936–)
BSSS	Regia deputazione subalpina di storia patria, *Bollettino della società di storia subalpina*
BV	*Bibliografia Valdese*, ed. G. Gonnet and A. Armand Hugon (Torre Pèllice, 1953)
Chevalier	J. A. Chevalier, *Mémoire historique sur les hérésies en Dauphiné avant le xvie siècle* (Valence, 1890)
CO	*Joannis Calvini Opera quae supersunt omnia,* ed. G. Baum, E. Cunitz, and E. Reuss (Corpus Reformatorum, vols. 29–87), Braunschweig, Berlin, 1853–1900
Crespin	*Actes des martyrs*, later *Histoire des martyrs*, (*s. l.*, numerous editions, 1554-1619). The edition used is cited with each reference.
Crespin-Baduel	*Actiones et Monumenta Martyrum* (1556 and subsequently), trans. C. Baduel. The edition of 1560 will be used for references.
CUL	Cambridge University Library
CUL G	CUL MS Dd. 3. 25
CUL H	CUL MS Dd. 3. 26

Fazy
: *Le Livre-Journal tenu par Fazy de Rame en langage embrunais (6 juin 1471 - 10 juillet 1507)*, ed. G. de Manteyer (Gap, 1932)

Fornier
: Marcellin Fornier, *Histoire générale des Alpes maritimes ou cottiennes*, ed. J. Guillaume (Paris, 1890-2)

Gilles
: P. Gilles, *Histoire ecclésiastique des églises réformées recueillies en quelques valées de Piedmont et circonvoisins, autrefois appelées églises vaudoises* (Genève, 1644); also ed. P. Lantaret (Pinerolo, 1881). The edition used is specified.

HE
: *Histoire ecclésiastique des églises réformées au royaume de France*, sometimes attributed to Théodore de Bèze ('Anvers', 1580)

Herminjard
: *Correspondance des réformateurs dans les pays de la langue Française*, ed. A.-L. Herminjard (Genève, Paris, 1866-97)

LHG
: *Le Livre des habitants de Genève*, ed. P. F. Geisendorf, vol. I (Genève, 1957)

LRAG
: *Le Livre du recteur de l'académie de Genève*, ed. Sven and Suzanne Stelling-Michaud (Genève, 1959-66)

Lentolo
: S. Lentolo, *Historia delle grandi e crudeli persecutioni fatti ai tempi nostri . . . contro il popolo che chiamano valdese*, ed. T. Gay (Torre Pèllice, 1906)

Lentolo MS
: Oxford, Bodleian Library, MS Barlow 8

Marx
: J. Marx, *L'Inquisition en Dauphiné* (Bibliothèque de l'École des Hautes Etudes, Sciences Historiques et Philologiques, 206e fasc., Paris, 1914)

RCPG
: *Registres de la compagnie des pasteurs de Genève au temps de Calvin*, ed. R. M. Kingdon, J.-F. Bergier, O. Fatio, and O. Labarthe, vols. I-III (Genève, 1962-5)

TCD
: Trinity College, Dublin

Note on the Spelling of Proper Names

Three languages at least were current in the region covered by this study in the early modern period: French, Italian, and forms of the local *patois*, which varied slightly from area to area. Proper names of individuals and places varied according to the language in which they were spoken. Almost all the early records, however, preserve proper names in Latin versions which are different again. For personal names, an attempt has been made to use the form of name most likely to have been used by the individual concerned himself: hence 'Johan' or 'Peyre' for inhabitants of the Waldensian valleys west of the passes, but 'Jehan' or 'Pierre', 'Giovanni' or 'Pietro', for higher churchmen or aristocrats, who seem normally to have used French or Italian. Dialect forms of Embrunais proper names have been taken from Fazy de Rame's *Livre-Journal*, one of the longest surviving texts in this dialect. This policy has not been followed when historical tradition has so far established one convention that it would be pedantic to depart from it: hence 'Gilles des Gilles' rather than 'Gilio de Gilio'. Place-names are usually given in the forms used today. Exceptions have been allowed for the same reason as above, for example 'Pragelas', not 'Pragelato'.

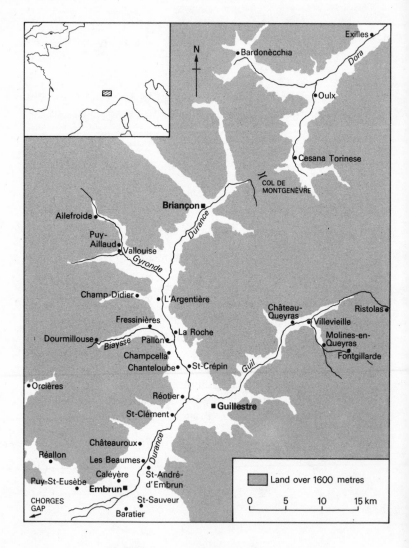

Map I. The Waldensian valleys west of the Alpine passes
(inset: the region covered by the two maps in
relation to France and Italy)

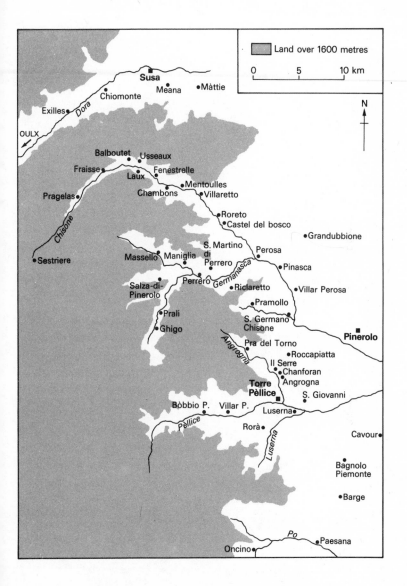

Map II. The Waldensian valleys east of the Alpine passes

Introduction

Obstinate dissent from the officially approved faith has been a common feature of most periods of Christian history. Such dissent, if raised into a system of belief (whether coherent or not) and followed as a rule of life, usually incurred the charge of heresy in the Middle Ages. That charge, once made against an uneducated believer, would ensure that the believer suffered disapproval, punishment perhaps, but above all misunderstanding. From the late twelfth century, the character of the 'Waldensian' or 'Vaudois' heresy was normally linked with the personality and image of its supposed founder, a merchant of Lyons called Waldo or Valdès. According to tradition, he was struck by a sudden anxiety for his soul's health; he immediately sold all his possessions and gave prodigally to the poor; he gathered around him a movement of pious, ascetic laymen who resisted the orders of the Church and were driven into the countryside. These 'Waldenses' taught from the Scriptures in the partial vernacular translations which they prepared; they regarded the visible Church as corrupt and its orders as invalid; they resisted or evaded all attempts to silence their puritanical and pacifist gospel. Their heresy duly spread to areas of southern France, northern Italy, and ultimately, it is claimed, to the Empire as well.

We probably can never discover whether there was any historical continuity between the followers of the pious merchant of Lyons and the 'Waldenses' of the south-western Alps whose presence was first officially noticed in the mid-fourteenth century, and those fifteenth-century descendants form the subjects of this study. Perhaps no more than a vague resemblance, or a conviction that all new dissent must necessarily follow old patterns, led the churchmen of the dioceses of Embrun and Pinerolo to stamp the epithet of 'Waldensian' on the most self-righteous and self-reliant of their mountain flocks. Although the name stuck, and was used by laymen as well as churchmen to describe these people, their behaviour in support of their 'sect' contrasted violently with the abhorrence of homicide and the monastic rigour traditionally associated with the followers of Valdès.

Two major assaults were made on the integrity and self-consciousness of the Waldensian communities of the Alps between 1480 and 1580. The first was an armed crusade, which ravaged several villages near the Alpine passes in the winter of 1487–8. The second assault was ideological rather than physical; it was the attempt made by the protestant reformers of Switzerland to bring the movement (with which protestantism was often associated in the polemics of its opponents) securely under their own organization and discipline. The records of these encounters have an important lesson to teach the social historian.

About 1500 Alberto Cattaneo, archdeacon of Cremona, reminisced about his role in the anti-Waldensian crusade of 1487–8. He remembered how his victims had been 'gifted neither with excellence of learning nor with sublimity of spirit' but had made up for their limitations in obstinacy. The Catholic army had attacked a group of heretics hidden in a cave above the valley of the Chisone; but the heretics 'protected by the nature of the place, threw huge rocks down the mountains, repulsed the Christians, killed some and wounded many, and threw them back from the crags. The fighting lasted from dawn to evening, and was most ferocious.' Only the next day, when the Catholics brought up siege-engines, did the defenders surrender. Another group of heretics, hidden in a cave under Mont Pelvoux named the Ailefroide, were only overwhelmed when soldiers climbed up beyond the entrance to the cave and let themselves down with ropes. In the assault more than ninety heretics were killed and thrown headlong from the rocks.

Perhaps some eighty years later, the protestant minister of Chiavenna (on the borders of Milan and the Swiss state of the Grisons), a Neapolitan named Scipione Lentolo, wrote a long account of the persecutions which God had inflicted on the 'Waldensian people'. Lentolo had been one of their ministers himself, and blamed their sufferings on their own sinfulness, which had caused God to punish them. In vain, he said, he had tried to persuade his flock not to rush into litigation before catholic judges. However, they insisted on doing so. What was more, they were incapable of behaving with proper protestant sobriety before their judges. 'You bawl, you shriek, you threaten', he told them, 'you carry on with calumny, lying, vindictiveness, and avarice . . . Then, though you behave in this way, you have the audacity to say that you fear God!' Worse still, some Vaudois made themselves 'fellows with the dissolute rogues amongst the catholics, and even exceed them in dissoluteness'. They raged with indignation if the ministers reproached them in public; they allowed criminals of various kinds to stay unpunished, by turning their valleys into a sanctuary for swindlers and even murderers from their own communities and from those outside.

Of the two assaults on the Waldensian identity just cited, neither the physical attack led by Cattaneo nor the spiritual hectoring administered by Lentolo was entirely successful. Both conflicts left a legacy of documents through which the tensions existing between two cultures may be observed. Formally, one would say that Cattaneo's encounter with the Waldenses was one of pure hostility, while Lentolo ran great risks to minister to them and took their side. In social terms, however, Lentolo was almost as alien to the Vaudois as Cattaneo. In both cases men from a literate background failed either to understand or to establish a rapport with the people of the mountains. The lessons of their experiences for the historian are that he should first of all be wary when using his evidence, since his sources are by definition produced by the literate; secondly, even to attempt to set a popular pattern of belief on paper involves a high risk of distortion, for the historian no less than for the inquisitor; thirdly, this barrier of incomprehension between learned churchmen and popular dissenters is a major historical fact in itself, perhaps even the key to any history of such heresy. A study which is to account for the balance of forces in the south-western Alps in this period must analyse the motives of churchmen as well as of heretics.

This case-study should have lessons for the religious history of its period as a whole. It helps to show who persecuted heretics, in what ways, and why. It shows that persecution was not seen as inevitable; if the cost to the economy and society of preserving orthodoxy was too high, then sometimes heretics might be left alone, or even restored to what they had lost. Protestantism, for its part, had much less effect on the Waldenses in the 1530s than on its second encounter with them over twenty years later. The reasons for that difference in results illustrate important features of Calvinist missionary work. The product of the protestant missions to the Alps was a distinctive rural, popular faith. That distinctiveness may be due to the survival of heretical ideas and practices in the post-Reformation period; it may also derive from the fact that the Waldenses were predominantly farmers and country people, rather than the prosperous guildsmen and bourgeois whose forms of protestantism have so far attracted most historians. If the latter is true, then the tensions in these small mountain communities may provide a paradigm for assessing the impact of the Reformation in the countryside elsewhere in Europe. This case, so exceptional in many respects, may perhaps contribute to an aspect of Reformation history which is still largely unwritten.

I An Alpine Heresy
and its Survival

1. The Background

Most of what we shall ever know about the dissident societies of heretics in the Middle Ages must be derived from the records of inquisitions. These records bring their own problems: the historian is anxious to see the heretics under normal circumstances, yet his records were made when their society was placed under great stress.[1] We must first discover how persecution was carried on, in order to understand how that process was likely to distort our evidence for Alpine society in general. This enquiry will help to explain who saw the heretics as a threat, and why; and also, since the victims of the crusade obtained a legal rehabilitation, why others saw them as much less of a threat.[2] For these social structures and stresses the physical and political geography of the Alps forms a striking and significant stage, a determining factor as well as a setting.

(i) The political and ecclesiastical geography of the Hautes-Alpes

By the fifteenth and sixteenth centuries the Waldensian heresy was rooted in a somewhat arbitrarily chosen series of valleys on either side of the mountains which separate the Dauphiné from the plain of Piedmont. These valleys are now bounded by the French *Départements* of the Hautes- and Basses-Alpes, and by the westernmost portions of the Italian Provinces of Turin and Cuneo. At other times the mountains of the region have been known by the name (now reserved for the hills just north of the Côte d'Azur) of Alpes-Maritimes, or as the Cottian Alps.

For the sake of completeness, this study will refer occasionally to groups of heretics based in the lowlands east and west

---

[1] See for instance E. Le Roy Ladurie, *Montaillou: village occitan de 1294 à 1324* (Paris, 1975); these problems of interpretation are raised rather than answered by Le Roy Ladurie's work.   [2] Marx, pp. 178–200.

of these ranges. For example, a small group of heretics was discovered in the 1490s in some villages on the western edge of the Vercors, in the diocese of Valence in the valley of the Rhône.[3] By the late fifteenth century at the latest, some groups of heretics were settled on lands just east of Avignon in the Comtat Venaissin, and on the southern edge of the Massif de Luberon in the Vaucluse.[4] Various forms of religious dissent had long since been detected in parts of the plain of Piedmont around Turin, and in the Valle di Susa.[5] The heretics in these regions will only be involved in this study when it is necessary to compare their experience with that of the Vaudois of the Alps themselves.

The 'Waldensian valleys' comprised the area described and included by a broad crescent drawn from the small archiepiscopal city of Embrun, through the frontier towns of Briançon and Oulx, down to the town of Pinerolo. These valleys were not, however, evenly and equally peopled with heretics; nor do we have sufficient evidence to allow us to discuss both sides of the Alps in equal detail throughout all stages of the story. For the fifteenth century, it is in the lands of the Dauphiné that the best records are found, both because the archbishopric of Embrun kept its records especially well, and also because an anti-heretical crusade relied upon troops provided by the Dauphiné, and so almost certainly did not attack Piedmont. For the sixteenth century, we know most about the Waldenses in the states of the Duchy of Savoy, east of the passes, because the dissenters in that region, unlike those in the Dauphiné, were not part of a protestant movement distributed over the whole province. From the Reformation on the 'Waldenses' of Piedmont were a special group, and retained their corporate name and identity.[6]

[3] N. Chorier, *Histoire générale du Dauphiné* (Valence, 1878-9), II, 494, P. Allix, *Some remarks upon the Ecclesiastical History of the Ancient Churches of Piedmont* (London, 1690), pp. 318-31; Chevalier, pp. 155-7.

[4] See below, chapter 10 (v).

[5] J. P. Perrin, *Histoire des Vaudois* (Genève, 1618 and 1619), part II, ch. 5; G. Boffito, 'Eretici in Piemonte al tempo del Gran Scisma', *Studi e Documenti di Storia e Diritto*, 18 (1897), 381-431; Marx, pp. 214-15; T. Kaeppeli, 'Un processo', *Rivista di Storia della Chiesa in Italia*, I (1947), 285-91.

[6] The point is made by G. Peyrot, 'Influenze franco-ginevrine', in *Ginevra e l'Italia* (Firenze, 1959), pp. 215-19.

This unevenness and imbalance in the evidence does not pose any insuperable problem. One of the Waldensian valleys, that of the Chisone, lay east of the passes in a part of the Dauphiné which overlapped with the diocese of Turin; one historian has already used its exceptionally continuous records.[7] Moreover, similar events happened on both sides of the Alps; there was enough commerce between Piedmont and Dauphiné and Provence to allow us to treat the region as a unity.[8]

The physical structure of the Hautes-Alpes is determined by the narrow, deep clefts in the rocks which carry streams and mountain passes. The region of the Embrunais, on the river Durance between the valley of the Gapençais and the passes at Briançon, marks the boundary between crystalline and calcareous rocks. Glaciation of the hard calcareous strata in the higher valleys deepened rather than broadened the lines of the rivers, creating valleys with precipitous edges.[9] For example, the Crête de l'Aiguille, which guards the entrance to the Val Freissinières, rises in a kilometre or so to 500 metres above the Durance; the inquisitor Cattaneo described that valley as 'closed in by the narrowest of gateways'.[10]

We do not know where the heretics came from, or if they were indigenous. In this period they occupied comparatively few valleys: west of the passes, they were found in those of the Biaysse and the Gyronde; although there were protestants in the valley of the Guil in the Queyras in the 1570s, there were apparently no Waldenses there in the fifteenth century.[11] East of the Montgenèvre, they were found in the middle of the high valley of the Chisone, and further south in the valleys of the Germanasca, the Pèllice, the Angrogna, and the Luserna. Further south still, in what is now the province of Cuneo, some heretics were found in the valleys of the Po, the Varàita,

---

[7] Bona Pazè Beda and Piercarlo Pazè, *Riforma e cattolicesimo in val pragelato 1555–1685* (Collana storica del Priorato di san Giusto in Mentoulles, 1, Pinerolo, 1975).

[8] *CUL G*, fo. 59ᵛ; also G. Audisio, 'Un aspect de relations', *BSHPF* 121 (1975), 484–515.

[9] P. and G. Veyret, *Atlas et géographie des Alpes françaises* (Genève, 1979), pp. 139 f.

[10] D. Godefroy, *Histoire de Charles VIII* (Paris, 1684), p. 282: 'perangustis clauditur faucibus'.

[11] Below, ch. 15 (iii).

and the Màira; these have generally been studied apart from the rest.[12]

For administrative and legal purposes, the valleys of the Durance and its tributaries fell under the dominion of the Dauphiné and of the *parlement* at Grenoble, the senior provincial court. The *juge-mage* of the Briançonnais, based on Briançon, was the secular judge most involved in the prosecution of heresy. His competence included not only the land west of the present-day frontier, but also the greater part of the Val Chisone, as far as a point near Casteldelbosco, just north-west of Perosa.[13] Hence the *parlement* of Grenoble was still dealing with heresy in this valley east of the Alps in the 1550s.[14]

The Piedmontese valleys fell within the Duchy of Savoy, and under the more immediate jurisdiction of the Lords of Luserna, the families of Manfredi, Rorenghi, and Bigliori.[15] However, in part of this period the Duchy of Savoy fell under French attack, and from 1536 to 1559 the power of the dukes in this region was extinguished.[16] This period of French rule, which altered the religious politics of the area, did not bring about a realignment of boundaries; the French governors created a French-style *parlement* in Turin, which acted against heresy in a similar way to its counterpart in Grenoble.[17] From 1548 to 1588, likewise, the marquisate of Saluzzo, which dominated the valleys south of the Po, fell into French hands.[18]

For church purposes the valleys of the western part of the Alps fell within the province of the archbishops of Embrun.

---

[12]   See A. Pascal, 'Margherita di Foix ed i Valdesi di Paesana', *Athenaeum*, IV (1916), 46–84, and his *Il Marchesato di Saluzzo e la riforma protestante durante il periodo della dominazione francese 1548-1588* (Firenze, 1960).

[13]   Pazè Beda, *Riforma e cattolicesimo*, pp. 11 f.

[14]   J. J. Hemardinquer, 'Les Vaudois du Dauphiné', *BSSV* 103 (1958), 53–63; P. Caffaro, *Notizie e documenti della chiesa pinerolese* (Pinerolo, 1891-1903), VI, 265–70.

[15]   See esp. P. Rivoire, 'Storia dei signori di Luserna', *BSHV* 11 (1894), 3–86; 13 (1896), 38–112; 14 (1897), 23–44; 17 (1899), 3–93, and subsequently; also A. Armand Hugon, 'Popolo e chiesa alle valli dal 1532 al 1561', *BSSV* 110 (1961), 7.

[16]   Carlo III (d. 1553) and Emanuele Filiberto (d. 1580).

[17]   L. Romier, 'Les Institutions françaises en Piémont sous Henri II', *Revue historique*, 106 (1911), 1–26.

[18]   Pascal, *Marchesato di Saluzzo*, as above; also F. Chiapusso, *Carlo Emanuele I e la sua impresa sul Marchesato di Saluzzo* (Torino, 1891).

Embrun's primacy over its province was, however, contested by the archbishopric of Vienne, which was to be significant in the litigation over the crusade.[19] East of the Alps, the inquisition in practice depended much upon support from the abbots and provosts of the Augustinian house at Oulx, and from the abbots of Pinerolo. In theory, however, inquisitorial commissions transcended conventional diocesan boundaries, and could be immense in their scope.[20]

Even in the late Middle Ages, these valleys supported quite a high level of population.[21] On 7 September 1483 the *universitas*, or body of heads of households, of Vallouise protested its ignorance of an appeal which some of its number, suspect of heresy, were pressing in the name of the whole valley. The disavowal attracted the signatures of 228 males, presumably all adults. Cited heretics in the same place numbered about 115.[22] The valley had 1,200 inhabitants in 1980, perhaps no more than in the 1480s. Cited heretics in the predominantly Vaudois village of Fressinières in 1488 numbered about 310, as against 200 inhabitants in 1980.[23]

The vast majority of the people of these valleys lived by agriculture, even those who might sustain some other calling, such as that of notary or innkeeper. Of seventeen witnesses whose occupations are supplied in a *procès-verbal* taken by Bishop Laurent Bureau in 1501 in the valleys of the Durance, four were priests (mostly from the episcopal manor of Champcella), two were described as 'farrier' or 'innkeeper', one was the lieutenant of Vallouise, one a notary, and all the rest were called 'labourers', which in this context clearly meant workers on the land.[24]

Agriculture could be fairly mixed. Cereals are now grown at up to 800 metres with ease; delays in growing crops make them impractical above 1,300 metres. We know that some heretics at least grew them.[25] Sheep were pastured on the

---

[19] Marx, p. 153.

[20] Fornier, II, 326; Marx, pp. 264-5; P. Guillaume, 'Notes et documents', *BCTHS* Ann. 1913 (1914), 424 f.

[21] Veyret, *Atlas et géographie*, p. 168.

[22] *CUL G*, fos. 78^r-9^v; *ADI B*, fos. 43^v-4^v.

[23] *ADI B*, fos. 50^r-6^v; modern population statistics are based on maps issued by the Institut Géographique National, Paris.   [24] *BP*, II, fos. 46^r-104^v.

[25] Veyret, *Atlas et géographie*, pp. 169 f.; *CUL H*, sect. 2, fo. 8^r; *Fazy, passim*.

higher lands.[26] Vines may be grown at up to 1,000 metres in good positions, and are now grown near Chanteloube, on the banks of the Durance. Some vineyards seized from heretics by the archbishop of Embrun were already a matter of contention by 1500.[27] One Jame Pascal kept an inn at Dourmillouse, the highest point in the Val Freissinières, at which travellers over the pass called to drink his wines.[28] In the summer, the inhabitants of the valleys would also seek to supplement their incomes by working in the plains.[29]

(ii) The social structures

The physical characteristics of the Alps obviously made them more difficult to rule than the plains. Likewise the traditional organization of the communities fostered a spirit of resistance to interference. By the late Middle Ages the burden of feudalism on the peasantry was much lighter than elsewhere in Europe. In the early fourteenth century those still under feudal lords were not very gravely restricted by the customs governing marriage outside the fief, nor by limits on inheritance; the main arbitrary tax, the *taille*, was levied on real property. Labour dues were much less than elsewhere.[30] Moreover, by no means all land was held by seigneurs: perhaps as little as a quarter, according to some estimates.[31] In contrast, a great deal of land was held as allodial property. Unless a seigneur could prove his title, land was legally presumed to be allodial.[32] Allods could also be created anew

[26] *CUL G*, fo. 111[r].

[27] Veyret, *Atlas et géographie*, p. 169; TCD MS 266, fo. 125[r-v].

[28] *CUL G*, fo. 116[r].

[29] Pazè Beda, *Riforma e cattolicesimo*, pp. 19–20 and n. 26, Veyret, *Atlas et géographie*, p. 171; the governor of the Piedmontese valleys, Sebastiano Castrocaro, reported in a letter of 30 June 1573 that it was impossible to do any business with the population, as they were mostly away in the plains and would not return until the end of August. See A. Pascal, 'Le lettere del governatore delle valli Sebastiano Graziolo Castrocaro', *BSHV* 26 (1909), 27.

[30] P. Vaillant, *Les Libertés des communautés dauphinoises (des origines au 5 janvier 1355)* (Paris, 1951), pp. 228–36.

[31] Veyret, *Atlas et géographie*, pp. 168 f.

[32] H. Pécout, *Études sur le droit privé des hautes vallées alpines de Provence et de Dauphiné au moyen âge* (Paris, 1907), pp. 79–84; G. Chianéa, *La Condition juridique des terres en Dauphiné au 18e siècle* (Paris, 1969), pp. 291 f.

by prescription; and within the allod, such dues or watch-service as might be imposed by the Dauphin would only constitute a moderate burden.[33]

These discrepant circumstances, which were not to cease until the Revolution, may perhaps have derived from the isolation and geography of the Alps, which made the military pressures for feudal subordination less acute. By the end of the Middle Ages allodialists had been joined by farmers as a free peasant class. Emphyteusis, or farming tenure, had particular advantages for the exploitation of marginal lands, and it was remarked on in the sixteenth century that the Waldenses of Provence developed their lands that way.[34] The *coseigneur* of Fressinières, Pallon, and Réallon, Fazy de Rame, regularly let out his *domaine* on short-term leases to improve the estate; by the late fifteenth century all the feudal dues on his estates had been commuted into an annual payment of 210 *setiers* of wheat, leaving only a tallage of $112\frac{1}{2}$ *livres* per annum owed in money.[35]

Not only were the individual inhabitants less oppressed; they also combined together to secure privileges for the communities as a whole. In the course of the fourteenth century charters of enfranchisement were gained by the communities of the Briançonnais from the Dauphin, and to some extent by those of the Embrunais from their arch-bishops.[36] These charters might provide for the communities to apportion their own charges and dues; they might also set out a form of self-government. Communities would be governed by consuls, who could be either designated by the *baile* (agent and rent-collector) of the seigneur or chosen by election; these could be assisted by syndics and *conseillers*, who would theoretically have shorter terms of office for specific purposes. Not all communities had consuls; on the other hand, there is evidence that the office of syndic grew

[33] Pécout, *Études*, pp. 86 f.; Chianéa, *Condition juridique*, pp. 294 f., 327 f. Compare twelfth-century Languedoc, as in R. I. Moore, *The Origins of European Dissent* (London, 1977), p. 234.

[34] Crespin-Baduel, fo. 88^{r}; also J. Camerarius, *Historica Narratio de fratrum orthodoxorum ecclesiis* (Heidelberg, 1605), p. 303.

[35] *Fazy*, I, 33-9; for similar commutations in the Piedmontese valleys in the early modern period, see Armand Hugon, 'Popolo e chiesa', 9-11.

[36] Vaillant, *Libertés*, pp. 457-62, 491-7.

more permanent.[37] The holding of a regular *consilium*, or meeting of heads of households, of a community seems to have been taken for granted in early modern Savoie.[38] In our period the predominantly catholic village of Vallouise used several meetings of its *universitas* to resolve to dissociate itself from the acts of its heretic members: it appealed to the archbishop three times in 1483, and again in 1487 and 1488.[39]

Over and above the self-government of the communities was the tradition, well-established in some areas by our period, of gathering together in *Escartons*, to which each community would send delegates to discuss common affairs. The *bailliage* of Briançon contained five *Escartons*, including three regions (Oulx, the Val Chisone, and Château-Dauphin) on the eastern side of the passes. Of the three *Escartons* in the *bailliage* of Embrun, one, that of Guillestre, was almost coterminous with the archiepiscopal manors, and included the communities enfranchised by the archbishop in 1331.[40] In the Briançonnais, moreover, the five *Escartons* would meet in a *Grand Escarton* to discuss the distribution of communal dues and obligations (the *exquartonamentum*, which gave the *Escarton* its name). Only the *tiers état* was entitled to a voice, and in 1552 the *parlement* of Grenoble tried, apparently in vain, to limit the number of delegates to these bodies.[41]

It is important not to make a facile equation between the presence of communal liberties and heresy. The area where the former were best developed, namely the town of Briançon, showed no tendency to religious dissidence. However, it was important that the assault on heresy was mounted in an area where seigneurial intervention was not taken for granted, and where the habits of the people as a whole provided some sort of scheme for the dissenting communities to follow. It has

---

[37]   Ibid., pp. 536–9, 553–8, 564 f.

[38]   J. and R. Nicolas, *La vie quotidienne en Savoie aux xviie et xviiie siècles* (*s. l.*, 1979), pp. 241–5.

[39]   *CUL G*, fos. 54^v, 57^v, 78^r–9^v; *ADI B*, fos. 12^v–13^r; Marx, pp. 239–40.

[40]   A. A. Fauché-Prunelle, *Essai sur les anciennes institutions autonomes ou populaires des Alpes cottiennes-briançonnaises* (Grenoble and Paris, 1856–7), II, 311–33; Fornier, III, 440–3; Vaillant, *Libertés*, p. 464, Pazè Beda, *Riforma e Cattolicesimo*, pp. 15–17; Veyret, *Atlas et géographie*, pp. 140, 169; J. R. Major, *Representative Government in Early Modern France* (New Haven, 1980), p. 76.

[41]   Fauché-Prunelle, *Essai*, II, 332.

been suggested that Calvinist organizations in Piedmont resembled the local political system;[42] Waldensian structures could follow local examples as well.

(iii) Rudimentary dissenting organization

One must now see how the Waldenses copied the ways of their country in organizing themselves to protect their heresy. One important point must be emphasized at once. This chapter does not claim to uncover the part played in the Vaudois organization at this period by the *'barbes'*, those most elusive, traditional pastors of the Waldensian laity, in any way which may be closely related to the history of persecution or rehabilitation.

There are several reasons for this omission. First, in the whole of the material studied there has not emerged a single full trial from the fifteenth century which indubitably involves one of these *barbes*. It was commonly thought that the trial of two Italian preachers from Spoleto, conducted at Oulx in 1492, revealed a great deal about the organization of the Vaudois. This illusion was created by the language of the notaries, who used the title of 'Waldensian *barbe*' to describe any heretic pastor who came into their grasp, of whatever sect. One of these preachers, Pietro di Jacopo, described himself as one of the 'fratres barloti' (*sic*) or 'brethren of the opinion'—in other words, of the Fraticelli who were still, in the late fifteenth century, surviving in the hills round Spoleto and the March of Ancona.[43] When they spoke of their heretic 'ordination', these preachers referred only to places near Spoleto or in the Abruzzi. It is not surprising to find a few errant Fraticelli wandering in the Alps; the same has been found in some evidence from fourteenth-century Piedmont.[44]

---

[42] Armand Hugon, 'Popolo e chiesa', 12.

[43] *CUL H*, sect. 6, and esp. fo. 9^r; Allix, *Some remarks*, pp. 307-17; D. L. Douie, *The nature and effect of the heresy of the Fraticelli* (Manchester, 1932), pp. 243-5; N. Cohn, *Europe's Inner Demons* (London, 1975), pp. 42-54.

[44] G. Amati, 'Processus contra Valdenses in Lombardia superiori, anno 1387', *Archivio Storico Italiano*, ser. 3 (1865), II, pt. i, 50-61; Boffito, 'Eretici in Piemonte', 381-412; G. G. Merlo, *Eretici e inquisitori nella società piemontese del trecento* (Torino, 1977), p. 20.

Moreover, it is unlikely that the *barbes*, as they have traditionally been represented, would have had much influence, since their followers often confessed to them only once in several years.[45] Nor would they have had any reason to involve themselves in the affairs of peasants anxious to protect their property, if they were, as was claimed, celibate and sworn to poverty, itinerant and independent of society.[46] In fact, the Fraticelli captured in 1492 looked on the villagers' lawsuits almost with detachment, admitting only to having heard some confessions.[47] A *barbe* captured at Pinerolo in 1507 said he had met the Vaudois litigants Angelin Palon and Antoni Marie, but had only discussed their suit in general terms, and had been asked to take messages asking for help to the Waldenses of the Val Germanasca, in Piedmont.[48]

Some witnesses early in March 1488 testified that there were *barbes* hidden in the caves with the obstinate heretics of the Val Chisone; if this was so, then the records of what happened after their capture have been irretrievably lost.[49] In fact, when one examines those *barbes* whose names and origins we know, they turn out to be local men of only modest status: Antoni Porte, Johan Bret, Jame Ruffi, and Johan and Antoni Brunet (all from the Alpine valleys); Thomas Tercian, of Meana di Susa; 'Symunt' from the Valentinois, and 'Estève' from Luserna.[50] Perhaps too much attention has been paid to the 'clandestine church organization' after all.[51]

Waldensian organization was, in short, very lay and very materialist; it was concerned with the defence of property,

---

[45]   Below, ch. 6 (iii).

[46]   See, e.g., Bernard Gui, *Manuel de l'inquisiteur*, ed. G. Mollat and G. Drioux (Paris, 1926–7), I, 48–59.

[47]   *CUL H*, sect. 6, fos. 7^{r-v}, 12^r.

[48]   *BP*, I, fos. 421^v-2^r; Marx, p. 193.

[49]   *BP*, I, fos. 282^{r-v}, 284^v-5^r, 287^{r-v}. The interrogations conducted in the Val Chisone after 2 March 1488 are missing from the Grenoble register.

[50]   *CUL G*, fo. 115^v; *CUL H*, sect. 4, fo. 4^r; *BP*, I, fos. 277^r-88^v; *ADI A*, fos. 303^v, 342^v; *ADI B*, fos. 299^v, 357^v; Fornier, II, 205.

[51]   See G. Audisio, 'Une organisation ecclésiale clandestine: les barbes vaudois', in *Histoire et clandestinité du moyen-âge à la première guerre mondiale: Colloque de Privas, Mai 1977*, ed. M. Tilloy, J. Chiffoleau, and G. Audisio (Albi, 1979), pp. 75–88, and also Audisio, 'Les barbes vaudois aux xve et xvie siècles', *BSSV* 139 (1976), 65–75.

by litigation and by force. As we would expect, therefore, the vast majority of Waldenses were small peasant farmers, either allodialists or free tenants. Since this class included most of the population, it was a class within which there was great inequality of income. A small and very unreliable guide to these differences is suggested by the differences in the rents collected by Fazy de Rame on behalf of his relative, Pierre de Rame, in 1486 and 1488; these rents varied between twenty to thirty *gros* for some tenants at Fressinières and one or two for others. The tenants who paid high rents seem in some cases, like that of Antoni Baridon, to have been the most influential heretics.[52]

Some were either not farmers at all, or combined farming with some other position. Michel Pelat, who later witnessed to the atrocities of the crusade, was notary of Fressinières.[53] The Vaudois also included the landless and servants. Especially after the crusade of 1488, many inhabitants of the valleys fled to towns further west. François Farel, notary of Gap (and grandfather of the reformer) was one of several from the noble and notarial classes of Gap who spoke in favour of the morals of their servants from Fressinières in 1501.[54] Three men from Fressinières explained in 1488 that they had not made heretic confessions for long periods while they were away in service.[55]

Neither the clergy nor the nobility was represented amongst the late medieval Waldenses. There were some clerical sympathizers only.[56] The hierarchy of the heresy was created amongst the third estate; it would have been especially difficult for the local nobility to be involved, as many of them were living in the towns and merging with the bourgeoisie.[57]

In those villages which were most given over to heresy, the defence of the community became the business of the elected leaders of society. On 19 April 1483 the consuls of Fressinières protested to the archbishop in strong and even vituperative terms, claiming that they had appeared on behalf of all those whom the archbishop had cited, on the deliberation

[52] *Fazy*, II, sects. 680–1, 740.
[53] *BP*, II, fo. 97v.
[54] *BP*, I, fos. 451r, 455v; II, fo. 1r–v.
[55] *ADI B*, fos. 128v–9r, 167r, 216r.
[56] See below, ch. 5 (i).
[57] *Fazy*, I, 26.

of the community, and 'to avoid expense'. They warned the archbishop not to inquire into the orthodoxy of those of Fressinières, because they said a case about this was being, and had long been, raised in the royal *Conseil*. A similar deputation, led by a consul of Fressinières and a notary, approached the archbishop at Guillestre on 25 April, presenting letters of the *Conseil* directing that the process of investigation be suspended. Pons Arnulphs (or Brunet) of Fressinières witnessed then that the consuls had said 'they would speak for all'.[58] On the other hand, on 1 October 1487 a deputation from Pragelas came before the commissary Alberto Cattaneo, complaining about the syndics of their village, who had raised an illegal levy to defend the heresy, and asking the commissary to remove the syndics and consuls, who were heretics.[59]

Led by these magistrates, the Waldenses engaged in three chief activities in defence of their communities: organizing appeals against and responses to the inquisition; levying a kind of 'tallage' or property tax to pay their legal costs; and punishing the minority who stepped out of line. Before the crusade overtook the Vaudois they appointed their own official proctors, to carry their affairs to Vienne, Paris, Rome, or elsewhere. Early in October 1487 François de la Roche reported that the people of the Val Chisone had nominated proctors without his approval; about the same time Peyre Griot reported that a meeting had taken place in Pragelas to establish a procuration.[60]

The proctor for those of Fressinières before the crusade appears to have been one Estève Rous, a tenant of the Sieur de Poët in Fressinières.[61] The sentence produced at the end of his trial before Cattaneo described how he had returned in the spring of 1487 to Fressinières to speak 'daulcunes matieres lesquelles il avoit pourchassez comme leur procureur et faucteur touchans et regardans les exploiz et exequcions par contre eulx faictes des lan a passe a cause de ceste matiere de vaudoisie'; the sentence accused him of pursuing the heretics' interests 'en court de Rome et du Roy et autre part'.[62] After

---

[58]   *CUL G*, fo. 56[r–v]; Marx, pp. 231–5.
[59]   *ADI A*, fo. 70[r].
[60]   Ibid., fos. 99[v]–100[r], 105[v].
[61]   *Fazy*, II, sect. 740.
[62]   *CUL H*, sect. 3, fo. 1[r–v].

the crusade the interests of the villagers of the western valleys were promoted by Angelin Palon of Fressinières and Antoni Marie of Vallouise. Palon enjoyed some status as a former *baile* of the landlord Fazy de Rame; the catholics tried several times to discredit him.[63] They alleged (quite correctly) that he had confessed and abjured heresy in 1488.[64] Antoni Marie had also been in service, with the chatelain of Vallouise, Hunet Jullian, who testified to his good character in 1501.[65]

Others went to the King of France and to Turin from the Val Chisone in their attempts to discredit the papal commissary.[66] A local notary 'went from house to house to draw up the instrument of procuration'; some Vaudois went to the Savoyard captain in the Val Perosa to ask him to come to Briançon and free Cattaneo's prisoners by force.[67]

When the suspected heretics of Fressinières were cited to appear before the commissary, they co-ordinated their replies. On 9 April 1488 three witnesses explained their not answering the summons by saying that the consuls or syndics of that village told them not to go, and made decisions for the whole community.[68] The ancient Guilhem Porte of l'Argentière said he did not answer because he was old, unable to walk, and passed the business off 'to others who had charge of it'. He said he had never been present in the discussions which he knew had taken place to prepare the heretics' appeals.[69]

Just as impressive as the way in which the Vaudois co-ordinated their response to persecution was the way in which they found money to pay for it. In the manner of the communities and *Escartons*, they levied a charge on themselves to pay for the prolonged lawsuits in which they were involved. When the Franciscan inquisitor Pierre Fabri interrogated some heretics in 1432, he found out that they had raised a tax on themselves, which had collected ninety

---

[63] *BP*, II, fo. 479^{r-v}; *Fazy*, II, sects. 681-92; Allix, *Some remarks*, p. 303; P. Guillaume, 'Sentence de réhabilitation des Vaudois des Alpes françaises', *BCTHS* Ann. 1891 (1891), 262.

[64] *ADI B*, fos. 114^v-16^v.

[65] *CUL G*, fos. 36^r, 53^v, for the Marie family; *BP*, II, fo. 84^r; Guillaume, loc. cit.

[66] *ADI A*, fos. 103^v, 137^r.

[67] Ibid., fos. 70^v, 101^v, 103^{r-v}.

[68] *ADI B*, fos. 161^v, 164^{r-v}, 173^r.

[69] *CUL H*, sect. 4, fo. 2^r.

florins, and had obtained permission to have their appeal heard by making their suit with an 'advocate' named Jehan Baile (later president of the Grenoble *parlement* from 1455 to 1461).[70]

Numerous witnesses from east and west of the passes referred to this tax in the late fifteenth century. Our first reference dates from 1486, when it was mentioned by Antoni Blanc and Odin Valoy of Fressinières.[71] From the depositions of the Valoy brothers we see it was a tax on property rather than income: Odin said he contributed 'only from the goods of his mother in Fressinières, for the burdens owed in the same place'; Peyre, on the other hand, paid 'according to the capacity of the goods he held both at Fressinières and St-André d'Embrun'.[72] Sperit Porte did not contribute, as he was not a householder; Guilhem Porte and the octogenarian Michel Bertrand 'Barbo' left paying the contributions to their sons.[73] The syndics and consuls of the villages made the collections, at least in Fressinières and Pragelas.[74] Of the villages by the Durance, Fressinières paid one half, and l'Argentière and Vallouise paid the other half between them. As one witness added, 'this was always the rule kept between them'.[75]

Fressinières, the smallest of the Vaudois villages of the Durance, paid proportionately more than the others because it was more peopled with heretics than elsewhere. Two witnesses from thereabouts said that they thought that all those who had been cited, including all of Fressinières, were heretics, because they all paid the costs of the tax.[76] One other said he contributed because everyone else in Fressinières did so.[77] In fact, several of Fressinières resisted the imposition, and some of them secured legal instruments from the archiepiscopal judge against the syndics to spare them the tax.[78]

Where solidarity was so important for common safety, it is not surprising that the Waldenses also disciplined those who stepped out of line. Antoni Blanc of Fressinières, who

[70] Fornier, II, 330, 355.   [71] *CUL G*, fo. 111ʳ; *CUL H*, sect. 2, fos. 2ᵛ–3ʳ.
[72] *CUL H*, sect. 2, fo. 3ʳ; Marx, p. 248, based on *CUL H*, sect. 5.
[73] *CUL H*, sect. 4, fos. 2ʳ, 5ʳ, 12ʳ.
[74] Ibid., fo. 10ʳ; Chevalier, p. 152; see above, note 59.
[75] *CUL H*, sect. 4, fos. 2ᵛ, 9ʳ; TCD MS 266, fo. 57ʳ; Chevalier, pp. 146, 148.
[76] *CUL H*, sect. 4, fos. 4ʳ, 9ʳ.   [77] Chevalier, p. 148.
[78] *ADI B*, fos. 100ʳ, 118ʳ, 122ʳ; Chevalier, pp. 150, 152.

was hardly involved in heresy at all, told how when he refused to pay the levy, Johan Reymunt and Michel Arbaud stole one of his sheep, sold it, and took the money as payment of his contribution. Previously, Blanc had been intimidated into keeping what he knew of Vaudois practices secret. One night in 1470 he met an acquaintance of his walking with two strangers, who ran away when Blanc approached. When he let this be known he was approached by the local heretic Pons Brunet; he told Blanc the names of these two *barbes*, and said they 'came in a good cause'; he made Blanc swear to give these men no hindrance, which Blanc promised to do.[79] When Odin Valoy first confessed to a *barbe*, he was warned to reveal nothing of what had happened, lest his tongue should be cut out 'the way one mutilates a goat', along with other threats.[80] On 3 April 1488 Fazy Ripert of Fressinières complained that when he wanted to answer the inquisitor's summons, the *conseillers* of Fressinières frightened him to prevent him from doing so; he also protested that he had always resisted pressure to confess to *barbes*.[81]

In the face of inquisitorial attack, the Waldenses were, on rare occasions, prepared to give up the 'clandestinity' which characterized their normal behaviour, and to dispute and advance the cause of their heresy in public.[82] When they spoke of Waldensianism, the Vaudois referred to it as 'our law', 'nostra ley', which they regarded as being better than the 'law' of the priests. In 1483, a catholic of Vallouise deposed that a Vaudois had said 'let us take twelve of your law and twelve of ours, and dispute to see who will turn out the better'; he had then apparently been struck blind.[83]

In his *Historiae Regum a Pharamundo*,[84] Alberto Cattaneo described how, when he started to deal with the Val Chisone, those of Usseaux and Fenestrelle sent two delegates to him. They offered to present 'the masters of our law, men distinguished in their lives and by their learning', who would

---

[79] *CUL G*, fos. 111^r, 115^v-16^r.

[80] *CUL H*, sect. 2, fo. 9^{r-v}.   [81] *ADI B*, fos. 134^v-5^r.

[82] On 'Clandestinité', see J. Gonnet and A. Molnár, *Les Vaudois au moyen âge* (Turin, 1974), ch. IV.   [83] Fornier, II, 413.

[84] BN, MS Latin 5938. The passage which relates to Charles VIII is printed in Godefroy, *Charles VIII*, pp. 277–83, and in Chevalier, pp. 85–92.

prove by scripture and by the councils that they were good Christians and praiseworthy. They warned Cattaneo not to provoke God's wrath against himself, saying they wished to obey God rather than men (an inquisitorial cliché about the Vaudois[85]), and did not fear those who would kill the body, but not the soul.[86] One of the two, Johan Disdier of Usseaux, later testified that some heretics had planned to bring a *barbe* to Briançon to dispute with Cattaneo.[87]

Later on, Johan Aufossi of l'Argentière admitted that he had exhorted the *barbes* Symunt and Louis about Easter 1488 to appear before Cattaneo to defend the sect. They said they would come, on condition Cattaneo gave them a safe conduct.[88] Perhaps in allusion to the same event, Fornier claimed that safe conducts were given, but the *barbes* still would not come.[89] This same disputatiousness was one of the charges levelled against the Vaudois in some articles presented to the judges-delegate for the rehabilitation in the summer of 1507.[90]

It is interesting to see similar behaviour amongst the Waldenses east of the mountains. In the early months of 1448 the Vaudois of the valleys of Luserna rose in force, and obliged the clergy to flee. The inquisitor Giacomo Buronzo was sent to deal with them. He was met in the middle of July by Claude Pastre, a *barbe*, with three hundred Vaudois in arms, who offered to hold a disputation on the piazza at Luserna. The catholics declined this invitation and instead placed an interdict on the valleys, which lasted until 1453.[91]

The case of Claude Pastre draws attention to the most striking aspect of heretical organization in this period, the readiness to resist by force of arms. Both in the Val Chisone and in the valleys of the Durance, the villagers were prepared to take to the hills and hide in caves when danger threatened. Five witnesses from the Val Chisone told in 1507 how they had fled to the *balma* (dialect for a large cavern) near Fenestrelle. A Vaudois of Usseaux fled to one mountain

---

[85] See Bernard Gui, *Manuel*, I, 36.   [86] Godefroy, *Charles VIII*, p. 280.
[87] *ADI A*, fo. 307ᵛ.   [88] *ADI B*, fo. 247ᵛ.
[89] Fornier, II, 426.   [90] *BP*, I, fo. 310ʳ.
[91] See F. Alessio, 'Luserna e l'interdetto di Giacomo Buronzo', *BSBS* VIII no. vi (1903), 413–14.

where he stayed with eighty men and women for three weeks. Another went to the *balma* 'de Traversier', which was defended by force. Other witnesses named yet other caves.[92] On the other side of the Montgenèvre the same tactics were used: the people of l'Argentière fled to the cave named after the Tête d'Oréac; some of those of Vallouise fled to the Ailefroide, or 'Alo Freydo', near Mont Pelvoux.[93]

These defenders expected their caves to be strong enough to withstand a siege. Three witnesses in April 1488 said those of l'Argentière stayed in the *balma* 'd'Oréac' until they saw it was not strong enough to stand assault.[94] Pons Violin admitted taking food and supplies to the *balma* 'd'Oréac'; Peyre Martin said that those hidden in the *balma* 'de Fenestrelle' kept their victuals in another cave named 'de l'Agniel' (perhaps near the present-day hamlet of Agnelli, north-east of Fenestrelle).[95]

Testimonies from 1488 and 1507 alike show that the Vaudois were, by local standards, fairly well armed. Estève David, interrogated on 8 March 1488, admitted that those hidden in the *balma* had 150 crossbows, and six or seven small firearms or culverins.[96] Johan Ruffi of Balboutet said that there were only two firearms (unless he was speaking of another cave); these two could not agree as to whether it was possible for the fugitives to escape across the Albergian to the Val Germanasca. When the attacks came, the Vaudois fought back. One group stayed in its cave for three weeks until it was stormed by Hippolyte de Bardonnèsche. Another had only been at the *balma* of Fenestrelle for seven or eight days when it was attacked; it defended itself with crossbows and slingshot, killing seven or eight soldiers. About fourteen defenders in the *balma* 'de Traversier' were killed in its storming, and one of the witnesses (who testified later) said he had been wounded by a crossbow quarrel.[97]

[92] *BP*, II, fos. 378^V, 387^V, 396^V, 400^V, 404^V, 407^V, 414^V, 416^V, 418^{r-v}, 419^V.

[93] Godefroy, *Charles VIII*, p. 281; Fornier, II, 431 f.; Marx, pp. 162 f. On the Ailefroide, see Godefroy, pp. 282 f.; Fornier, II, 443 f.; Marx, pp. 164 f.; and on the *balma* 'd'Oréac', *CUL H*, sect. 4, fo. 4^r; TCD MS 266, fo. 57^r; Marx, pp. 165 f.

[94] *ADI B*, fos. 267^{r-v}, 269^r, 278^{r-v}.

[95] *CUL H*, sect. 4, fo. 4^r; *BP*, II, fo. 387^V.   [96] *Colobrinas* in the latin text.

[97] *BP*, I, fos. 277^V-287^V; II, fos. 378^V-9^r, 387^V-8^r, 400^V-1^r, 414^V-15^r.

To explain the structures of the heresy, we have had to examine some aspects of its history which have yet to be outlined in detail. Some conclusions about the Waldenses are already apparent. For an amorphous body of peasant dissenters, their resources were as remarkable as their self-consciousness and confidence. Their behaviour in this period perhaps helps to explain how, in the age of the reformation, they turned their struggle for survival into a spiritual conflict with repercussions throughout Europe.

2. Why Persecution Failed

This title begs a question. Some catholic polemicists in the seventeenth century were determined to claim that the assault against the Waldenses of the Alps in the last quarter of the fifteenth century was a complete success. The Jesuit Marcellin Fornier, in his *Histoire Générale* (written between 1626 and 1643), described the crusade at this time as bringing about 'l'entière extirpation de l'hérésie Vaudoise'; he ridiculed the Huguenot minister Perrin's suggestion that there were churches of the Vaudois in the Dauphiné about 1560, and insisted that the heresy had been obliterated at least fifty-nine years earlier.[1] *Pace* Fornier, however, the inquisitors did not eradicate heresy; they saw the whole business of the inquisitions denounced as abusive; in the early days of the reform a few Vaudois and some reformers groped towards a mutual understanding and achieved a precarious continuity into the modern era. Persecution failed; and if we see why it failed, we shall be that much closer to understanding the role of Waldensianism in its society.

(i) The course of events *c*.1400–1514

The history of persecution of the Waldenses in the late medieval Dauphiné began with the appointment of the Franciscan François Borelli in 1369, as inquisitor for the dioceses of Arles, Aix, Embrun, and Gap. With the coming of the Great Schism Borelli apparently extended his powers and received a commission in 1380 from Clement VII extending his brief to Vienne, Geneva, Aubonne, Savoie, Avignon, the Comtat Venaissin, Orange, Diois, and Forez. In that same year he cited the inhabitants of the valleys of Fressinières, l'Argentière, and Valpute (as Vallouise was called before the time of Louis XI) and remitted 150 heretics

[1] Fornier, II, 367–8, 544–5.

to the secular arm. In 1385, with the help of some of the people of the Queyras, he mounted an expedition against the heretics of the Val Chisone. Between 1388 and 1396 Borelli was particularly active in Valpute, enjoying the assistance of the local chatelain. One account claims that in 1393 he pronounced a massive sentence against 230 Vaudois, although his *vacations* for those years show only seven individuals burnt within the jurisdiction of Valpute.[2]

At about the same time the Waldenses of the Piedmontese Alps were under attack. In 1375 Gregory XI had complained to Amadeus VI of Savoy that in his states some heretics were working their evil in safety, since they enjoyed the protection of the nobility of that region, and inquisitors who tried to deal with them were frustrated. In 1387 the Dominican Antonio de Septo, or Settimo, began a long series of processes based on Pinerolo, in which he uncovered much besides usual Waldensian heresy. In 1395 Fra Giovanni di Susa tried and sentenced a heretic from Carmagnola named Jame Ristolas, and in 1412 he sentenced some of the last remnants of the Cathar heresy at Chieri.[3]

Persecution was less frantic in the early fifteenth century. In 1419 the Franciscan Pierre Fabri was appointed as inquisitor to the Dauphiné, to assist the resident Pons Feugeron. His commission, like Borelli's, was vast, covering Arles, Aix, Embrun, Vienne, Tarentaise, Provence, Forcalquier, Venaissin, Diois, Valentinois, and Albon. He was one of a succession of inquisitors based in the Minorite house built at Briançon, which had originally been intended for Valpute. In 1429 Fabri examined some Vaudois on the article of their refusing to betray the sect. Guilhèm Porte said in 1488 that he remembered being interrogated by Fabri, but denied that he had been declared relapsed by him. In 1432 Fabri uncovered the first recorded case of the Vaudois tallage. In 1437 he was in collaboration with another Franciscan called Fazy Fabri; in that year they together sentenced the heretic Estève Bleyn,

---

[2] Perrin, *Vaudois*, pp. 109–15; Chorier, *Histoire générale du Dauphiné*, II, 391–2; Marx, pp. 145, 202–13, based on ADI, B 2992, 4349, 4352.

[3] Amati, 'Processus contra Valdenses', *Archivio Storico Italiano*, ser. 3 (1865), I, pt. ii, 3–52, II, pt. i, 3–61; Boffito, 'Eretici in Piemonte', 391–402, 421–4; Merlo, *Eretici e inquisitori, passim.*

of Puy-St-Roman, near Valpute.[4]

In 1457 the persecuting archbishop, Jehan Baile, was elected to the see of Embrun. Meanwhile, Perre Fabri having died in 1452, his place was taken by another minorite, Glaude Martin, who dealt with some Vaudois in 1459-60.[5] In 1483 a witness deposed that Martin had interrogated Michel Bertrand 'Barbo'[6] of Fressinières; Bertrand admitted five years later that he had abjured heresy before Martin thirty-five years previously.[7] When news of heresy in the region reached Louis XI of France, he sent a *conseiller* named Ascars to investigate in 1471; according to the Gapençais lawyer Jacques Arnaud, who accompanied Ascars, they were quite satisfied with the catholicity of the people of l'Argentière.[8]

By a bull of 15 January 1472 the Franciscan Jehan Veyleti was appointed to succeed Fazy Fabri and Jehan Franconis, sacristan of Embrun, as inquisitor over the range of provinces which 'had been the custom with his predecessor Pons Feugeyron.'[9] From July 1473 he set to work in earnest, although the records of his activities seem to have been lost.[10] Veyleti was accused by the historian Perrin, almost certainly wrongly, of falsifying the testimonies of his victims.[11] In any case, he managed to arouse much hostility. In 1474 he was attacked as he travelled between the Montgenèvre and Cesana Torinese on his way to Rome. He was robbed of his papers and money and wounded; two assistants, Jehan Desventes and Jacques Robertet, were also assaulted. Two men were later hanged for this attack.[12]

[4] *CUL H*, sect. 4, fo. 2ʳ; Fornier, II, 326-30; Marx, pp. 215-17; Chorier, *Histoire générale*, loc. cit.; E. Arnaud, 'Histoire des persécutions', *BSHV* 12 (1895), 64.   [5] Fornier, II, 358; Arnaud, 'Histoire des persécutions', 67.

[6] 'Barbo' is an alternative surname or nickname for the family of Bertrand of Fressinières, and has nothing to do with *barbes* in the religious sense.

[7] *CUL G*, fo. 53ᵛ; *CUL H*, sect. 4, fo. 5ʳ.

[8] Marx, pp. 145-7; *BP*, II, fos. 17ᵛ-19ʳ.

[9] Fornier, II, 367-8; Marx, pp. 52, 55.

[10] Fornier, II, 370-1; Marx, p. 195, based on *BP*, II, fos. 494 ff. This part of the Bureau-Pascal dossier contains an inventory of the inquisitorial archive of the diocese of Embrun as it stood in 1507, with the titles of many documents which have since perished, either in 1585 or 1790.

[11] Perrin, *Vaudois*, p. 127.

[12] *CUL G*, fos. 53ʳ, 116ᵛ-17ʳ; *CUL H*, sect. 4, fos. 2ʳ⁻ᵛ, 5ʳ, 10ʳ; *BP*, II, fos. 445ʳ-6ᵛ; Godefroy, *Charles VIII*, p. 280; Fornier, II, 371-3.

The villagers oppressed by Veyleti appealed to Louis XI, who was known to be hostile to Archbishop Baile; on 18 May 1478 the King issued letters ordering the inquisitors to desist from troubling those of Vallouise, and accusing them of corruption and extortion. Because the Grenoble *parlement* hesitated over these letters, they were repeated on 31 March 1479. About the same time, two of the most determined promoters of the crusade of 1488, Oronce Émé and Jordanon Cordi, were placed under arrest by the *Grand Conseil*. However, this respite for the Vaudois was not total, as Louis had fallen foul of the liberties of the Dauphiné, and in any case the letters exempted obstinate heretics from the amnesty, which gave the inquisitors a loophole.[13]

Shortly before the death of Louis XI Archbishop Jehan Baile was able to take up an interest in prosecuting Waldensianism once more. On 2 April 1483 he started to take down some general testimonies about the people of the villages of the Durance. In the course of these proceedings he gathered information later used in the trial in absence of the leading Waldensian Antoni Baridon of Châteauroux. Three days later he summoned the consuls of Fressinières, and told them he 'did not intend to afflict them in their persons or goods, but solely to lead them kindly back to the faith'; they replied that they would consult and decide how to answer him.[14]

On 17 April a deputation from Vallouise, consisting of the priest, Estève Garnier, and the syndics, asked the archbishop to inquire into the evil reputation the valley suffered for heresy and to separate the good from the bad. That same day Baile began to interrogate suspects. Two days later, the consuls of Fressinières appeared before Baile and protested that the whole case now stood undecided in the King's court, and also asked for a copy of the process so far. Baile ignored an outburst from one of the consuls, Michel Ruffi, and insisted on interrogating him on matters of faith. On 30 April he asked Ruffi what the gathering at Fressinières had decided and got no answer. Ruffi asked again for a copy of the process;

---

[13] Perrin, *Vaudois*, pp. 118-24, based on *CUL G*, fos. 46-50; E. Arnaud, 'Louis XI et les Vaudois du Dauphiné', *BCTHS* Ann. 1895 (1896), 513-18; Fornier, II, 409-10; Marx, pp. 147-9; also *BP*, I, fos. 381^r-2^v.

[14] *CUL G*, fos. 53^r-4^r, 98^v-9^r.

when this was refused, he appealed to the King.[15]

On 2 May the catholics of Vallouise again asked the archbishop to conduct an inquisition. On 7 June a proctor
appeared for Vallouise, saying that the consuls there wished
to dissociate themselves from the supplication lately presented
on the Vaudois' behalf to the governor of the Dauphiné by
Guilhem Orsière, of Fressinières.[16] On 23 July the suspects
obtained royal letters which suspended the prosecution
while the case stood in the *Conseil*, and ordered that the
excommunicates be absolved meanwhile. These letters were
presented by deputies from Fressinières and l'Argentière to
the archbishop in an acrimonious meeting at Guillestre on
25 August. On 7 September all the adult male catholics of
Vallouise signed a protest against heresy; they may have done
this because the Vaudois had refused to identify themselves
by name.[17]

Baile evidently respected these legal to-ings and fro-ings; it
seems that nothing further was done against heresy for over
two years. Early in February 1486 Baile visited his diocese,
and in the course of his travels preached against the Waldensian
heresy in the small village of Châteauroux.[18] In the course of
the summer and autumn of 1486 Baile began some very
tentative moves to prosecute some of those who lived outside
the main foyers of dissent, or who were not much involved in
the recent protests. In these trials he took long records and
was meticulous in interrogation.[19]

If Baile thought that by these careful opening moves he
would escape the inveterate litigiousness of the people of the
Durance villages, he was mistaken. Trouble started late in
1486 when the archbishop launched a mass excommunication
against those of Fressinières and elsewhere.[20] On 5 February
1487 Peyre Roux and Estève Roux of Fressinières presented
a formal protest to the archbishop in which they appealed to

---

[15] Ibid., fos. 54^v-6^v.   [16] Ibid., fo. 57^v.
[17] Ibid., fos. 78^r-9^v; TCD MS 265, fos. 23^r-9^r; TCD MS 266, fos. 15^r-18^v;
Marx, pp. 149-51, 231-5.
[18] *CUL G*, fos. 99^r-^{v}.
[19] Arnaud, 'Histoire des persécutions', 76.
[20] The written sentence of excommunication has not been found, but
numerous witnesses early in 1488 testified that they had been excommunicated
by the archbishop some eighteen months before.

the Holy See and to the *legatus a latere*, in the shape of the Archbishop of Vienne. In March Baile was cited to Vienne, but refused to appear save by a proctor. He refused thereafter to take any part in the case at Vienne, which dragged on until October. At the same time an appeal was made to the Pope, who supplied an apostolic rescript for Vienne's benefit: the proctors for the archbishop and the appellants met on 5 October. Baile meanwhile appealed to Rome in his turn, and secured the appointment of a judge-delegate, Pietro Accolti.[21]

Perhaps these inconclusive legal wrangles frustrated those in the archiepiscopal entourage who lacked Baile's scrupulousness or patience. Whatever the reason, the whole business was suddenly short-circuited. On 27 April 1487 the archdeacon of Cremona, Alberto de Capitaneis or Cattaneo, obtained a papal bull authorizing him to act against heresy in the Dauphiné, Savoy, Piedmont, and wherever appropriate. We do not know how he became involved, nor whom he knew in the region, although he did correspond with a fellow-inquisitor, Blaise de Berra. On 26 June Cattaneo reached Pinerolo, where he issued general letters of citation, in which the appeal to Vienne was denounced as inadmissible. On 5 August he arrived at Grenoble, there to secure the support of Hugues de la Palu, Sieur de Varax, and Jehan Rabot, who acted for the *parlement* of Grenoble. In spite of the general nature of his commission, Cattaneo was never to do anything about heresy in the states of Savoy.[22]

On 28 August Cattaneo directed the Franciscan Jehan Columbi to go to Pragelas and preach to those suspect of heresy and exhort them to repent. By 1 September Cattaneo was at Briançon collecting information about the heretics of the Val Chisone. On 18 September the first letter of citation was issued, listing thirty-seven suspected heretics.[23] On 24 September Cattaneo was better informed, and a fresh citation listed no less than 331 suspects from Pragelas,

[21] *BP*, II, fos. 105–373, used by Marx, pp. 152–8; Fornier, II, 427, and III, 413 ff.

[22] *CUL G*, sect. 2, as printed in S. Morland, *A History of the Evangelical Churches of the Valleys of Piemont* (London, 1658), pp. 196–214; Marx, pp. 158–9; D. Carutti, *La crociata valdese del 1488 e la maschera di ferro, con alcune appendici alla storia di Pinerolo* (Pinerolo, 1894), pp. 11–23.

[23] Chevalier, pp. 139, 142 f.

Usseaux, and Mentoulles. Further mass citations followed, with only meagre results. On 3 October the *procureur* of the faith (who acted as prosecutor) called for the excommunication of those who had not answered the summons, which was granted. The excommunication was renewed on 6 October, with a fine of twenty-five ducats imposed on each of the contumacious. Citation was tried again without effect, and on 16 November the obstinate heretics of the Val Chisone were formally remitted to the secular arm for punishment.[24] Cattaneo asked for confirmation of his right to invoke the secular arm, which he received on 27 November. Meanwhile the catholic villagers west of the passes had disowned their neighbours yet again.[25]

Perhaps a hundred or so suspected Vaudois who had come to Cattaneo of their own accord, or been tricked into coming to Briançon, were interrogated and absolved between October 1487 and early March 1488.[26] After that the crusade proper could begin. The chronology of this crusade is far from clear. It seems, however, that the first invasion of the Val Chisone by the Dauphin's troops took place in early March, at a time when the paths into the Val Germanasca, according to one witness, were still impassable because of the depth of the snows.[27] On the eighth there were still some heretics hidden in caves around Fenestrelle. These were stormed, and the survivors presumably captured and interrogated. Then the leaders of the army returned to Briançon where they met the seigneurs of Fressinières. The formal process of citation and excommunication had been gone through for the people of Fressinières, l'Argentière, and Vallouise, with apparently even less effect than in the Val Chisone.[28] The crusaders went south and imprisoned the subjects of Fressinières by using a mixture of threats, persuasion, and force. Late in March or early in April a final attack was made on the Vaudois of

[24] *ADI A*, fos. 53ᵛ–68ᵛ, 80ᵛ–8ʳ, 90ʳ–4ᵛ, 107ʳ–12ʳ, 121ᵛ–7ᵛ.
[25] Marx, p. 159; *CUL G*, fo. 57ᵛ.
[26] *ADI A*, esp. fos. 145ʳ–366ᵛ. It is impossible to arrive at exact statistics for this period, because a hundred or so folios of this manuscript have been made wholly or partly illegible by damp.
[27] *BP*, I, fo. 282ʳ⁻ᵛ.
[28] *ADI B*, fos. 16ʳ–27ᵛ, 29ʳ–30ᵛ, 32ʳ–6ᵛ, 40ᵛ–56ʳ, 60ʳ–74ʳ.

of Vallouise who had hidden in the Ailefroide.[29]

At this stage the immense burden of mass interrogations was undertaken by Cattaneo and his sub-delegates.[30] So great was the task that it was necessary to parcel out some of the inquisitorial duties in commissions. Robert Laugier, later precentor of Embrun, dealt with some of those of l'Argentière; Pierre Sabine, *official* (archbishop's administrator) of Embrun, with others; Pierre Grand, a canon lawyer, interrogated yet more in the house of Pons Brunet, consul of Fressinières.[31] Ysoard Eymar, *curé* of St-Crépin, interrogated numerous Vaudois of Fressinières in his parish; one Philippe de Plesance also shared the task.[32] With a mass absolution pronounced at Embrun on 27 April, the proceedings drew towards a close.[33] According to proctors in 1507, some 160 suspected Vaudois had been killed, whether by 'hanging, burning, being slaughtered in their own homes, or being thrown from rocks', in the crusade and in the executions which followed.[34]

Not surprisingly, with the end of the crusade the persecutions of the Vaudois lost momentum. Cattaneo left; Archbishop Baile grew old and died in 1494. Most important of all, the outraged and dispossessed survivors speedily made their way to the King, and began that process of investigation and counter-inquisition which will be discussed below.[35]

Persecution, however, did not cease altogether. After Cattaneo's departure another inquisitor, a Franciscan from Valence named François Plouvier, was appointed by the Pope to deal with heresy in the Dauphiné and the Viennois, and specifically the valleys subjected to the late crusade. He took part in haggling with the victims for the commutation of their penances; in March 1489 he took some evidence against Thomas Guot of Pragelas and tried Peyre Valoy

[29] *BP*, I, fos. 276ᵛ-90ᵛ; Godefroy, *Charles VIII*, pp. 281-3; Chevalier, pp. 44-94; Fornier, II, 429-45; Marx, pp. 158-67; S. dei Conti da Foligno, *Le storie de' suoi tempi dal 1475 al 1510* (Roma, 1883), I, 299-307.

[30] *ADI B*, fos. 82ʳ-360ʳ, *passim.*

[31] *CUL H*, sect. 4; *Fazy*, II, sect. 1269; *ADI B*, fos. 192ʳ-6ʳ.

[32] *ADI B*, fos. 143ᵛ-71ʳ, 220ᵛ-42ᵛ.

[33] Chevalier, pp. 152-5, based on *ADI B*, fos. 208ʳ-14ʳ.

[34] *BP*, I, fos. 386ᵛ-7ʳ.

[35] See below, ch. 3.

of St-André d'Embrun.[36]

The court of the penitentiary of Oulx, Barthélemi Pascal, carried out an infamous trial in 1492 of two wandering heretic confessors from Spoleto, the last remnants of the Fraticelli. In 1495 the same court tried for heresy Thomas Guot of Pragelas, who had fled from the crusaders. When Charles VIII was on his way to Italy in 1494, he stopped at the provostship of Oulx: there he was shown 'un grand homme fort robuste, natif de la Pouille, lequel estant interrogé, fut accusé d'être un des principaux maistres de la Vaux-Pute'. After this summary trial the man was hanged in public on a convenient tree.[37]

At about the same time the bishop of Valence, Jehan d'Espinai (1491-1503), took in hand the elimination of Waldensianism in the Valentinois. The heresy was reputed to be gaining ground in the villages east of Valence, especially in Chabueil, Alixan, Châteaudouble, and their environs. Two Franciscan inquisitors were assassinated while trying to investigate the heretics. In 1494 Antoine Fabri, canon of Embrun, took charge of the interrogations; two trials of his, against heretics from the villages of Beauregard and Saint-Mamans, survive.[38]

Only in 1514 do we have clear evidence that persecution had recommenced on any scale in the lands ravaged by the crusade. Some lawyers and aristocrats, aided by the vicar of the provost of Oulx, Guillaume Coste, enlisted the aid of the bishop of Angoulême, Antoine d'Estaing, to purge heresy around Bardonècchia and Oulx. On 5 April 1514 the heads of families in the area were directed to reveal all they knew about local heretics to the authorities; some penances of crosses were imposed in this period.[39] However, no documentary evidence survives from this period and no further conclusions may be drawn.

[36] *CUL G*, fo. 32ʳ; *BP*, I, fos. 218ᵛ, 232ᵛ, and II, fos. 377ᵛ-8ʳ, 389ʳⁱᵛ; Perrin, *Vaudois*, p. 131; P. Guillaume, 'Notes et documents', *BCTHS* Ann. 1913 (1914), 422-6; Marx, pp. 244-54, 263-6; Chorier, *Histoire générale*, II, 502.

[37] *CUL H*, sect. 6; *BP*, I, fos. 215ʳ-76ᵛ; Godefroy, *Charles VIII*, p. 195, from the narrative of Pierre Desprey.

[38] *CUL H*, sect. 7; Allix, *Some remarks*, pp. 318-31; J. Columbi, *Opuscula Varia* (Lyon, 1668), pp. 330-1, cited by Chevalier, pp. 155-7; Chorier, *Histoire générale*, II, 494; Arnaud, 'Histoire des persécutions', 27-44.

[39] Chorier, *Histoire générale*, II, 512; J. Taulier, *Histoire du Dauphiné depuis les temps les plus reculés jusqu'à nos jours* (Grenoble, 1855), p. 228.

While we know so much about the troubles of the Dauphiné, we are in deep ignorance about the state of things in Piedmont. However, about 11 November 1475 Giovanni Andrea di Aquapendente, sub-delegate and vicar of the archbishop of Turin, Giovanni di Campesio (1469–82), began to proceed against the heretics of Luserna. When the *podestà* there resisted the ordinances he issued on 28 November, he obtained an edict from Duchess Yolande of Savoy on 23 January 1476 which directed that help be given to the inquisitors. The war with Burgundy seems to have cut short this venture. There was a revolt against seigneurs in the same region in 1483 which may or may not have been to do with religion.[40] According to the inventory of the Embrun archive in 1507, the inquisitor originally nominated to act alongside Cattaneo, Blaise de Berra of Mondovì, tried a suspected *barbe* named Philippe Nazarot at Luserna.[41]

In 1491 a papal bull, nearly identical to that produced for Cattaneo and de Berra in 1487, was issued authorizing Angelo Carletti of Chivasso and the bishop of St-Jean-de-Maurienne to proceed by force against heresy in the eastern valleys. It may be that Carletti and Philippe de Bresse invaded the Piedmontese valleys in 1493 as a result of this commission; this hypothesis is, however, speculative.[42] To all intents and purposes we must analyse the means and motives of the persecutors from the records of the Dauphiné alone. However, that region was most likely not unique in its experience.

(ii)   Harassment or crusade? Inquisitorial technique

A one-dimensional chronology of the inquisitorial process, like that just supplied, is apt to conceal the vast difference in patterns of behaviour which separated one inquisitor from another, or one occasion, when time was plentiful, from another when haste was needed. If we compare, however

---

[40] Fornier, II, 373–4; Carutti, *Crociata valdese*, pp. 7–10; Gilles, 1881 edn., I, 37–9; M. A. Rorengo-Lucerna, *Memorie historiche dell' introduttione dell' heresie nelle valli di Lucerna . . .* (Torino, 1649), pp. 22–5.

[41] *CUL G*, fo. 75^{r-v}; Marx, p. 195, based on the Embrun inventory.

[42] See esp. M. Viora, 'Le Persecuzioni contro i Valdesi nel secolo xv^o: la crociata di Filippo II', *BSHV* 47 (1925), 5–19.

briefly, the different types of inquisitorial procedure, we may reach some tentative conclusions about the natures and methods of those responsible. This exercise has a twofold importance: it allows us to see why the attitudes of orthodox laymen to inquisitors were so variable; it also performs the crucial task of telling us how far we can trust trial registers as evidence for Waldensian beliefs.

The trial of a heretic could involve months of deliberation; or it could be finished within minutes. At one extreme, on 4 February 1486 a heretic from the diocese of Sisteron called Antoni Blasii was captured by the inquisitors. On 25 February he was made to swear not to leave the territory of Embrun, where he was to be tried.[43] On 13 March his trial opened before Archbishop Baile; his interrogations ended on 27 July, and his abjuration and penance took place on 14 September.[44]

At the opposite extreme, during the crusade everything was done in haste. On 9 April 1488 Cattaneo and his colleagues processed the interrogations of no less than twenty-three suspected heretics. On 28 April they dealt with thirty-six; at this stage they divided themselves into groups across the country. Other days were nearly as busy as these.[45]

Some details of the archbishop's procedure bear further witness to his meticulousness and persistence. For example, canon law required that the accused be formally cited to appear, so that he could not claim ignorance of the case. In September 1486 Baile summoned a heretic named Antoni Baridon of Châteauroux, one who had been responsible for introducing others to the sect.[46] Baile cited him a total of seven times, only excluded him from defence on the seventh occasion, and kept all the records.[47] When the accused's wife asked for a copy of the dossier, she was given it.[48] Meanwhile, of course, Baridon had fled to Provence.[49] The citations used in the crusade were formalities based only on rumour and suspicion, and were generally recognized as a prelude to

---

[43] TCD MS 266, fo. 48^v.   [44] *CUL G*, fos. 59^r-77^v.

[45] *ADI B*, fos. 143^v-73^v, 220^v-42^v, 244^r-6^r, 324^r-40^r.

[46] He had introduced, amongst others, Antoni Blanc, as in *CUL G*, fo. 116^r, and Odin Valoy, as in *CUL H*, sect. 2, fos. 3^v, 12^{r-v}, 14^v.

[47] *CUL G*, fos. 81^{r-v}, 82^v-3^v, 86^{r-v}, 87^{r-v}, 88^v-9^r, 91^r-2^v, 93^v-4^r.

[48] Ibid., fols. 89^v-91^r.

[49] As he admitted in 1501, in *CUL G*, fo. 37^r, and *BP*, II, fo. 86^{r-v}.

armed assault. Their wording admitted the problems faced, when it said 'since perhaps those due to be cited and listed below may not be able to be conveniently reached and found, we direct that a copy of these presents be fixed to the doors of the churches of Mentoulles, Usseaux, and Pragelas; we wish and decree that by means of this posting the suspects be deemed to be lawfully cited as if they had been cited in person.'[50]

Much more important than the citation is the interrogation itself. Baile's interrogation records seem to be trustworthy.[51] Sometimes they show his abrasive technique in interrogation, as when he remarked sarcastically to a suspect who denied knowledge of a heretical doctrine 'you are ignorant indeed!'[52] The opposite extreme to Baile's detailed and idiosyncratic dossiers of interrogations was reached by Cattaneo in the Val Chisone, and by Antoine Fabri in the Valentinois. In each of these cases the records present a series of confessions from the victims in short paragraphs; the wording of these paragraphs is almost identical, in the Latin version, for page after page, although the order in which they are reproduced may and does differ.[53] Where there is variety in language, it is by a gradual evolution of the notary's technique and phraseology, not by variations at random between one witness and another. By late March 1488 one inhabitant of Fressinières was put off going to the commissaries because he had been warned that they took things down in writing which the victims had never admitted.[54] Thereafter, it is true, the records became more plausible.

The major dichotomy in inquisitorial technique is that between local clergy, content to deal with heretics patiently in the hope of securing a permanent (and possibly sincere)

---

[50]   Chevalier, p. 142.

[51]   Compare successive versions of the same interrogation, in TCD MS 266, fo. 46^v, and *CUL G*, fo. 63^v; or two accounts of the same torture session, in *CUL G*, fos. 65^r–6^v (quoted by Marx, pp. 237–9) and in TCD MS 266, fos. 46^v–7^v.

[52]   *CUL G*, fo. 111^v.

[53]   *ADI A*, *passim*; also *BP*, I, fos. 278^r–9^r, 281^r–2^r, 283^v–4^v, 286^r–7^r, 288^v–90^r; *CUL H*, sect. 7, fos. 6^r–8^v; Allix, *Some remarks*, pp. 322–5; Chevalier, pp. 156–7.   [54]   *ADI B*, fos. 117 (*bis*)^r, 121^v.

abjuration, and visitors, determined to obtain a quick and standard confession which would justify the punishment meted out, and the crusade itself.[55] This is more than a difference between two types of record. It is a difference in approach which hides a difference in motive: one approach would simply be an irritant to these dissenting communities, the other would drive them, and everybody else, to desperation. When we see who was chiefly responsible for the crusade, this result becomes less surprising.

(iii) The clique of persecutors

Social historians would no doubt prefer to see in the events just described the workings of a fundamental tension within the society of the Alps. It seems plausible to assume that some common grievance held against the Vaudois, whether economic or institutional, would have been needed to provoke such a frenetic outburst of persecution. However, try as one may, every attempt to find some specific social group responsible crumbles before a mass of important exceptions.

The crusade was not the work of the higher clergy, because the archbishop himself was not much involved. Although Jehan Baile's rapacity was notorious,[56] and his family parvenu,[57] there is no evidence that Baile involved himself much in Cattaneo's doings; he was already old, and some of the worst atrocities took place outside Embrun's sphere altogether, in the Val Chisone in the diocese of Turin.[58] Nor was it the work of the aristocracy as a whole. Fazy de Rame, *coseigneur* of Fressinières, warned his tenants about the persecutions, and tried to mediate between them and the

---

[55] This dichotomy has some similarity to that suggested by R. Kieckhefer, *Repression of heresy in medieval Germany* (Liverpool, 1979), p. 111.

[56] This was the opinion of Louis XI, in A. Fabre, *Recherches historiques sur le pélerinage des rois de France à Notre-Dame d'Embrun* (Grenoble, 1860), p. 146; of a Chorges innkeeper, in *BP*, II, fo. 40ʳ, cited by Marx, pp. 172-3 and nn.; and of the villagers of the valleys by the Durance, in TCD MS 266, fo. 125ʳ⁻ᵛ.

[57] The family came from Villar-St-Pancrace, near Briançon, and most of its members were lawyers; some other Bailes seem to have been servants. See Fornier, II, 352-5 and nn.; *Fazy*, I, 19-20, and II, sects. 723-4, 628; also *BP*, I, fos. 458ᵛ-9ʳ.

[58] As set down in *BP*, II, fos. 374ʳ-425ʳ.

commissioners to prevent bloodshed.[59] The crusade nearly ruined him financially.[60] Aymar de la Roche, governor of Mentoulles, also tried to mediate, and helped some prisoners to ransom their relatives under sentence of death.[61] Finally, although on several occasions the catholics in villages of divided religious allegiance protested about the heretics, and some of the syndics and *conseillers* of Vallouise gained confiscated lands,[62] there is no evidence that they initiated the persecution; the Vaudois' neighbours all spoke up for them in 1501 and 1507.[63]

All attempts, in fact, to find a reason grounded solely in the social fabric of the Alps for the crusade of 1487-8 are equally unsatisfactory. One is drawn to conclude that there was no such reason at all; and that one must look at each member of the group of men who were most involved in the campaign, and assess their motives from the records of their activities. Here one is not looking for a class of people with interests (whether spiritual or economic) at heart; one is studying a gang of institutionalized plunderers, who exploited the heresy laws ruthlessly for their own gain. Alberto Cattaneo, archdeacon of Cremona, commands attention first. Opinions differ as to his competence, his reliability, and even his age. He does not appear in the story until his appointment as inquisitor by papal letters of 21 April 1487, and by the bull *Id nostri cordis*, dated six days later.[64] According to proctors who acted for the Vaudois in 1507, he was not more than twenty-two at the time of the crusade, and took very little part in the interrogations; he was wholly controlled by his coadjutors, Oronce Émé and Jordanon Cordi; he did not even understand the local *patois*, as he spoke 'a Tuscan or

[59] *CUL H*, sect. 4, fo. 3ʳ; *ADI B*, fos. 138ʳ, 162ᵛ; *Fazy*, II, sect. 1493; Fornier, II, 434-5; Marx, pp. 163-4. For similar behaviour on the part of landlords during the war in Piedmont in 1560-1, see P. Rivoire, 'Storia dei Signori di Luserna', *BSHV* 13 (1896), 83-5.

[60] *Fazy*, I, 24, 356; II, sects. 673, 715-21, 754-6, 859-61.

[61] *BP*, II, fos. 415ʳ⁻ᵛ, 419ᵛ-20ᵛ; Fornier, II, 421-2, 424; Godefroy, *Charles VIII*, p. 281.

[62] *CUL G*, fos. 54ᵛ, 57ᵛ, 78ʳ-9ᵛ; *CUL H*, sect. 13, fo. 2ʳ⁻ᵛ; *BP*, I, fos. 317ᵛ-18ʳ.

[63] *CUL G*, fos. 25ʳ-38ᵛ; *BP*, I, fos. 439ʳ-64ᵛ; II, fos. 1ʳ-104ʳ.

[64] *CUL G*, fos. 8 ff., 75ʳ⁻ᵛ; Morland, *History of the Evangelical Churches*, pp. 196-214.

Italian tongue'.[65] According to proctors for the catholics in the same year, however, he was a doctor in both laws, 'full of all learning', and authorized to deal with the matter. Twenty years later, they pointed out, he was in the service of the French King as a senator at Milan, and could produce his copies of the documents if called on to do so.[66]

Cattaneo's victims provide more details with an inevitable bias. Fazy Gay and Fransez Ruffi both complained in 1501 that Cattaneo had threatened them with death unless they confessed to heresy.[67] Other witnesses said that, at the mass absolution of Vaudois before the *Grand Réal* at Embrun, Cattaneo made those whom he absolved swear that they would never appeal to the Pope or the King against his judgement.[68] Others told how the absolved heretics were fined a sum of four hundred 'gold pieces' (presumably *écus*) for each village of Fressinières, l'Argentière, and Vallouise; of this money Cattaneo was said to have received four hundred, in payment of his 'salary and expenses'.[69]

Cattaneo's experience as an inquisitor clearly did not teach him to trouble over-much about the precise description of heterodox doctrine. When he wrote his account of the crusade in his history, he prefaced the narrative of the campaign with a brief description of the heretics' beliefs. This list of doctrines he copied, with only minor alterations, from the description of 'Waldensian' Hussitism found in the *Historia Bohemica* of Pope Pius II, one of the least apposite of texts for the case.[70] In prefering a literary source to an empirical one, however, he was typical of his age.[71]

Another obvious member of this group of persecutors was the senior lay judge of Briançon, Oronce Émé or Aymé.

---

[65] *BP*, I, fo. 354ᵛ: 'ydioma tuscanum seu ytallicum'; Marx, p. 259, based on *BP*, I, fos. 294ʳ-305ᵛ.

[66] *BP*, II, fos. 446ᵛ-7ʳ, 471ʳ⁻ᵛ.

[67] *CUL G*, fo. 25ᵛ; *BP*, II, fos. 47ᵛ-8ʳ, 51ᵛ.

[68] e.g. *BP*, II, fos. 66ʳ, 75ʳ, 94ᵛ; Marx, p. 262; needless to say, this detail is not found in the text of the abjuration, in Chevalier, p. 154.

[69] *BP*, II, fos. 95ʳ, 100ʳ, 102ʳ, 104ʳ.

[70] A. S. Piccolomini (Pius II), *Opera Omnia* (Basel, 1551), pp. 103-4; compare Godefroy, *Charles VIII*, p. 278.

[71] Compare B. de Lutzenburgo, *Catalogus hereticorum* (Cologne, 1522), art. *Waldenses*, which employs the passage from Pius II in the same sense.

According to some protests made in 1507, he, along with
Jordanon Cordi, was placed under arrest in the time of
Louis XI for abuses committed against those of the valleys.
Émé and Cordi escaped from prison, and their case was
referred to the *parlement* of Grenoble, 'where', the proctors
claimed, 'it is still undiscussed'.[72] In other articles the proctors
alleged that Émé and Cordi had used Cattaneo as an instrument
to pursue their vendetta.[73] Four witnesses complained that
Émé was one of those who threatened to kill them if they did
not confess their heresy.[74] The Fraticelli tried at Oulx in
1492 also deposed that those of the valleys of the Dauphiné
regarded Émé as one of the worst of the persecutors—in spite
of the fact that Émé was present at that very trial.[75]

All that has been said about Émé applies equally well to
Jordanon Cordi, *procureur-fiscal* of the Briançonnais. In
depositions made by the people of the Val Chisone, moreover,
he appears to have paid special attention to his duties as
executor of the financial business of the crusade. Johan
Mathiou of Pragelas complained how Cordi sent a servant to
him, to ask him to come to Briançon to give evidence as a
witness; immediately Mathiou arrived he was imprisoned.
When he had been absolved and told to wear a yellow cross,
Cattaneo let him know that he might be released from this
penance for twenty-five ducats. Mathiou protested that he
was too poor; after four or five months, however, Cordi came
to him and said that if he paid fifteen florins, ' "as atonement
for his wrongs", as he said, then he would be free from all
constraints.' A series of witnesses listed sums which they had
lost to the *procureur-fiscal*, either to redeem the property of
relatives killed in the fighting, or as a result of plain robbery.[76]
Two witnesses said that the redemption of confiscated
property in the Val Chisone cost its people over 6,000 *écus*,
and one added that this also was paid to Cordi.[77]

The trio of notorious persecutors, according to the report
that Fraticelli had heard, was completed by Pons Pons,

[72] *BP*, I, fos. 381^r-2^r.   [73] Marx, p. 259.
[74] *CUL G*, fos. 31^r, 38^r; *BP*, II, fos. 65^v-6^r, 93^r, 98^r, 100^v-1^r.
[75] *CUL H*, sect. 6, fos. 1^r, 7^v, 9^r; Allix, *Some remarks*, p. 315.
[76] *BP*, II, fos. 383^r-5^r, 401^v-3^v, 410^v-11^r, 416^v-17^v, 418^r-19^r, 422^r.
[77] Ibid., II, fos. 390^r, 401^r-^{v}, 402^v-3^r.

conseiller in the *parlement* at Grenoble.[78] He seems mostly to have been busy in the western region of the lands affected by the crusade. Johan Arnulphs of Fressinières had been captured by Pons twice, once at Embrun and once at Gap. Three witnesses from the town of Chorges, between Embrun and Gap, were outraged when Pons, as a punishment for their providing shelter for some of those escaping from the crusaders, insisted on levying a fine of eighty *écus* on the town. When they took this to the treasurer of the Dauphiné, he was apparently reluctant to accept it, and doubted its legality.[79] Several of those who testified had doubts about the legality of the way in which Pons's victims were put to death.[80]

Besides lawyers, there were a few in the clique who simply provided military muscle; this group included a few small landowners in the valleys. The most notable was the leader of the crusaders' army, the lieutenant of the governor of the Dauphiné, Hugues de la Palu, lord of Varax. According to Peyre Jordan of Fressinières and three other witnesses, it was Varax, along with Poët and Antoine Baile, who persuaded the people of Fressinières, who had fled from the army to the highest points in the valley, with 'sweet and smiling words', to come down from their refuges; the villagers were then taken, the women dragged by the hair, and all were shut up in a building to which burning faggots were laid, while Palu and the others shouted to those inside 'You will all be burnt if you do not say that you are Waldenses'.[81] Varax also led the armed attacks on the heretics of the Val Chisone who had hidden in various caves. It was claimed that, when he captured those in the *balma* of Fenestrelle, he said that he did not know whether they were good or bad; but he shut them up in a large barn and abused them anyway.[82]

Varax was assisted by Jehan Rabot, a *conseiller* in the *parlement* of Grenoble like Pons. Those who deposed about the violence and threats used by the commissaries included

---

[78] Allix, *Some remarks*, p. 315 as above.
[79] *CUL G*, fo. 30ᵛ; *BP*, II, fos. 31ᵛ-2ʳ, 34ᵛ-5ʳ, 36ʳ.
[80] *BP*, II, fos. 43ᵛ-4ʳ, 75ᵛ.
[81] *CUL G*, fo. 34ʳ⁻ᵛ; *BP*, II, fos. 73ʳ-5ᵛ, 92ᵛ-4ᵛ, 98ʳ-9ᵛ, 100ᵛ-1ᵛ; Marx, p. 169.   [82] *BP*, II, fos. 388ʳ, 404ᵛ.

him in their denunciations. Rabot was still embroiled in the confiscations in 1498, when Rostain d'Ancezune, archbishop of Embrun, referred Louis XII's chancellor to him when questioned in Paris about the suit of those of Fressinières.[83]

Lanthelme Eynard, Sieur de Monteynard and seigneur of l'Argentière, was named several times as retaining the goods confiscated from heretics.[84] Lanthelme d'Avançon, one of the family of Saint-Marcel of which at least three members were involved in the crusade, acquired an evil reputation. Peyre Martin of Usseaux was captured by him and led to the house of Guilhem Blanc at Fenestrelle; there he was tortured and told that, unless he paid 200 *écus*, he would be hanged the next day. Antoni Pinatel had to ransom his father from d'Avançon in the same way.[85]

This exploitation of a curious form of the laws of war was made into a fine art by Hippolyte de Bardonnèsche, *coseigneur* of Bardonècchia. He had a gibbet raised near Usseaux and blackmailed those of that village with the threat of hanging, some for eleven *écus*, some for four. Other witnesses recorded the violence he used in the military attack in the Val Chisone.[86] Antoine Baile, brother of the archbishop and one of the *coseigneurs* of Fressinières, agreed with Cattaneo that if a servant of his were punished with wearing a cross for heresy, he would be exempt from the penance as long as he stayed in Baile's service. This small favour would have preserved Baile's dignity without stripping him of his servants.[87]

Pierre Sabine, *official* of the bishop of Embrun, was one of the most indefatigable witnesses in the early heresy trials; he was also accused of extorting confessions with threats.[88] Moreover, as prior of the little abbey of Les Beaumes, north-east of Embrun, Sabine was landlord to the Valoy

---

[83] *CUL G*, fo. 2ᵛ; G. Allard, *La Vie de Jean Rabot, conseiller au parlement de Grenoble* (H. Gariel, *Dephinalia*, pt. ii, Grenoble, 1852).

[84] *CUL G*, fo. 33ᵛ; *CUL H*, sect. 13, fo. 2ʳ; *BP*, I, fos. 341ʳ, 347ᵛ–8ʳ; Marx, p. 256.   [85] *BP*, II, fos. 388ʳ–9ʳ, 397ʳ; Fornier, II, 429.

[86] *CUL H*, sect. 13, fo. 2ᵛ; *BP*, I, fo. 385ᵛ; II, fos. 378ᵛ–9ʳ; Fornier, II, 429–30; Marx, pp. 261–2.

[87] P. Guillaume, 'Notes et documents', 420–1, based on ADH-A G 2763, fo. 140ᵛ; *CUL H*, sect. 4, fo. 16ᵛ.

[88] *CUL G*, fos. 25ᵛ, 31ʳ, 32ᵛ, 34ʳ; *BP*, II, fos. 48ʳ, 65ᵛ–6ʳ, 68ᵛ, 74ᵛ.

brothers at St-André, just across the Durance. Both these brothers were subjected to long trials for heresy: Odin broke out of prison, Peyre was burnt.[89]

It will already perhaps be apparent why structural explanations of the crusade against the Waldenses are so insufficient. The crusaders came from all the different ranks of the privileged, and in that was the chief source of their strength. They included ecclesiastics like Cattaneo and Sabine, church lawyers in Cordi and the notaries, secular judges in Émé, Rabot, and Pons, military and political force in Varax, and local landed influence in Baile, Poët, Bardonnèsche, d'Avançon, and Monteynard. This combination of powers was very hard to resist. It was, however, only a temporarily successful alliance which caused much damage to society and the economy, and represented no clear group besides itself. Before discussing the process by which this group was discredited, however, we must try to analyse the motives of its participants more closely.

(iv) The motives for persecution

It was suggested above[90] that the motives which animated the archbishop, and those who led the slower, more methodical dealings with heretics were probably very different from those which inspired the clique who perpetrated the crusade of 1487-8. This distinction becomes even clearer if we look at the punishments which the crusaders imposed. These punishments suggest that the crusaders had no concern, even according to the standards of the age, for their victims' souls; and that they wanted money, quickly and in liquid form.

The standard punishment for a heretic in this period was redolent with moral overtones.[91] If the forms were followed exactly, the inquisitor could have little more than moral satisfaction as the reward for his work. A penitent heretic, who was a first offender, would be absolved with a penance, which usually involved the saying of a number of prayers, the carrying out of pilgrimages and fasts, and the wearing

---

[89] Marx, pp. 246, 248, 252-4.   [90] Above, section (ii).
[91] On this see H. C. Lea, *History of the Inquisition of the Middle Ages* (London, 1888), I, 459-62.

of a yellow cross on the front and back of the clothing for a specified period of time. Since these punishments were intended to reform the penitent's attitude towards the Church and the faith, they ought not to have been commuted. Furthermore, in some cases the absolved heretic was required to be available to visit the inquisitor at specified times after absolution to give proof of repentance. In the case of a relapsed or obstinate heretic, the punishment of remission to the secular arm, and burning, had the same moral content: the corrupt member was to be cut off to purify the rest of the body. Up to 1378 it was also argued that the house where a heretic had lived should be razed to the ground, although the normal tenurial system made this prescription so unpopular that it was usually waived after that time. The only case of a heretic's house being burnt in this region and period dates from Bioletto, in the marquisate of Saluzzo, in 1510.[92]

As far as the evidence tells us, in the long trials both before and after the crusade these prescriptions were more or less obeyed. The *procès-verbal* illustrates the heretic's breakdown and contrition; penances for first and minor offenders were fairly mild; they did not involve loss of money, save in the costs of pilgrimages and other pious works. In the crusade itself, on the other hand, canonical form or convention was breached in several ways which allow us to see the workings of the crusaders' minds: the commutation of penances for money, the levying of fines and ransoms, the sale of confiscated lands, and the use of informal and unusual means of execution.[93]

In principle a penance imposed for heresy should not have been commuted for a sum of money: but many of the crusaders' penances were. Fransez Lanterme, of Pragelas, told how three months after he had been sentenced to wear a cross, Cattaneo sent for him and two others, and offered to remove their crosses for a payment of four *écus*. A month later François Plouvier absolved him for half a ducat. In several other cases apparently random sums were charged to

---

[92] Marx, pp. 136-7; V. Promis, 'Memoriale', *Miscellanea di storia italiana*, VIII (1869), 496.

[93] On these see also Lea, *History of the Inquisition*, I, 471-80.

the victims to have their crosses removed.[94]

These measures were evidently aimed at translating spiritual punishments into liquid cash as soon as possible. Other moves served the same ends. Those who fled from the crusaders found that the archbishop's officers occupied their property and stripped its assets.[95] We saw above that the main heretic villages were each fined 400 *écus*.[96] Ransoms were also demanded of suspected heretics, either for their own lives or for those of their close relatives. In one case the price rose as high as a hundred ducats, for Martin Flote of Pragelas: the money could not be found, and he was hanged.[97] The prosecutors generally made the offer of ransom, rather than the victims; in some cases aristocrats such as Aymar de la Roche took pity and negotiated such bargains.[98] Even quite small sums of money were taken from heretics while they were in prison.[99]

Although by strict canon law it was not permitted for the heirs of heretics to inherit their lands, it had been discovered in the past that this land often could not pass to anyone else, and exceptions had been allowed in the fourteenth century.[100] In this crusade, however, resale of lands became something of an industry. Several Vaudois of the Val Chisone bought back their family possessions for sums which ranged from sixteen florins to two hundred, and to ninety *écus*. Those of that valley reckoned their losses in many thousands of *livres*.[101]

The canonical penalty of death by burning for obstinate or repeated heresy was dramatic, but slow; it also required certain formality in its application. The crusaders, with their need for haste, frequently resorted to hanging as a more effective means of terror. Manuscript sources refer to the hanging of those accused of heresy eleven times.[102] In the heat of the campaign other methods were used. Some of those captured in the storming of the caves were thrown

---

[94]   *BP*, II, fos. 377v–8r, 386v, 389r–v, 415v–16r.
[95]   *CUL G*, fo. 36v, and *BP*, II, fo. 86v, for Antoni Baridon; for the Jauvents of Caléyère, *CUL H*, sect. 12, fos. 1v–2v.
[96]   *BP*, II, fos. 99v–100r, 102r, 103v–4r, as above.   [97]   Ibid., II, fo. 424v.
[98]   Ibid., II, fos. 388r–9r, 397r, 399v–400r, 411r, 415r–16r, 420r–v.
[99]   Ibid., II, fos. 381r–2r, 410v–11r.   [100]   Marx, pp. 126–7.
[101]   *BP*, II, fos. 385r, 401v, 402v–3v, 417v, 418v–19r, 422r, 423v, 424v–5r.
[102]   *CUL G*, fos. 32v, 34v, 36v–7r; *BP*, II, fos. 3r, 17r, 64r, 69r, 86r, 416r, 424v.

from rocks.[103] One heretic was simply run through with a sword, apparently a simpleton whom the commissaries had killed in cold blood. Another, Antoni Brunet, was taken from his home at Baratier and drowned without form of law. Fransez Pastre claimed that he had been told that the commissaries intended to flog his brother, Philippe Pastre, to death; he paid ten *écus soleil* to Oronce Émé, and his brother escaped.[104]

It is fairly clear that the commissaries chose their tactics to terrorize, intimidate, and eventually despoil the communities in their way; there is no reason even to argue that those at the head of the persecution acted out of any high spiritual concern for the good of the souls of their victims. We may go a little further than this conclusion. The commissaries wanted ready cash, rather than land; so this conspiracy was concocted, not permanently to alter the structure of local society, but simply to enrich a few at the expense of a marginal group. Hence the events of 1487–8 should not be seen, for example, as an attempt by a landed aristocracy to repair the damage which they had suffered from the economic trends of the late Middle Ages. A few aristocrats, like Pierre de Rame, *coseigneur* of Fressinières and Sieur de Poët, may have been driven by bad housekeeping to try to exploit the crusade; but for those aristocrats outside Cattaneo's clique the crusade cost more than it earned. Of course, once the crusaders were on their lands, landlords like Fazy de Rame had to find money to pay their expenses; so they were drawn willy-nilly into the proceedings. They may then appear to participate in a process with which they were unsympathetic.[105]

Beyond this crude explanation one proceeds with difficulty. The clergy would have had no particular reason to prosecute the heretics for refusing the tithe; although they accused the Vaudois of this in 1501, this charge was expressly denied by

---

[103] *CUL G*, fo. 36[r–v]; *BP*, I, fo. 386[v]; Godefroy, *Charles VIII*, p. 283. The latter reference is from Cattaneo's own account.

[104] *BP*, II, fos. 61[r–v], 64[r–v], 411[r].

[105] Marx, pp. 122–3. In one sentence half of the confiscated goods was reserved to the *coseigneurs* of Fressinières: see Marx, p. 243, based on *ADI B*, fos. 264[r]–8[v]. It is hard to see that any of this reached Fazy de Rame; but cf. Promis, 'Memoriale', 492–3, 496.

them.[106] In 1483 and 1497, indeed, representatives from Fressinières actually asked the clergy to visit their church and preach there. The Waldenses may have used the services of the catholic church in a heterodox way, but there is no evidence that they avoided them deliberately in a way which aroused clerical jealousy.[107]

Alberto Cattaneo may have been interested in pure self-aggrandizement. Fransez Ruffi of Fressinières, asked about his handling by Cattaneo, said that the inquisitor had had him imprisoned, and threatened that he would die if he did not confess to being a Vaudois, and said 'you will have your appeal to the Pope and the King—well, behold the Pope and the King!'—whereat Ruffi made his confession.[108]

The unscrupulousness of the crusaders, finally, was not lost on the local population. Of those interviewed at Chorges and Gap in 1501, sixteen said that the persecution had been motivated by greed for goods rather than zeal for justice. A proverb had been formed: 'their heresy was in their wallets; and if they had been poor, they would never have been accused of such things.'[109]

We are now in a better position to say exactly why persecution failed as it did. An effective persecution would have taken more than a few months, since one could not kill all the Vaudois, and only by piecemeal processes could they have been persuaded to give up their old ways. Likewise, if persecution were to succeed it would have needed a consistent and broad base of catholic support; instead support for the crusaders was patchy and sporadic. For this alienation the rift between those who worked with and through Cattaneo and the group around the archbishop must bear much of the blame. Finally, a persecution which would have rivalled those of Jacques Fournier, Bernard Gui, or their kind would have needed a man of dedication and experience at its head, not a Milanese lawyer who was inexperienced, ignorant of local

---

[106] *CUL H*, sect. 2, fo. 4ᵛ; *BP*, II, fo. 62ʳ; compare *CUL G*, sect. 3, as in Allix, *Some remarks*, p. 300.

[107] *CUL G*, fo. 2ʳ, 56ᵛ.   [108] *BP*, II, fo. 51ᵛ.

[109] Ibid., II, fo. 11ᵛ; other references of the same sort are found at *CUL G*, fos. 30ʳ, 33ᵛ; *BP*, I, fos. 443ᵛ, 457ᵛ, 459ᵛ, 463ᵛ-4ʳ; II, fos. 2ᵛ-3ʳ, 6ʳ-ᵛ, 10ᵛ, 12ᵛ, 15ʳ, 16ᵛ, 21ʳ-2ᵛ, 26ᵛ, 44ʳ, 64ᵛ.

language and customs, and impatient. Nevertheless, the persecution did not fail simply because of the failings or vices of its instigators. It failed as a result of a long lawsuit which finally vindicated the legal stand of the people of the Alpine valleys. The mechanism of that lawsuit, and especially of the investigations in the Alps which accompanied it, are of great importance in telling us yet more about the standing of the Waldenses in the catholic society of their time.

3. The Rehabilitation of the Persecuted

(i) The case in the *Grand Conseil*, 1489-1509

Understandably enough, those who had been compelled to take an oath to Archdeacon Cattaneo never to appeal against his judgement to the King of France or the Pope[1] did not feel themselves bound by that provision. According to their own account, almost as soon as the crusade was over, they went off to appeal to Charles VIII, with, as they put it, 'much carnage amongst the population'.[2] In 1491 some villagers of l'Argentière appealed to the *parlement* of Grenoble against the extortion being practised by the seigneurs of l'Argentière; it seems they won their case.[3] Some time during this period the chancellor Adam Fumée demanded from Jehan Baile the records of the heresy trials in his diocese; he arrested Baile and his secretary, and did not allow them to keep any copies of the documents, which were apparently sent up to the *Grand Conseil*.[4] With Baile's death and the start of the Italian wars, however, this stage of the case went no further.[5]

Baile was succeeded by Rostain d'Ancezune, bishop of Fréjus and relative of a counsellor of Charles VIII, at the King's express bidding.[6] Three years after his translation, Rostain was visiting Champcella when he was approached by Fazy Gay, of Fressinières, who asked him to visit that parish. Rostain explained that the people of Fressinières were excommunicate,[7] and that the matter was in the hands of the papal commissioners; he wanted to visit, but his hands were

---

[1] *BP*, II, fos. 66^r, 75^r, 94^v, and above, ch. 2, n. 68.

[2] *BP*, I, fo. 349^r: 'non sine magna hominum strage.'

[3] Arnaud, 'Histoire des persécutions', *BSHV* 12 (1895), 107 ff.

[4] *CUL G*, fo. 3^v; Marx, p. 178, dates the event to 1494, but without citing evidence.   [5] *BP*, I, fos. 349^v-50^r.

[6] Fabre, *Recherches historiques*, pp. 189, 299-302; A. Sauret, *Essai historique sur la ville d'Embrun* (Gap, 1860), pp. 236-44.

[7] Apparently notwithstanding the absolutions accorded to penitent heretics by Cattaneo; Rostain's objection must have been to visiting those who had fled from the region before the crusade and had not been absolved.

tied. Gay protested that by now the people had been absolved. Rostain gave Gay six months in which to produce proof of this absolution, which he never did; he also inquired at Rome through his emissary, without any results.[8]

The villagers were given a more sympathetic hearing in Paris after the accession of Louis XII in 1498. When Rostain went there for the coronation, he was called before the chancellor to explain why the villagers were being deprived of the sacraments. After a brief investigation, however, the *Grand Conseil*, according to Rostain, gave its approval to his scruples about giving the sacraments to unabsolved heretics.[9]

In this same year it was agreed that the King should write to the Pope to request a formal commission to investigate the whole matter, in collaboration with the archbishop. On 11 March 1500/1 Alexander VI formally assented to this request in the bull *Carissimus in Cristo*, given to Laurent Bureau, bishop of Sisteron, Geoffroy Boussart, canon of Le Mans, Jehan Saulnier, *official* of Autun, and Thomas Pascal, *official* of Orléans, to correct and ratify the acts of past commissioners.[10] By a further bull of 5 April 1501 the Cardinal of Rouen, Georges d'Amboise, was given authority to absolve heretics as a papal legate.[11]

In the first instance only two of the new appointees, Laurent Bureau and Thomas Pascal, were delegated to investigate the events of the previous decades where they had taken place. Some idea of the importance attached to the mission, however, may be gained from the fact that Bureau took time from his duties as Louis's confessor to carry out the inquiry. On 15 July 1501 the commissioners were at Grenoble, from where they issued a general letter directing all those who held information and documents about the inquisitions to produce it for them.[12] The *parlement* of Grenoble ratified this demand, and Bureau and Pascal proceeded to Gap, which they reached on 20 July. There they presented their credentials to the bishop, and conducted interviews on the 21st and 22nd. On the 23rd they did the

[8] *CUL G*, fo. 2[r]; Marx, p. 179.   [9] *CUL G*, fos. 2[v]-3[r]; Marx, pp. 179-80.
[10] *BP*, I, fos. 432[r]-4[r]; Guillaume, 'Sentence de réhabilitation', 256-7; Fornier, III, 410-12; Marx, pp. 180-1.
[11] *CUL H*, sect. 8; Marx, pp. 181, 254-5.   [12] *BP*, I, fos. 431[r]-7[v].

same at Chorges.[13]

On 24 July 1501 the commissioners reached Embrun and presented their commissions to Rostain d'Ancezune. Almost at once an argument began over access to papers relating to the prosecution of heretics. The following day was a Sunday; on 26 July Bureau and Pascal insisted on riding up to Fressinières themselves to take testimonies. The day after that, Rostain stayed at his manor of Champcella, where he heard that Bureau had preached and said mass at Fressinières.[14] Further testimonies were taken, both at Fressinières and Champcella, until 29 July.[15]

The initial reaction of the commissioners was so favourable that in the autumn of 1501 procedures for absolution and restitution of goods were set in motion. On 7 October a fresh bull confirmed the Cardinal of Rouen's powers of absolution.[16] On 12 October the *Grand Conseil* sent letters to the *parlement* of Grenoble, ordering the *parlement* to command those who held lands claimed by the appellants to surrender them, or appear before the King.[17] On 23 October the *parlement* agreed to pass on these commands, but would not consent to the evocation of individuals to courts outside the Dauphiné. Nevertheless, on 3 November Pierre ·Arabi, usher of the court, commanded Nicolas Paris, former secretary to Baile (and also the notary who kept the records of the early heresy trials) to surrender a house, mill, and some lands belonging to Jame and Antoni Jouans (or Jauvent) of Caléyère, who were associated with the Vaudois appellants, and to pay them 100 *écus* for the damage done to their property in the mean time; Paris refused, and was assigned to appear before the King on 1 January 1501/2. His may have been a test case.[18]

With these events in the Embrunais the case in the *Grand Conseil* resumed in all its legal perplexity. On 1 January 1501/2 the proctors for the defendants and the Vaudois plaintiffs made their appearance. The defendants asked for

[13] Ibid., I, fos. 437^v-64^v, and II, 1^r-4^v; II, fos. 4^v-46^r; Marx, p. 181.

[14] *CUL G*, fos. 3^v-5^v; Perrin, *Vaudois*, pp. 140-3; Marx, pp. 181-5.

[15] *CUL G*, fos. 25^r-38^v; *BP*, II, fos. 46^r-104^r.

[16] *CUL H*, sect. 10; Marx, pp. 185, 256-7.

[17] *CUL H*, sect. 11, fo. 1^{r-v}, and sect. 12, fo. 1^{r-v}; Perrin, *Vaudois*, p. 145.

[18] *CUL H*, sect. 12, fos. 1^v-2^v; Marx, pp. 186-7. On the previous association of the Jauvents and the Baridons, see Marx, p. 250, and *CUL H*, sect. 5, fo. 6^v.

the case to be transferred to the *parlement* of the Dauphiné, which was formally refused on 24 January. On 6 April (or perhaps 16 April) the catholic proctor defaulted to appear after citation. On 21 April the defendants defaulted again. The Vaudois proctors requested that their opponents be declared contumacious, and a decree in their favour was issued on 27 May 1502.[19] This decree named a large number of those still holding seized property (*détenteurs*) who were thus told to surrender these lands; any who resisted were to be constrained by seizure of their own property. On 6 July the *parlement* at Grenoble registered this decree also, again with a proviso against any evocation of subjects outside the Dauphiné.[20]

This edict, like those before it, settled nothing. When Laurent Bureau died in July 1504, the senior position in the commission passed to Geoffroy Boussart, canon of Le Mans. It was decided that the only way to avoid the problems of the legal relations between the *Grand Conseil* and the Dauphiné was to send Boussart and Pascal to the Dauphiné to pass sentence there as officers of the *Roi Dauphin*. In late 1506, these two cited a group of *détenteurs* to Vienne, in two groups for 25 September and 1 October. These citations were resisted, as being outside the jurisdiction of the ordinary of Embrun; the lesson of 1487 had not been forgotten. In January 1507 the commissioners finally bowed to the invincible parochialism of Dauphinois lawyers and travelled to the Embrunais. However, objections were then raised to Pascal's sub-delegate, Antoine de la Colombière, who had acted for the appellants in the case in 1487.[21]

Only in July 1507 were investigations under way once more. On 12 July Boussart and de la Colombière took depositions in the Val Chisone. Three days later one of the catholic proctors made a submission to justify the crusaders. On 23 July, at Embrun, the villagers' proctors described in a detailed written submission the atrocities to which their clients had been subjected in the crusade. Their articles were

[19]   *CUL H*, sect. 13, fos. 1^r-6^r. It is hard to reconcile the dates given in the documents one with another.

[20]   *CUL H*, sect. 13, fo. 6^{r-v}.

[21]   Marx, pp. 187-9, based on *BP*, I, fos. 1-100.

answered in a process of counter-accusation which lasted into the first week of August. On 17 and 18 August Raymond Émé wrote to say that a *barbe* had been captured at Pinerolo, and would the commissioners please come to hear his confession? The latter reached Pinerolo on 20 August.[22] On 25 August a new series of catholic procuratorial articles was presented in the Val Chisone, and on 2 September an inventory of the archive of Embrun was made, which allows us to judge the extent of our loss.[23]

After this Paris made a further attempt to assert its authority. In the summer of 1508 the parties were cited to appear yet again. On 8 October the judges cited, to an ecclesiastical court at the bar of the chapter of Notre-Dame, the archbishop of Embrun, the provost of Oulx, Alberto Cattaneo, François Plouvier, and the procurator of the faith in the Embrunais, who all failed to appear, and were declared contumacious. On 27 February 1508/9 sentence was finally given in favour of the appellants. The wording of that sentence is noteworthy: it pronounced that 'although . . . regarding the catholic faith, there was good reason . . . to inquire and proceed by means of inquisition against the said plaintiffs, as we are well and sufficiently aware; however, these processes . . . because of not keeping to the form of law, we void, annul and invalidate'.[24] Even after this pronouncement some villagers were still complaining about the de Rame families; but they had won their point, and on 7 November 1509 a decision in favour of the people of Fressinières was given against the de Rame at Grenoble.[25] One of the oddest episodes in the history of the late medival inquisition was over.

(ii) Can we trust the evidence?

An important unanswered question hangs over the rehabilitation. Its records are a rich source for the way in which the

---

[22] The full trial record for this *barbe*, Jean-François Gignoux, either is lost or was never made. Its *incipit* is found at the end of the last existing leaf of *BP*, II.

[23] *BP*, I, fos. 290ᵛ–430ᵛ, and II, fos. 430ʳ–71ᵛ, 494 ff.; Marx, pp. 191–5.

[24] Guillaume, 'Sentence de réhabilitation', 261–5; Fornier, III, 418–23; Marx, pp. 195–7.

[25] Marx, p. 197; Arnaud, 'Histoire des persécutions', 137.

inquisitors behaved; yet those same records lie under suspicion. It was suggested as soon as they were made that the commissioners had cheated so as to obtain a favourable report of the life and morals of those suspected as Vaudois; that they were selective in calling witnesses and in taking down evidence alike. Only by a brief study of the evidence may we resolve this question.[26]

A total of ninety-two witnesses were interrogated. We are told the occupations of forty-nine, and the spread of these appears quite natural, including besides farmers and labourers two nobles, five merchants, ten notaries, and twelve priests. Of the ninety-two it is probable that fifty at most were Waldenses, although all denied holding heretical beliefs. This is not the sort of sample which suggests that only witnesses likely to be favourable were called.

It was also alleged that, when witnesses were interrogated, the commissioners only had recorded what they wanted to hear, and that they refused to have a record kept of the suspects' reputation for heresy.[27] Fortunately, in the early stages of the inquiry at Fressinières, Rostain insisted on having his own secretary present, who kept separate notes of the interrogations. This secretary, Vincens Gobaut, was himself suspect as a *détenteur*.[28]

Both Gobaut's version of the Fressinières inquiry and that taken by Gaultier, the notary for the judges-delegate, show signs of tampering. The Embrun version omits the testimonies of seven witnesses altogether.[29] Its records of interrogations on matters of faith are much shorter than Gaultier's version, in spite of Rostain's protests.[30] It also tends to omit the damaging stories of the treachery used when the people of Fressinières were persuaded to surrender.[31]

On the other hand, the record kept for Bureau and Pascal says much less about the fact that some of the witnesses were given penances for heresy, and ignores the admissions that

---

[26]   Marx, pp. 177–8, discusses this issue in a rather perfunctory way.

[27]   *CUL G*, fos. 4^v-5^r, 6^r; cf. Perrin, *Vaudois*, pp. 143 ff.

[28]   *CUL G*, fo. 38^v. For Gobaut as a *détenteur*, see *CUL H*, sect. 13, fo. 2^r.

[29]   They are only found in *BP*, II, fos. 88^r-90^v, 96^r-104^r.

[30]   *CUL G*, fos. 25^r-6^v, 34^r, for example; and compare *BP*, II, fos. 46^v-53^v, 72^v-3^r.

[31]   *CUL G*, fo. 34^v; compare *BP*, II, fos. 73^r-5^r, 92^v-5^r, 98^r-102^r.

some Vaudois had laid aside their penitential crosses illegally.[32] In a few comparatively trifling cases there are small discrepancies between testimonies, and in that of Honoré du Bourg, of St-Crépin, a direct contradiction regarding his opinion of the heretical reputation of Fressinières.[33]

In spite of these differences, and a clumsy attempt by the *official* of Embrun to prevent records being kept of the atrocities,[34] there is in fact no reason to suppose that the evidence collected by Bureau and Pascal is worthless. Neither side ignores altogether the facts adduced by the other, although both try to shift the emphasis. However, an examination of the evidence certainly does prove that by the time they came to Embrun the commissioners had formed a tolerant view of those suspected of heresy. This attitude is further proven, if not totally explained, by the abundant evidence supplied by Rostain about his quarrel with Laurent Bureau.[35] This same attitude, where some of the most senior clergy in France chose to take the side of some oppressed mountain folk against a section of the nobility and higher clergy of the region, is striking enough, and must be explained.

(iii) The motives for rehabilitation

The rehabilitation meant different things to the lawyers, notaries, and priests who testified so readily to the perfect catholic conduct of the Vaudois, and to the bishops and ecclesiastical judges who pronounced sentence in the decree of February 1509. One must consider these different meanings in turn.

Boussart and Pascal did not say in 1509, as most of the witnesses in the previous eight years had done, that the people of the valleys were faultless in life and doctrine. The sentence admitted that there was good reason to proceed against them by inquisition.[36] However, it did go on to say that the appellants had been found 'not to be heretics, nor

---

[32] These admissions are only recorded in *CUL G*, fos, 27ʳ, 31ʳ⁻ᵛ, 34ᵛ, 38ᵛ. Cases where a penance was abridged by inquisitors, without money changing hands, are found in *BP*, II, fos. 391ᵛ, 410ʳ.

[33] *CUL G*, fos. 37ᵛ-8ʳ, and *BP*, II, fos. 91ᵛ-2ʳ.

[34] *CUL G*, fo. 34ᵛ.   [35] *CUL G*, fos. 3ʳ-5ʳ, 6ʳ.

[36] Guillaume, 'Sentence de réhabilitation', 263, and above, n. 24.

pertinaciously deviant from the faith'. The apparent contradiction was explained as follows: the judges exhorted the
priests in the region to keep diligent watch over their flocks,
and both by spiritual and corporal weapons to drive away
from the fold those 'wolves and false apostles, who by animal
deceits and secret preachings, deceive the simple and careless,
and destroy the Lord's vine . . .'. In other words, the judges
drew, as inquisitors hitherto had generally not done, a
distinction between the *barbes*, who were to be uprooted by
all means to hand, and the common people, who were easily
misled, and for whose care the priesthood was responsible,
not simply as a disciplinary body, but also as a pastoral one.[37]
It is a moot point whether the organization of Waldensianism
did represent the deceit of the simple by the caste of *barbes*:
here we have suggested that it did not; however, this explanation is the attitude for which we have to account.[38]

Amongst the witnesses for the inquiry in 1501 a different
motive must be sought. They had learned in previous decades
that there were those who would use any aspersion of heresy
to uproot rural society. These witnesses evidently decided, in
their attempts to obliterate all mention of heresy in the
valleys, that peace was more important than purity of religion.
This is an unusual attitude to have to explain, although it
does make the unique state of these valleys in the sixteenth
century more comprehensible.

A simple institutional explanation must be discarded. The
rehabilitation was not the result of a conflict between the
secular and spiritual authorities in which the inquisition, as
a spiritual one, was gradually discredited and subordinated
towards the end of the Middle Ages. Lea ascribes the loss of
prestige suffered by the inquisition to the jealousy shown to
papal inquisitors by their rivals among both local episcopal
clergy and lay authorities.[39] Marx seems to suggest something
similar when he remarks that by the end of the fifteenth
century the inquisition had lost prestige, as in this case where

[37]   Ibid., 264 and 254.
[38]   Above, ch. 1 (iii).
[39]   Lea, *History of the Inquisition*, I, 356-7, and, for the episode under
discussion, II, 158-61. The secularization of the process of inquisition in France
was to be completed in 1539 and subsequently.

the *Grand Conseil* treated it like any other secular office.[40] Lea's interpretation of the politics of the early inquisition has recently been disputed by Kieckhefer;[41] a similar revision is due here. No clear institutional reasons, grounded in antipathy between distinct and identifiable groups, explain the rehabilitation by themselves. The rehabilitation, like the crusade itself, split the units of the social hierarchy down the middle: some priests, papal officers, and laymen were amongst the persecutors; other bishops, priests, and laity were in favour of rehabilitation, and came from the same classes and types as the persecutors.

Amongst the higher clergy there were undoubtedly both personal and ideological rivalries at work, which prompted the commissioners to side with the villagers against other clergymen. The officious brusqueness with which Laurent Bureau treated Rostain d'Ancezune shows how there was bad blood between the two men. When Rostain sent Bureau some wine when he arrived in Embrun, the confessor's servants returned asking him to send no more. When Rostain invited Bureau to lunch at Champcella on 26 July 1501, Bureau said that Rostain 'came as a spy to watch on him', although he accepted the invitation. At Fressinières Bureau refused to tolerate the archbishop's lodging in the same house as himself.[42]

Some remarks Bureau made suggest that the rivalry ran deeper than an exclusively personal hostility. At their first stormy encounter, Bureau remarked 'voz autres clerjaux ne sçavez que deux C. c. et deux ff. . . . et voulez entreprendre de supprimer la théologie . . .'.[43] If we consider this statement in the light of the 1509 sentence, it takes on a new significance: the clergy ought to send competent preachers, and see that their flocks are not seduced, rather than neglect them and punish them when they go astray. The sentence, like Bureau's remarks, represents the resentment of theologians (and Bureau and Boussart were masters of theology[44]) against

[40]   Marx, pp. 197–8.   [41]   Kieckhefer, *Repression of heresy*, pp. 40–1.
[42]   *CUL G*, fos. 3^v, 4^v.
[43]   Ibid., fo. 4^r; see Marx, p. 182. 'C. c.' refers to 'codice et capitulo', and 'ff.' to the current designations of civil law texts.
[44]   *BP*, I, fo. 432^r.

those who only studied civil and canon law. The judges pointed out that the heretics were not 'pertinaciously' heretical: the point of this was that, if they were preached to at all competently, they would listen, so the local clergy had no excuse not to convert them to the truth. As Bureau and Pascal recognized, one could not kill all the heretics, one had to convert a few; this was, moreover, just what Baile had tried to do before 1487. This attitude may explain another remark allegedly made by Thomas Pascal at the Inn of the Angel at Embrun, about which Rostain fumed and over which hagiographers have crowed ever since Perrin's time: that he wished he were as good as the worst of Fressinières.[45]

Moreover, even though the formal, legal rehabilitation was unusual, it was not at all rare for inquisitors to find themselves rebuked for excesses, even in this region and period. François Borelli's excessive zeal was criticized in 1376.[46] A papal brief of 16 July 1453, obtained after protests from the Vaudois of Luserna, lifted the interdict imposed following the mission of the inquisitor Giacomo Buronzo.[47] In 1497 an inquisitor named Jérome, who had been over-active in persecuting heresy in the Alpes-Maritimes, was told to restrain himself.[48] In 1513 the Vaudois of Paesana, whom Angelo Ricciardino had attacked in 1509-10, were formally pardoned by Pope Leo X.[49] In the sixteenth century such rebukes, now delivered by the secular authorities, were to be found again. Jehan de Roma, the violent and notorious persecutor of the Vaudois of Provence, was expelled from the Comtat Venaissin by the Cardinal de Clermont and inhibited by the *parlement* of Aix. Later Jehan Meynier, president of the *parlement* and leader of the massacre of 1545, was put on trial for his life.[50]

---

[45] *CUL G*, fo. 6ʳ; Perrin, *Vaudois*, p. 144; see also E. Comba, *History of the Waldenses of Italy*, trans. T. E. Comba (London, 1889), p. 139.

[46] Marx, pp. 145, 202-3.

[47] Alessio, 'Luserna e l'interdetto', 414-17; Rorengo-Lucerna, *Memorie historiche*, pp. 19-20.

[48] L. Biau, *Essai sur les protestants du xviᵉ siècle dans les Alpes-Maritimes* (Cahors, 1903), p. 19; P. Degiovanni, 'Gli Eretici di Tenda, Briga e Sospello', *Rivista Cristiana*, 9 (1881), 256-7 and document II.

[49] Promis, 'Memoriale', 518.

[50] Herminjard, VII, 469-71; P. Gaffarel, 'Les Massacres de Cabrières et de Mérindol en 1545', *Revue historique*, 107 (1911), 241-71; and below, ch. 10 (v).

From the point of view of the judges-delegate, these particular inquisitors and crusaders had managed to place themselves in total discredit with most of the local population, clerical and lay alike. The self-centredness of the clique of the crusaders was to blame for this. It is even arguable that it was this indiscriminate rapacity, rather than strict 'not keeping to the forms of law', which made it necessary to reject the whole process of inquisition and restore the state of affairs before 1461. There are serious grounds for doubting whether Cattaneo's procedures really were illegal.[51] Canon law offered such scope to the inquisitor that it would have been very difficult to prove specific breaches of form: nor did the sentence attempt to establish exactly where the crusaders had gone wrong. On the other hand, if one looks at the inquisitions in the light of the differences in technique discussed above[52] one might surmise that the crusaders had so far exceeded the accepted conventions of inquisitorial behaviour that the only way left was to revoke the whole business and end the legal process which had lasted over three reigns.

From the point of view of the secular power other reasons weighed as importantly. Bureau apparently said to Rostain on 24 July 1501 that the King, Louis XII, 'had said to him with his own lips that the archbishop of Embrun would be contrary to him, and to his commission, and a formal party against the Vaudois'. Thomas Pascal said at about the same time that the King had been given to understand that 'the people of Fressinières were powerful enough to provide for his needs, when the King should ask, forty or fifty thousand ducats; so the said lord did not intend to lose such subjects . . .'.[53] These figures are not as 'improbable' as has been thought;[54] an explanation is there for the seeking.

Embrun and the Montgenèvre mattered a great deal to the Kings of France. Louis XI's devotion to Our Lady of Embrun was famous, and from 1482 the Kings of France were honorary canons in the cathedral chapter.[55] The interest shown by

[51] Marx, p. 177.   [52] Above, ch. 2 (ii).
[53] *CUL G*, fos. 4[r], 6[v].   [54] Marx, p. 185.
[55] Fabre, *Recherches historiques*, pp. 127, 296–8; Sauret, *Essai historique*, pp. 216–19.

Charles VIII and his successor was more material. The Montgenèvre guarded the best and safest route into Italy; only one other little-known route existed in this corner of the Alps at the time, over the Col de la Traversette by Monte Viso. It was the Montgenèvre which was used in 1494.[56] The co-operation of the people of this region could be essential for the passage of armies, in which vast sums of money could indeed be at stake. In 1515 the extent of this usefulness was shown when François I passed the Alps, not by the usual routes, but by travelling south-east from Guillestre, over the Col de Vars, past St-Paul and the Col de l'Arche into the Stura di Demonte. Paolo Giovio described how this route was discovered by Giacomo Trivulzio, then in François's service, 'with the help of those most expert in that territory'.[57]

Less specific reasons probably built up that sympathy for the persecuted which was evidently so rife in the valleys during the investigations in the 1500s, and which gave the judges evidence on which to work. The disruption caused by the elimination or displacement of these useful, if puritanical individuals clearly weighed on the region. An innkeeper of Chorges remarked in 1501 how 'rumour had it that if they [the Vaudois] had been poor they would not have been persecuted, but their goods were the cause of their destruction'; he added that 'before these executions, the country was much more fruitful, but from that time he reckoned there had always been barrenness; he believed this proceeded from so great an injustice done to these poor people, which was still not repaid . . .'. Other witnesses testified to the enormous shock inflicted by the spectacle of the crusade on the neighbourhood. The vicar of Chorges told how the executions were, he thought, 'done unjustly, and rather to have their goods than from any good zeal for justice', and he believed this, he said, 'because there were fair maids and girls,

---

[56] Godefroy, *Charles VIII*, p. 195; Y. Labande-Mailfert, *Charles VIII et son milieu (1470–1498)* (Paris, 1975), pp. 277–8; P. Gioffredo, *Storia delle Alpi Marittime*, ed. C. Gazzera (Monumenta Historiae Patriae, Scriptorum t. II, Turin, 1839), col. 1161; H.-F. Delaborde, *L'Expédition de Charles VIII en Italie* (Paris, 1888), p. 391.

[57] Sauret, *Essai Historique*, pp. 262–3; P. Giovio, *Historiae sui temporis* (Paris, 1558), I, 168v–9v; Gioffredo, *Alpi Marittime*, col. 1234; R. J. Knecht, *Francis I* (Cambridge, 1982), p. 42.

fleeing on their own, and in the gravest danger of prostitution; about all these things people felt pity at such inhumanity, that no-one would dare to receive them in his house . . .'.[58]

Faced with these testimonies, one is bound to wonder what distinguished the 'heretics' from their neighbours at all. They must have believed or practised something alien to catholicism, and yet have been sufficiently mild in their dissent not to become objectionable to all those around them. The belief of the heretics, then, that most thorny of regions for investigation, requires a more detailed survey than it has received in the past, and one which takes more account of its popular manifestations. So far, it may be concluded that, thanks both to the disrepute into which the inquisition fell, by the indiscriminate and profiteering way in which the crusade was run, and to the moderation towards heretics felt by catholics for political and intellectual reasons, it was not the inquisition as an 'institution' alone which had lost prestige on the eve of the Reformation; it was the legal enforcement of religious orthodoxy itself.

[58] *BP*, II, fos. 44^r, 26^v.

II The Beliefs of the Heretics before the Reformation

4. Worship and the Fate of
the Soul

Some apology and explanation is called for before we embark
on this detailed analysis of the forms which the Waldensian
heresy assumed. It may seem strange to take quite so long to
examine the available evidence, ample though it is, and reach
conclusions. It may also be objected that Waldensian beliefs
have already been the object of numerous and full studies.[1]
Jean Marx decided, on the basis of the same documents as
those used here, that 'the essentials of Waldensian doctrine
are represented more or less the same' in the sources as they
have come down to us, and that a schematic portrayal of
these ideas was perfectly possible.[2]

Perhaps at the end of his researches, with the qualifications
'à peu près', 'en ce qu'elles ont d'essentiel', 'de manière plus
ou moins explicite' appended to that claim, Marx's assurance
was wearing rather thin. Our information regarding heretical
beliefs in this period is, in fact, neither unanimous nor easy
to interpret: it is contradictory, full of ambiguities, and of
very varying reliability and completeness.[3] One is entitled to
scramble together all the references to the heresies of the sect
and create a 'radical' picture of Waldensianism if one wishes.[4]
However, if a heresy is not studied as it was believed, and as
it may reasonably be shown to have been believed by a fair
proportion of those who were accused of being its followers,

[1] For example G. Gonnet, 'Le Confessioni di fede valdesi prima della riforma',
BSSV 117 (1965), 61-95; *Le Confessioni di fede valdesi prima della riforma*
(Torino, 1967), *passim*; 'Le Développement des doctrines vaudoises de Lyon à
Chanforan 1170-1532', *Revue d'histoire et de philosophie religieuses* 52 (1972),
397-406.
[2] Marx, p. 19, and pp. 19-23 for his summary of beliefs.
[3] Compare G. Vinay, 'Il Valdismo alla viglia della riforma', *BSSV* 63 (1935),
69: 'L'unità valdese anteriore alla riforma che si è fino ad oggi affermata o sottin-
tesa non è che parziale'.
[4] As in G. H. Williams, *The Radical Reformation* (London, 1962), pp. 525-9,
a picture of Waldensianism which is not endorsed by the present study.

then our description of it is flawed.

Here we shall make detailed use of the records of the trials, bearing in mind the problems presented by the different sorts of record which have come down to us. This choice of route is not one followed by many who have written on these Waldenses; most have preferred to trust theologians and inquisitorial authorities.[5] There is, however, one important objection to relying solely on the trial records. There are in existence scattered copies of religious tracts generally agreed to have heretical associations, and written in the dialect used for the Morel-Masson dossier of the 1530s, itself a rare heretical document.[6] One might expect to supplement this study by means of these much prized manuscripts.

The objections to using this material here are, however, even stronger. In the first place, Waldensian beliefs seem to have been overwhelmingly oral, and there is very little evidence of pastors actually using books to preach. Four witnesses in the 1480s referred to the *barbes* carrying a book or books with them, but did not refer to their using them.[7] Moreover, the milieu of some of the surviving so-called 'Waldensian manuscripts' appears to have little to do with popular dissent. One of the collection includes a Latin grammar;[8] another, according to Enea Balmas, is written in the style of a highly cultivated scriptorium.[9]

The manuscripts look even less Waldensian when one considers their content. These writings have been classified as either Cathar tracts translated into forms of Provençal, or translations and compilations of catholic moral treatises

---

[5] Gonnet, *Confessioni di fede*, pp. 126-38, when dealing with this stage in Waldensian ideas, relies entirely on printed sources, and does not even use Marx's *pièces justificatives*; G. G. Merlo, *Eretici e inquisitori*, uses the fourteenth-century Piedmontese material in a valuable, if occasionally uncritical, way.

[6] M. Esposito, 'Sur quelques MSS de l'ancienne littérature religieuse des Vaudois du Piémont', *Revue d'histoire ecclésiastique* 46 (1951), 127-59; E. Montet, *Histoire littéraire des Vaudois du Piémont* (Paris, 1885), *passim*; Gonnet and Molnár, *Vaudois au moyen âge*, pp. 319-70, 443-50; E. Balmas, *Manoscritti valdesi di Ginevra* (Torino, 1977).

[7] *CUL G*, fo. 59^v; *ADI A*, fos. 87^v, 119^v, 301^r.

[8] CUL, MS Dd XV. 33 (E in Morland's Catalogue of 1658); see also Gonnet and Molnár, *Vaudois au moyen âge*, p. 444.

[9] Genève, Bibliothèque Publique et Universitaire, MS 208: see Balmas, *Manoscritti*, pp. 9, 59-60.

(such as the *Somme le Roy* of Laurent de Bois, of 1279), or compilations of Taborite, and later of protestant origin, or finally the 'Waldensian' texts properly so called. Of these last the list is far from ample: the 'Profession of faith of Valdès' dated to 1180, the *Liber Antiheresis* of Durand of Osca or Huesca, the rescript of the Bérgamo conference of 1218, and the correspondence dating from the late fourteenth century between the Lombard and the Austrian Waldenses.[10] Besides these there are two very minor tracts of pastoral exhortation, the so-called 'Pistola de li amic', whose heretical nature has been disputed, and the letter of *barbe* Bartolomeo Tertiano, of Meana di Susa, one of a family of *barbes*.[11] Both these texts probably date from the late fourteenth or early fifteenth centuries.[12] In short, if we are seeking material which clearly was either written or used amongst the Alpine heretics in the late fifteenth century and which expresses the ideas of that form of popular dissent, there are no texts to use whatever. The presence in the region of some Taborite heretical tracts on themes such as 'the dream of purgatory' in dialect suggests that there may have been other forms of heterodoxy current besides that which is found in the high mountains: but that theme is not one which can be developed here, even if sufficient evidence were forthcoming.

Since we are forced back on the trial records, we must read them critically. Not every confession is equally trustworthy, although none will be discarded without consideration here, however improbable. Where there is a complete trial dossier, evidence given before torture is to be preferred, normally, to that given after torture, except at the very start, when the accused normally denied everything. Of those cases where full records survive, Antoni Blasii and Odin Valoy were tortured,[13] while Antoni Blanc and Thomas Guot were threatened with it;[14] so allowance must be made for discrepancies.

---

[10] On this last see esp. P. P. A. Biller, 'Aspects of the Waldenses in the fourteenth century including an edition of their correspondence' (Oxford University D. Phil. thesis, 1977).

[11] A *barbe* named Thomas Tercian of Meana was active in the 1480s: *ADI A*, fo. 342[v].

[12] Gonnet and Molnár, *Vaudois au moyen âge*, pp. 336-40, 451-4. The letter of *barbe* Tertian is printed in Pazè Beda, *Riforma e cattolicesimo*, pp. 33-5.

[13] *CUL G*, fos. 65[r]-6[v]; *CUL H*, sect. 2, fo. 11[r].

[14] *CUL G*, fos. 112[r], 114-15[r]; *BP*, I, fo. 260[r].

Where there was only a short interrogation, torture was less likely, although threats, as described by some of the crusade victims from Fressinières, could have a similar effect.[15] The accuracy of the notaries, however, did vary. Broadly speaking, the records kept by Cattaneo east of the Mont-genèvre show stereotyping to a greater or lesser extent; while those taken later, on the western side, and those taken under commission by Cattaneo's delegates, do not and may be used with some confidence. The only statements about beliefs which will not be used at all are those taken in 1501 and 1507 before the commissioners for the rehabilitation, where the suspects denied every article of heresy automatically.

The result of this intricate sifting will be a greatly reduced vision of the extent and seriousness of the attack made by Waldensian ideas on catholic doctrine, let alone on catholic practice. In this we are not trying to reopen the debate on the authenticity of the Waldenses as forerunners of the Reformation.[16] That issue will be considered below, chiefly as part of the historiography of the sect.[17] The evidence forces us to restrict the nature of the heresy; however, this has the advantage of explaining why the Vaudois continued to use the offices of catholic priests, and shows how the Waldenses, who only saw their pastors for confession at long intervals,[18] did not maintain a body of ideas which was coherent, interlinked, or utterly unchanging.

It may be objected that the mildness of the heresy found in the Alps is an illusion produced by the ignorance of its adherents, or by their lack of understanding or memory. Did not Bernard Gui say of some Waldensian ideas '[the *barbes*] do not reveal these openly to their followers, but hold them amongst the *parfaits* of that sect'?[19] We return, in other words, to the problem encountered with heretical organization: should we concentrate on the 'believers' or the *barbes*?

In the first place, all we have are the depositions of the

[15] *CUL G*, fos. 31[r], 34[r-v], 38[r]; *BP*, II, fos. 65[v]-6[r], 93[r], 98[r], 100[v]-1[r].
[16] Cf. P. Melia, *The Origins, persecutions and doctrines of the Waldenses* (London, 1870), *passim*, and even Pazè Beda, *Riforma e cattolicesimo*, pp. 32-3, 37-9, for the case against regarding the Vaudois as early protestants.
[17] Below, chs. 16 and 17.   [18] Below, ch. 6 (iii).
[19] Gui, *Manuel de l'inquisiteur*, I, 48-9.

'believers', and we must use what we have. Secondly, illogicality in Waldensian beliefs is not necessarily a problem. There are reasons to suppose that beliefs were not transmitted as logically linked syllogisms, but as proverbs. If Waldensianism was proverbial rather than logical, a reduction of its coherence may bring us closer to its essence for its believers, rather than take us further away.[20]

There is a third answer, more tentative but potentially more important. The inquisitors were obsessed with the *barbes*. They built up a stereotyped account of their organization: the *barbes* were itinerant preachers based in Apulia, where they were ordained by an elder or pontiff. On 24 April 1387 a native of Valpute, living at Barge, confessed that he knew two *barbes*, called Baridon and Johan, who were both from Apulia; there they had their 'supreme pontiff'.[21] Vincent Ferrer, who visited the valleys in 1403, said that their heretic preachers came from Apulia twice a year.[22] One Philippe Regis revealed in 1451 that he acted as a 'lieutenant' in Piedmont for the *barbes* during their absence; he said that they came from Fressinières or Manfredonia in Apulia; each year a collection was made and sent to Apulia, which once raised 300 ducats.[23] In the light of this tradition it is perhaps surprising that only two crusade victims referred to the 'master of the Waldenses' ordaining the *barbes* in Apulia.[24] The vast majority made no such statement; and those *barbes* whom we can identify were mostly local men of no special standing in the heretics' organization.[25]

Without doubt there were Vaudois in Apulia: their migrations, especially in the late fifteenth century, are well-

[20] Earlier in this century the valleys were very rich in proverbial lore: see T. G. Pons, 'I nostri proverbi' *BSHV/BSSV* 57 (1931), 98-130; 58 (1932), 98-133; 59 (1933), 70-106; 64 (1935), 87-114; 70 (1938), 39-63; and 116 (1964), 71-89.

[21] Amati, 'Processus contra Valdenses', *Archivio Storico Italiano* (1865), I, pt. ii, 37, 39.

[22] Comba, *History of the Waldenses*, pp. 149, 325.

[23] Gonnet and Molnár, *Vaudois au moyen âge*, pp. 265-6; J. Jalla, 'Notice historique', *BSHV* 14 (1897), 8-9.

[24] *ADI A*, fos. 104ᵛ, 154, 265ʳ.

[25] Above, ch. 1 (iii).

attested.[26] In 1532 Pierre Griot (a native of Cesana then living in Provence) told how the Vaudois in Apulia sent money to the gatherings of the *barbes*.[27] There were also, undoubtedly, gatherings and an organization, however informal and obscure, of Vaudois pastors: the evidence of sixteenth-century heretics confirms this beyond doubt.[28] However, as with self-government, so with beliefs: it is possible to pay far too much attention to these shadowy figures, who obsessed the inquisitors only because they confirmed their assumption that every heresy was an anti-church with church trappings, and then to ⁻omit the far more obvious facts about less spectacular individuals about whom there is more to know. It was to the Alps, finally, not to Apulia, that the missions of the 1530s and the 1550s were directed. The local situation before then, where no settled pastorate of the heresy existed, is of cardinal importance.

(i) God and the saints

'The medieval Waldensian protest, based on the Sermon on the Mount and on other fundamental sayings of the Gospel', writes Valdo Vinay, 'had a character more moral, social, and disciplinary than theological in the exact sense of the term.'[29] Perhaps this should warn us off topics as general as this one. However, there are some statements in Vaudois confessions of this period which are nothing if not theological.

Repeatedly the victims of the inquisition said, as a major element in their confessions, that they were taught that 'God alone was to be prayed to', or, in Embrunais dialect, 'lon devio tant solement prear Dieu'.[30] This is one of the most frequent statements in about 250 cases which survive from

---

[26] *CUL G*, fo. 63ʳ, and TCD MS 266, fo. 43ʳ; F. Reynaud, 'Quelques documents sur l'émigration des Vaudois au xvᵉ siècle', *Provincia*, V, no. 263 (1964), 155-7; P. Rivoire, 'Les Colonies provençales et vaudoises de la Pouille', *BSHV* 19 (1902), 53-4.

[27] G. Audisio, *Le Barbe et l'inquisiteur* (Aix-en-Provence, 1979), p. 105.

[28] Audisio, *Barbe et l'inquisiteur*, pp. 52-5, and 'Une organisation ecclésiale clandestine', 85-7; T. G. Pons, 'Barba, barbi e barbetti nel tempo e nello spazio', *BSSV* 122 (1967), 47-76.

[29] V. Vinay, *Le Confessioni di fede dei Valdesi riformati* (Torino, 1975), p. 11.

[30] *CUL H*, sect. 5, fo. 7ʳ.

this period. One Fraticello tried in 1492 at Oulx added to this admission some Christological heresy: he believed 'only in God the Father [born] of the Virgin, but born from the seed of man and in original sin'.[31] This heretic, Pietro di Jacopo, was unique in his eccentric admission.

Usually, of course, the stress laid on 'God alone' was intended to contrast with the worship which late medieval catholicism in practice paid (whatever the theologians might say) to the saints. In most cases those who deposed on this doctrine also said they had been told not to pray to saints. In a few cases, however, like that of Johan Viollin of Champ-Didier, they simply said the saints had not been mentioned in their confession, or said they forgot what had been said about them.[32] Learned authors of inquisitorial treatises made this rejection of the saints' worship part of a logical schema. The author of the *De inquisitione hereticorum* treatise (formerly ascribed to David of Augsburg) thought that the Vaudois believed the saints to be so absorbed in the contemplation of the divine majesty that they could not hear the prayers of the faithful. This effort to explain by logic the Waldensian position was quite misplaced; and indeed later authors, like Pius II or Alfonso de Castro, presented a simpler picture.[33]

If most witnesses, whether Vaudois or catholic, agreed that the Vaudois generally did not pray to saints,[34] there were still a few exceptions and dissenters. Some Vaudois were disobedient, like Fazy Reymunt, who prayed to saints though the *barbes* told him not to;[35] others were perplexed. Jame Bérard of l'Argentière said he thought the saints were to be 'venerated as holy martyrs and confessors and should be prayed to', although God alone was to be worshipped.[36] Peyre Roux of Fressinières said that saints should be venerated

[31] Ibid., sect. 6, fo. 9ᵛ.   [32] Ibid., sect. 4, fo. 1ʳ.

[33] E. Martène and U. Durand, *Thesaurus Novus Anecdotorum* (Paris, 1717), V, col. 1780; A. S. Piccolomini, *Opera*, p. 104; A. de Castro, *Adversus omnes hereses* (Coloniae, 1539), col. CXCIXʳ; Gui, *Manuel*, I, 46-7.

[34] *CUL G*, fos. 54ᵛ, 55ᵛ, 57ʳ, 73ᵛ, 116ᵛ; *CUL H*, sect. 2, fo. 11ᵛ; sect. 3, fo. 2ᵛ; *BP*, I, fos. 270ᵛ–88ᵛ; Chevalier, pp. 146-56.

[35] *ADI B*, fo. 129ᵛ.

[36] *CUL H*, sect. 4, fo. 10ᵛ; there is a variant version of Bérard's deposition in *ADI B*, fos. 318ᵛ–19ᵛ.

although they did not hear prayers.[37] Johan Baridon of Fressinières said that although the saints and the Virgin were not to be 'honoured', 'neither should they be despised'.[38]

Finally, several victims said they accorded a special status to the Virgin: at least thirteen of those from Fressinières and l'Argentière included the Virgin with God as the sole recipients of their prayers.[39] Thomas Guot of Pragelas insisted in 1495 that he 'believed in the Virgin', although he did not think she had the power to forgive sins.[40] Perhaps less credibly, the other Fraticello, Francesco di Girundino, said the 'Waldenses' believed in Saints Peter, Gregory, Silvester, and John, but not in Saint Paul.[41]

Even on an issue which should have been completely straightforward there turn out to be inconsistencies in the evidence, and not only those found in eccentric texts like the Fraticelli case. Possibly in some cases an accused heretic might repeat under pressure what he had heard from the village priests rather than from the heretics; but perhaps also he might form an independent position which did not make him any the less 'Waldensian' for that. This pattern will recur in other points of doctrine.

(ii) Purgatory and good works

Scholastic theorists about heresy had to find a reason for everything which they supposed the heretics believed. Hence, on the theme of purgatory, one finds in the *De inquisitione hereticorum* treatise: 'They say there is no purgatory, but that everyone who dies goes at once to heaven or to hell . . . they say that offerings for the dead benefit the clerics who devour them, not the souls who do not need them. . . .'[42] This became a topos of inquisitorial wisdom about Waldensianism, that it blamed the errors of the Roman Church on its avarice.

---

[37] *CUL H*, sect. 4, fo. 8[v].   [38] *ADI B*, fo. 175[v]; see also fo. 180[r].
[39] *ADI B*, fos. 124[v], 126[r], 127[r–v], 167[v], 169[r], 170[r], 178[v], 180[r], 218[v], 304[r], 307[v], 345[v].   [40] *BP* I, fos. 249[v], 250[v], 257[v].
[41] *CUL H*, sect. 6, fos. 3[r]-4[r]; Allix, *Some remarks*, pp. 309-10. Alongside these passages in the MS an annotator has written 'figmenta'.
[42] *Thesaurus Novus Anecdotorum*, V, col. 1780.

Very few indeed of those accused employ such concepts. Brunet Bertrand of Fressinières related in 1488 how, when he lived in the Champsaur, a man came 'collecting money continuously for the dead' (presumably for indulgences). When he mentioned this to a *barbe* as a reason for believing in purgatory, the latter said there was no need to believe in it, as the Church invented it to extort money.[43] Only Francesco di Girundino besides this *barbe* made the same assertion.[44] Most of the numerous references to purgatory taken down before and during the crusade years simply contain a straightforward denial of the existence of such a place.[45] On this was made one of the most familiar of the Vaudois proverbs: 'In the other world there are only two ways, that is to say Paradise and Hell, and there is no such thing as purgatory.'[46] It is not absolutely certain that these short statements derive from the people themselves, rather than the churchmen. However, in this case the idea of 'two ways' is so concise and undialectical, that the case for its being a popular saying must be very strong.

Sometimes the 'purgatory' theme casts light on Vaudois debate. In the earliest stages of his long trial, Antoni Blasii, of Dauphin near Manosque, tried to clear himself of the aspersion of heresy by saying that when he and his wife were quarrelling, she said there was no such thing as purgatory: at which he was so angry that he beat her. When confronted with his later admission that he had been taught this idea himself, he explained that he beat her 'because he had heard too much about the heresy already and wished to hear no more'.[47]

On the other hand, of those interrogated in 1488, two women said that purgatory had not been mentioned by the *barbe* to them. Peyre Roux or Ruffi deposed that when he was told by a *barbe* that there was no such thing as purgatory,

---

[43] *ADI B*, fo. 199r.   [44] *CUL H*, sect. 6, fo. 4r.

[45] *CUL G*, fos. 53r-v, 54v, 57r, 116v; *CUL H*, sect. 2, fo. 11r; sect. 4, fos. 4r-v, 10v, 11r, 12r, 13r-v, 15r-v; *BP*, I, fos. 244v, 247r, 249v-50r, 261v-2r, 270r, 278v, 281v, 284r-v, 286v, 289r; *ADI A* and *B, passim.*

[46] *CUL H*, sect. 5, fo. 7r: 'En laultre monde non avio que dos chamins soes assaber de Paradis et de Infert et que non ero ges de purgatori . . .'.

[47] *CUL G*, fos. 61r, 61v, 63v.

he pointed out that there was a reference to purgatory in the Book of Maccabees.[48] Florence Fabri of l'Argentière said that, although the *barbe* told her there was no purgatory, she preferred her *curé*'s teaching on this point. Some witnesses were less certain than most even about the *barbes*' teaching: one said that the *barbes*, because they could not find a reference to purgatory in scripture, did not know it existed, but 'neither did they deny it'. Malan Reymunt said a *barbe* told him there was a purgatory, 'but he did not know where'.[49]

There is a clear paradox, for some of those deeply implicated in heresy also claimed that their fathers had left money for masses for their souls.[50] One even claimed that a *barbe* had told him to have a mass said for his parents.[51] The catholic priest of Orcières-en-Champsaur also confirmed this.[52] These claims may simply have been an attempt to avoid suspicion. They may also, however, have been part of a belt-and-braces attitude which tried to employ all the available means of salvation simultaneously. This would accord with a state of affairs where the heretics thought of themselves as better than the catholics, but not as inherently antagonistic to them.

There is no trace, moreover, that the Vaudois evolved at this stage any alternative theology of grace to make salvation any the less a matter for the individual. The Vaudois of the Vercors said that good works were more use if done before death than after;[53] Aymonet Porte of l'Argentière said he thought good works were only possible in this world.[54] No one else mentioned good works at all; but clearly there was no debate between Vaudois and catholic as to their importance. The moral puritanism of the Waldenses had a place for them in the scheme of salvation which protestantism would find it very hard to remove.

[48] *CUL H*, sect. 4, fos. 3^{r-v}, 8^v.
[49] *ADI B*, fos. 327^r, 255^r, 285^r.
[50] *CUL G*, fos. 33^r, 35^v; *BP*, II, fos. 70^r, 78^v.
[51] *ADI B*, fo. 268^v.
[52] *CUL G*, fo. 29^r; *BP*, II, fo. 58^v; a suggestion explicitly resisted by some proctors' articles in 1507, *BP*, II, fo. 437^{r-v}.
[53] *CUL H*, sect. 7, fo. 6^r; Allix, *Some remarks*, p. 323; Chevalier, p. 156.
[54] *ADI B*, fo. 245^r.

(iii) Heretics alone saved?

This section is only necessary because of some clauses of inquisitorial theory. The *De inquisitione hereticorum* treatise, along with other medieval material, alleged that the Vaudois thought, because of their breach with Rome, that they were themselves the sole true church, and that only they were saved.[55] The same suggestion was taken for granted in the Embrun proctors' articles of 1501.[56]

The references to such an idea in the trial material are sparse and not very convincing. In the summary of Antoni Blasii's trial read out at his abjuration—but at no other point—he was said to have believed that only those within the sect will be saved.[57] Johan Lantelme of Pragelas, in the midst of a deposition about the *barbes*, said they believed that all those in their sect were saved, which is not quite the same thing.[58] Francesco di Girundino in 1492, and Thomas Guot in 1495, made admissions similar to that attributed to Blasii.[59]

The absence of any body of really convincing admissions to this belief helps to reinforce the point suggested earlier: that the Vaudois in this period did not 'un-church' the catholics, nor did they exclude themselves from the services purveyed by the catholic church. It was protestantism which was to insist (and vainly, until military and political conditions were favourable) that there be a total separation.[60] In the mean time those who were asked in 1501 if they thought only the Waldenses were saved, replied indignantly that they expected salvation in the Roman Church; and Bureau rapidly gave up asking that question.[61] Already, then, it is clear that the trial material will not supply us with a unanimous monochrome picture of the beliefs current amongst the Vaudois. Moreover, it is also clear that we must examine the heretics' relations with the priesthood, since all their ideas impinge again and again on this issue. If practice seems to betray theory, we must not be surprised.

---

[55] *Thesaurus Novus Anecdotorum*, V, col. 1779; compare col. 1756.
[56] *CUL G*, sect. 3, as in Allix, *Some remarks*, p. 301.
[57] *CUL G*, fo. 73^v; TCD MS 266, fo. 43^r.
[58] *ADI A*, fo. 130^v. See also ibid., fo. 134^r, for the usual version.
[59] *CUL H*, sect. 6, fo. 2^{r-v}; *BP*, I, fo. 262^r.
[60] Below, ch. 14 (i).   [61] *CUL G*, fo. 25^v; *BP*, II, fo. 48^v.

5. Relations with the Catholic Church

(i) The priesthood and the Pope

[The Waldenses] come feignedly to Church to conceal their error; I was curé in that parish for two years, and in the third I gave it to be looked after by a chaplain from the Champsaur. He left because of their lack of devotion. I myself, considering their behaviour, ways, and manners, wished to give up that charge . . .

Michel Peyre, *curé* of Fressinières, 1483[1]

For eight years I have been vicar of Orcières, where many of the Val Fressinières lived for many years. They lived and received the sacraments of the Church, and in other ways behaved like other Christians . . . An old man, whose name I forget . . . confessed after the manner of a Christian, and in his confession I never heard nor understood anything about heresy . . . he received confession and the sacrament of the Eucharist from me humbly and devoutly . . .

Johan Lagier, vicar of Orcières, 1501[2]

One could duplicate these conflicting testimonies. They show how the relationship between the Vaudois and the clergy depended, at the local level, much more on individuals and the political climate than on heretical ideas at their purest.[3] Yet the theoretical attitude of the heretics to Rome was an obsession which the older inquisitorial treatises could never lay aside. Pseudo-Reinerius, in the section of his treatise where he listed the errors with which they 'blasphemed' the church of Rome, gave up counting after listing nineteen or twenty doctrines which the Waldenses held against the Church.[4] Even Claude de Seyssel, after his experience as

---

[1] *CUL G*, fo. 57ʳ.

[2] Ibid., fo. 29ʳ; compare *BP*, II, fos. 58ʳ–9ᵛ.

[3] Compare the tributes made by other priests, as above, ch. 3 (ii).

[4] (Matthias Flacius Illyricus), *Catalogus Testium Veritatis*, ed. Simon Goulart (Geneva, 1608), cols. 1509–10; M. Nickson, 'The "Pseudo-Reinerius" treatise', *Archives d'histoire doctrinale et littéraire du moyen âge*, 42 (1967/8), 296–7; *Thesaurus Novus Anecdotorum*, V, col. 1779.

archbishop of Turin in the early sixteenth century, dwelt at great length on the error of the belief that mortal sin made the ministrations of priests invalid.[5]

The references to the Pope or the priesthood in the materials are very numerous, and not all equally trustworthy. They are agreed, however, that Waldensian teaching was that because priests lived too fast and loose, they had lost the power to absolve sins, or even to administer the sacraments, according to some; the *barbes*, by contrast, were saintly men, imitators of the apostles, and had at least as much, or possibly more power, when compared with the priests.

In the case of the Pope, first of all, there were problems when the implications of this doctrine were worked out. According to Antoni Blasii, some *barbes* who came to see him at Dauphin claimed that their power to absolve sins had actually been given them by the supreme pontiff! After torture, however, he remembered his aunt's telling him long ago how, since some Pope he did not know of, none of Peter's successors had lived his life or received his power.[6]

This last suggestion, that the papacy had lost its purity and power since the time of Sylvester, was an inquisitorial cliché developed by the *De inquisitione hereticorum* treatise and taken up by the Embrunais clergy in their articles in the 1500s.[7] Most of the Vaudois, however, did not echo it. Odin Valoy said that only the first Pope was instituted by Christ;[8] five others simply said that the Pope's sins deprived him of his power.[9]

More detailed statements were made about the priesthood in general, which was something much closer to the concerns of the people of the valleys. However, our information about their attitudes leaves questions unanswered. Did the faulty morals of the priesthood make it obligatory to reject only

[5] C. de Seyssel, *Adversus errores et sectam Valdensium disputationes* (Paris, 1520), fos. 10–49; also *De Divina Providentia* (Paris, 1520), fos. 108^r-9^r; A. Caviglia, 'Claudio di Seyssel (1450-1520)', *Miscellanea di storia d'Italia*, 3rd series, 23 (1928), 397–421.

[6] *CUL G*, fos. 59^v, 65^v-6^r.

[7] *Thesaurus Novus Anecdotorum*, V, col. 1779; compare *BP*, I, fo. 403^v; ibid., II, fos. 439^v, 441^r-2^r, 481^r; Allix, *Some remarks*, p. 299.

[8] *CUL H*, sect. 2, fo. 14^r.

[9] Ibid., sect. 4, fos. 1^v, 8^v; sect. 5, fo. 7^v; sect. 7, fo. 7^r; *BP*, I, fo. 251^r; Allix, *Some remarks*, p. 323; Marx, p. 250.

certain priests? Or on the other hand, was it necessary to reject the whole caste and form a rival church? The heretics were fairly clear that the *barbes* had more power to absolve sins effectively than the priests;[10] however, the evidence which suggests that they thought their pastors were able to consecrate the host as well is stereotyped and so suspect;[11] the only reference to *barbes* actually carrying out their own consecrations is found in the worthless ramblings of one of the Fraticelli.[12] Indeed, in Luserna in 1453, and in the valleys of the Durance in 1497 and 1501, the Vaudois made strenuous efforts to have themselves restored to the Roman communion.[13] Hence we must conclude that a general disapproval of the priesthood amongst the Vaudois seems to have remained purely theoretical, and that its implications were not worked out to their logical ends.

As we have suggested above, the state of relations with the priests probably depended on those priests themselves.[14] There was probably some tension in Fressinières: in 1501 Peyre Romanet had to deny before Laurent Bureau that he had threatened the *curé* to such effect that he had been driven away;[15] Rostain Payan also seems to have been badly treated before 1483, when he said mass as vicar at l'Argentière.[16] On the other hand, Honoré Die, vicar of Orcières, was one of those to whom Peyre Valoy, while wanted by the inquisitors, turned for advice. Die tried to act as a reconciler, and suggested that Valoy surrender himself to the archbishop. He also allowed Valoy to stay with him and make some tubs in the priest's stable, in spite of the canonical penalties for receiving and abetting excommunicates.[17] Valoy

---

[10]   *CUL G*, fos. 59ᵛ, 61ʳ, 63ᵛ; *CUL H*, sect. 2, fos. 11ᵛ, 14ʳ; sect. 3, fo. 2ʳ; sect. 4, fos. 1ᵛ, 8ᵛ, 11ʳ, 12ʳ; *BP*, I, fos. 255ʳ, 256ᵛ-7ʳ, 279ʳ, 282ʳ, 289ᵛ-90ʳ; Chevalier, pp. 146, 147, 149, 150, 151; Marx, p. 241.

[11]   *ADI A, passim*, for example fo. 251ᵛ: 'Ecclesiastici ecclesie Romane tenent vitam nimis largam et amplam dicentes etiam tantam habere potestatem celebrandi et consecrandi prout ipsi habent si vellent hoc facere digniores dictorum sacerdotum. . . .' In ibid., fo. 355ʳ, we find 'si velent possent consecrare corpus cristi sed ipsi nolunt'. The only instance of this sort of stereotype in *ADI B* is found on fo. 182ʳ.   [12]   *CUL H*, sect. 6, fo. 4ᵛ; compare Gui, *Manuel*, I, 42-5.

[13]   Alessio, 'Luserna e l'interdetto', 417-18; above, ch. 3.

[14]   Above; see also *CUL G*, fos. 53ᵛ-4ᵛ, 57ʳ.   [15]   *BP*, II, fo. 62ʳ.

[16]   *CUL G*, fos. 53ᵛ-4ʳ. This testimony has been partially obliterated by damage to the MS.   [17]   *CUL H*, sect. 5, fo. 6ᵛ; Marx, pp. 246, 250.

did not, on the other hand, follow Die's advice.

The paradox on this issue is like that just noticed in the case of purgatory. The Vaudois would confess, sometimes even without much pressure being used, to having held certain beliefs; but often the application of those beliefs was vague to the point of nebulousness. One might hold certain attitudes to the morality of the clergy in the abstract, but that did not necessarily imply that one ostracized all its representatives or neglected its services. Vaudois ideas had an emblematic function: they were not so much guides for conduct as verbal tags around which the self-consciousness of the morally superior would gather. The expression of this, again, was a proverb.

(ii)   Sanctity and power

As much as one has sanctity, just so much has one of power.

Thus one clause of the summary of the trial of Peyre Valoy.[18] This aphorism occurs in various different, and certainly not stereotyped forms, at least twelve times in short and long depositions, from genuine Vaudois and Fraticelli alike.[19] It is reflected in those distorting mirrors, the proctors' articles, on two occasions;[20] it also appears in the *Errores Valdensium* compiled after Angelo Ricciardino's activities against the Vaudois in Paesana around 1510.[21] Although it refers to the question of the church, and was therefore likely to interest inquisitors, it is also characteristically popular, since it creates no argument centred round the priests themselves; it simply bypasses them.

The consequences of this idea were, in theory at least, anarchic. It did not encompass any unitary notion of a church which would be either in grace or out of it; in this sense it could pose problems for protestant ministers, who

---

[18]   *CUL H*, sect. 5, fo. 7^v.

[19]   *CUL G*, fo. 73^r; *CUL H*, sect. 4, fo. 8^v, sect. 6, fos. 4^v, 10^r; *BP*, I, fo. 261^v; *ADI B*, fos. 124^v, 181^r, 215^r, 248^r; Chevalier, pp. 146, 150-1; Marx, p. 250.

[20]   *BP*, II, fo. 481^r; Allix, *Some remarks*, p. 299.

[21]   A. Pascal, 'Margherita di Foix ed i Valdesi di Paesana', *Athenaeum*, IV (1916), 85.

would be as prone to faults of 'sanctity' as anyone else.[22] In fact, it did not tie in at all well with any concept of a ministry, since spiritual power was related to performance, and not to the sacral character conferred by vocation or ordination.

One strange postscript must be added, which fits in oddly with this conclusion on 'sanctity' as a Waldensian concept. In the last admissions of Antoni Blasii, we find the suggestion that if one of the Waldensian sect is on a ship, that ship will never founder. This revelation is not corroborated by any other testimony; possibly the Provençal Vaudois were at that time more self-conscious as a sect.[23]

(iii) Communities without priests?

There was no sense in which even the most Waldensian of the Alpine valleys were forbidden to the Roman clergy. Even Fressinières had its unhappy parish priest.[24] Yet the catholics accused the heretics, as a sign of their heresy, of never promoting any of their offspring into the priesthood; we find this charge repeated often enough for it to merit separate consideration. In Archbishop Baile's early inquiry into Waldensianism in 1483, three witnesses from the catholic side pointed out that none of those suspect of heresy had ever been admitted to holy orders.[25] Three of those subjected to full trials also admitted that they did not know of anyone in the sect who had ever become a priest or a monk.[26]

The point was only really taken up in the inquiry of Bureau and Pascal in 1501. Here the testimonies differed. Johan Fabri, vicar of l'Argentière, said that none of those under suspicion had ever been made a priest. Fransez Ruffi of Fressinières, asked why the people of that valley were not ordained, said that the people did not have the resources to support them. In one version he is alleged to have said 'it is better to be a well-off farmer than a poor priest'.[27] Other

---

[22] Below, ch. 15 (i).   [23] *CUL G*, fo. 69ᵛ; TCD MS 266, fo. 48ʳ.

[24] Michel Peyre: *CUL G*, fo. 57ʳ, and above.

[25] *CUL G*, fos. 53ᵛ, 54ʳ⁻ᵛ, 57ʳ. Of these witnesses four were themselves priests in Vallouise or Fressinières.

[26] Ibid., fo. 55ʳ; *CUL H*, sect. 2, fo. 13ʳ; *BP*, I, fo. 261ᵛ.

[27] *CUL G*, fos. 27ʳ, 33ᵛ; *BP*, II, fo. 52ʳ: 'melius est esse dives laborator quam pauper presbiter'.

witnesses were less certain: Peyre Reymunt said that he did not know why the people of Fressinières did not become priests, and was not sure that they did not. Johan Daniel or Arnulphs, of Fressinières, asked if he had seen any of the parish tonsured, said that he had seen this done for two of them.[28] In the legal debates in 1507, the articles of the catholic proctors felt it was necessary expressly to contradict the suggestion that suspected Vaudois were ever taken into the religious life.[29]

In logic, of course, no Waldenses should ever have wished to be ordained. Yet it is interesting that they were thought by some to be of sufficient standing to support ordinands, and that their not doing so was linked with their alleged prohibition on marriage with catholics[30] as proof of their heretical aloofness, and refusal to deign to act like ordinary believers.

(iv) Censure, betrayal, and death

The most critical area of relations between Waldenses and clergy was that which concerned the disciplinary function of the church. The Waldenses were traditionally said to despise the censures of the church, either because they believed that no Christian could excommunicate another, or because they despised the catholic church itself.[31]

Our evidence on this theme is abundant, since Jehan Baile had issued a mass excommunication some time late in 1486; numerous witnesses admitted that they had been excommunicate for eighteen months by spring 1488.[32] Of these several said that they had been taught that the censures of the church could harm no one and should be ignored.[33] Martin Deyrin of Villaretto said on 2 March 1488 that he had been taught to take no heed of censures, bulls, or indulgences, as these had been invented to extort money.[34] Once again,

---

[28] *CUL G*, fo. 30r; *BP*, II, fo. 63r.
[29] *BP*, II, fos. 437v–8r, 482v.   [30] Below, ch. 8 (ii).
[31] See Gui, *Manuel*, I, 38–9, and *CUL H*, sect. 2, fo. 9r.
[32] *CUL H*, sect. 4, fos. 1r, 3r, 4v, 5v, 6r–v, 11r–v, 12v, and *ADI B, passim.*
[33] *CUL G*, fo. 69v; TCD MS 266, fo. 48r; *CUL H*, sect. 4, fos. 1v, 4r, 8v, 12r; *ADI B*, fos. 182r, 286v, 289r, 290v. Chevalier, pp. 146, 150.
[34] *ADI A*, fo. 362v; see also *ADI B*, fo. 199r.

this logical explanation is rare. There were a few exceptions to this resistance; at least five from Fressinières claimed that they had been ready to answer the archbishop's summonses, but were prevented by the leading heretics in their village.[35] Peyre Valoy was sufficiently worried about his excommunication to discuss it with a priest.[36]

If this contempt for ecclesiastical censure was perhaps not unique to heretics in late medieval Europe,[37] possibly the way in which they maintained their solidarity was more unusual. The Waldenses were supposed to hold it to be the one unpardonable sin, the sin against the Holy Spirit for which there was no forgiveness, to betray one of their sect.[38] This inquisitorial cliché illustrates very well the different ways in which intellectuals and ordinary people understood religious dissent. For our evidence for the pains threatened against betrayers in the next world, which was the clerical version, comes from very doubtful sources: depositions taken from trial summaries, from evidence after torture, or from the Fraticelli.[39] It is also found in the stereotyped first 'carnetus' of Cattaneo's interrogations; at one stage the witnesses are quoted as believing that the sins of the flesh are less serious than the sin of betrayal;[40] at a later stage it is simply said that betrayal is unpardonable and the sin against the Holy Spirit.[41] Only one witness in these prolix accounts said the *barbes* 'told him on no account to come to penance, because those who came were lost and damned'.[42] These spiritual pains were, incidentally, very rarely reported in the sixth 'carnetus' of interrogations, which is generally more reliable and convincing.[43]

---

[35] *CUL H*, sect. 4, fo. 3ᵛ; *ADI B*, fos. 110ʳ, 120ᵛ, 135ʳ, 173ʳ, etc.

[36] *CUL H*, sect. 5, fos. 6ᵛ–7ʳ; Marx, p. 246.

[37] J. Toussaert, *Le Sentiment religieux en Flandre à la fin du moyen-âge* (Paris, 1962), pp. 435–46; P. Adam, *La Vie paroissiale en France au xivᵉ siècle* (Paris, 1964), pp. 179–206.

[38] *Thesaurus Novus Anecdotorum*, V, col. 1780.

[39] *CUL G*, fos. 69ʳ, 73ᵛ; *CUL H*, sect. 2, fos. 12ʳ, 14ᵛ; ibid., sect. 6, fo. 1ᵛ.

[40] *ADI A*, fos. 131ʳ, 132ᵛ, 134ʳ⁻ᵛ, 139ᵛ: 'si aliquo casu aliquis corrumperetur est peccatum irremissibile propterea debent pocius uti seminis quia non est peccatum magnum . . . .'

[41] Ibid., fos. 252ʳ, 254ᵛ, 256ᵛ, 258ᵛ–9ʳ, 261ᵛ, 263ʳ, 266ᵛ, 269ᵛ, 278ᵛ, 281ʳ, etc.; *BP*, I, fo. 271ʳ.   [42] *ADI A*, fo. 265ʳ.

[43] Chevalier, p. 147; *ADI B*, fos. 229ᵛ, 248ʳ, 283ᵛ, 289ʳ.

On the other hand, we have some lurid and realistic testimony from Odin Valoy that the heretics would exact punishment from their betrayers in this present world. When Odin was introduced to a *barbe* who helped to cure his infected leg, he was warned by those who led him to meet the stranger never to speak of the meeting, or his tongue would be cut and he would be slaughtered 'the way one strikes down a goat'.[44] At another point he was told not to reveal the sect to the priests, and that 'if a man were known to have revealed the sect he would have his tongue ripped out from his neck and his flesh torn into little pieces like goats' meat'.[45]

Although this particularly bloodthirsty series of threats is not found anywhere else, it is significant that as late as 1530 Georges Morel was asking the reformer Oecolampadius whether the *barbes* were right to advise the Vaudois to kill their betrayers.[46] Certainly as far as the late Middle Ages are concerned the 'non-violence' and abhorrence of homicide traditionally ascribed to the Waldenses (as well as to the Czech 'Unity of Brethren') can, in this context, be much overrated.[47]

Since the Vaudois went to such lengths to avoid detection, one would not expect them to hold a martyr's death in very high esteem. There is one text, however, which suggests just that. Late in the trial of Antoni Blasii, he related how the Vaudois believed that the fires which consumed an unrepentant heretic would be called the 'fire of blessing' and would save him from the fires of hell. About this they had a proverb: 'He who is burnt by the blessed fire, is not burnt by the accursed fire.'[48] However, this piece of evidence stands on its own: only one set of proctors' articles repeated the suggestion that patient suffering of execution allowed a heretic to rank as a martyr.[49] In much later years a protestant minister was to complain of how few former Vaudois were prepared to 'seal their faith with their blood'.[50]

---

[44] *CUL H*, sect. 2, fo. 9^{r-v}: 'sicut chaplatur unus caprinus.'

[45] Ibid., sect. 2, fo. 14^{r-v}: 'extraheretur ling[u]a talium post collum seu post capitem [?] et carnes sue scinderentur minute sicut carnes edorum.'

[46] Vinay, *Confessioni de fede... riformati*, pp. 44 f.; TCD MS 259, pp. 110-11.

[47] Cf. G. Scuderi, 'I Fondamenti teologici della non violenza nel Valdismo', *BSSV* 129 (1971), 3-14.

[48] *CUL G*, fo. 69^v; TCD MS 266, fo. 48^r: 'Qui eys crema dal fuoc benet/non eis crema dal fuoc malet.' [49] *BP*, II, fo. 440^{r-v}.

[50] *Lentolo MS*, p. 492; compare TCD MS 259, pp. 2-5.

6. The Sacraments:
Rome and its Competitors

(i) A general rejection?

The sacraments were the marketable goods of late medieval catholicism. A church which could deliver them to its faithful without inpairing its credibility would be able to hold the allegiance of its flock. On the other hand, if a heretic regarded the church as corrupt, surely he would not wish to participate in its sacraments? This seems to have been the logic of those catholic clergy in the Embrunais who chorused that the Waldenses did not believe in the sacraments of the church;[1] or of the authors of two sets of proctors' articles which made the same claim in 1501 and 1507.[2] They would evidently not have understood the double-think which allowed Georges Morel to report that 'the symbols of the sacraments are not administered to our little flock by ourselves, but by the limbs of Antichrist'.[3]

A chestnut of inquisitorial wisdom was once again to blame here. Both pseudo-Reinerius and the *De inquisitione hereticorum* treatise listed a great succession of errors against the sacraments one by one; the former began its second section of errors by saying 'they condemn all the sacraments of the Church'.[4] After this general statement several diverse and specific criticisms were recorded; some sacraments were regarded as erroneous in their very existence, others as wrongly administered by the catholics.

Two heresies, indeed two forms of heresy, were being

[1] *CUL G*, fos. 53ᵛ, 54ᵛ, 57ʳ. These were Vincent Rolland, Antoni Stodi, Estève Garnier, Michel Peyre, and Clément Garcin.

[2] Allix, *Some remarks*, p. 300, based on *CUL G*, sect. 3; *BP*, II, fo. 483ʳ.

[3] Vinay, *Confessioni di fede . . . riformati*, pp. 42–3; compare TCD MS 259, p. 52.

[4] *Thesaurus Novus Anecdotorum*, V, cols. 1779–80; Flacius Illyricus, *Catalogus*, cols. 1510–12; Nickson, '"Pseudo-Reinerius" Treatise', 297–9.

confused here. Some authors believed that the Vaudois rejected the sacraments because of the faults of the priests; others that they regarded certain details of ritual as wrong, for example the use of Latin, or of the pax.[5] These issues are quite separate. The statements of Baile's clerical witnesses are therefore meaningless; and they are not supported by any admissions found in the trial material or elsewhere. On the contrary, when interdicted by the catholics the Waldenses did their best to have pressure put on the clergy to restore the sacraments to them.[6] They might understand them in an unusual way, or make unconventional use of them; but they would not go without them.

(ii) Baptism

There is no credible trial evidence from this period to prove that the Waldenses of the western Alps entertained any heresy about baptism whatever. Only one witness, Fransez Ruffi of Fressinières, was even asked in 1501 if he believed in it.[7] In spite of this, theory intrudes in two forms: first, that of two standard and much used inquisitors' manuals which said that the Vaudois denied or diminished the value attached to infant baptism;[8] secondly, in that of the ideas studied by those interested in the so-called 'internationale' of East European Waldensianism and Hussitism, who make a similar claim.[9]

Some material from the Fraticelli trial illustrates how myths can be built up about a heresy, when the interrogators lacked skill or caution. The first of these victims, Franceso di Girundino, said that at the ordination of the *barbes* (as his sect is described all through the record), the ordinands took oaths to maintain the laws of the sect; then their superior

---

[5] Nickson, '"Pseudo-Reinerius" Treatise', p. 298; compare also Pius II's views on Waldensian baptism, *Opera*, p. 103.

[6] Above, ch. 2, and *CUL G*, fos. 2^r-3^r.   [7] *CUL G*, fo. 27^r.

[8] *Thesaurus Novus Anecdotorum*, V, col. 1779; Flacius Illyricus, *Catalogus*, col. 1510; Nickson, '"Pseudo-Reinerius" Treatise', 297.

[9] Gonnet and Molnár, *Vaudois au moyen âge*, pp. 434-7; also G. Scuderi, 'Il Sacramento del battesimo nella fede, nella pietà, e nella teologia del valdismo medioevale', *BSSV* 124 (1968), 3-16, which ignores the evidence from the Alps at this period.

gave each new pastor some wine to drink, and gave him a new name (in this case the new name was Martin). At the end of the paragraph is the remark 'and this ritual they keep in place of baptism'.[10]

The second Fraticello, Pietro di Jacopo, told instead how, 'when a child has been baptised by a priest, and they [the barbes] are in the house, they wash his forehead to remove the stigma of baptism; then they shave a part of his head, as a sign that this baptism has been recovered'.[11] Fortunately, with a little guesswork we may discern how these statements were made. In the *De inquisitione hereticorum* treatise there is the statement 'they say that a man is first truly baptized, when he has been inducted into their sect'.[12] On this single sentence, it would seem, the prisoners at Oulx were interrogated; and as the meaning of the sentence is far from clear, they produced totally different rhapsodic variations. In spite of this, the text probably meant no more than that the Vaudois regarded their initiation processes[13] as more holy than catholic baptism.

(iii) Confession: the alternative rite

Although confession is by far the best documented, and was probably the most important religious activity for the Waldenses in this period, it has not been studied in great detail; perhaps this has been a consequence of the anxiety shown as late as the nineteenth century by Calvinist pastors about such a Romish practice.[14] Even Emilio Comba was slightly cagey about the role of this rite.[15]

Both pseudo-Reinerius and Bernard Gui noted how the Vaudois believed that laymen of their sect had the power to absolve sins, and that confession was best directed to them rather than to priests.[16] Several witnesses in 1483 recalled

---

[10]   *CUL H*, sect. 6, fos. 5ᵛ–6ʳ; Allix, *Some remarks*, p. 313: 'et quod illa solempnitas habetur loco baptismi.'

[11]   *CUL H*, sect. 6, fo. 10ʳ⁻ᵛ.

[12]   *Thesaurus Novus Anecdotorum*, V, col. 1779.   [13] See below, ch. 8 (i).

[14]   See e.g. A. Monastier, *A History of the Vaudois Church* (London, 1848), pp. 141–2, 143.

[15]   Comba, *History of the Waldenses*, p. 299, answering Monastier's point.

[16]   Flacius Illyricus, *Catalogus*, cols. 1510–11; Nickson, '"Pseudo-Reinerius" Treatise', 298; Gui, *Manuel*, I, 42–3.

this suggestion; others added that the laymen who heard confessions came from remote parts, and their arrival was awaited eagerly by the heretics.[17]

Our records provide very impressive evidence for the spread of the practice. Of several hundred witnesses whose depositions survive, at least 260 admitted confessing to *barbes*, and in some cases on quite a significant number of occasions.[18] Besides these, several Vaudois admitted seeing the *barbes* but denied confessing to them; Catherine Ripert, for example, said she had met a *barbe* and intended to confess, but then did not have the opportunity.[19] For those brought up in Vaudois households the *barbes* were hard to avoid; Gabriel Orsel had had a *barbe* eating and drinking in his house, although he rejected his wife's suggestion that he confess to him; one also stayed at the house of Gabriel Vincent of Pragelas, although his mother could not induce him to make confession.[20]

This confession to *barbes* was not an exclusive thing. Inquisitors admitted that the Vaudois would confess to their catholic clergy once a year, although they claimed this was done only to escape detection. However, some notorious heretics also said they confessed to their *curés*: Pons Arnulphs or Brunet, Estève Roux, and Thomas Guot all said that they confessed yearly before Easter communion.[21] These could hardly have expected to conceal their heresy by this devotion.

Compared to this annual confession, the Waldenses confessed their sins to *barbes* irregularly, even sporadically. In 255 cases where one is able to make any statement, the greatest number was that of those who had confessed to a *barbe* only once: these were seventy of the sample. Apart from them, fifty-one had confessed twice; thirty-four had done so three times, twenty-three four times, fifteen five times, eleven six times, fourteen seven times, four eight times, two nine times, six ten times, and nine had done so more

---

[17] *CUL G*, fos. 53ʳ⁻ᵛ, 54ᵛ, 57ʳ.

[18] The statistics in this section are derived from the whole of the available corpus of records. They are not exact, as the documents contain gaps (*ADI A* and *B* are only the first and sixth books of crusade confessions respectively) and parts of *ADI A* are all but illegible because of damp, and cannot be used.

[19] *CUL H*, sect. 4, fos. 16ᵛ, 17ʳ.   [20] *ADI A*, fos. 137ᵛ, 279ʳ⁻ᵛ.

[21] Chevalier, p. 146; *CUL H*, sect. 3, fo. 2ᵛ; *BP*, I, fo. 246ʳ.

than ten times; besides these, sixteen said that they had confessed 'many' times, which could mean anything.[22]

If one collates these figures with the ages of those deposing, and the number of years which they said had passed since their first confession, the normal frequency of heretic confessions emerges as less than once a year;[23] often it is less than every two years and sometimes much less frequent than that, even amongst the most apparently dedicated. Estève Roux, the Vaudois proctor for Fressinières, had confessed no more than four times in twenty years in the sect.[24] Odin Valoy, after torture, said that the confessors usually came twice a year to hear confessions; but he himself had only confessed at most four times in four years just past. His statements about the regularity of *barbes*' visits do not fit in with the claim that the arrival of one was a notable event for these people.[25]

We have less information about the details of how the Vaudois were introduced to these confessors. Generally they met them through a contact or a relative who was already a believer, sometimes under some extraneous pretext. Antoni Blasii had asked one Vincent, a Piedmontese by birth like himself, to let him know of anyone in Provence who might be ready to take Blasii's letters to Angrogna. This Vincent later returned with two men who spoke Piedmontese, who took Blasii behind his clothier's shop and offered to hear his confession.[26]

Odin Valoy had gone up to Fressinières one Sunday to collect three *setiers* of wheat to sow in his plot at St-André. There he met his uncle, Fazion Jullian, who remarked that Odin had something wrong with his leg, and offered to take him to a 'great clerk' who could heal him. They went to the house of Michel Barbo at Dourmillouse, the highest settlement in the Val Freissinières, where Odin was introduced to a man who spoke 'the dialect of Angrogna', who then gave him

---

[22] Again, these statistics are not precise data, as deposition evidence is incomplete and sometimes ambiguous.

[23] There are rare exceptions: for example Estève David, *BP*, I, fo. 277^{r-v}, admitted confessing six times in four years.

[24] *CUL H*, sect. 3, fo. 2^r.

[25] Ibid., sect. 2, fo. 12^r; cf. *CUL G*, fo. 57^r.   [26] *CUL G*, fo. 59^v.

a herb to cure his leg, and offered to hear his confession, saying he was sent 'on God's behalf'.[27]

Antoni Blanc's introduction was more accidental. He had stopped at the wine shop kept by Jame Pascal at Dourmillouse while travelling from Poët over the Col de Freissinières, and found a dozen people gathered there. Then Antoni Baridon introduced him to an old man who spoke 'the dialect of that region', and whom Baridon called 'a good man of God', who wished to say some 'good words' to him. Blanc duly made his confession.[28] Bonet Martin of Mentoulles was enticed on his own to a house at Villaretto, but fled as soon as he realized the man who led him there was a *barbe*.[29]

Most other witnesses said that their family or their friends and neighbours had introduced them to the heretics, without providing many details; this was probably the most common way. Some, like Catherine Ripert, met the pastors on their own while looking after flocks on the high pastures.[30] According to theory, the Waldenses were supposed to meet only behind closed doors at night;[31] but the testimony of Thomas Guot partially contradicts this.[32] The only general rule was that the heretics tended to meet as far up their valley as possible.

As far as we can tell, there was nothing in the substance of confession to *barbes* which could not have been confessed as well to priests, although the moral priorities of the two types differed.[33] The Vaudois almost certainly did both, and the only statement which suggests they were told only to confess to *barbes* is very suspect.[34] There is no obvious reason, therefore, why the Waldenses should have felt this supplementary confession to be necessary. Presumably it was an act of emulation; the *barbes* claimed to do something which the priests did, only better, so the people would regard their penances as conferring more merit towards salvation. Confession, then, was simply the most important expression

---

[27] *CUL H*, sect. 2, fos. 8^r-9^r. [28] *CUL G*, fo. 116^r.
[29] *BP*, II, fos. 405^v-6^v. [30] *CUL H*, sect. 4, fos. 15^r, 17^r.
[31] Compare *CUL G*, fo. 53^{r-v}: testimonies of Turin Gontier and Vincent Rolland; also Comba, *History of the Waldenses*, pp. 274-7, where this custom is used to explain the stories of the 'congregations' or 'synagogues'.
[32] *BP*, I, fo. 248^v, where he said that the *barbes* preached both by day and by night. [33] See below, ch. 8.
[34] *CUL G*, fos. 69^r, 73^r; TCD MS 266, fo. 48^r.

of the solidarity and distinctive character of Waldensianism.

(iv) Penance

We have very little information about the kinds of penances which followed heretic confessions, or how they were regarded. We cannot prove or disprove the endearing suggestion of pseudo-Reinerius, that the Waldenses were opposed to the imposition of heavy penances, and preferred those which Christ imposed, when he said 'go away, and sin no more'.[35] We can address ourselves to two questions: first, whether the Ave Maria was prescribed as a penance; secondly, whether the saying of prayers was intended to be in fixed quantities, or was directed by the *barbes* as a general injunction to regular piety.

The prayer Ave Maria, derived from Luke 1:28, was and is an integral part of Roman Catholic ritual. Because it involved the invocation of a saint rather than of God, Bernard Gui and Nicholas Eymeric supposed the Vaudois could not use it.[36] There was an inquisitorial saw that the Vaudois regarded the Ave as 'not a prayer but a greeting'.[37]

This cliché is rarely found in the trials. It occurs in the trials of the Fraticelli, and that of Thomas Guot, all three carried out at Oulx.[38] It is found in the third interrogation of Peyre Griot of Pragelas on 11 October 1487, which contained much other improbable material, and in two other instances.[39] On the other hand, we saw that some Vaudois at least claimed to place a special emphasis on the Virgin as distinct from the other saints;[40] so it is not surprising to find at least a dozen cases where victims said the *barbes* had told them to say both the Pater Noster and the Ave Maria as penances.[41]

Sometimes the Ave was enjoined in odd contexts: Antoni Blasii's aunt told him to say it, along with the Pater, before

---

[35] Flacius Illyricus, *Catalogus*, col. 1511; Nickson, '"Pseudo-Reinerius" Treatise', 298.

[36] Gui, *Manuel*, I, 54-5; N. Eymericus, *Directorium Inquisitorum*, ed. F. Pegna (Rome, 1578), II, 205.

[37] 'Non oracio sed salutacio.'

[38] *CUL H*, sect. 6, fos. 4ʳ, 9ᵛ, and compare fos. 8ʳ, 12ʳ; also *BP*, I, fo. 250ᵛ.

[39] *ADI A*, fos. 104ᵛ, 251ʳ; *ADI B*, fo. 256ʳ⁻ᵛ.   [40] Above, ch. 4 (i).

[41] *CUL G*, fo. 67ᵛ; *CUL H*, sect. 2, fo. 4ʳ; ibid., sect. 4, fos. 1ʳ, 4ʳ, 5ᵛ, 6ʳ⁻ᵛ, 10ᵛ, 11ᵛ; *ADI B*, fos. 116ʳ⁻ᵛ, 306ᵛ; Chevalier, p. 151.

he ate or drank, while a *barbe* who heard him told him to say a continuous succession of prayers until he fell asleep.[42] Odin Valoy, when asked if his parents had taught him any heresy, at first said they had not, unless it were the Pater Noster and the Ave Maria.[43] Only one victim said that any alteration was to be made to the prayer: Angelin Palon (later to be a Vaudois proctor) said he had been given a penance of the Pater Noster, and the Ave 'as far as "Holy Mary, mother of God" only', presumably omitting, rather ungrammatically, the request that she pray for him.[44] Surely, then, this standard prayer did play a role which was hardly to be distinguished from that which it served for the catholics. In any case, both believed that the ritual repetition of prayers was a meritorious act.

Since Waldensian prayer did involve ritual repetition, one is bound to ask whether this was a repetition of fixed quantities set by *barbes*, or a regular practice regardless of sins to be atoned for. Certainly some Vaudois were given penances which must have had fixed limits: for example those who were told to say prayers 'for a whole year', or the believer told to say a hundred Paters, which could hardly have been a regular imposition.[45] Quite a number of cases simply referred to a 'certain quantity' of prayers.[46]

Other instances, however, seem to refer to the confessional being used to inculcate regular and permanent habits of prayer. We noted how Blasii was told to say the Pater until he fell asleep. Antoni Blanc was told to say ten Paters every day, with no limit set.[47] Odin Valoy, Dauphine Viollin, and Estève Roux were all told to say ten night and morning, and were not aware of any limits to this practice.[48] Antoinette Viollin of l'Argentière was told to say fifteen Paters each morning, but only one at night.[49] Other witnesses interrogated during the crusade said they were told to say certain numbers of prayers every day, without limit.[50]

[42] *CUL G*, fos. 67ᵛ, 69ʳ.   [43] *CUL H*, sect. 2, fo. 4ʳ, as above.
[44] *ADI B*, fo. 116ʳ⁻ᵛ.   [45] *CUL H*, sect. 4, fos. 1ʳ, 3ᵛ, 12ʳ.
[46] *CUL H*, sect. 4, fos. 5ᵛ, 6ʳ⁻ᵛ; *BP*, I, fo. 248ᵛ; Marx, p. 249.
[47] *CUL G*, fos. 69ʳ, as above, and 116ᵛ.
[48] *CUL H*, sect. 2, fo. 9ʳ, sect. 3, fo. 2ᵛ; *ADI B*, fo. 344ʳ⁻ᵛ.
[49] *ADI B*, fo. 345ʳ.   [50] *CUL H*, sect. 4, fos. 10ᵛ, 11ᵛ, 15ʳ; sect. 7, fo. 11ʳ.

Moreover, this habit of saying prayers does seem to have had some success. It would need to have done, since a regular habit of prayer was the only way in which any form of religious practice could be continued across the years which normally separated confession to a *barbe*. However, numerous witnesses recalled afterwards how suspected Vaudois whom they knew were able to say the standard prayers of the Church, and the creed, clearly and distinctly.[51] Such a level of religious instruction, basic though it was, perhaps helped to make the Vaudois respectable in the eyes of their catholic neighbours; it was also to form a base for protestant pedagogy in the next century.[52]

(v)   The Mass, and Eucharistic doubts

Various issues are raised by the question of the Eucharist and its place in Vaudois ideas, although all these points are rather peripheral to what seem to have been the heretics' chief concerns. Since the Vaudois believed that the power to bind and loose, to condemn vice and to give absolution, resided in a good layman or one who was truly 'holy', they were also supposed to believe that a good layman might consecrate the host as well.

Our evidence for the Vaudois in the Alps in this period believing the theory is very suspect and comes from stereotyped depositions.[53] What is more, even in that evidence we find one testimony according to which the *barbes*, although they have the power to consecrate, choose not to do so.[54] Outside this material, references to the same belief are few and far between.[55]

As regards the practice, we saw earlier that more than one staunch Vaudois insisted that he communicated every Easter.[56] At least two crusade victims said that a *barbe* had

---

[51] *BP*, I, fos. 446ʳ, 455ʳ⁻ᵛ, 457ʳ, 458ᵛ, 463ᵛ; II, fos. 2ʳ, 9ᵛ, 12ᵛ, 14ʳ⁻ᵛ, 16ʳ⁻ᵛ. Some witnesses said that those of Fressinières could say the prayers in Latin as well as in the vernacular.

[52] *Lentolo MS*, pp. 518–20.

[53] See above, ch. 5 (i), and *ADI A, passim; ADI B*, fo. 182ʳ.

[54] *ADI A*, fo. 355ʳ.

[55] *CUL G*, fo. 57ʳ; *CUL H*, sect. 3, fo. 3ʳ, sect. 4, fo. 9ʳ.

[56] Chevalier, p. 146; *BP*, I, fos. 246ʳ, 250ʳ⁻ᵛ, 257ʳ.

actually told them to go to Mass.[57] Before we postulate 'religious dissimulation' to explain this behaviour, we should be sure that the Vaudois really believed that the catholic Eucharist was invalid; and such evidence does not exist in sufficient quantity.[58] The two Fraticelli made slightly inconsistent references to the 'blessed bread' which their 'Waldenses' were supposed to make for themselves and use instead of the Eucharistic Host.[59] This suggestion perhaps derived from the *Dialogue between a Catholic and a Patarene*, possibly via Bernard Gui's manual,[60] or from a misunderstanding of part of the *De inquisitione hereticorum* treatise which deals with doubts about the real presence.[61] These two also echoed the catholic allegation that the Vaudois received the Mass in pretence.[62]

Evidence for doubts about the real presence is almost nonexistent. Some witnesses in 1501 were asked about their beliefs on the Eucharist, but this seems to have been an oddity of Bureau's.[63] Our only statement from a trial of a heretic regarding this doctrine is totally orthodox.[64] Under protestant influence, it is true, sacramentarian heresy was to make some headway, at least amongst the Vaudois of Provence in the 1530s; but this was in a new age.[65]

In this study of the sacraments we have come upon a fresh paradox. In these activities, confessing sins, saying prayers, and attending religious services, the Waldenses were practising the rites nearest to the heart of their belief and presumably most important to them. However, when we examine these

---

[57] *CUL H*, sect. 4, fo. 10ᵛ; TCD MS 266, fo. 57; *ADI B*, fo. 115ᵛ.

[58] So-called 'Nicodemism' became an issue when, under protestant influence, some Vaudois felt a logical need to establish whether they should share in catholic worship or not. See below, ch. 14 (i).

[59] *CUL H*, sect. 6, fos. 4ᵛ, 10ʳ.

[60] *Thesaurus Novus Anecdotorum*, V, cols. 1754-5; Gui, *Manuel*, I, 42-5.

[61] *Thesaurus Novus Anecdotorum*, V, col. 1779: 'Corpus Christi et sanguinem non credunt vere esse, sed tantum panem benedictum, qui in figura quadam dicitur corpus christi. . . .'

[62] *CUL H*, sect. 6, fos. 6ʳ, 10ᵛ; compare *CUL G*, fos. 54ᵛ, 57ʳ.

[63] *CUL G*, fos. 26ʳ, 27ʳ, 28ʳ⁻ᵛ; *BP*, II, fos. 49ʳ⁻ᵛ, 51ᵛ⁻2ʳ, 55ᵛ, 57ʳ.

[64] *BP*, I, fo. 257ʳ.

[65] Audisio, *Barbe et l'inquisiteur*, pp. 81, 91; see also J. Aubéry, *Histoire de l'exécution de Cabrières et de Mérindol et d'autres lieux de Provence* (Paris, 1645), pp. 22, 47.

same practices, they turn out to be almost unreservedly catholic in content, although carried out by heterodox individuals. Most of the core of Waldensianism turns out to be only barely heretical. Therefore, we must to some extent redefine the concept of 'heresy' if we are to understand these groups of people. They were certainly self-aware as a distinct group; but that did not prevent them from distinguishing themselves only by minor details, or specific rituals, rather than by the essentials of faith. Their rivalry with catholicism was moral rather than ideological. Above all, they were not 'radical' heretics, if by that one means heretics who questioned any fundamentals of religion. Turning now to much more minor elements in religious faith and conduct, we may begin to see some of these distinctive elements forming a pattern.

7. The Lesser Ministrations and the Church's Year

... The feasts, vigils of holidays, orders, blessings, offices of the Church and all such like they utterly reject, along with consecrated churches and cemeteries: they blaspheme against all such things, and say they were only set up through the avarice of priests ...[1]

(i) The church building, the cemetery, and prayers for the dead

Here, as in so much else, there could be a difference between theory, as suspected Waldenses could be persuaded to confess it, and actual practice as it is occasionally recorded. The Fraticelli, and one set of proctors' articles, asserted that the Vaudois believed it was as profitable to pray in a stable as in a church.[2] Some victims of the inquisition (some tortured) said that prayer might as well be made in a field;[3] some depositions taken by Cattaneo, which contain formal repetitive language on this point even in the second register, asserted that prayer was as well made either at home or in a stable, as in church.[4]

As for practice, Jame Gobaut of Embrun reported in 1483 that he had been in l'Argentière, and very few of those of Fressinières, who were in the village, entered the church; but since he was dealing with a lawsuit at the time involving these people, his testimony is suspect.[5] It does little in the face of numerous testimonies that the Vaudois did in fact attend catholic services.[6]

[1] *Thesaurus Novus Anecdotorum*, V, col. 1779.
[2] *CUL G*, sect. 3, as in Allix, *Some remarks*, p. 300; *CUL H*, sect. 6, fos. 4r–v, 10r.
[3] *CUL G*, fo. 73v; *CUL H*, sect. 2, fo. 12r, sect. 4, fos. 1v, 4v.
[4] *BP*, I, fos. 279r, 282r, 284v, 287r, 289v; *ADI A*, e.g. fo. 252r and subsequently; *ADI B*, fos. 102r, 115r, 117r–v, 119r, 136r, etc.; Chevalier, p. 146; also the case of Thomas Guot, *BP*, I, fo. 257r–v.
[5] *CUL G*, fos. 54v–5r.
[6] From sympathetic clergy in 1501, and also in *CUL G*, fo. 99r–v.

The case of cemeteries reveals a similar conflict, or, if one prefers, a lack of willingness among Vaudois to practise what they were supposed to believe. Several victims of the inquisition confessed they had been told that they had no special value, and not only in the inevitably repeated wisdom of the first Cattaneo register;[7] yet we know that Antoni Blanc's wife Alise, who died early in 1490 and probably received the Vaudois last rites, was buried in the village churchyard of Fressinières.[8] Some circumstantial evidence about these last rites suggests that in fact the Vaudois did not neglect the ceremonies of burial, and there is no suggestion that they avoided the facilities provided by the orthodox church when they did so.[9]

Surprisingly enough, there is even some doubt as to the total rejection of prayers for the dead amongst the Vaudois. It would seem to stretch illogicality to absurd lengths to suggest that they would pray for souls in a purgatory which they did not believe to exist. However, our evidence that such prayers were explicitly rejected is quite weak: two trial summaries,[10] some catholic claims in 1483,[11] some admissions by Thomas Guot,[12] and some stereotyped confessions extracted by Antoine Fabri in 1494.[13] Even the victims in the Cattaneo registers did not specifically exclude them very often.[14]

This evidence is supplemented by some more useful insights. Three suspected heretics interviewed by Archbishop Baile in 1483 said that when they prayed for their parents' souls they prayed 'may God have pardoned them'.[15] One of the procuratorial treatises on heresy submitted in 1507 remarked on this, commenting that the Vaudois prayed 'may God have pardoned them' rather than 'may God pardon them', since

---

[7] *CUL G*, fo. 73ᵛ; *CUL H*, sect. 2, fo. 12ʳ, sect. 4, fo. 4ᵛ; *ADI A*, fo. 252ʳ and subsequently; *ADI B*, fos. 115ʳ, 132ᵛ.

[8] *CUL G*, fo. 113ʳ.   [9] Below, ch. 8 (v).

[10] *CUL G*, fo. 73ᵛ; *CUL H*, sect. 3, fo. 2ᵛ.

[11] *CUL G*, fos. 53ᵛ, 54ᵛ. Of these Estève Garnier only said 'parum offerant et parum faciunt celebrari pro mortuis'.

[12] *BP* I, fos. 244ᵛ, 257ᵛ, 262ʳ, 270ʳ.

[13] *CUL H*, sect. 7, fo. 7ʳ, as in Allix, *Some remarks*, p. 323; Chevalier, p. 156.

[14] *ADI B*, fos. 146ᵛ, 150ʳ, for example.

[15] *CUL G*, fos. 55ʳ⁻ᵛ, 56ʳ: 'Dieu ly ayo perdona.'

they believed that when a man died, he was at once either saved or damned.[16] On these grounds the articles contradicted the claim of favourable witnesses that some Vaudois left money for prayers for their souls.[17] This positive and distinctive stance, rather than mere rejection, was probably the Vaudois characteristic.

(ii) Fasts and feasts, and the Ambrosian Lent

Thirteenth-century inquisitorial wisdom in this issue had been that the Waldenses rejected the calendar of the Church altogether.[18] Such an attitude would have been interesting, both as repelling the suggestion that the Church year was so much a part of rural life in the Middle Ages that it could not be escaped, and also as anticipating the attitudes of puritan Calvinism. However, later and more moderate experts on the Waldenses like Bernard Gui said that the *parfaits* of the sect kept Sundays and the Feasts of the Virgin, and some also the days of the Apostles and Evangelists; while they abstained from meat in Lent, though only to avoid shocking their neighbours.[19]

On the issue of keeping Church feasts, we should not be surprised to find contradictions, since the theorists themselves were at odds. The extreme view, that all saints' days, or even all holy days besides Sunday, should not be kept, is only suggested or stated by Antoni Blasii, Thomas Guot, some stereotyped admissions extracted by Cattaneo in the Val Chisone, and three clerical witnesses for Baile in 1483.[20] After torture Odin Valoy said that he had been told only Sunday was to be kept; later he added that one should keep Ascensiontide.[21]

Other, and perhaps better, sources reveal a picture of indescribable confusion or uncertainty. Antoni Blanc was

---

[16] *BP*, II, fos. 436^V-7^r.

[17] *CUL G*, fo. 29^r. Compare also ibid., fo. 33^V.

[18] *Thesaurus Novus Anecdotorum*, V, col. 1780; Flacius Illyricus, *Catalogus*, cols. 1511-12; Nickson, '"Pseudo-Reinerius" Treatise', 301.

[19] Gui, *Manuel*, I, 48-51.

[20] *CUL G*, fos. 54^V, 57^r, 61^r, 67^V, 73^V; *BP*, I, fos. 245^V, 270^V, 278^V, 281^V, 284^r, 286^V, 289^r; *ADI A*, e.g. fo. 265^V.

[21] *CUL H*, sect. 2, fos. 11^V, 14^r.

simply mystified when asked about Vaudois precepts on Church feasts.[22] Some Vaudois, interrogated during the early stages of the crusade, said the 'four great feasts', and Michaelmas, should be kept.[23] In the later crusade records there is enormous variety and contradiction, although a number of victims emphasized the main feasts of the life of Jesus, Christmas, Easter, and Pentecost; some would add Corpus Christi or the Apostles' days; some simply said they believed in keeping the 'greater feasts', without saying which.[24] The two Fraticelli were at odds on this issue; Peyre Valoy said that he did not know which feasts the Church said should be kept.[25]

Hence we find that the catholic emphasis on the purely negative aspects of Waldensianism, on its rejection of all the details of catholic belief and practice, is somewhat misplaced. Moreover, the absence of agreement on this point is perhaps a reminder that for the scattered communities of the hills the whole business of which feast-days should or should not be observed was much less important than for the corporate towns, where those not ceasing from work would be obvious at once.

Fasting (that is, abstaining from certain foods, especially meat) played two roles in the late medieval church. It was a ritual preparation for the major feast-days, in so far as the eves or 'vigils' of saints were observed as fasts. It was also used as a penance for the individual. We may look at each of these uses in turn. Fasting as a part of the calendar was not, according to the trial records, usually rejected altogether, save in dubious evidence like the summary of the Blasii trial, which contradicts what has gone before it.[26] Some specific vigils were rejected: for example those before saints' days, by those heretics who rejected feasting for them as well; or yet again the four Ember days.[27] Other heretics rejected some fasts and kept others, just as they had done with feasts.[28]

---

[22] *CUL G*, fo. 111^v.   [23] *ADI A*, fos. 268^v, 270^v, 273^{r-v}.

[24] *CUL H*, sect. 4; *ADI B, passim*; Chevalier, pp. 146–51.

[25] *CUL H*, sect. 6, fos. 4^{r-v}, 10^r; Marx, p. 247.   [26] *CUL G*, fo. 73^v.

[27] *CUL H*, sect. 4, fos. 1^v, 4^r, 8^v, 12^r; *BP*, I, fos. 278^v, 281^v, 284^r, 286^v, 289^r; *ADI A*, fos. 268^v, 270^v, 273^{r-v}, 276^r, etc.; Marx, p. 241.

[28] *CUL H*, sect. 4, fos. 3^v, 4^v, sect. 5, fo. 7^r, sect. 7, fo. 8^r, as in Allix, *Some remarks*, p. 324; Chevalier, pp. 146, 147, 149.

Some confessed Vaudois said they adhered to catholic teaching on this issue, and one actually claimed that a *barbe* had instructed her to fast Ember days and vigils.[29] Odin Valoy only fasted before St. Matthew's day, for some reason.[30]

On the other hand, the puritan mentality of Waldensianism was not at all averse to using fasting as a penance. A variety of victims said that *barbes* had told them to fast, sometimes on Fridays on bread and water.[31] As with prayer, therefore, we see the rituals of the religious life serving almost exactly the same social and moral function as in Roman catholicism. The Waldenses simply organized the patterns of their worship along different and artificially distinctive lines.

This same attitude is found in Waldensian attitudes to Lent. A simplistic author like Alfonso de Castro, writing in the early sixteenth century, could claim that the Waldenses rejected abstinence in that period of the year altogether.[32] In fact, the Vaudois in this period regarded Lent in exactly the same way as the catholics, but they taught that it should begin, not on Ash Wednesday, but on the following Monday, which the Vaudois themselves called the 'Old Lent'.[33] Alberto Cattaneo, a native of Piacenza, not far from Milan, was able to identify this in some of his earliest interrogations as the custom of the Ambrosian rite.[34] Peyre Roux claimed that he began his Lent on Ash Wednesday, but admitted that the *barbes* had told him to begin it later.[35] Several depositions which alleged that suspected Vaudois had been seen eating meat in the first Sunday in Lent confirm that this practice was in fact followed.[36]

(iii) Images and pilgrimages

The pattern found in this and the following section is as before. Theory, and logic, required that the Waldenses should

[29] *CUL G*, fo. 111ᵛ; *CUL H*, sect. 4, fos. 3ʳ, 6ʳ; *ADI B*, fo. 129ᵛ.

[30] *CUL H*, sect. 2, fo. 11ᵛ.

[31] Ibid., sect. 3, fo. 2ᵛ, sect. 4, fos. 6ᵛ, 10ᵛ, 11ᵛ, 12ʳ, sect. 7, fo. 11ʳ; *BP*, I, fos. 254ᵛ-5ʳ; *ADI A*, fo. 315ᵛ; *ADI B*, fo. 190ᵛ; Chevalier, p. 156.

[32] de Castro, *Adversus omnes hereses*, fo. LXVIIʳ.

[33] *CUL H* sect. 4, fos. 1ᵛ, 3ᵛ, 4ʳ, 10ᵛ, 11ʳ, sect. 5, fo. 7ʳ; *BP*, I, fos. 278ᵛ-9ʳ, 281ᵛ, 284ᵛ, 287ʳ, 289ᵛ; Chevalier, p. 150; Marx, p. 247.

[34] *ADI A*, fos. 117ᵛ, 134ᵛ; Marx, p. 21.

[35] *CUL H*, sect. 4, fo. 8ᵛ.   [36] *CUL G*, fos. 67ᵛ, 100ᵛ.

reject some part of catholic ritual which was surely irrelevant to their needs and beliefs; yet our evidence that they were aware of this logical duty is poor or unreliable; and we have testimonies that some individuals involved in the heresy did the reverse.

Images should have been as irrelevant to the spiritual needs of the Vaudois as the saints they normally represented — although that, as we have seen, is an argument which cuts several ways. Aeneas Sylvius even suggested that the Vaudois advocated iconoclasm.[37] Yet the documents which suggest that they rejected images are typical of weak inquisitorial material: two trial summaries; a stereotyped admission by both the Vaudois in the Vercors; and an admission extracted from Odin Valoy after torture.[38] Even the crusade registers provide only infrequent mentions.[39] Of the Fraticelli, Pietro di Jacopo spoke wistfully of some churches of which he had heard, which were in Apulia, 'absolutely white', and where the priests were of their sect.[40] If the Vaudois of Apulia built places of worship without images, those of Fressinières had Rostain d'Ancezune summoned to restore the ornaments to their village church.[41]

One witness in 1483 who mentioned pilgrimages said the Vaudois made very few, as opposed to none.[42] The same sort of dubious evidence testifies to the Vaudois' rejection of them.[43] References even in the crusade registers are sparse.[44] This evidence might be adequate on other issues; but it is surprising here, as Embrun was a centre of pilgrimage, and the Vaudois would hardly ignore it in their teaching if they objected to the practice so strongly. We know in fact that Antoni Blanc was on pilgrimage to the shrine of Our Lady of Embrun when his wife died.[45]

---

[37] Piccolomini, *Opera*, p. 103; compare Cattaneo in Godefroy, *Charles VIII*, p. 278.

[38] *CUL H*, sect. 2, fo. 11^v, sect. 7, fo. 8^r, as in Allix, *Some remarks*, p. 324; *BP*, I, fo. 270^v; Chevalier, p. 156; Marx, p. 241.

[39] e.g. *ADI A*, fos. 251^v-2^r.   [40] *CUL H*, sect. 6, fo. 10^r.

[41] *CUL G*, fo. 3^r.   [42] Ibid., fo. 54^v.

[43] *CUL H*, sect. 2, fo. 12^r, sect. 3, fo. 2^v, sect. 6, fos. 8^r, 10^r, sect. 7, fo. 8^r; Marx, p. 241.

[44] e.g. *ADI B*, fo. 145^r.   [45] *CUL G*, fo. 112^v.

(iv)   Holy bread and water

'Holy bread', presumably in the shape of the reserved sacrament, hardly appears at all in the materials. We learn that the
Waldenses attached no importance or sanctity to it through a
confession by Odin Valoy, and the reports of one priest and
of Peyre Roux, who said he followed catholic teaching on
this issue as well.[46] We find much more about holy water.
The witnesses for the inquiry of 1483 all said the Vaudois did
not believe in it, yet curiously showed how the heretics did
not abandon it altogether: Clément Garcin said that 'when
they take Holy Water they throw it back on to themselves,
taking no special care for it'.[47] One wonders if his understanding of what he saw was influenced by his reading.

However, in the inquisitions a wide variety of deponents
said they had been taught that holy water had no special
power;[48] almost inevitably Peyre Roux said that he had
been taught this but had not believed it.[49] Some could not
remember that the *barbes* had said anything about it.[50] On
the other hand, Antoni Blasii, on the brink of breaking down
under torture, asked to be given some holy water to drink,
'to help him tell the truth'.[51]

How far we believe the evidence suggested by these
materials depends upon a difficult exercise of judgement.
Some of the 'heresies' ascribed to the Waldenses would mark
them as more obsessively determined to differ from Rome in
all things than the more credible of the evidence suggests.
On the other hand, country folk who were simply suspicious
and a little contemptuous of the clergy might cast doubts on
holy water, for instance, without any need for ideological
underpinning.[52] There is no clear line which divides the
essence of 'popular heresy' from the simple neglect of

[46]   Ibid., fo. 54^v; *CUL H*, sect. 2, fo. 12^r, sect. 4, fo. 8^v.

[47]   *CUL G*, fos. 53^v, 54^v, 57^r.

[48]   Ibid., fos. 61^r, 73^v; *CUL H*, sect. 2, fo. 12^r, sect. 3, fo. 3^r, sect. 5, fo.7^r,
sect. 6, fos. 4^r, 10^r, sect. 7, fo. 7^v; *BP*, I, fos. 279^r, 282^r, 287^r, 289^v; Chevalier,
pp. 146, 156; Marx, p. 250; *ADI A, passim*.

[49]   *CUL H*, sect. 4, fo. 8^v.

[50]   Ibid., sect. 4, fos. 3^v, 4^r; *BP*, I, fo. 249^v.

[51]   *CUL G*, fo. 66^{r-v}; TCD MS 266, fos. 46^v-7^r; Marx, p. 239.

[52]   See, e.g. K. Thomas, *Religion and the Decline of Magic* (London, 1971),
pp. 51-5, 75, 86.

conventional piety by ordinary country folk: nor should we try to construct one. However, once the clergy had become convinced of their 'heretical' nature all forms of dissent were grist to the inquisitorial mill. In the end, a clearer picture of the Vaudois identity may be gained from the moral and social order of their culture, to which we now turn.

8. A Waldensian Morality – or Counter-morality?

(i) Initiation

As a partially closed, and partially clandestine community, the Waldenses of the late medieval Dauphiné had their own forms of initiation for entrants to the sect. Normally this took the form of the first confession to a *barbe* made by the entrant and his or her formal instruction in the distinctive ideas which have been described. In spite of the fact that many children must have been brought up in an atmosphere where heretical ideas were already prevalent, they seem not to have been told anything specific about those ideas until a certain age.

Odin Valoy said at his trial that his uncle only told him about the sect when he was about twenty; and added that it was common practice to tell children nothing about it until that age, because at any younger they might give the heretics away.[1] This explicit statement is unique; moreover, it places initiation slightly later in life than the other sources suggest. Antoni Blasii was told about the heresy at nineteen or so, but his aunt said she was surprised that he had not been told about it earlier.[2] Others fairly deeply involved in the sect, like Peyre Valoy or Johan Pellegrin, learned at about the age of fourteen or fifteen.[3] Taking the evidence as a whole, in 151 cases where details are supplied, four heretics were inducted under the age of ten; twenty-six learned before they were sixteen; eighty-nine between sixteen and twenty-five; seventeen between twenty-five and thirty, and fifteen later.[4]

Since Waldensianism placed such emphasis on 'law' and on

---

[1] *CUL H*, sect. 2, fos. 12ᵛ, 14ᵛ.   [2] *CUL G*, fos. 60ᵛ–1ʳ.

[3] Ibid., fos. 55ᵛ, 110ʳ, 114ᵛ; Marx, p. 249.

[4] The difference in numbers between those inducted before and after the age of twenty is not significant. These statistics exclude all those recorded in *ADI A*, whose ages were not supplied.

forms of ritual and behaviour, it could not be inculcated in the cradle nor practised by proxy. Such an attitude might have helped to create an otherwise unfounded suspicion that the Waldenses rejected the practice of infant baptism.[5] Moreover, in this initiation we see the lay nature of the heresy once again. The *barbes* were in the background to hear confessions, but the actual introduction was done by parents or relatives; in the same way, although the *barbes* were on hand for disputations in the 1480s, resistance was led by those who had no explicit spiritual function.[6]

(ii)   Marriage and divorce

From the fairly sparse information available, it would seem that by the 1480s a pattern of comparatively late marriage, with an average age in the mid-twenties, was already established in this region. Of a sample of ninety-two women over the age of fifteen, between the ages of sixteen and twenty, twenty-eight were single as against nine married; between the ages of twenty-one and twenty-five, six were single and seven married; between the ages of twenty-six and thirty, five were single and eleven married; over the age of thirty, there were still three unmarried as against fifteen married and eight widowed.[7]

In pre-Tridentine fashion, betrothal rather than solemnization seems to have been the important threshold to married life. When Odin Valoy married Françoise Meyffred she was living in the *muanda*[8] which the Valoy brothers rented from the prior of Les Beaumes, Pierre Sabine; Odin described how he 'contracted' with her 'in his own home, that is, his wife's and his own'.[9] Some sort of ceremony seems to have been involved, however. Estève Garnier of Vallouise said in 1483 that the Vaudois would not intermarry with catholics, because

---

[5]   Above, ch. 6 (ii).   [6]   Above, ch. 1 (iii).

[7]   These statistics also exclude *ADI A*. They are also imprecise because some women did not know their ages exactly, or had them taken down differently by different notaries.

[8]   Possibly equivalent to the Piedmontese *miando*, meaning a summer steading; Marx, p. 246, interprets it as 'bergerie'.

[9]   *CUL H*, sect. 2, fos. 4ʳ, 13ʳ, 15ʳ: 'in suis parietibus ipsius loquentis et uxoris sue.'

their 'rites, customs, and ceremonies' were quite different from the catholics'.[10] He could here only have been referring to folk-customs rather than the rituals of the church; however, he provided no more details.

A favourite suggestion of catholic witnesses against the Vaudois was that the latter scorned marriage links with non-Vaudois. This claim is found seven times in the evidence taken in 1483, in depositions against the Baridon family, and in two sets of proctors' articles.[11] Monet Regis, of St-Mamans near Valence, admitted this tenet.[12] Odin Valoy, who married a girl from the catholic family of Meyffred, said that no one of his family wanted to come to the wedding, as his wife was from outside the sect.[13] On 12 October 1487 Peyre Don, of Villaretto in the Val Chisone, said that in the past he had wished to marry Jehannette, sister of Fazy Veylier. She refused to marry him unless he became a Vaudois; he would not, so she married Guilhem Bonet instead.[14] Antoni Blasii told how an acquaintance of his called Nicolas Grilhet had married at Manosque, but speedily took his new wife off to Angrogna for a while after their wedding, so that she should learn the faith.[15]

Some suspected Vaudois alleged in 1501 that it was the catholics who put up the resistance to marriage links between those of Fressinières and those outside.[16] In spite of this, such fastidiousness as was ascribed to the Vaudois fits in with their strictness in other matters. It also probably affected daughters most of all, who might be supposed to find it more difficult to convert catholic husbands; this might in turn explain their marrying fairly late. Nevertheless, the heresy was not sealed perpetually in a few family names and entirely within those names. Amongst the protesting catholics in Vallouise in 1483 are found several names, such as Reymunt, Ruffi, Aufossi, and Alard, which were associated with heresy in the same region. The interrelation of Waldensian families could at best

    [10] *CUL G*, fo. 54ᵛ.
    [11] Ibid., fos. 53ʳ⁻ᵛ, 54ᵛ, 57ʳ, 100ᵛ-1ʳ; *BP*, II, fo. 442ᵛ; Allix, *Some remarks*, p. 301.   [12] Chevalier, p. 156.
    [13] *CUL H*, sect. 2, fos. 4ʳ, 13ʳ.   [14] *ADI A*, fo. 106ʳ.
    [15] *CUL G*, fo. 65ᵛ; TCD MS 266, fo. 46ᵛ; Marx, p. 238.
    [16] *CUL G*, fos. 25ᵛ, 27ᵛ; *BP*, II, fos. 48ʳ⁻ᵛ, 53ʳ.

only have been partially exclusive.

The inquisitors also alleged that the Waldenses rejected the elaborate system of prohibited degrees of consanguinity, and that they married within them.[17] Antoni Blasii, Estève David, and Thomas Guot all admitted they thought marriage was permitted either within the fourth or third degree (still fairly remote relations);[18] Blasii believed he was related to his wife through his brother.[19] In the first Cattaneo register this accusation is used to promote an otherwise almost unsupported charge of libertinage: 'they taught him that one can marry in the second and third degree without sin, and that to be coupled with women is not evil, because the sins of the flesh are reckoned amongst the least of the sins.'[20] This charge relating to prohibited degrees is nearly always tied to the second allegation, which has nothing to do with the charges relating to the notorious, supposedly immoral 'synagogues', which will be considered later.[21]

In practice, the prohibited degrees were far too many for comfort as far as these mountain communities were concerned. In the valley of the Queyras alone, between 1497 and 1507 ten marriages needed dispensation from the rules of consanguinity.[22] These dispensations had to be paid for: which was presumably what the Vaudois refused to do. Of only six dispensations issued in the 1490s and 1500s relating to couples from l'Argentière and Vallouise, there is no clear evidence that any of those asking for such documents were Vaudois; and none were issued to couples from Fressinières.[23]

The same free will and informality which were used in marriage seem, oddly enough, also to have applied to divorce

---

[17] *BP*, II, fos. 438r, 482v.

[18] *CUL G*, fos. 69r–v, 73v; TCD MS 266, fo. 48r; *BP*, I, fos. 255r–v, 279r.

[19] TCD MS 266, fo. 45r.

[20] *ADI A*, fos. 252r–v, 254r–v, 256r–v, 260v–1r, 263r, 266r, 269r, 273v–4r, 275v–6r, 278r, and so on to 362r: 'eundem docuerunt quod possunt contrahere matrimonium in secundo et tercio gradu sine peccato et quod habere copulam cum mulieribus non est malefactum quia peccatum carnis inter cetera vicia pro minimo reputatur.'

[21] Below, (iii).

[22] ADH-A MS G 2767, fos. 98v, 100r, 102v, 136r, 159r, 187r, 232r, 410r, 414r, 542v.

[23] Ibid., fos. 1v, 10v, 74r, 135r, 186(*bis*)r, 476v; the interdict sustained by Rostain d'Ancezune against Fressinières might possibly be the sole reason for the absence of dispensations issued for couples here.

in this period. Although the inquisitors did not follow up the suggestions of theoretical heresy about divorce which some manuals referred to,[24] some witnesses discussed the possibility. Antoni Blasii's brother Barthélemi had married the daughter of another clothier from Angrogna, Laurent Falquet, at L'Isle-sur-la-Sorgue; all three then decided to emigrate to Apulia. While at Genoa, Barthélemi discovered his wife had contracted to another man; so he let her go, returned to Provence, and settled and remarried in Draguignan, and accepted the whole business.[25] Blasii himself offered to prove his repentance at his abjuration by divorcing his wife if she would not leave the sect.[26] Peyre Valoy mentioned in his trial how his father and mother were living apart, one at Fressinières and one at St-André.[27]

(iii) Sexual matters and witchcraft charges

The material on Alpine Waldensianism does not offer the same opportunities for the exploration of the salacious or the romantic as does the Fournier register on Catharism. This is ironic, however, since for much of the past few centuries the allegations of incest and debauchery in the Waldensian trials have been far more notorious.

A few minor questions affecting sexual relations must be dealt with first, before these central allegations. One is the suggestion made by Monet Regis of St-Mamans, that the Vaudois people should abstain from marital relations on Fridays, and also at obviously unfruitful times, during menstruation and pregnancy.[28] This is repeated nowhere else in this century, although it has similarities to a clause of the pseudo-Reinerius treatise.[29] Yet in 1530 Georges Morel consulted the reformers on this very same point, and was told to be more sympathetic to human frailty.[30]

At the opposite extreme, it was alleged that the Waldenses

---

[24] *Thesaurus Novus Anecdotorum*, V, col. 1756.
[25] *CUL G*, fo. 63ʳ; TCD MS 266, fo. 43ʳ.   [26] *CUL G*, fo. 69ʳ.
[27] Marx, p. 245.   [28] Chevalier, p. 156.
[29] Flacius Illyricus, *Catalogus*, col. 1511; Nickson, '"Pseudo-Reinerius" Treatise', 298: 'mortaliter peccare coniuges si absque spe prolis conveniant.'
[30] TCD MS 259, p. 49; Vinay, *Confessioni di fede . . . riformati*, pp. 42, 84.

did not regard simple fornication as a sin, and that for this purpose they also limited the scope of incest very narrowly.[31] Besides the rather dubious crusade depositions which supported these claims, the Fraticelli said the women of the sect would offer themselves freely to the *barbes*;[32] one of them said that lechery, unless between mother and son, was no sin, and quoted the words 'be fruitful and multiply, and fill the earth; Saint John keep you and you shall be saved'. This curious phrase was taken up in proctors' articles in 1507.[33]

These general allegations were usually presented as riders, as it were, to the chief charge: that at their nightly gatherings, the Waldenses would put out the lamps after the preaching and indulge in a promiscuous and incestuous orgy. The argument as to whether this orgy ever happened is not dead yet. Normal Cohn dismisses the stories as part of a literary tradition; while Bona Pazè Beda remarks of these meetings, 'they are symptoms of the habits of sexual play which permeated the society of the time, and against which reformers and catholics alike thundered...'.[34] Since even modern authors can differ so totally, and none has yet surveyed all the evidence in print, a detailed discussion is perhaps worth while.

Very little evidence about the 'congregation' is forthcoming before the crusade. In 1483 Johan Pellegrin said he had heard how, when the Vaudois were gathered together at night, they 'do things with the women saying "who has, let him hold" '.[35] After torture, Odin Valoy admitted that before his marriage he had been present in the house of Pons Arnulphs, or Brunet, where about a dozen men and women were gathered. The *barbe* preached, and then took hold of a woman to have sex with, as a lead to the others. Odin then followed suit. However, he said that the gathering took place in the daytime, and that the house where it took place had several rooms, so that the couples could be separate from one another. At the 'repetition' of his evidence at the end of the

<hr/>

[31] *BP*, II, fo. 443[r] (these articles also permitted adultery); compare *ADI B*, fos. 267[r], 308[r].

[32] *CUL H*, sect. 6, fos. 5[r-v], 11[r].   [33] *BP*, I, fos. 403[v]-4[r].

[34] N. Cohn, *Europe's inner demons* (London, 1975), pp. 38-42; Pazè Beda, *Riforma e Cattolicesimo*, p. 36.   [35] *CUL G*, fo. 55[v].

trial Odin tried to withdraw some of his admissions, saying that some things which he had said were true and some were not.[36]

Considering the numbers interrogated, even in the crusade the yield was meagre. On 3 October 1487 Guigo Boc or Bosc, of Mentoulles, said he had been to Waldensian meetings in the house of Thomas Ruffi at Villaretto; asked if his wife had committed adultery at these meetings, he said at first he did not know, then that he thought so. Then he added that as one of the sect he was able to enjoy all the women of the sect outside the meetings, and that this was why he joined the sect; besides which his brothers despised him for being a catholic.[37] On his third interrogation on 11 October, but not before, Peyre Griot of Pragelas admitted the standard inquisitors' tale, saying he had been at meetings where orgies took place four or five years before. He added that any child conceived at these meetings was regarded as a *barbe* without any further consecration.[38]

Besides these two cases, there is virtually no firm evidence. Three witnesses said they had heard of such meetings happening, but had never been present.[39] Several members of the Bérard family of l'Argentière, who had been the object of, as they said, malicious rumours to this effect, denied the charge vehemently and repeatedly.[40] Several other witnesses from Fressinières or l'Argentière either denied the suggestion of such meetings taking place, or said they knew nothing whatever about them.[41] The manuscripts take us no further. In the seventeenth century the catholic polemicists Martin and Rorengo both claimed to have found further documentary evidence. The admissions from which Martin quoted either

---

[36] *CUL H*, sect. 2, fos. 12^v, 15^v.

[37] *ADI A*, fos. 74^v-5^r; G. Martin, *Inscription en faux... contre le livre intitulé 'De la puissance du Pape' par le sieur Marc Vulson* (Grenoble, 1640), pp. 220-1.

[38] *ADI A*, fos. 104^v-5^v, 154^v; Marx, p. 26; Pazè Beda, *Riforma e Cattolicesimo*, p. 36, n. 81.

[39] *CUL H*, sect. 4, fo. 8^v; *ADI B*, fos. 182^r, 294^v.

[40] *CUL H*, sect. 4, fo. 11^r; *ADI B*, fos. 262^r, 278^v, 279^v-80^v, 286^{r-v}, 304^v, 319^r. Of these Johan Bérard (fo. 262^r) said he had been at a preaching session at the end of which the *barbe* had put out the light, but he knew of nothing else which happened then.

[41] *CUL H*, sect. 4, fos. 1^{r-v}, 3^v, 4^r, 5^r, 6^v, 12^r, 15^r; *ADI B*, fos. 119^r, 126^r, 131^r, 157^r, 164^r.

are inconsistent with the depositions of other similar witnesses, or derive from manuscripts of the Cattaneo register for Vallouise, which no longer exists.[42]

After the crusade, the trial of the Fraticelli does contain some full traditional admissions. Yet, for example, Pietro di Jacopo's first statement about the 'congregation' is very muddled, and it is only in the second version that he explains that the dancing around each other done by the participants in the darkness was intended to make sure that no one could identify his or her sexual partner. At the end of his first description of such orgies the record simply cross-refers back to the confession of the first Fraticello, as though exact details were not regarded as important.[43]

There are numerous objections to the stories of these orgies. They are inconsistent with what we hear from elsewhere about the moral tone adopted by the Waldenses. At least four witnesses deposed that they believed that after one was married, to breach the bond by adultery was a mortal sin.[44] The pieces of evidence for the 'congregations' used above all derive from the sort of sources we are least likely to credit.[45] When, in 1507, some proctors' articles took up the allegations and asserted that a house at Balboutet in the Val Chisone had been identified as the place where these meetings took place, the catholic party was desperate for anything to discredit the appellants.[46]

Such admissions as confirm the allegations follow almost exactly the pattern of confessions extracted by Antonio Settimo in the Pinerolese in the 1380s. In 1387 one heretic had deposed rather standard beliefs, describing the 'congregation' as simply a preaching gathering. At the end of the meeting, he said, the *barbe* put out the light, said 'let him who has [this message] keep it', and after a while everyone

[42]   Rorengo-Lucerna, *Memorie historiche*, pp. 12-13; Martin, *Inscription en faux*, pp. 221-6. Martin reproduces the confessions of seven victims from Puy-Aillaud, Vallouise, or l'Argentière. His quotation from Guigo Boc is quite accurate (above, n. 37) but we cannot judge in these cases.

[43]   *CUL H*, sect. 6, fos. 9ᵛ-10ᵛ.

[44]   *CUL H*, sect. 7, fo. 6ʳ; *BP*, I, fo. 248ʳ; *ADI B*, fo. 267ʳ; Allix, *Some remarks*, p. 323; Chevalier, p. 156; Marx, p. 26, n. 10.

[45]   See above, ch. 2 (ii).

[46]   *BP*, I, fos. 307ᵛ-8ʳ, 404ʳ.

left.[47] Only the following year, when Settimo investigated a possibly unstable Franciscan tertiary called Antonio Galosna did he extract evidence of a multitude of licentious and devilish synagogues; as each town in Piedmont was named, many of these far from Waldensian country, he produced a stream of information.[48] Moreover, the tradition established by these heresy trials was to survive the reformation. In the early years of the reformation in France similar orgiastic excesses were supposed to take place at clandestine Huguenot meetings;[49] heresy continued to be linked with sorcery and sexual licence.[50]

Laurent Bureau and Thomas Pascal went to great pains to ask those whom they interviewed in the summer of 1501 if there had been any substance to these charges. Without exception priests, notaries, and suspected Vaudois alike said the charges were false. The *curé* of Gap, Arnulph des Vallars, said the girls from Fressinières were so chaste they would rather starve than consent to fornication, although they were much solicited, and he had told them to complain to him when this happened. François Farel said he had often asked the suspects about the 'congregation', especially the simple-tons, who had all replied with shocked denials, and pointed out that none of their women ever became pregnant before marriage.[51] .

Even if we consider the numbers of the testimonies, quite apart from their different quality, it is evident that the claims made in favour of the existence of such meetings are insufficiently supported and discredited. The odium and outrage such rumours created, moreover, allied to the force presumably used to extort such confessions, may have helped the case for the heretics' legal rehabilitation.

---

[47] Amati, 'Processus contra Valdenses', *Archivio Storico Italiano*, series 3 (1865), I, pt. ii, 22, 39–40; the phrase was 'qui habet teneat'; cf. the account of Johan Bérard, above.

[48] Ibid., II, pt. i, 3–45; Marx, pp. 24–5; Cohn, *Europe's inner demons*, pp. 37–8.

[49] C. Haton, *Mémoires*, ed. F. Bourquelot (Paris, 1857), pp. 49–50; J.-A. de Thou, *Historiarum sui temporis* (Paris, 1604–8), II, 718; N. Z. Davis, *Society and Culture in Early Modern France* (London, 1975), pp. 158, 317.

[50] Haton, *Mémoires*, p. 511; C. de Rubys, *Histoire veritable de la ville de Lyon* (Lyon, 1604), p. 269.

[51] *BP*, I, fos. 447^r-v, 451^v-2^r.

A few scanty insinuations circulated linking Waldensian heresy with forms of idolatry, witchcraft, or *maleficium*; these stories are not altogether connected with the 'congregations' but neither are they completely distinct. Antoni Blasii reported how he had heard that almost all of his native valley of Angrogna were thought to be Waldenses, and were alleged to hold a 'synagogue', in which they kissed the anus of a goat.[52] This hearsay smacked of the stories of the 'Vauderie' at Arras twenty years before;[53] the inquisitor, however, did not follow up the admission. At Odin Valoy's first heretic confession, a *barbe* told him that 'to deny God and the Virgin Mary is the greatest of sins; they are Waldenses who do such things'. From that time he had assumed that 'Waldensian' meant God-denying, and never equated the term with his beliefs.[54] Pietro di Jacopo, last of all, made some perplexing admissions about his sect worshipping the idols 'Bacus', 'Sibilla', and 'Fadas' at their meetings.[55]

Some vague suggestions of *maleficium* by natural or supernatural means seem to have troubled l'Argentière just before the crusade. Jame Bérard and Sperit Porte seem to have been in a plot to intimidate the catholic Guigo Alfand, who was collaborating with the archbishop, with threats of burning his house down. The matter was left to the secular judge of the place.[56]

In the 1430s and 1440s, some inquisitors uncovered or claimed to have uncovered a large number of magicians and folk-witches of one sort or another in the Dauphiné, including the area of Valpute.[57] However, as far as concerns allegations of something like later witchcraft, one must conclude with Marx that, in this area and period, inquisitors did not confuse

[52]　*CUL G*, fo. 62^r; TCD MS 266, fo. 45^r; Marx, p. 25, no. 3.

[53]　Cf. F. Bourquelot, 'Les Vaudois au xve siècle', *Bibliothèque de l'école des chartes*, 2nd series, III (1846), 81-109; A. Duverger, *Le Premier Grand Procès de sorcellerie aux Pays-Bas: La Vauderie dans les états de Philippe le bon* (Arras, 1885); Cohn, *Europe's inner demons*, pp. 229-32.

[54]　*CUL H*, sect. 2, fos. 9^r, 7^v.

[55]　Ibid., sect. 6, fo. 9^v; Marx, p. 26, n. 6, Cohn, *Europe's inner demons*, p. 41.

[56]　*CUL H*, sect. 4, fo. 11^{r-v}; the threats included 'faciemus taliter quod aliqui ex vicinis videbant stellas de fundo domorum . . .' (*sic*), and also 'qui aure paor de sa mayson si la garde . . .'.

[57]　Marx, pp. 27-50; Cohn, *Europe's inner demons*, pp. 226-7; ADI, B 4356.

sorcerers of that type with Waldenses, and the latter were condemned always on fairly traditional charges.[58] Those who were condemned for witchcraft in the 1480s, for example the sorcerers from the Champsaur burnt by Jacques Brunenche in 1484-6, do not seem to have had any links with the Vaudois.[59]

(iv) Swearing and lying

It has long been assumed to be one of the most characteristic traits both of Waldensianism[60] and of Catharism[61] that these heresies abhorred all lies, and all oaths. Under the influence of a literalist reading of the Bible, the heretics are supposed to have felt that the swearing of any oath, even in a legal or commercial context, was forbidden by Christ, and to have refused ever to swear, unless perhaps to avoid detection by inquisitors.[62] Here, in spite of the weight behind the orthodox view, we are forced to suggest that, in the Alps in the late fifteenth century, the Waldenses only rejected the casual, blasphemous, prophane oath, and that they made no more fuss about lies than about any other normal sins.[63]

Scholastic theory was fairly consistent about the absoluteness of the Waldensian position. Pseudo-Reinerius said that the Vaudois regarded one who forced the taking of an oath as worse than a murderer.[64] The *De inquisitione hereticorum* set out the supposed Vaudois casuistry for atoning for oaths which one was forced to take.[65] The inquisitorial articles of 1501 and 1507 were unanimous that the Vaudois were conspicuous by their refusal to swear, and one of them even cited the great canonist Henry of Ostia (archbishop of Embrun 1250-61) in support of the same point.[66]

---

[58] Marx, p. 48; cf. also F. Gabotto, 'Valdesi, catari e streghe', *BSHV* 18 (1900), esp. 12–17. [59] Marx, pp. 235–6.

[60] See e.g. Vinay, *Confessioni di fede . . . riformati*, p. 27.

[61] J. Duvernoy, *Le Catharisme: la religion des cathares* (Toulouse, 1976), pp. 189–91. [62] Gui, *Manuel*, I, 38–41.

[63] For corroboration of this result see Audisio, *Barbe et l'inquisiteur*, pp. 59–60; also 'Il Sentimento religioso dei Valdesi della Provenza attraverso gli atti notarili, 1460–1520', *Quaderni Storici*, 41 (1979), 451–69, esp. 460–1.

[64] Flacius Illyricus, *Catalogus*, col. 1513; Nickson, '"Pseudo-Reinerius" Treatise', 303. [65] *Thesaurus Novus Anecdotorum*, V. cols. 1780, 1784.

[66] *CUL G*, sect. 3, as in Allix, *Some remarks*, p. 300; *BP*, II, fos. 434ʳ, 438ᵛ–9ʳ, 481ᵛ; cf. Henricus de Bartholomaeis, de Segusio, alias Ostiensis, *Aurea Summa* (Venice, 1605), col. 1531.

The testimonies given in 1483, and indeed most of the records of the Cattaneo crusade, are too ambiguous and devoid of context to help on this question.[67] The absolute categorical rejection of all oaths is found in some unimpressive evidence: three trial summaries;[68] the confession of Odin Valoy after torture;[69] and the admissions of Peyre Valoy and Francesco di Girundino.[70] The two trials from the Valentinois included a totally stereotyped confession as follows: 'that to swear in any circumstances or for any reason, whether for true or false, or to make any oath whatever where the phrase "by so-and-so" is used was a great sin. . . .'[71] Peyre Chiolet of Usseaux went even further in his admission: he had been told 'that to swear or lie in whatever instance is a mortal sin; therefore he should never affirm anything, but say "I believe so or not", "I think so or not". . . .'[72]

In the fuller and more convincing evidence of the long trials we find a more complicated picture. Antoni Blasii was only averse to swearing 'by God', or perhaps by the Virgin.[73] Thomas Guot at first said he only refused to swear 'by God or the saints'.[74] Antoni Blanc was asked by the archbishop 'if one swears without cause or need, not taking care not to swear, is that a sin or not?' He replied that it was a mortal sin, and later said he had been told not to swear 'by God'.[75] When Odin Valoy was first introduced to a *barbe*, the latter at once asked if he swore by God; Odin replied that he did, more than he needed to. The *barbe* replied 'swearers and blasphemers of God are the firebrands of Hell'.[76]

Some contemporaries referred explicitly to a reluctance to swear amongst the Vaudois which had no heretical overtones. The vicar of l'Argentière said in 1501 that he knew many who were suspected of heresy, whom he thought were good

[67]   *CUL G*, fos. 54[V], 55[V], 57[r].

[68]   Ibid., fo. 73[V]; *CUL H*, sect. 5, fo. 7[r]; *BP*, I, fo. 271[r]. In two of these cases the summaries do not match the trial records.

[69]   *CUL H*, sect. 2, fo. 12[V].   [70]   Ibid., sect. 6, fo. 5[V]; Marx, p. 249.

[71]   *CUL H*, sect. 7, fo. 6[r]; Chevalier, p. 156.

[72]   *ADI A*, fos. 132[V]-3[r]. This admission is unique.

[73]   *CUL G*, fos. 67[r], 69[r].   [74]   *BP*, I, fos. 244[V]-5[r].

[75]   *CUL G*, fos. 111[r], 116[V].

[76]   *CUL H*, sect. 2, fo. 8[V]: 'Juradors et blasphemadors de dieu sont tisons de enfern.'

catholics, but who were different from the rest because they
did not care to swear.[77] The proctors for the Vaudois tried in
1507 to vindicate their clients' reputations by saying the
latter were 'accustomed, so far as is possible for them, to
abstain from oaths and blaspheming of the name of our Lord
Jesus Christ, . . . and to keep their contracts and promises
according to the law . . .'.[78]

Similar testimonies to the Vaudois' dislike of profanity are
found well into the sixteenth century. Claude de Seyssel
noted how the Vaudois helped their cause by their godly way
of life. This godliness consisted mainly in their 'not swearing
unless forced to, and not taking the name of God in vain.'[79]
When Georges Morel reported that the *barbes* advised the
people against swearing, he linked oaths with dancing and
loose living.[80] When Scipione Lentolo reflected on the faults
of his former flocks, he had to admit that they could partially
excuse themselves by saying 'how is it that we do not love
God, or are not zealous for his honour, since we . . . do not
blaspheme, nor do we swear unless when in great need?'[81]

We have overwhelming testimony to show that, even
outside the context of a heresy trial, the Vaudois used the
formal, sacramental oath to make covenants one with another
as regularly as anyone. Antoni Blasii was held on parole from
the archbishop's prisons on simple oath.[82] When Antoni
Blanc encountered some *barbes* at night near Pallon, and later
discussed the matter with the local heretic Pons Brunet, the
latter made him swear on the scriptures not to hinder these
men.[83] Early in his trial Odin Valoy offered to find those
who would swear that he was not a heretic. Peyronette
Beraud was made to swear not to reveal the *barbes'* presence
to anyone by her neighbour in Beauregard, Telmon Pascal.
Francesco di Girundino and Antoni Blasii both, apparently,
swore not to reveal the sect; the former took an oath not to

[77] *CUL G*, fo. 33[r].   [78] *BP*, I, fo. 356[v].
[79] Seyssel, *Adversus errores*, fo. 8.
[80] TCD MS 259, p. 48; Vinay, *Confessioni di fede . . . riformati*, p. 42. There
is a separate discussion of the ceremonial oath on p. 76 of the MS, for which see
Vinay, pp. 46, 56.
[81] *Lentolo MS*, pp. 483-4, 496-7. The same was reported of the Vaudois of
Provence in the 1540s.
[82] *CUL G*, fo. 73[r–v]; TCD MS 266, fo. 48[v].   [83] *CUL G*, fos. 115[v]-16[r].

swear by God.[84]

As regards lying, several witnesses, mostly from the crusade inquiries, said they had been told not to lie or bear false witness, usually in combination with the instruction not to swear.[85] However, there was no special emphasis laid on this command; a *barbe* might equally ask his pupil 'not to swear or do evil'.

Puritanical and self-conscious strictness, rather than 'heresy' as such, was the motive for the behaviour of the Vaudois on this article. Hence the discrepancy between theory and practice is easily accounted for. The inquisitors discovered a sanctimonious habit of the morally superior; they had to turn it into a theological 'crime' so as to make it fit the stereotype they had received of what Waldensianism was about. At least none of them explored the consequences and logical implications of the Waldensian precept on oaths with the same obsessive attention to detail as Jacques Fournier.[86]

(v)   Funerary rites

These last two sections afford only glimpses into the folk-customs which accrued around religious dissent; thanks to the way in which the inquisitors worked they are almost irrecoverable. Here we are concerned with the custom of putting a cord of rope about the neck of a dying heretic. This cord was then supposed to be left about the neck of the body and buried with it.

Estèver Garnier pointed out in 1483 that the Waldenses did not seek the last rites of the Church, 'unless from dissimulation'. Clément Garcin said that he had seen two or three of the dead of Fressinières, bound with a halter about the neck when they were led to burial, 'and such things he had not seen done amongst good Christians'. He claimed the Vaudois said this was done 'because of vomiting'. He had also heard that amongst the Waldenses corpses were laid with the head facing into the grave, contrary to normal practice.[87]

---

[84] *CUL H*, sect. 2, fo. 5^r; sect. 7, fo. 9^v; sect. 6, fos. 1^v, 5^v-6^r; TCD MS 266, fo. 48^r.   [85] e.g. *BP*, I, fo. 248^{r-v}; *ADI B*, fo. 226^v; Chevalier, pp. 147, 151.
[86] Cf. J. Duvernoy, *Le Registre d'inquisition de Jacques Fournier* (Toulouse, 1965), I, 40-122.   [87] *CUL G*, fos. 54^v, 57^r.

According to information, now lost, on the basis of which the trial of Antoni Blanc was conducted, the halter was used at the deaths of Johan Alard, at Baratier about 1470, and of Antoni Blanc's wife Alise, who died at Fressinières on 25 March 1490. In the Alard case, the young Vaudois Johan Pellegrin rashly applied the cord in the presence of catholic witnesses, explaining that this was something done by the people of Fressinières to prevent the soul from expiring through the mouth of the dying person.[88] No other evidence of this practice exists in the manuscripts save an ambiguous reference in Jame Bérard's interrogation.[89]

It is far from certain that this peculiar rite was, as Marx claimed without citing evidence, a survival or borrowing from Catharism.[90] It may have had nothing to do with the *barbes* and their teaching at all, and have been rather an antique custom amongst these tightly bound communities which resisted more normal 'Christianizing'.

This custom doubtless gained its associations with Catharism and the supposed *endura*, or heretical last rites, because of a legend which circulated in clerical circles. Marcellin Fornier included in his seventeenth-century history of Embrun a description of an alleged Vaudois *endura*: he claimed that a number of witnesses had said in 1505 that the *barbes* asked those on the point of death, or disabled by disease, if they wished to die confessors or martyrs. If they replied the first, nature was allowed to take its course; if the second, they were strangled. This was proved, Fornier claimed, by the fact that the tombs of many who had died this way were opened, and they were found to have a halter about their necks.[91]

Fornier was here confusing the Vaudois rite with a custom referred to in the trial of Giacomo Bech, the Fraticello *de paupere vita* who confessed teaching various dualist doctrines to Antonio Settimo at Turin in the summer of 1388. Bech said that confessors of his sect would say to the sick, 'do you wish to die a confessor or a martyr?' If the sick person

---

[88] Ibid, fos. 110^r, 111^v-13^r, 114^{r-v}.
[89] *CUL H*, sect. 4, fo. 10^v: 'si deberet transire collem. . . .'
[90] Marx, p. 24.
[91] Fornier, II, 209. For a similar legend regarding the Cathars, see Moore, *Origins of European Dissent*, pp. 224–5.

claimed that he wished to be a martyr, they placed a bolster over his face. If he died in the course of this process, he was called a martyr; if he recovered, he was called a 'parfait' and acquired the right to give a similar *consolamentum* to others.[92] It seems, therefore, that the inquisitors, and Fornier after them, seized on a confession of a traditional supposed Cathar practice and used it to explain the evidence of a genuine Vaudois folk-rite. This attitude on the part of the clergy is, as we shall see, typical.

(vi) Needles and emblems

All we can do here is note the occasional mention of some of the material symbols loosely associated with dissent. The Valoy brothers, Peyronette Beraud, and Catherine Ripert all said that the *barbes* had given them pins or needles when they met them.[93] Peyre Valoy said he was given them as playthings when a child; but adults also received them. They may have been intended to authenticate the *barbes'* pretended function as *colporteurs*.[94] Odin Valoy put them in his felt hat, and later lost them.[95]

As no one seems to have been quite sure what to do with these pins, it seems fairly clear that they were intended first of all as emblems. We know that the *barbes* carried emblematic containers for them too. When two *barbes* from Piedmont offered to hear Blasii's confession, they showed him two things: one was a book, which the *barbes* showed him but did not read from; the other was a needle-case[96] covered in black leather divided into four sections, which the *barbe*

---

[92] Amati, 'Processus contra Valdenses', *Archivio Storico Italiano*, series 3 (1865), II, pt. i, 57.

[93] *CUL H*, sect. 2, fo. 10^v, sect. 5, fo. 7^r, sect. 7, fo. 13^r; *ADI B*, fo. 225^v; Marx, p. 249. They were called 'agulhes' in dialect.

[94] Pins or needles were generally carried about the country by *colporteurs* or pedlars in the pre-industrial period; cf. R. Mandrou, *De la culture populaire aux 17e et 18e siècles: la bibliothèque bleue de Troyes* (Paris, 1964), p. 19. In a Wycliffite tract there is a reference to members of religious orders becoming 'pedderis [pedlars] berynge knyves, pynnys and girdlis and spices and sylk and precious pellure and forrouris for wymmen . . .'. See *The English works of Wyclif*, ed. by F. D. Matthew (EETS, OS 74, 1880), p. 12.

[95] *CUL H*, sect. 2, fo. 15^r.

[96] 'Agulherium', probably equivalent to the Provençal 'agulhier', meaning a pincushion, although something more solid is obviously meant here.

carried hidden away in his clothing. One of them said to Blasii that this container was a token or sign carried by the confessors on their travels, by which they were known to their believers.[97]

These details are not made less plausible, in this case, because they are only attested by a few records. The inquisitors were not interested much in these relations of the accused, and it is by pure chance that mention of them has survived at all. In general, the moral attitudes of the Vaudois have here confirmed what their doctrinal attitudes suggested: that they were not engaged in a constant struggle to be different from and opposed to catholicism in all things; rather they were travelling alongside, in the same direction, but aware of themselves as a distinct and better class of Christian, and determined to show that fact. They would not bother with the formalities of dispensation in marriage, where no moral issue could be seen to be involved. They would show their spiritual isolation by marrying amongst themselves and by keeping their language purer than was normal; and recognize amongst themselves their private rites and emblems. No wonder, then, if they were far more obnoxious in the eyes of visiting clergy who could believe any calumny, than in the sight of those who lived with them all the time and accepted their ways.

[97] *CUL G*, fos. 59^v-60^r.

9. The Churchmen's View: The Inquisitorial Articles

(i) The documents and their context

The preceding five chapters have attempted to build up a picture of the beliefs which the Waldenses themselves held, seen through the distortions produced by the sources. However, these very distortions also have an important lesson. In a few documents the churchmen of the Embrunais and Briançonnais set out the heresy as they saw it, and explained why it posed a threat to the church and the faith. A brief comparison between the churchmen's picture of Waldensianism and the above analysis will offer some relief and context in which to see the heretics' beliefs themselves.

The churchmen's view was set out in four tracts of varying lengths dating from 1501 and 1507. Three originated from Embrun. The first of these was a legal submission presented to Laurent Bureau, Thomas Pascal, and Rostain d'Ancezune on 26 July 1501, to protest against the behaviour of the judges-delegate and justify past persecutions.[1] Its author was probably the procurator of the faith for Embrun, one Jame Brianson.[2] The other two Embrun articles were presented by Jehan Richan, the procurator for the vicar-general of Embrun, to the judges-delegate on 25 and 30 August 1507.[3] All three of these tracts followed a pattern. They claimed that Waldensian heresy was notoriously prevalent in the region; they described its organization and its heresies; they then described

---

[1] *CUL G*, sect. 3; Morland, *History of the Evangelical Churches*, pp. 215–22; Allix, *Some remarks*, pp. 297–306. For the context of the document see *CUL G*, fo. 4v and Marx, p. 183 and n. 2.

[2] *CUL H*, sect. 13, fo. 2r; *Fazy*, II, sects. 859, 1057; not Cattaneo, as claimed by Gonnet and Molnár, *Vaudois au moyen âge*, pp. 270, 368, and 423; *BV*, no. 744; and E. Comba, 'I Valdesi prima del sinodo di Cianforan', *BSHV* 58 (1932), 25.

[3] *BP*, II, fos. 425v, 427r, 477r, 478v.

the moves made to extirpate this dissent, often trying to justify Cattaneo and discredit the Vaudois' proctors.[4] A fourth treatise was presented by the procurator of the faith of Oulx, Jehan Rostellan, on 17 August 1507;[5] it used a slightly different order.[6]

All these documents were designed to press the case for the persecutions, and so tended to exaggerate the threat posed by Waldensianism. Nevertheless, they employed a common method in analysing the heresy; although they are not, in fact, local 'inquisitors' manuals' they may fairly safely be used as though they were so.

(ii) Literary sources

Here we must confine ourselves to those parts of the articles which deal with doctrine. The only tract which refers to any source is the first of Jehan Richan's submissions, which quotes Ostiensis, and also refers to Turrecremata's description of the errors of the Vaudois in his *Summa de Ecclesia*.[7] Probably even these were used in some sort of collection or florilegium.[8]

However, even without citing sources, these tracts still reflect a literary approach to the heresy. The first sign of this approach is an intense preoccupation with the heretics' attitudes towards the Church of Rome. The short entry in Turrecremata on the Waldenses was in fact simply a paraphrase of the first paragraph of the description of Waldensianism in *De inquisitione hereticorum*; it described how the heretics treated Rome with contempt, said they were the only true church, and that all catholics were damned, and so on.[9] This same approach was used in Richan's second tract and in Brianson's, which both concentrated on the faults of Rome in the heretics' eyes.[10]

---

[4] Ibid., II, fos. 430^r-71^v, 479^r-88^r.

[5] Ibid., I, fos. 397^v, 398^v.   [6] Ibid., I, fos. 399^r-406^r.

[7] Ibid., II, fo. 434^r; J. de Turrecremata, *Summa de Ecclesia* (Lyon, 1496), IV, pt. 2, ca. xxxv.

[8] As suggested by *BP*, II, fo. 433^{r-v}, which refers to the *Mare Historiarum*. Although this is the title of a work by Giovanni Colonna (BN MS Latin 4914-15) this seems unlikely to be the same text.

[9] Turrecremata, *Summa*, loc. cit.; compare *Thesaurus Novus Anecdotorum*, V, col. 1779.   [10] *BP*, II, fo. 481^r; Allix, *Some remarks*, pp. 299-300.

More specifically, the articles made much of the supposed heretical tenet about the decline of the church since Sylvester. This did not appear often in the trials;[11] yet all the articles quoted the claim, and Richan's first tract developed it at length.[12]

In general, the articles stated several of those charges which the trials prove to have been least justified, and in their most extreme form. They said the Waldenses believed that no one was saved except in the heresy;[13] that all fasting on the eves of feast-days was to be avoided;[14] that no honour whatever was to be paid to the saints;[15] or that betraying one of the sect was an unpardonable sin.[16] Brianson's articles even added some new heresies: that tithes and alms should not be given to the church, and that obedience should not be paid to temporal lords who were not of the sect.[17]

(iii) Use of local material

The authors of these collections did not rely solely on a few old manuals and treatises for their picture of the sect, however. They used the records of some trials to amplify their knowledge, for example about the *barbes*. In one instance, Brianson said that the *barbes* were sent out two by two by their superior from 'the city of Aquilla in the Kingdom of Naples'.[18] This clearly referred to the statement of Pietro di Jacopo, the Fraticello, that he and his companions had been elected at l'Aquilla, near Cittareale in the Abruzzi.[19] Likewise, when Richan's first tract described why the *barbes* had to go about the world in secret, it borrowed almost word for word from the trial of the Valentinois Vaudois carried out in 1494.[20] Immediately after that, the same tract quoted

---

[11] See *CUL G*, fos. 65ᵛ-6ʳ.

[12] *BP*, I, fo. 403ᵛ; II, fos. 439ᵛ, 441ʳ-2ʳ, 481ʳ; Allix, *Some remarks*, p. 299.

[13] Allix, *Some remarks*, p. 301.

[14] *BP*, II, fos. 438ʳ⁻ᵛ, 439ᵛ, 482ʳ⁻ᵛ; Allix, loc. cit.

[15] *BP*, I, fo. 403ᵛ; II, fos. 439ʳ, 481ᵛ; Allix, loc. cit.

[16] *BP*, II, fos. 440ᵛ-1ʳ; Allix, loc. cit.

[17] Allix, *Some remarks*, pp. 300-1; compare *Thesaurus Novus Anecdotorum*, V, col. 1756.   [18] Allix, *Some remarks*, pp. 297-8.

[19] *CUL H*, sect. 6, fo. 6 attachment, 9ᵛ.

[20] *BP*, II, fo. 442ʳ; compare *CUL H*, sect. 7, fo. 8ʳ⁻ᵛ; Chevalier, pp. 156 f.

Francesco di Girundino to the effect that the *barbes* had their mission 'because of the evil life and conversation of the churchmen'.[21]

Evidently the compilers of the articles were most attracted either by confessions with stereotyped and improbable admissions, or by those containing weird fantasies, extorted by pressure, and having nothing to do with actual Waldensianism. This trait emerges especially in the discussion of the 'congregations', which are described in all the articles save the second of Richan's.[22] In Richan's first submission one reads that 'many entered the sect for the sake of fulfilling their lusts'; this was derived from the odd admissions of Guigo Boc of Mentoulles.[23] Rostellan's articles quoted the Girundino trial verbatim on the supposed justifications for Waldensian libertinage.[24]

However, if the articles did use the least typical and credible trial records most freely, they did at times reach deeper into the local language of dissent. The proverb about 'two ways', which expressed the Waldensian denial of purgatory, was cited in all three sets of articles presented in 1507; two of these mentioned it first of all the heads of doctrine.[25] The first tract by Richan also quoted the Vaudois form of prayer for the dead.[26] That same tract, and also Brianson's, quoted the saying about 'God alone';[27] Brianson and Richan's second tract quoted the saying about sanctity being the source of spiritual authority.[28]

The authors of the articles were also aware of some social customs and habits of the heretics which the old inquisitors' manuals did not discuss. Brianson and Richan's first tract both cited the fact that the Vaudois persuaded their followers not to marry outside the sect.[29] The latter also observed how the Vaudois separated themselves from the company of their

---

[21] *BP*, II, fo. 442^v; compare *CUL H*, sect. 6, fo. 2^{r-v}.

[22] *BP*, I, fos. 307^v-8^r, 403^v-4^r; II, fo. 443^r; Allix, *Some remarks*, p. 300.

[23] *BP*, II, fo. 443^r; compare *ADI A*, fo. 75^r, and Marx, p. 25.

[24] Above, ch. 8 (iii).

[25] *BP*, I, fo. 493^r, II, fos. 436^v-7^r, 481^v.

[26] Ibid., II, fo. 437^r.

[27] Ibid., II. fo. 439^r; Allix, *Some remarks*, p. 301.

[28] *BP*, II, fo. 481^r; Allix, *Some remarks*, p. 299.

[29] *BP*, II, fos. 442^v-3^r; Allix, *Some remarks*, p. 301.

neighbours because they felt they were better than the rest.[30]
When theory and practice clashed, the result was very odd:
Brianson said that the Waldenses, because they believed they
could eat meat at any time of the year, felt themselves entitled
to begin their Lent on Monday after the first Sunday in
Lent;[31] evidently they made little use of their freedom.

(iv) Conclusions

These articles have shown us a perplexing and ambivalent
vision of the inquisitors on which to end this survey. In fact,
the Janus-like character of the articles demonstrates the
ambiguity of the position the local churchmen occupied.
On the one hand, they were close enough to the Vaudois to
understand their language and pick up some of their stock
phrases. However, they had been imbued with just enough of
scholastic habits to wish to understand everything about the
Waldenses within the terms of reference of scholastic logic.
Hence they worked out to their extremes the implications of
Waldensian beliefs; hence they insisted on seeing Waldensianism as a rival church, which should parody and controvert
Rome in everything. This explains why they were so ready to
use the material of the Fraticelli trial; and why they would
especially welcome stereotyped confessions like those from
Valence, which gave a clear and simple reason for everything
which the Vaudois did. The churchmen of the Embrunais
were, then, representatives of an élite approach and an intellectual tradition; but they were also on the periphery of that
intellectual culture (unlike the protestant ministers) and so
were doomed to uneasy compromises in understanding a
culture which was oral, marginal, and popular.

  Everything one learns about the relationship of churchmen
and Vaudois warns one against the risks involved in any glib
summing-up of the heretics' ideas and mental universe.
However, the task must be undertaken. First of all, the
Waldenses, by their rejection of purgatory, incomplete as it
was, cut a few knots of late medieval religion. They might
not dispense altogether with the spiritual aids of catholicism;

---

[30] *BP*, II, fos. 443ᵛ–4ʳ.   [31] Allix, loc. cit.

but they rid themselves of the pressing need for them. If there was, in the country, such a thing as the 'burden of late medieval religion', it was not allowed to weigh on the Waldenses to the extent of pursuing them into the next world.[32] The doubts which they entertained about the clergy had the same effect. The Vaudois could still use the clergy; but by their sanctimonious contempt for the prestige of the caste as a whole they escaped from any servile obedience to the sanctions that body might impose — in theory, if not in actual fact. They achieved a moral liberation which made them masters of their own consciences.

Secondly, since the 'heretical' nature of Waldensianism consisted almost as much in matters of spiritual government as in questions of fundamental belief, the Waldenses felt justified in carrying on a lay religion, with separate confession, slightly different fasts and feasts, and a slightly altered practice of prayer, which implied almost no difference in the essentials of Christian dogma. In this parallel devotion the *barbes* were like the lesser clergy, only more reputable; they were useful intermediaries for worship rather than spiritual taskmasters.

There is still a serious problem. The Waldenses fairly readily admitted a theoretical rejection of many symbols and religious forms which they appear not to have given up in fact. One is forced to assume either that they accepted some unimportant parts of the catholic 'package' even though some of those elements seemed to them superfluous; or that what mattered was not so much behaving differently in these points, but being able to feel free from the obligation to respect conventional cults and consecrations. 'Rejection' of churches or of holy water would then be a symbolic verbal assurance rather than a guide for actual behaviour.

Finally, just as the 'lay' elements in heretical organization turned out to be more crucial to its fate than its 'spiritual' personnel, so perhaps the Waldenses would ultimately have been much more conspicuous by those traits which did not actually involve religious acts. Their tendency to endogamy,

---

[32] See, e.g., S. E. Ozment, *The Reformation in the Cities* (New Haven, 1975), pp. 22-32.

their unwillingness to allow themselves the usual profanities of speech, their living apart from their neighbours and using their own signs and emblems, would have been a far more regular part of Waldensian life and conduct than a heretical confession made less often than once every two years. Ultimately, perhaps, the Vaudois were that most striking of phenomena: a rural, popular, marginal élite with a highly developed self-consciousness and communal pride.

The remaining chapters will not provide any further opportunity to conduct such a detailed survey of the attitudes of a popular culture. However, if the essentials of this picture are borne in mind much of the trouble surrounding the attempts of protestant clergy to absorb the movement may be understood.

III The Waldenses and the Protestant Ministers, 1520–1580

10. Setting the Record Straight

Up to the end of the Middle Ages the Waldenses did not always show the traits which have traditionally been ascribed to them. They were not always a clandestine body, for they sometimes asserted their superiority before their neighbours and their priests. They were not always the sufferers of persecution; they could fight back, both at law and with force, when the occasion demanded. They were not by any means absolute pacifists who abhorred the thought of killing anyone. Their ideas had neither that taboo-like quality and heterodox mythology which has been found in the Cathars, nor the clear determination altogether to reject catholicism which the priests expected. The simple proverbial statements which enshrined their beliefs, and the few rituals which expressed their individuality, hardly broke at all with the traditional theology of west European Christianity.

Setting a conventional image of Waldensianism against protestant ideas would be difficult; the problems are far worse now that the evidence has forced us into a complicated and shaded vision of heretical belief and conduct. These complexities are made harder to handle because of the poverty of the sources. Whereas inquisitors in the late Middle Ages kept their records jealously,[1] judges in the French *parlements* which dealt with heresy for much of this period were less careful, and may even have been in the habit of burning the record of the trial along with the victim.[2]

The martyrologies, which must be used, often claim to include authentic records, but obviously involve the risk of distortion, as do the reformers' letters. There are for the first time some sources originating from the Waldensian pastorate of the period in question: the dossier of the talks between Morel and Oecolampadius and Bucer in 1530, and the histories

---

[1] Compare the attitude of Archbishop Rostain, *CUL G*, fos. 5ᵛ–6ʳ, and above, ch. 3, n. 4. [2] As suggested by *HE*, I, 23.

written by ministers in Waldensian parishes such as Girolamo Miolo and Scipione Lentolo.[3] However, these documents require careful handling like the rest, and are less useful than they at first appear.[4] The eighth book of Lentolo's history, on the other hand, provides a unique insight into the relations between one pastor and his flock.[5]

In the past most of the attention given to the absorption of Waldensianism into protestant forms of worship and theology has been concentrated on the realm of pure ideas and confessions of faith.[6] One may also study the personalities and the politics involved; more elusive, but as worthwhile, is the attempt to see the evolution of the attitudes of the Waldenses, and how they responded to a new type of pastor in their midst. Inevitably, since protestants corresponded much more amongst themselves about the Waldenses than with them, one has to trace the evolution of protestant attitudes as well. These are shown especially well in the organizing of embassies to plead the Vaudois' cause, in which a few protestants tried to stir their fellows to show solidarity with their slightly suspect new allies.[7]

To present these developments clearly, one must eschew the assumption that one protestant church is just as organized and tightly knit as another. This assumption produced the belief, found in early protestant writers, that the Vaudois joined the reform at a single meeting, at which the problem was resolved by discussion once and for all.[8] Eugène Arnaud could still say in 1895 that at a meeting in 1533 'The conversion of the Vaudois to the Reform became a *fait accompli* from that moment on.'[9] In a work published in 1974, there is likewise a statement that 'the adherence, pure and simple,

---

[3] TCD MS 259; Vinay, *Confessioni di fede... riformati*, pp. 36-137; Lentolo; CUL MS Dd. 3. 35, fos. 30^r-41^v; G. Miolo, *Historia breve e vera de gl'affari de i valdesi delle valli*, ed. E. Balmas (Torino, 1971).

[4] See below, chs. 14 (i), 16 (i).   [5] *Lentolo MS*, pp. 473-583.

[6] See Vinay, *Confessioni di fede ... riformati*, pp. 11-34; 'Der Anschluss der romanischen Waldenser an die Reformation und seine theologische Bedeutung', *Theologische Literaturzeitung*, 87 (1962), 89-100.

[7] See below, ch. 13 (ii); also A. Pascal, 'Ambasciere', *BSBS* XVIII (1913), nos. 1-3, 80-119, nos. 5-6, 314-36; XIX (1914), nos. 1-3, 26-38.

[8] See for instance Gilles, 1644 edn., pp. 29-32; 1881 edn., I, 47-52.

[9] E. Arnaud, 'Récit historique de la conversion', *Revue de théologie et des questions religieuses* (1895), 43.

of the Vaudois of the Alps to the Swiss Reformation' was achieved at one fixed time in the 1530s.[10] Quite apart from the questions which it begs about the nature of protestantism at the time, such a notion makes assumptions about the unity of the *barbes*, and their power over the people, which we have seen reason to doubt.[11]

Subsequent chapters will examine the development of attitudes and religious ideas amongst the leaders of the two sorts of dissenters; they will also suggest that the Waldenses had a reciprocal effect on the protestant ministers as profound as the change which the ministers brought about in the heretics. First we must try to resolve some of the technical problems surrounding the course of events which led the two groups into contact. The changes which must be suggested in the generally accepted picture are, however, of more than technical or pedantic significance.

(i) The traditional picture

The traditional interpretation of the adhesion of the Waldenses to the reform tends to make all the changes derive from a series of collective decisions taken at annual synods of the *barbes*, like those described by Georges Morel or Pierre Griot.[12] Recent scholarship has constructed a series of these synods which are claimed as being especially important for the decision-making process.[13] The modern accounts may be summarized as follows. At a meeting in Laux in the Val Chisone in 1526, the Waldenses decided to send two representatives, a *barbe* from Calabria and one from Angrogna called

---

[10] Gonnet and Molnár, *Vaudois au moyen âge*, p. 307; compare Vinay, *Confessioni di fede . . . riformati*, pp. 27-8.

[11] See above, ch. 1 (iii).

[12] TCD MS 259, pp. 11-12; Vinay, *Confessioni di fede . . . riformati*, pp. 38-40; Audisio, *Barbe et l'inquisiteur*, pp. 54, 103; 'Organisation ecclésiale clandestine', 86.

[13] G. Gonnet, 'Le Premier Synode de Chanforan de 1532 avec une note sur les itinéraires vaudois', *BSHPF* 90 (1953), 201-21; 'I Rapporti tra i valdesi franco-italiani e i riformatori d'oltralpe prima di Calvino', in *Ginevra e l'Italia* (collected essays), (Florence, 1959), pp. 1-63; 'Les Relations des Vaudois des Alpes avec les réformateurs en 1532', *Bulletin d'humanisme et renaissance*, 23 (1961), 34-52; Gonnet and Molnár, *Vaudois au moyen âge*, pp. 283-318; Pazè Beda, *Riforma e cattolicesimo*, pp. 301ff.

Martin Gonin, to see Guillaume Farel at Aigle; later in that year these two returned to the valleys bringing printed books of the Reformation. In 1530, a synod held at Mérindol, on the south-western edge of the Montagne de Luberon, in Provence, drew up a list of disputed points of doctrine; it then sent two *barbes*, Georges Morel of Fressinières, and Pierre Masson, simply called 'de Bourgogne' in the records, to see Guillaume Farel, Berthold Haller of Berne, Oecolampadius of Basel, and Martin Bucer at Strasbourg. On the way back from Strasbourg Masson was imprisoned at Dijon; the traditional story was that he was martyred there, but one recent author suggests he may have abjured.[14]

At a subsequent synod, also held at Mérindol, a new confession of faith was drawn up on the basis of the discussions which the *barbes* had held with the reformers. In his recent work on the documents of these discussions, Valdo Vinay has shown this confession of faith to have no historical foundation other than in the imagination of the seventeenth-century historian Jean-Paul Perrin; he nevertheless accepts the theory according to which this process of debate was essential to the fusion of Vaudois and protestant.[15]

In the summer of 1532 Martin Gonin and another pastor called Guido were sent to the Canton de Vaud to see Guillaume Farel; they called both him and Antoine Saunier, the pastor of Payerne, to a synod in the Val d'Angrogna, which took place over six days from 12 September; as a result a new confession of faith was drawn up which incorporated the ideas of the reformers of Neuchâtel and the Pays de Vaud. This synod is claimed by most authorities to have taken place in the tiny hamlet of Chanforan, close to the village of Il Serre, a few miles north of the main village of the valley, Angrogna San Lorenzo.

After the synod of Chanforan two *barbes*, Daniel de Valence and Jean de Molines, left in protest at the acceptance of the reformers' ideas. They went to stay for a while with

[14] Crespin, 1565 edn., p. 189; Perrin, *Vaudois*, p. 216; J.-F. Gilmont, 'Le Pseudo-Martyre du Vaudois Pierre Masson', *BSSV* 133 (1973), 43-8.

[15] V. Vinay, 'Mémoires de George Morel', *BSSV* 132 (1972), 38-41; *Confessioni di fede . . . riformati*, pp. 22-7; but compare Gonnet and Molnár, *Vaudois au moyen âge*, p. 305.

the Czech 'Unity of Brethren' at Mlada Boleslav. The brethren there sent a letter of reproach to the valleys of Piedmont, urging the Waldenses not to accept too easily the doctrines of those whose reform was only just begun. This letter was debated at a fresh synod at Prali, in the Val Germanasca, in 1533; there the brethren's criticisms were rejected, and the decisions of Chanforan were confirmed and ratified.

One of the results of the synod of Chanforan was the publishing of a French translation of the Bible. The Waldenses apparently raised between 500 and 800 *écus* to pay for its printing, while Olivétan worked at the translation from 1533 to 1535. In the latter year it appeared in an enormous folio edition from the presses of Pierre de Vingle at Neuchâtel. In some of the earlier accounts it was claimed that Olivétan had been at Chanforan along with Farel and Saunier; this is no longer accepted by authoritative historians.[16]

After 1535 there was an enormous silence, which suggests that the penetration of reformed ideas was perhaps less absolute than the 'definitive' nature of the synod of Chanforan would lead one to suppose.[17] In 1545 the Vaudois of Provence were the victims of a notorious massacre at the hands of the *parlement* of Aix; but only in the mid-1550s did missionary pastors from Geneva settle in the valleys, when the Vaudois Protestant church took on a structured character. At a pair of synods held in 1563 and 1564, long since described by Jalla,[18] the organization of the Piedmontese Waldensian churches along the lines of Genevan and French Calvinism was completed.[19]

[16] H. Delarue, 'Olivétan et Pierre de Vingle à Genève, 1532-3', *Bulletin d'Humanisme et Renaissance*, 8 (1946), 106-8; G. Gonnet, 'Olivétan e il primo sinodo di Chanforan: itinerari alpini valdesi', *Ricerche di storia religiosa*, 1 (1954), 120-8.

[17] But to very few historians; see for example Pazè Beda, *Riforma e cattolicesimo*, pp. 42-3.

[18] J. Jalla, 'Synodes vaudois de la réformation à l'exil, 1536-1686', *BSHPF* 50 (1901), 471, 474-81. This article also appeared in *BSHV* 20 (1903), 93-133, with numerous sequels.

[19] Some traditional accounts do not even go so far as this; cf. *Vaudois au moyen âge*, pp. 316-18.

(ii)   The first approaches, 1520–31

The drastic and vicious harassment which the Waldenses of the Alps suffered in the late 1480s was probably far from typical of priestly conduct in the period, and certainly was not approved of by all the clergy. Nevertheless, the heretics entered the 1520s still subject to occasional harassment. In 1521 one 'Gioanni Bartolomeo, maestro della setta dei valdesi o dei poveri di Lione' was tried at Perosa; we only know these bare details of his case. In March 1526 one Giacomo Resaudio (or Jacob Ressent), of the Bec-Dauphin, deposed before the vicar-general of the bishop of Geneva at Pinerolo about the sect.[20] Meanwhile the Reformation began to make inroads in the Alps. Guillaume Farel possibly preached at Gap in 1522, although this is uncertain.[21] More impressive was the work of Pierre Sébiville and Aimé Meigret, two friars who between 1523 and 1526 corresponded with the reformers and indulged in some fiery Lutheran preaching at Grenoble. In 1528 one Étienne Renier, who had preached reformed ideas at Annonay, was burnt at Vienne.[22] These individuals began their work in the towns, not in the countryside, and had no evident connection with Waldensianism.[23]

In 1526 it is claimed that the 'synod of Laux' took place. Doubts have already been expressed as to whether this ever happened.[24] According to the minister Girolamo Miolo, who wrote in 1587, a meeting did take place in Laux at some stage; he said that he had heard that the *barbes* used to meet every September, and they had 'once' met, 140 in number, at Laux in the Val Chisone.[25] The seventeenth-century historian and minister of Torre Pèllice, Pierre Gilles, amplified this story with characteristic redundancy of style.[26] The only

---

[20] P. Caffaro, *Notizie . . . della chiesa Pinerolese*, VI, 58; J. Jalla, *Storia della riforma in Piemonte* (Firenze, 1914), p. 22; Pazè Beda, *Riforma e cattolicesimo*, pp. 31, 35, 302.
[21] E. Arnaud, *Histoire des protestants du Dauphiné, aux xvie, xviie, et xviiie siècles* (Paris, 1875–6, and repr. Genève, 1970), I, 3–8.
[22] *HE*, I, 8–9; Arnaud, *Protestants du Dauphiné*, I, 10–17.
[23] See below, ch. 11 (i).
[24] Gonnet, 'Rapporti tra i valdesi . . . e i riformatori', 6, 12; Pazè Beda, *Riforma e cattolicesimo*, p. 41; Caffaro, *Notizie . . . della chiesa Pinerolese*, VI, 261–2.   [25] Miolo, *Historia breve e vera*, ed. Balmas, p. 100.
[26] Gilles, 1644 edn., p. 17.

reason for placing the meeting at Laux in 1526 appears to be a quite separate reference by Gilles to a document in which he had read that in 1526 'Barbe Martin of Val Luserne' returned to the valleys of Piedmont bearing printed books about the Reformation; to suppose that a synod sent him on this mission is pure speculation.[27] Moreover, it is possible, but by no means certain, that this 'Martin of Val Luserne' was the same as the Martin Gonin of Angrogna who features later in the story.

There is supposed to have been a gathering at Mérindol in 1530, from which the *barbes* Morel and Masson set out on their mission for talks with the protestant leaders. The only evidence for such a gathering appears to be the fact that these two were actually sent. However, it is fairly clear that it was the Provençal Vaudois who sent these emissaries: Crespin included their mission as part of the preliminaries to the massacre of 1545; he said that after Masson's capture Morel 'returned' to Mérindol.[28] From the comparison between Morel's account of the Vaudois organization in his letter to Oecolampadius, and Pierre Griot's at his trial, it is clear that the same people are being described.[29]

Morel and Masson went first to Neuchâtel, then on to Morat (now Murten), and Berne, from where they were sent to Basel to consult Oecolampadius. This must have been towards the end of September, as Oecolampadius's first reply to their queries is dated 13 October 1530. Four days later, Oecolampadius wrote to Bucer at Strasbourg to ask him to receive the pastors, to read what he had written to them, and to comment on it; if he was too busy, he was to pass on the task to Wolfgang Capito.[30] No record other than a bare mention in Morel's letter tells of the treatment the pastors received at Neuchâtel or Morat, although Crespin also noted that they called at Berne to see Berthold Haller.[31] Their itinerary implies that these two travelled up the valley of the

---

[27] Ibid., p. 29. [28] Crespin, 1565 edn., p. 189.
[29] Vinay, *Confessioni di fede . . . riformati*, pp. 36–44; Audisio, *Barbe et l'inquisiteur*, pp. 52–5. Morel is discussed in detail below, ch. 12 (ii).
[30] Vinay, *Confessioni di fede . . . riformati*, pp. 72, 62, 70; J. Oecolampadius and H. Zuinglius, *Epistolarum libri quatuor* (Basel, 1536, but attributed to 1548), fos. 3[V], 199[V]. [31] Crespin, loc. cit.

Rhône from Provence to the Pays de Vaud, rather than taking the route which Saunier later followed, across the Alps to Turin, then approaching the lands of the Piedmontese Vaudois from the east.

The letter which ostensibly presents the first impressions and queries of Morel and Masson was only printed in full as late as 1620.[32] Two replies of Oecolampadius, without address or attribution, were printed in the collected letters of Oecolampadius and Zwingli; Bucer's reply, or a draft of it, survives in the Thomassarchiv in Strasbourg and has been edited.[33] That mysterious piece of continuous prose in Provençal dialect, TCD MS 259, cuts across all these texts. It is anterior to some of the Latin letters (since it alone contains some questions to which the Latin texts give answers), and posterior to some parts of them as well, since it translates the Latin word for word with a very un-vernacular idiom and vocabulary.[34] Clearly, then, the debates in 1530 were not a simple exchange of letters, but a long discussion involving drafts and redrafts, of which the surviving texts are fragments.[35]

The aftermath of these discussions is wrapped in the profoundest obscurity. The French version of Crespin's martyrology says only that the stir which these contacts caused stimulated persecution leading up to the massacre of 1545.[36] The Latin version of 1556, the *Actiones et Monumenta Martyrum*, printed an influential interpretation, for which the evidence is nevertheless rather nebulous:

[32] A. Scultetus, *Annalium Evangelii passim per Europam decimo quinto salutis partae seculo renovati decades duae* (Heidelberg, 1618-20), II, 295-306. In the margin of the Latin text Scultetus added 'ex reliquis bibliothecae Oecolampadii', as though to indicate that he had used a manuscript original.

[33] Oecolampadius, *Epistolae*, fos. 2ʳ-4ᵛ; J. J. Herzog, 'Ein wichtiges Document', *Zeitschrift für die historische Theologie*, 3 (1866), 311-38; also Vinay, *Confessioni di fede . . . riformati*, pp. 74-116.

[34] See TCD MS 259, pp. 67-75, 81-96, 106-9, and 114-16, besides Vinay, *Confessioni di fede . . . riformati*, pp. 118-37, for passages of significant length found in the dialect versions of Bucer's replies and not in the Latin texts which survive.

[35] The editor of Oecolampadius's letters concluded that the first 'request' of Morel was written as an *aide-memoire* for Oecolampadius and did not represent true 'correspondence'; see Vinay, *Confessioni di fede . . . riformati*, p. 50; but cf. ibid., p. 14. For the theological content of these debates see below, ch. 14 (i).

[36] Crespin, 1565 edn., pp. 189-90.

When the people had heard these things [Morel's report], they were moved by such a zeal for reforming their church, that they summoned those of their fellows in Apulia and Calabria who were oldest and most experienced, to take counsel with them regarding the reform and correction of the church . . .[37]

These words were reprinted later in the sixteenth century by Heinrich Pantaleon and Joachim Camerarius; they were translated into Italian by Lentolo and paraphrased in French by the *Histoire ecclésiastique*.[38] Perrin confused the issue by providing two different accounts of the mission: in one, Morel's report was read to a gathering at Angrogna; in another, it led at once on to the decree against the Vaudois of Provence.[39]

On this slim basis it has been claimed that after Morel's return there was a second synod at Mérindol, where a new confession of faith, based on the recommendations of the reformers, was drawn up. Until recently it was assumed that the confession of faith was that which constituted chapter 12 of the first book of Perrin's history.[40] As early as 1841 J. H. Todd pointed out that parts of the 'confession' were somewhat similar, though not identical, to phrases found in pp. 21-5 of the Dublin dossier, dating from autumn 1530; the confession appeared to be pieced together from statements made by both Vaudois and reformers.[41] Valdo Vinay recently suggested that the confession was invented by Perrin alone.[42] Amedeo Molnár attempted to repel this charge of fabrication by pointing out that some phrases in the 'confession' were characteristically 'Hussite', and these Perrin could not have invented.[43] This perplexity is astonishing; for

[37] Crespin-Baduel, 1560 edn., fo. 89[r].
[38] H. Pantaleon, *Martyrum Historia* (Basel, 1563), pp. 111 ff.; J. Camerarius, *Historica Narratio de fratrum orthodoxorum ecclesiis* (Heidelberg, 1605), pp. 305-6; Lentolo, p. 23; *HE* I, 36. [39] Perrin, *Vaudois*, pp. 157, 216.
[40] Perrin, *Vaudois*, pp. 79-87; this text was reprinted in 1658 by Morland, with the date 1120 appended: see Morland, *History of the Evangelical Churches*, pp. 30-4.
[41] J. H. Todd, 'The Waldensian Manuscripts in the library of Trinity College, Dublin', *The British Magazine and Monthly Register*, XIX (1841), 399-402.
[42] Vinay, 'Mémoires de George Morel', 38-41; *Confessioni di fede . . . riformati*, pp. 22-7.
[43] Gonnet and Molnár, *Vaudois au moyen âge*, p. 305, n. 94; this study has uncovered no evidence whatever of such an interpenetration of Waldensian and Hussite ideas, at least in the western Alps.

in the margin of the original edition Perrin acknowledged he had taken the 'confession' from 'the book entitled "Spiritual Almanac" and the memoirs of Georges Morel'.[44] Perrin was thus admitting that he constructed this document from two manuscripts he himself owned: these were probably the present Dublin MSS 259 and 260.[45] The translations of Taborite treatises which were the source of the 'Hussite' elements in the confession may or may not have been used by Morel's circle; there is almost no evidence that popular Waldensianism was anything other than proverbial, local, and oral, so we should beware of attaching much importance to them.[46]

Since the confession is indeed a synthesis of materials without historical foundation, both it and the 'second synod of Mérindol' vanish into thin air. The talks of Morel and Masson may have helped to lead the Waldenses as a whole, or even only those of Provence, in a protestant direction; all we lack is the evidence.

(iii) The myth of Chanforan, 1532–3

The year 1532 has been presented as one of the cardinal points of this story: the year when the culmination of one stage, if not of the whole process of the absorption of the Waldensian heresy into the Reformation, is traditionally said to have taken place.[47] It is therefore necessary to deal with the events of this year in more detail than the sources would normally deserve or permit. The traditional story of the 'synod of Chanforan' has been set out in a sequence of articles

---

[44] Perrin, *Vaudois*, p. 79: 'Extraite du liv. intitulé *Almanach Spirituel*, et des mémoires de George Morel'. For the 'Hussite' character of the former MS, see Gonnet and Molnár, *Vaudois au moyen âge*, p. 353.

[45] The title *Almanach Spirituel* appears to derive from the ecclesiastical calendar written on the first few leaves of some MSS. TCD MSS 260 and 267 both have this feature; MSS 260, 263, and 267 contain tracts of Taborite or of catholic origins, which mostly comprise pieces of moral instruction and are of uncertain dates. On these see Todd, 'The Waldensian Manuscripts', *British Magazine*, XIX (1841), 507–11.   [46] See above, ch. 4.

[47] In 1932 one whole number of the Vaudois *Bulletin* was devoted to this centenary. See *BSHV* 58 (1932): 'Bollettino commemorativo del sinodo di Cianforan (Angrogna), 1532–1932'. The spelling 'Cianforan', a concession to Italian phonetic custom, is no longer used even by Italian authors.

since one by Emilio Comba in 1876 transcribed for the first time that series of theological theses which we shall call here the 'Angrogna propositions'.[48] Perhaps the most concise version of the familiar account is that set in the plaque near the monumental *stele* raised on the hillside at Chanforan itself in 1932, which reads:

In September 1532 the 'Barbes' and the people, having gathered together in this place, held a six days conference, where it was decided that the Ancient Waldensian heresy would acknowledge itself in the recently-born Reformation and that the first complete translation of the Bible into French should be made by Olivetanus, the cost of it being met by the Waldenses.[49]

The synod of Chanforan, as it has been presented in the past, is a myth in both the technical and the loose sense. It gives Waldensianism, and for that matter the Reformation, a coherence and organization which it did not possess at this period. Hence this debate about an issue of chronology is important for our whole vision of the way the two forms of dissent related one with another. Our confusion dates chiefly from the work of protestant authors, who shaped the Waldenses after their own mould.[50] The evidence for a unanimous and epoch-making synod does not exist; and the information we possess regarding the ideas discussed at this time in the Alps suggests that they were occasions of confrontation rather than reconciliation.[51]

Nevertheless, in 1532-3 there were contacts of some kind, tentative and inconclusive though they were, between the Waldenses and some of the reformers. There must have been several meetings, in different places and involving different people; these meetings make more sense if one does not try to fit them to the Procrustean bed of the 'synod of Chanforan'.

Pierre Griot, the Vaudois from Cesana Torinese, said that he had heard of a gathering in 'Vauluserne', probably in

---

[48] E. Comba, 'Il Sinodo di Chanforan e le sue conclusioni', *Rivista Cristiana*, 4 (1876), 265-9, based on work by Karl Benrath; Vinay, *Confessioni di fede . . . riformati*, p. 143.

[49] The claim that Olivétan's Bible was the first translation into French is of course an error.

[50] To avoid cluttering the narrative with a long excursus on the origin of the 'myth of Chanforan', a detailed historiographical discussion is offered in an appendix.   [51] See below, ch. 14 (ii).

1531, at 'Le Serre',·which may be Il Serre, the hamlet north of Angrogna and near Chanforan in the Val d'Angrogna.[52] Perhaps after this, but before autumn 1532, Antoine Saunier paid an initial visit to the Vaudois, since in his letter of November 1532 he said the 'brethren' thanked Farel for sending Saunier and his companions to them 'again'.[53] A congregation of *barbes* was held in late August 1532, although we do not know where: this was the first which Pierre Griot attended, and he claimed he went against his will, along with one 'Johannet', or Jehan Gérault, from the Embrunais.[54]

Griot found that strange things were afoot. There were 'Grands clercz et docteurs' at the congregation, two 'gentilz-hommes' called Charles and Adam, from the region of Grenoble, and two 'religieux' called Augustin and Thomas. These two carried out a public disputation about justification by faith. The *religieux*, perhaps surprisingly, adopted the protestant stance and argued that works were of no value for justification, while the 'gentlemen' said that faith without works was dead.[55]

After this meeting (assuming it took place, as Griot said, some time in late August), a further disputation was held early in September in the region of Angrogna. It is the record of points disputed at this meeting which survives in the Dublin MS, and is nowadays usually called the 'declaration of the synod of Chanforan'.[56] The document is headed simply 'the propositions which were disputed in Angrogna, the year of Our Lord 1532. And on the day 12 September, in the presence of all the ministers and also of the populace'.[57] This disputation record lists no participants, and does not mention justification by faith amongst its theses.[58] Since the

---

[52] Audisio, *Barbe et l'inquisiteur*, p. 103. *Luserne* tended to be used as an overall name for the valleys of Luserna, Angrogna, and Pèllice. There is also a hamlet called 'Serre' between Massello and Salza di Pinerolo in the Val Germanasca.

[53] Herminjard, II, 452: 'quod ad se nos remiseris'.

[54] 'Johannet' may have been a standard alias for a *barbe*; a namesake preached in the region of Fressinières in 1488. See Chevalier, p. 140.

[55] Audisio, *Barbe et l'inquisiteur*, pp. 103-20.

[56] TCD MS 259, pp. 118-25; compare Vinay, 'La Dichiarazione del Sinodo di Chanforan 1532', *BSSV* 133 (1973), 37-42.

[57] Vinay, *Confessioni di fede . . . riformati*, p. 139: 'Le proposicione che sono disputate en angronia lanno del segnor 1532. Et adi 12. de setembro. Enpresencia de tuti li ministri et ecian dio del populo . . . .'   [58] See below, ch. 14 (ii).

date and the issues are different, there seems no reason to suppose this is the same meeting which Griot described.

None of the participants in the August colloquy may be identified with certainty, in spite of 'Adam' being Saunier's pseudonym (Saunier would hardly have disputed against justification by faith). However, it has usually been stated that Farel and Saunier went to the Piedmontese valleys in September 1532. We cannot deny the suggestion; but neither is it satisfactorily proved. One of the best authorities for the claim was the Genevan chronicler Antoine Fromment, close enough to the reformers for his testimony to have considerable weight. His version of events runs thus:

> Mre Guillaume Farel avec Antoine Sonnier, tous deux du Dauphiné, et ministres soubz la principauté de Berne, furent requis par certains aultres ministres, Georges Mourel de Fressinières, et Pierre Masson de Bourgogne . . . de se trouver à ung synode, . . . qui se debvoyt tenir en Piémont, et là estre assemblée certain nombre de fidelles chrestiens, qu'on souloit appeller Valdences, ou Pauperes de Lugduno, et maintenant Luthériens, tant de Callabre, de la Poille, du Piémont, de la Provence, de Dauphiné, et de Laurreyne, que de plusieurs aultres contrées de la terre . . .
>
> Or après avoir esté assemblés, consultèrent . . . des affayres de leur religion, . . . que fut faict à la grande utilité de toute la chrestienté . . . et ne fust que par l'impression seulement de la Bible, imprimée à Neufchastel, à leurs propres despens translatée d'Hébreu en Françoys, par Pierre Robert, dit Olivétanus . . . [59]

Fromment then went on to speak of Farel's first visit to Geneva. Although perhaps written before 1550, Fromment's account contains some unlikely details; his claim that Morel and Masson initiated the synod is unsupported, and shows signs of extrapolation from limited sources later used in the martyrologies.

Nevertheless, Fromment's statements were repeated by several other authors, in a rather bald fashion. Michel Roset, a former secretary to the *Petit Conseil* of Geneva, wrote how in September 1532, Farel and Saunier had been in Piedmont 'for the religion of the gospel which was flourishing there, bearing letters of recommendation from the *Seigneurs* of

[59] A. Fromment, *Les Actes et gestes merveilleux de la cité de Genève*, ed. G. Revilliod (Genève, 1854), pp. 2 f.

Berne . . .'.[60] Savion followed Roset to the letter, and Scultetus's *Annales Evangelii* translated his account exactly.[61]
Spanheim's *Geneva Restituta* of 1635 seems to have borrowed
from Fromment, or Crespin, or both, when it relates how the
Waldenses sent two *barbes* to speak with Oecolampadius,
Bucer, and Capito, and then called Farel and Saunier to a
synod at Angrogna 'to form a union'; after this the two
reformers went on to Geneva.[62]

Several points must be borne in mind about these con-
cordant witnesses. Some are vague about dates, or include
factual errors. There is some uncertainty as to whether it was
possible to travel from the Pays de Vaud to Piedmont and
back again within two months, as was pointed out by the
eighteenth-century Swiss historian Abraham Ruchat.[63] It is
possible to read into the epistles to Olivétan's Bible of 1535
a reference to a visit to the 'bons frères' by both Farel and
Saunier in 1532, but the text is too cryptic to be certain.[64]
The most this text does is to forestall any claim that Olivétan
also made the journey.[65]

A further problem is presented by Saunier's itinerary. If
he were in Piedmont in September, and in Geneva later in the
same month, it is hard to see how, by 5 November, he could
write to Farel in these terms, having evidently just arrived
amongst the Piedmontese Vaudois:

> We are teaching the ministers and the people, though not openly;
> they hear us willingly, and some travel as much as two days' journey
> only for the sake of hearing the words of truth. We do not yet have
> public schools, but we soon shall have. About this point we have had
> a council summoned, but it *has not yet come to pass*.
> The brethren wish you every happiness and are most grateful that

[60] M. Roset, *Les Chronicques de Genève*, ed. H. Fazy (Genève, 1894), p. 163.

[61] P. F. Geisendorf, *Les Annalistes genevoises du début du dix-septième siècle, Savion, Piaget, Perrin: Études et textes* (Genève, 1942), p. 401; Scultetus, *Annales Evangelii*, II, 383.

[62] F. Spanheim, *Geneva Restituta, Oratio* (Genevae, 1635), p. 42.

[63] A. Ruchat, *Histoire de la réformation de la Suisse* (Genève, 1740), IV, 301-2 and note.

[64] Herminjard, II, 453, n. 19: 'Je suis assez recordz que toy Cusemeth et toy Almeutes . . . allastes, troys ans y a, visiter les églises chrestiennes, noz bons frères.'

[65] Delarue, 'Olivétan et Pierre de Vingle', 105 ff.; Gonnet, 'Olivétan e il primo sinodo', loc. cit.

you have sent us to them again. The printer has been given five hundred gold pieces by Martin, to have things printed as soon as possible. See to a *Unio*, well corrected, in French, for it will be of the greatest use to us . . . See to the Bible being edited and printed as I suggested, one column in large letters of French, and another smaller column in small letters in Latin . . .[66]

This visit, in late September or early November, by Saunier and Olivétan alone, is surely the occasion of the main attempt by the reformers of the Pays de Vaud to bring the Waldenses under their wing; doubtless others, who had inspired the previous meetings and missions, were trying as well. Our information on the visit is very sparse, most of Saunier's letter being taken up with details of the itinerary.

A disaffected faction, unhappy with the *pourparlers* of autumn 1532, transmitted to the Bohemian brethren in Bohemia and Moravia news of these events. The brethren wrote a general letter on 25 June 1533, which criticized the Vaudois for dealing so readily with a newfangled movement.[67] There is manuscript evidence that the leaders of this faction were known as Daniel and Jean, generally called Daniel de Valence and Jean de Molines.[68] According to Gilles, after this letter came, a synod was called for 15 August 1533; it met in the Val Germanasca, and there the brethren's letter was read and deemed irrelevant.[69] It does seem likely that a meeting took place at that time; Saunier complained on 22 September that he had been held up at Turin by the students and the lameness of his horse, and could not go to an 'assembly' which had only lasted three days.[70]

The series of events described above may now be summarized. Late in 1531 there seems to have been the gathering at 'Le Serre' which Griot had heard of but not attended. Saunier may have made an early visit before the autumn of 1532. Late in August, somewhere in the Alps, there was held the congregation, described by Griot, to which the

---

[66] Herminjard, II, 452–4; B. J. Kidd, *Documents illustrative of the Continental Reformation* (Oxford, 1911), pp. 491 f., my italics.

[67] Herminjard, III, 63–9; Arnaud, 'Récit historique de la conversion', 36–41; Vinay, *Confessioni di fede . . . riformati*, pp. 144–51.

[68] Gilles, 1644 edn., p. 33; Vinay, *Confessioni di fede . . . riformati*, p. 144.

[69] Gilles, 1644 edn., pp. 33–5.   [70] Herminjard, III, 80 f.

two *religieux* and the two gentlemen went to dispute. On 12 September, in Angrogna, the propositions regarding some Vaudois rituals were argued over by some unknown disputants. Late in September or early in November Saunier and Olivétan arrived in the Piedmontese valleys and started to preach and write back to Farel for books. These two continued to work in Piedmont into 1533, in Turin, and also occasionally in the Alps. This framework of events is no more than approximate; but to make any more definite claims would be to exceed the limits of the evidence which survives.

(iv) The years of silence, 1534–49

A short and violent assault on the Vaudois of Piedmont led by the lord of the tiny hamlet of Roccapiatta, Pantaleone Bersatore, seems to have caused only limited trouble. Bersatore had been in correspondence with the bishop of Cavaillon about some Piedmontese Vaudois who had been preaching heresy in Provence. Armed with this evidence he obtained a commission from the Duke of Savoy, dated 28 August 1535, which authorized him to seize the Vaudois, if need be by force.[71] A few heretics were captured and their depositions were taken down; a few of these may have been burnt. However, Blanche, widow of the Count of Luserna, protested at these attacks made on her subjects without her permission; as the Duke of Savoy was under threat of invasion by François I, he thought it prudent to withdraw the commission the following year.[72]

On 28 September 1535 the consuls of Payerne, in the Pays de Vaud, wrote to the *Conseil* of Berne, asking it to intercede for their pastor Antoine Saunier, who had been imprisoned, along with a companion, at Pinerolo. Berne took the affair seriously and wrote to the Duke of Savoy at once. The reply came back that he was in the hands of the Papal commissary and that little could be done.[73] However, when François I's invasion of Piedmont made him master of the prisoners, the Swiss wrote to him in turn, and an exchange was agreed

---

[71] L. C. Bollea, 'Alcuni documenti di storia valdese (1354–1573)', *BSHV* 45 (1923), 5–7.

[72] Gilles, 1644 edn., pp. 36–41.   [73] Herminjard, III, 351, 355, n. 4.

between Saunier and other protestants on one hand, and on the other the friar Furbitti, who was then in prison in Geneva. Saunier had been freed by early April 1536.[74]

For a period during the French occupation the governor of the valleys of Angrogna, Luserna, Perosa, and Germanasca was none other than Gauchier Farel, brother of Guillaume the reformer. Gauchier had entered the service of Wilhelm von Furstenberg late in 1535. Furstenberg was in 1536 commanding a force of German mercenaries in François's pay; he used his influence with the King to intercede for the reformed cause of which he was a partisan. Late in 1537 or early in 1538, as a result of his connection with Furstenberg, Gauchier Farel was appointed to organize the administration of the lands to the north of the Po along the lines of a French territory. Gauchier used his position to be of help to the protestants and heretics. He is said to have had catholic churches in the Val d'Angrogna destroyed; and to have accused the Lords of Luserna, who had imprisoned some Vaudois, of siding with the imperialists, and condemned them to confiscations.[75]

In spite of this protection, the Piedmontese lost one of those who had perhaps formed one of their strongest links with the small clique of reformers. In April 1536 the Sieur de Champoléon, a seigneur in the Champsaur north of Gap, captured Martin Gonin on his way from Geneva to Angrogna, on suspicion of being a spy. Apparently it was only by accident that he was discovered to be carrying heretical papers. On 26 April, after an examination at Grenoble, he was drowned by night in the Isère.[76]

In 1540 persecution claimed a victim in the Dauphiné. Estienne or Estève Brun came from Réotier in the Embrunais.

[74] A. Pascal, 'Ambasciere', *BSBS* XVIII, nos. 1-3 (1913), 82; based on Herminjard, III, 321-5, 370, 398, and as above.

[75] Gilles, 1644 edn., pp. 44 f.; P. E. Martin, 'Une lettre inédite de Guillaume Farel relative aux Vaudois du Piémont (8 mars 1538)', *BSHPF* 61 (1912), 204-13; Pascal, 'Ambasciere', *BSBS* XVIII, nos. 1-3 (1913), 83-5; R. Peter, 'Le Comte Guillaume de Furstenberg et les Vaudois', *BSSV* 143 (1978), 30-2; F.-X. Provana di Collegno, 'Rapports de Guillaume Farel', *BSEHA* (1891), 267-73.

[76] Crespin, 1565 edn., pp. 138-40; L. Rabus, *Historien der . . . Martyren* (Strasbourg, 1554-7), VI, fos. 121ᵛ ff.; Pantaleon, *Martyrum Historia*, p. 73; T. de Bèze, *Icones* (s. l., 1580), sig. Cc i v; *HE*, I, 23. For a full discussion of Gonin see below, ch. 12 (ii).

He had decided to improve his study of the scriptures by reading them in Latin as well as in the vernacular. He was imprisoned in 1538 in the prisons of Embrun, and abjured; interrogated two years later by a Franciscan inquisitor called Domicelli, he was declared relapsed and burnt.[77]

In 1538 the favour shown to the Vaudois by Gauchier Farel brought its own problems. Gauchier was at odds with the French governor in Turin, René de Montjehan, who resented the favour Gauchier was showing towards heretics. With the connivance of the *Connétable* Anne de Montmorency, Montjehan led a plundering raid into the Piedmontese valleys and enriched his soldiers with confiscated goods. When Gauchier, who was now in Switzerland, heard of this, he applied to the *Conseil* of Berne, which wrote to ask Fursten-berg to take more care of the people of Luserna and San Martino and protect them from the 'tyranny' which was weighing upon them. Saunier and Calvin also involved them-selves in stirring up the support of the *Conseil* of Geneva. The matter entangled itself with a personal quarrel between Furstenberg and Montjehan. When the latter died soon after, in 1539, the valleys returned to a state of calm under Furstenberg's successors.[78]

In spite of these alarms, the most striking feature of this period is the tremendous silence which covers not only the news of generalized persecution, but also the evidence of active evangelizing and preaching of heresy, protestant or Waldensian. Indeed, when Cardinal Innocenzo Cibò made his visitation in 1545 of the churches of Angrogna, Bòbbio, Villar, Torre, Luserna, San Germano, and Pragelato, there appeared in his register no mention whatever of Vaudois or heretics, although a decree was issued forbidding the receiving of foreign preachers.[79] The French *parlement* in Turin, set up after the invasion, did little more than threaten the fomenters

[77] *HE*, I, 26; Crespin, 1565 edn., pp. 154 f.; Arnaud, *Protestants du Dauphiné*, I, 21-3.

[78] Herminjard, V, 149 and note, 170f., 281; VI, 122-3; IX, 459f.; Pascal, 'Ambasciere', *BSBS* XVIII, nos. 1-3 (1913), 86-9, and XIX, nos. 1-3 (1914), 26f.; Peter, 'Guillaume de Furstenberg', 32.

[79] A. Pascal, 'Comunità eretiche', *BSHV* 30 (1912), 62.

of heresy.[80] In Dauphiné the Archbishop of Embrun did express anxiety about heresy in 1540, and in 1545 a victim of the inquisitor Tommasso Giacomelli and of the vicar-general of Oulx appealed to the *parlement* at Grenoble; but these incidents have hardly left a trace.[81]

This silence has led one author[82] to conclude that in the pre-Calvinist period the protestant message lacked any coherent means of infiltrating these valleys. Jean Delumeau has warned against uncritical acceptance of the stereotype introduced by Théodore de Bèze, according to which the Calvinist organizational machine is responsible for any lasting process which the Reformation made.[83] Evidently we have seen enough activity before 1555 to support such qualifications. Nevertheless, the pattern in this period is of small-scale evangelizing by an obscure group of enthusiasts, nothing more. The difference between this phase and that of the organized Genevan ministry in the valleys is very striking indeed.[84]

(v) The massacres in Provence, 1532–45

So far it has been possible to describe the affairs of the Waldenses of the Alps to the virtual exclusion of other groups of heretics. Here it is necessary to deal briefly with the Vaudois of Provence. This has the value of allowing comparisons; in some cases we are even dealing with the same people as before, since some Vaudois from Fressinières were settled in Provence by the 1500s.[85] It is also necessary to mention the Provençal Vaudois when discussing the attitudes of the reformers, who paid especial attention to the heretics after the notorious massacres in the Luberon in 1545.

---

[80] Pascal, 'Ambasciere', *BSBS* XVIII, nos. 1–3 (1913), 90, based on his *I Valdesi e il parlamento francese di Torino* (Pinerolo, 1912), pp. 7–9, 26–8; J. Jalla, 'Le Refuge français', *BSHPF* 83 (1934), 577.

[81] J. A. Chabrand, *Vaudois et Protestants des Alpes* (Grenoble, 1886), p. 82 and n.1; J.-J. Hemardinquer, 'Les Vaudois du Dauphiné', *BSSV* 103 (1958), 53, 57.

[82] Pazè Beda, *Riforma e Cattolicesimo*, pp. 42 f.

[83] In his *Naissance et affirmation de la réforme* (Paris, 1973), pp. 144–53.

[84] Compare (vi) below.

[85] See G. Audisio, 'Un aspect des relations', 513, for a list of inhabitants of Cabrières-d'Aigues who had migrated there from Fressinières by 1495.

The Vaudois in Provence were distinctly precocious in establishing contact with the early protestants. The one most responsible for introducing Pierre Griot to the heretic communities in the Luberon was one Anthoine Guérin, described as 'le bonnetier d'Avignon', who told Griot he had been a Dominican friar, and had laid aside his habit, and had taken to preaching clandestinely at Paris, Meaux, and Rouen. He taught Griot most of what this 'Vaudois *barbe*' knew about heresy.[86] The case of Jehan Serre, *dit* Bérard, 'le boiteux de Murs', seems to have been similar, and he also taught Griot.[87] When Colin Pellenc, of Plan d'Apt, was burnt in 1540, the inventory of his goods included a copy of Olivétan's French Bible of 1535, a work attributed to Farel, and a letter which it has been conjectured may have been from Calvin to the Vaudois.[88]

Several renegade priests were mixing amongst the Vaudois in this region from the 1530s on. It is likely, thanks to the ferment produced by the publicity of the early Reformation, that these clerical converts adhered more closely to protestantism than to traditional heresy. A bookbinder at Mérindol had married an ex-nun; an ex-Franciscan was also spreading protestantism in Mérindol; a former priest confessed in 1540 that he had been at Geneva before coming to Provence.[89] By 1545 the heretic pastor at Cabrières was an ex-Franciscan from Normandy; the former *curés* of Mérindol and Cabrières were also preaching heresy. The latter had previously been a domestic chaplain to the bishop of Cavaillon.[90]

The traditional accounts tend to date the beginning in earnest of the persecution from the decree of 18 November 1540, which pronounced a sentence of total destruction on the village of Mérindol.[91] However, from the *procès-verbal*

[86]   Audisio, *Barbe et l'inquisiteur*, p. 104. See below, ch. 12 (ii).

[87]   Audisio, *Barbe et l'inquisiteur*, pp. 96, 107, 126.

[88]   M. Villard, 'Vaudois d'Apt au xvie siècle', *BCTHS*, Ann. 1965 (1966), 649-51; Audisio, *Barbe et l'inquisiteur*, pp. 61f., 75, 127.

[89]   J. Aubéry, *Histoire de l'exécution de Cabrières et de Mérindol et d'autres lieux de Provence* (Paris, 1645), pp. 23f., 26.

[90]   E. Arnaud, *Histoire des protestants de Provence, du Comtat Venaissin, et de la Principauté d'Orange* (Paris, 1884), I, 97-8.

[91]   (Jean Crespin), *Histoire mémorable de la persécution et saccagement du peuple de Mérindol et Cabrières et autres circonvoisins, appelez Vaduois* (s. l., 1556); Crespin, 1565 edn., pp. 189-217; for other entries in the martyrologies see ch. 16 (iii) below.

prepared by the *Lieutenant-Général* for Provence, Jacques Guérin, in 1541, we see that by the early 1530s the spiritual court at Aix had already begun to act against heresy. Letters issued by François I on 17 July 1531 ordered an inquisition into 'Lutherans' in the diocese of Aix. The archbishop sent his *official*, Victor Peyronet, together with the *procureur-fiscal* and the inquisitor, to take down information; this process lasted the whole of 1532. In 1533 the spiritual court at Aix began to try suspects. Carmelite preachers were sent to regions supposed to be heretical, and a number of Piedmontese living in Lourmarin were examined and abjured their errors. Further legal processes, with excommunication of the recalcitrant, were carried out at Villelaure and La Roque d'Antheron, then at Peypin d'Aigues.[92]

Alongside these formal and legal inquisitions one inquisitor was working with much less caution. The Dominican Jehan de Roma seems to have begin his activities against heretics in Provence in 1528. He had been ejected from the Comtat Venaissin by the Cardinal François de Clermont;[93] by the early 1530s he was concentrating his efforts on the diocese of Apt. On 3 October 1532 Claude de Savoie, Comte de Tende, then *Lieutenant-Général* in Provence, gave orders that de Roma be helped; on 17 March the Sieur de Cental was specifically directed to aid him.[94] On 8 April 1533 the Archbishop of Aix and the president of the *parlement* began to try de Roma himself, having received royal letters of 12 February demanding that the inquisitor be stopped and investigated.[95] He was to die of the plague at Avignon in the summer of 1533.[96]

De Roma presented a long submission in his own defence, in which he strove to present himself as a scrupulous and dedicated seeker out of heretics; his editor seems to accept that view of his character.[97] On the other hand, the wording

[92] J.-H. Albanès, 'Premières années du protestantisme en Provence', *BCTHS* Ann. 1884 (1884), 32-4; P. Gaffarel, 'Les Massacres de Cabrières et de Mérindol en 1545', *Revue Historique*, 107 (1911), 243; Aubéry, *Histoire de l'exécution*, pp. 18f.; E. Arnaud, 'Histoire des premières persécutions', *BSHV* 9 (1892), 4ff.

[93] Herminjard, VII, 469f.   [94] Audisio, *Barbe et l'inquisiteur*, pp. 19f.

[95] Herminjard, VII, 470-88.

[96] Audisio, *Barbe et l'inquisiteur*, pp. 34f.; Arnaud, 'Histoire des premières persécutions', *BSHV* 8 (1891), 45-58, and 9 (1892), 3f.

[97] Audisio, *Barbe et l'inquisiteur*, *passim*, but esp. pp. 7-35.

of the royal commission against him, the complaints made by
the Vaudois to the royal commissioners, and de Roma's
own blustering letters defending his practices, present him as
a violent, arrogant bully with a smattering of theological
terms and learning, who tried to browbeat heretics and royal
commissioners alike in the attempt to continue his work.[98]

Meanwhile the court at Aix continued the prosecutions.
In 1533 the hands of the judges of Aix were strengthened
by bulls of Clement VII and letters from François I of
8 November, which all urged on the prosecution of heresy.
In March 1534 the Archbishop of Aix sent the prior of the
Carmelites of Pertuis, Elzias Philip, to spread the word of the
papal bulls, which ordered all heretics to abjure. After two
months, several heretics of Villelaure, Cucuron, and Lourmarin
were dealt with.[99] Meanwhile two victims from Cabrières
d'Aigues deposed about the *barbes* in that village.[100]

In 1535 the archbishop took further action against those
who had refused to answer his summonses. Several heretics
of Pertuis were arrested, interrogated, and burnt. On the
other hand, when the officers of the spiritual court tried to
arrest one who was suspected of being a *barbe*, no sooner
had they seized him than they were assailed by a troop of
forty or fifty armed heretics, who recovered the prisoner,
chased his captors as far as the abbey of Saulvecane, and
beseiged them in the abbey. When the *juge ordinaire* of Aix
sent a force to make reprisals, the Vaudois fled, and only a
few were captured and burnt.[101]

This activity was restrained somewhat in the same year. On
the one hand, François I issued the edict of Coucy on 16 July
1535; this gave those accused of heresy an amnesty for six
months, to allow them to return to their homes and repent of
their errors. Although the edict excluded 'sacramentarian'
heretics (which some of the protestants moving amongst the
Vaudois may have been), apparently several heretics did

[98]   Herminjard, loc. cit.
[99]   Albanès, 'Premières années du protestantisme', 34–6; Gaffarel, 'Les Massacres', 243f.
[100]   Aubéry, *Histoire de l'exécution*, p. 19.
[101]   Albanès, 'Premières années du protestantisme', 36f.; Gaffarel, 'Les Massacres', 244.

receive the benefit of this edict.[102] On the other hand, Guillaume Farel and Pierre Viret wrote a substantial manifesto to the Swiss protestants advertising the Vaudois cause on 4 August; about the same time the Vaudois themselves wrote in their own defence.[103] These letters evoked a sympathetic reply from Wolfgang Capito of Strasbourg. Farel also wrote to Guillaume du Bellay, Sieur de Langeay, about the possibility of his interceding with François I.[104]

François's military preoccupations did rather more for the Vaudois at this stage than these first attempts at intercession. When the edict of Coucy expired on 17 May 1536, it was renewed at the end of the same month. At the end of hostilities between France and Savoy in 1537, informations were taken against some Lutheran priests and others at Tourves, in the Var. On hearing of this, Wilhelm von Furstenberg wrote on 27 October to protest at the mishandling of priests who had been forced to leave wives and children because of the threat of imprisonment by the archbishop. Despite this the trials lasted into 1538.[105]

On 24 June 1539 further royal letters turned over jurisdiction in heresy cases to the secular courts, *baillis*, and *sénéchaux*, in collaboration with diocesans. In 1540 these royal letters were supplemented by patents issued for the *parlement* of Aix on 31 May, and to the archbishop on 31 August, which directed that heresy be proceeded against.[106] In the mean time the inquisitors made some alarming discoveries during the interrogations of four heretics in the course of 1539. These admitted that the Vaudois were preparing to defend themselves against attack by force; one witness confessed that they all hoped to join Furstenberg's *Landsknechts*.[107]

[102] Albanès, 'Premières années du protestantisme', 37f.; *HE*, I, 37; Arnaud, *Protestants de Provence*, I, 14f.
[103] Herminjard, III, 327–32; C. Schmidt, 'Aktenstücke, besonders zur Geschichte der Waldenser', *Zeitschrift für die historische Theologie*, 22 (1852), 252–6; Arnaud, *Protestants de Provence*, I, 16ff.
[104] Herminjard, III, 335, 359.
[105] Aubéry, *Histoire de l'exécution*, p. 20; *HE*, loc. cit.; Albanès, 'Premières années du protestanisme', 38f.; Gaffarel, 'Les Massacres', 245; Peter, 'Guillaume de Furstenberg', 30, 35f.
[106] Albanès, 'Premières années du protestantisme', 39f.; Gaffarel, 'Les Massacres', 245f.
[107] Aubéry, *Histoire de l'exécution*, pp. 22–7; Peter, 'Guillaume de Furstenberg', 33.

Such pieces of information as these gave the *parlement* the impetus to issue the *Arrêt de Mérindol* on 18 November 1540. This handed over (somewhat archaically) the inhabitants of whole villages to the 'secular arm', and directed that the village of Mérindol should be razed to the ground. However, the decree was only the start of a series of diplomatic and legal moves surrounding these villagers. The *président*, Barthélemi Chassanée or Chasseneuz, decided not to have the decree put into effect at once. François I then seems to have asked Guillaume du Bellay, then his lieutenant in Piedmont, to supply a report on the life and morals of the Vaudois. In view of his correspondence with Farel, it is perhaps not surprising that his report was sufficiently favourable for further letters to be sent by the King in mitigation of the penalties decreed against the Vaudois, on condition that they abjured within three months.[108]

In the spring of 1541 the people of Mérindol made their protests to the *parlement* of Provence, and appended to their appeal a confession of faith. Various forms of the protest and confession are preserved, but all seem to derive from those published by Crespin.[109] The main confession was dated 6 April 1541, and was headed by the names of André and Martin Mainard, two of those cited in the original decrees. These confessions, including one submitted by Cabrières d'Avignon in the Comtat Venaissin, were sent to the bishops of Cavaillon and Carpentras for opinions. The bishop of Carpentras was then Giacomo Sadoleto, who had said in a letter to Farnese in July 1539 how much he preferred the arms of persuasion to those of force as a means to win the souls of heretics.[110] According to protestant sources, Sadoleto said that the confessions might be acceptable if only a few phrases could be changed. He has been credited with preventing the attempts made by the vice-legate at Avignon

---

[108] The letters of grace were dated 8 February 1541. See Crespin, 1565 edn., pp. 198f.; *HE*, I, 38; Gaffarel, 'Les Massacres', 247; Arnaud, *Protestants de Provence*, I, 27–34; V.-L. Bourilly, *Guillaume du Bellay, Seigneur de Langey* (Paris, 1905), pp. 314–17.

[109] Crespin, 1565 edn., pp. 202–5; *HE*, I, 39–41; Camerarius, *Historica Narratio*, pp. 365–84; Herminjard, VII, 80–2; Arnaud, *Protestants de Provence*, I, 34, 41.

[110] Herminjard, V, 361–3.

to execute the edict in the Comtat in 1542.[111] More recent authors are slightly more sceptical about the extent of Sadoleto's sympathies.[112]

Meanwhile the protestants abroad renewed their efforts; on 23 May 1541 a gathering at Ratisbon wrote to François I on the Vaudois' behalf.[113] Catholic attempts to convert some Vaudois were unsuccessful, and piecemeal armed attacks only brought on reprisals from the heretics.[114] Several factors aggravated the situation. The first was the death of the scrupulous legalist Chassanée, rapidly followed by that of his successor. On 23 December 1543 he was in turn succeeded by Jehan Meynier, Sieur d'Oppède. The new *président* was not only intolerant; he also held the lands directly between Cabrières d'Avignon and Mérindol. The rising influence and self-assurance of the heretics, as in the Dauphiné of the 1480s, was a threat to his security as a landlord, and also an opportunity to pay off his debts and enrich his estates.[115]

Further trouble was created by rumours about the Vaudois' organizing themselves for self-defence. Meynier is said to have been exasperated by the way the Vaudois had established themselves in strongholds in the Luberon. He also spread the rumour that the Vaudois intended to rebel and turn Provence into a protestant canton after the Swiss model.[116]

Nevertheless, following a deputation to the King, the letters of grace postponing the execution of the decree were renewed in 1542 and 1543, although Meynier subsequently had them revoked.[117] When, later in 1543, the Vaudois of Cabrières fortified themselves in their village, and those of Mérindol pillaged the abbey of Sinanque, it was only the intercession of the landlords of these villages (whose tenants were increasing the value of their lands manyfold) which

---

[111] *HE*, I, 41-2; Camerarius, *Historica Narratio*, pp. 385-7; Arnaud, *Protestants de Provence*, I, 37 ff.

[112] R. M. Douglas, *Jacopo Sadoleto 1477-1547, Humanist and Reformer* (Cambridge, Mass., 1959), pp. 186-94; M. Venard, 'Jacques Sadolet, évêque de Carpentras, et les Vaudois', *BSSV* 143 (1978), 44-9.

[113] Arnaud, *Protestants de Provence*, I, 43-5, based on *CO*, XI, letter no. 311.

[114] Arnaud, *Protestants de Provence*, I, 45-51.

[115] Gaffarel, 'Les Massacres', 248; *HE*, I, 43.

[116] Gaffarel, 'Les Massacres', 249 f.

[117] Arnaud, *Protestants de Provence*, I, 52 ff.

prevented immediate execution. An inquiry was ordered into the conduct of the villagers, which by urgent lobbying Meynier forestalled. By making the most of their contacts at court the *parlementaires* were able to obtain letters patent from the King, on 1 February 1545, by which it was ordered that the edict be enforced, the villagers killed, and their dwellings razed.[118] The Cardinal François de Tournon was supposed to have been particularly important in securing these letters; certainly the protestants believed this at the time.[119]

Execution of the *Arrêt* was delayed until April, probably because of the need to arrange the support of an army led by Polin de la Garde.[120] From 18 April the army swept westwards along the southern edge of the Luberon where the Vaudois were settled. Mérindol, Cabrières, and Tourves were amongst the last places to be devastated. The savagery and brutality of this attack became notorious throughout Europe; the Wars of Religion had not yet brought about a revision of standards in these matters. At first, the authorities approved. In mid-May François was said to have smiled when he heard the news, and commented 'c'est une belle defaicte'. Pope Paul III accorded Meynier various honours of the Empire, which François allowed him to accept.[121]

Retribution followed, however. With the new reign, Henri II bowed to widespread sympathy with the victims of the massacre; letters issued on 17 March 1549, less than four full years after the execution, directed that the cases against Meynier, Polin de la Garde, and the other persecutors should be heard by the *parlement* of Paris. The trial lasted from autumn 1550 to February 1551; Meynier, Polin, and all but one of the other defendants were ultimately acquitted, although Meynier had not long recovered his lands before he died in 1558.[122]

The parallel between the crusade in the Alps in the 1480s and this episode is not exact. The sudden savagery of the

[118] Crespin, 1565 edn., pp. 212–15; *HE*, I, 43 f.; Gaffarel, 'Les Massacres', 250 f.
[119] *CO*, XII, cols. 58 f., 78 f., 111; but see M. François, *Le Cardinal François de Tournon* (Paris, 1951), pp. 219–21.
[120] Gaffarel, 'Les Massacres', 252; but compare *HE*, I, 44.
[121] *CO*, XII, cols. 79–81; Gaffarel, 'Les Massacres', 262 f.
[122] Gaffarel, 'Les Massacres', 265–70; Arnaud, *Protestants de Provence*, I, 89 ff., 98 ff.

attack seems to have been less the result of hatred of orthodox Waldensianism, than of a fear that the radical protestants who were stirring up the Vaudois would present a serious threat to public order. In any event, the persecution did not in any way eradicate protestantism in Provence. In the 1550s numerous inhabitants of the villages of Cabrières, Lourmarin, Tourves, Mérindol, Cadenet, and elsewhere went to live in Geneva and subscribed to the Calvinist settlement of religion.[123] In 1556 some of these exiles returned to their homes in Provence.[124] In May 1561 the protestants of Lourmarin wrote a letter of sympathy and solidarity to the Piedmontese, under attack by Emanuele Filiberto.[125] In December 1561 the minister of Cesana, Humbert Artus, wrote to the Company of Pastors at Geneva to say how the churches of Provence were pressing for a minister to visit them.[126] In 1563 the former minister of Mérindol, Jean Poirier, who had since 1545 been at Sisteron and in the marquisate of Saluzzo, was being recalled by Mérindol.[127] In 1563 and 1568 there were uprisings in Provence on behalf of the reformed cause.[128] In fact, the protestant tradition became firmly entrenched in the former Vaudois villages of the Luberon, and in at least one case was still strong up to the time of the Revocation of the Edict of Nantes and beyond.[129]

(vi) A church is formed, 1550–70

Most historians have not attached nearly so much importance to this later phase of Waldensian history; there is not nearly so much myth to disentangle as surrounds the years 1532–3. For all that, these are some of the most formative and

[123] *LHG*, pp. 46, 47, 54, 56–8, 60, 71, 78, 106, 110, 113, 116, 120, etc.

[124] Arnaud, *Protestants de Provence*, I, 108ff.

[125] Letter of 5 May 1561, in Gilles, 1644 edn., p. 167.

[126] J. Jalla, 'Correspondance ecclésiastique vaudoise du seizième siècle', *BSHV* 33 (1914), 83f.

[127] E. Comba, 'Lettres ecclésiastiques à la vén. Compagnie des pasteurs de Genève aux 16ᵉ et 17ᵉ siècles avec quelques réponses de la V. C. au sujet des églises de nos vallées', *BSHV* 16 (1898), 23; Jalla, 'Correspondance ecclésiastique vaudoise', 85–8; *CO* XIX, cols. 534–6.

[128] Gaffarel, 'Les Massacres', 270f.

[129] See, e.g., T. F. Sheppard, *Lourmarin in the Eighteenth Century* (Baltimore and London, 1971), pp. 152–72.

important times for the dissident communities in the Alps.

In October 1539 the French, secure in Turin after the expulsion of the Duke of Savoy, established a *parlement* there to take care of criminal cases, including heresy, in the same way as the French provincial *parlements*.[130] We only hear of its making real moves against heresy from 1550. This may simply be the result of the loss of most of its registers; however, two distinct sources date its activities from that time. In 1550 the inquisitor-general in Turin, Tommasso Giacomelli, summoned the people of Angrogna, in the persons of their syndics, to the Dominican convent at Turin to answer on matters of faith. Those of Angrogna sent two proctors, who were promptly imprisoned. The villagers protested at this and insisted on a safe conduct for those whom they sent. This was eventually given, and they sent their syndics to promise that they would live 'Christianly'.[131]

At the same time other heretics whom the *parlement* had seized were being prosecuted. In June 1550 the *parlement* ordered the inquisitor and the vicar of the Abbey of St. Mary at Pinerolo to proceed against two heretics, while reserving its right to pass judgement. In November 1550 the court acted against one of those who had thwarted an attempt to promote the catholic cause in the Val d'Angrogna. The inquisitor and a counsellor had gone to the valleys, but one Collet Stringa had warned the Vaudois, and the inquisitor was ambushed so that 'the said commission could not be fully executed according to the intentions of the said court . . .'; Stringa was cited to appear.[132]

Meanwhile the *parlement* dealt with other non-Waldensian cases; between December 1550 and early 1552 it considered the cases of an apostate Franciscan of Fenile, the Lutheran schoolmaster of Vigone, a heretic *colporteur* and a priest, both from Bair, and some suspected witches of Barge and Bagnolo Piemonte.[133] These cases show that there was a will

---

[130] L. Romier, 'Les Vaudois et le parlement français de Turin', *Mélanges d'archaeologie et d'histoire*, 30 (1910), 195; 'Les Institutions françaises en Piémont sous Henri II', *Revue historique*, 106 (1911), 7 ff.

[131] Gilles, 1644 edn., p. 50.

[132] Romier, 'Vaudois et le parlement français', 199–201.

[133] Ibid., 201–7.

to prosecute, despite unfavourable circumstances;[134] but such selective persecutions did not arouse much alarm amongst protestants elsewhere.[135]

In 1555 Calvin's organization gained undoubted hegemony in Geneva; in that year also the first Calvinist ministers arrived in Piedmont. Jean Vernou came originally from Poitiers, but was an associate of Calvin at Geneva. Late in 1554 or early in 1555 he and another minister made a journey to the Waldensian valleys. They preached first at a village called 'Barbotté'[136] and subsequently at Fenestrelle, one of the chief Vaudois villages of the region. There they met some hostility, and had to be protected. They preached two long sermons and administered the communion. They refused, however, to go too far in acquiescing in 'that insane fancy that it is preferable to preach in the open than in secret', and pointed out to the Waldenses the case of the primitive clandestine church.[137]

Thereafter they went to Angrogna with an armed escort. They preached there in the house of one of the pastors, where the crowd was so great that they had to hold a service in 'a great yard surrounded with galleries'. Most important of all, at this point Vernou and his companion told the Vaudois they should obtain 'harvesters to help those whom they already possessed', and offered, 'if they would tell the ministers the number of places where pastors were needed, to be of assistance'.[138]

Vernou reported all these details of his mission in a letter to Geneva dated 22 April 1555. There seems no reason to suppose that this was not the beginning of the first serious conversion of the Waldensian valleys into a protestant canton; for everything follows from these contacts in the spring of 1555. In that year the schoolmaster in Angrogna found that

[134] Gilles, loc. cit.

[135] Pascal, 'Ambasciere', *BSBS* XVIII, nos. 1-3 (1913), 90; Pascal, *I Valdesi e il parlamento francese di Torino* (Pinerolo, 1912), *passim*.

[136] Actually Balboutet, west of Usseaux in the Val Chisone.

[137] On this issue see below, ch. 14 (i).

[138] 'Une mission en Piémont', *BSHPF* 17 (1868), 16-19; *CO*, XV, cols. 575-8; Pazè Beda, *Riforma e cattolicesimo*, pp. 43-5; Hemardinquer, 'Les Vaudois du Dauphiné', 54; R. M. Kingdon, *Geneva and the Coming of the Wars of Religion in France 1555-63* (Geneva, 1956), pp. 2, 56.

the numbers attending his preaching were so great that the traditional focus of preaching, the pastor's house, was too small; so two 'temples' were built in the valley that August, one near the church of San Lorenzo (now in the main village in Angrogna), and another a mile higher up, probably at Il Serre, where one now exists. Later that year the same was done in the valleys of the Pèllice and the Luserna, and in March 1556 a church was built in the Val Germanasca.[139]

Shortly afterwards ministers started to leave Geneva for the valleys in a rapid succession. After Vernou's letter of 22 April had been read to the Compagnie des Pasteurs, he and his companion were appointed to assist the people of Piedmont.[140] In June 1555, however, it was reported that Vernou, along with four other companions, had been captured and led to Chambéry, where he was burnt that autumn.[141] One of the first and the most distinguished of their successors was Estienne Noel. A native of Champagne, he had been expelled from Montbéliard in 1555. In that year he met the indigenous Vaudois pastor Gilles des Gilles, who was then returning from southern Italy. Gilles met Noel at Lausanne, and brought him back to be minister at Angrogna. By the spring of 1556 he was corresponding with Calvin and Farel about Piedmontese affairs.[142]

In June 1556 Viret wrote to Calvin about sending a further minister to the 'Alpine Churches', and recommended Pierre Guérin, who had recently been busy in the Dauphiné. A year later he had been sent.[143] Viret also suggested Estienne Fago (or Favonius).[144] Still more were sent following petitions to

---

[139] Crespin, 1619 edn., fo. 584r; Gilles, 1644 edn., pp. 51 f.; Lentolo, pp. 78 f.; *Storia delle persecuzioni e guerre contro il popolo chiamato valdese che abita nelle valli del Piemonte, di Angrogna, Luserna, San Martino, Perosa e altre, a far tempo dall' anno 1555 fino al 1561*, ed. E. Balmas and C. A. Theiller, (Torino, 1975), pp. 73 f., 232 f.   [140] *RCPG*, II, 62.

[141] Crespin, 1565 edn., pp. 624–56; Pantaleon, *Martyrum Historia*, pp. 310–28; Gilles, 1644 edn., p. 52; *CO*, XV, cols. 689–91, 694–7, 707–9, 740–5, 805–7, 808–9; *RCPG*, II, 64, 126 f.

[142] Gilles, 1644 edn., pp. 53–5; *CO*, XV, cols. 102–4, 108–10, 146–7; Bèze, *Corresp.*, II, 41–2 and notes.

[143] *CO*, XV, col. 189; XVI, col. 532.

[144] *CO*, XVI, cols. 153 f.; Jalla, 'Correspondance ecclésiastique vaudoise', 76; *Quelques lettres inédites de Pierre Viret*, ed. J. Barnaud (Saint-Amans, 1911), p. 103 and notes. He was sent either in 1556 or 1557.

the Compagnie des Pasteurs: Jehan 'Vineannus' in June 1556, Jehan Lauversat (or Lauvergeat), the survivor of the first mission of 1555, in September, and a 'M. Albert' from the Albigeois on 27 November.[145]

About the same time there arrived in Piedmont Humbert Rémond (or Artus) and Dominique Vignaux, a Gascon, and also one of the first Italian speakers to be sent from Geneva, Giafredo Varaglia of Busca. The latter had been a Capuchin and friend of Ochino; in 1556 he copied his general's apostasy and went to Geneva. In the spring of 1557 he was sent to be minister at Angrogna alongside Estienne Noel.[146] On 14 September 1557 the Company approved the sending of Pasquier Bacnot (or Barnot) as a minister to Piedmont, although it is not known what became of him thereafter.[147] In the autumn of 1559 another Italian was sent; this was Scipione Lentolo from Naples, who had been since 1558 in the Italian Church at Geneva. He arrived in Angrogna in November, to succeed the then martyred Varaglia.[148]

The same process was meanwhile providing ministers for the Val Chisone. In January 1557 Jean Chambeli of Issoudun was appointed to be a minister in Piedmont, while in April or May Martin Tachard was delegated to follow him, although he probably did not set out until June 1558. Estienne Vidal became a minister in the Val Pragelato about the same time. Of these, however, Chambeli was to stay only twenty months, and Tachard had ceased to minister in the region by late in 1561.[149] Vidal, on the other hand, was still in the Val Chisone in 1571.[150]

However, at the same stage, the *parlements* of Turin and Grenoble had begun an energetic repression of heresy. From

[145] *RCPG*, II, 68–70; Jalla, 'Correspondance ecclésiastique vaudoise', 77.

[146] Crespin, 1565 edn., p. 891; Gilles, 1644 edn., pp. 53–5; Jalla, 'Correspondance ecclésiastique vaudoise', 74 f.; Miolo, *Historia breve e vera*, ed. Balmas, pp. 94 f.; *RCPG*, II, 74.

[147] Jalla, 'Correspondance ecclésiastique vaudoise', 77; Bèze, *Corresp.*, II, 138 and notes; *RCPG*, II, 79. On the ministers sent to Piedmont by the Company of Pastors see the list in *BSHPF* 8 (1859), 76.

[148] *CO*, XVII, cols. 668 f.; Lentolo, pp. 4 f., 87; Jalla, 'Le Refuge français dans les vallées vaudoises', 580–9.

[149] Pazè Beda, *Riforma e cattolicesimo*, p. 46; Jalla, *Storia della Riforma in Piemonte*, pp. 86, 185 f.; 'Correspondance ecclésiastique vaudoise', 77; *RCPG*, II, 70, 74, 81, 83.   [150] *RCPG*, III, 264–6.

March 1556 the latter court took a variety of steps; it issued edicts requiring those of the Val Chisone to reaffirm their loyalty to the Catholic Church; it imprisoned those whom it could capture, and prosecuted others in their absence.[151] Likewise, in December 1555 the *parlement* at Turin issued an edict ordering the imprisonment of those who in Lent 1555 had received 'ministers coming from Geneva'; this was obviously in response to the mission of Vernou and Lauversat.[152]

Further edicts were promulgated in an attempt to bring those of Angrogna to heel. On 20 December 1555 the *parlement* at Turin appointed two of its members, Agostino della Chiesa and Bartolomeo di Termes, to inquire into the Waldenses; shortly afterwards one of the *présidents*, Bartolomeo Émé, seigneur de St-Julien, was substituted for Termes. In March 1556 these two visited the Piedmontese valleys; on the 23rd they issued an order directing the Vaudois to employ the catholic rites and to follow catholic worship, and to hand over their pastors to the authorities. The Vaudois replied with a confession of faith, and refused to submit. On 27 November 1556 Henri II issued an edict ordering that the persecution be enforced; this order was apparently kept secret until 22 March 1557, when further orders were given that the congregations should abandon and surrender their ministers. This edict named forty-three inhabitants of the communities of Angrogna, San Giovanni, Rorà, Bòbbio Pèllice, and Villar Pèllice, who were to appear before the commission in Turin.[153]

The Vaudois had not forgotten the example of those of Mérindol, and wrote to Geneva to ask for the help of the protestant cantons of Switzerland in interceding with the King of France. This form of assistance had already been

---

[151] Pazè Beda, *Riforma e cattolicesimo*, pp. 45–52, based on Jalla, *Storia della riforma in Piemonte*, pp. 185–92; Caffaro, *Notizie della chiesa pinerolese*, VI, 264–9; Hemardinquer, 'Les Vaudois du Dauphiné', 54 f., 57–63.

[152] Jalla, *Storia della riforma in Piemonte*, pp. 80–2, quoted by Pazè Beda, *Riforma e cattolicesimo*, p. 46.

[153] Crespin, 1565 edn., p. 870; 1619 edn., fos. 584^r–6^v; R. Dinoth, *De Bello Civili Gallico* (Basel, 1582), p. 6; Gilles, 1644 edn., pp. 54–62, 67–70; Lentolo, pp. 79–86; Pascal, 'Ambasciere', *BSBS* XVIII, nos. 1–3 (1913), 91 f.; Jalla, *Storia della riforma in Piemonte*, pp. 86–90; *Storia delle persecuzioni*, ed. Balmas and Theiller, pp. 75–86, 234–40.

invoked three times before, in 1535 in the case of the Provençal Vaudois and of Antoine Saunier's imprisonment, and in
1538 for the Piedmontese when they were attacked by
Montjehan.[154] In this case it was Farel and Théodore de Bèze
who instigated the appeal, when they made their case to
the Senate of Berne on 23 April 1557. Berne agreed to an
embassy and sent the two with letters to the rulers of Zürich.
Eventually a diet was arranged of the four cities in the
confederation, Berne, Zürich, Basel, and Schaffhausen; this
began on 10 May. A Swiss embassy was put in hand, and
meanwhile Farel and Bèze set about securing the support of
Strasbourg, and of Georges of Montbéliard, Christoph of
Württemberg, and the Elector Palatine. The embassy of the
Swiss towns left for Paris on 1 June, and that of the German
princes in mid-July. Henri II met both embassies, and gave
ambiguous replies which satisfied no one.[155] However, the
Vaudois were left in peace for a while, for which they thanked
the protestants.[156] Only in June 1558 was a fresh summons
issued which named thirteen individuals accused of being
'prescheurs' coming from Geneva.[157]

In the later 1550s the mission to Piedmont was one of the
most dangerous of all postings for a protestant minister, and
several of those involved in evangelizing were captured and
burnt in this period. Barthélemi Hector, a Poitevin like
Vernou, was a carrier of religious books and Bibles working
from Geneva. He was arrested while crossing from the Val
Germanasca to the Val d'Angrogna in 1556. He was taken to
Turin, tried, and executed.[158] Much more important for the
valleys was the loss of the minister of Angrogna, Giafredo

---

[154] See (iv) and (v) above.

[155] Pascal, 'Ambasciere', *BSBS* XVIII, nos. 1–3 (1913), 91–119, and 5–6
(1913), 314–36; XIX, nos. 1–3 (1914), 27–38; A. Hollaender, 'Eine Schweizer
Gesandtschaftsreise an den Französischen Hof im Jahre 1557', *Historische Zeitschrift*, N. S. 33 (1892), 385–410; *CO*, XVI, cols. 459–61, 462f., 469–81, 481–6,
499f., 500–2, 502f., 538–41, 554–6, 567–8, 586–7, 590–6, 609–17; Bèze,
Corresp., II, 62, 75, 82f., 86–94, 118–20; Lentolo, pp. 86f.; *Storia delle persecuzioni*, pp. 91f., 243.

[156] A. Vinay, 'Lettre de Busca', *BSHV* 7 (1890), 44–7.

[157] Gilles, 1644 edn., p. 70.

[158] Crespin, 1565 edn., pp. 839–43; *HE*, I, 111; J. Foxe, *Actes and Monuments* (London, 1583 edn.), p. 955; Gilles, 1644 edn., p. 53; Morland, *History of
the Evangelical Churches*, p. 225; Vinay, 'Lettre de Busca', 49f.

Varaglia. He had only been a few months in the valleys when he was captured late in 1557 while returning from Dragoniere,[159] where he had been talking with an aristocratic convert. After long interrogations he was burnt at Turin on 29 March 1558.[160] Two other protestants suffered at Turin after that: Elia Golla of Carmagna, burnt in 1559 by Giovanni Caracciolo, prince of Melfi, and Paolo Rappi of Vigone, burnt at Turin in 1560.[161]

Two points emerge about the attack against the Waldenses in the wars of 1560-1. First, it had been very well prepared by events in the *parlements* on both sides of the Alps ever since ministers first started to infiltrate the valleys. The presence of these new and impressive dissenters had provoked an immediate and informed reaction. Secondly, the war broke out more or less simultaneously, although under two different political dispensations, on either side of the political divide between Piedmont and the Dauphiné as established by the peace of Cateau-Cambrésis in 1559. The whole scheme may even have been a result of the clause in that peace treaty whereby the participant powers bound one another to purge their own lands of heresy.[162] In histories of the reign of Emanuele Filiberto it has, despite this possibility, been traditional to claim that the war was the idea of the duke alone, because of his anxiety for religious purity.[163] Probably the only role which the attack on Angrogna played in purely Savoyard concerns was as a substitute for the impractical ambition of the reconquest of Geneva; this was to be attempted

---

[159] Or possibly Dronero, in the Marquisate of Saluzzo.

[160] Crespin, 1565 edn., pp. 890-5; Pantaleon, *Martyrum Historia*, pp. 334f.; Bèze, *Icones*, sig. Cc. i r; Gilles, 1644 edn., p. 65; Morland, *History of the Evanglical Churches*, p. 226; *CO*, XVII, cols. 73f.; Lentolo, pp. 87-115; Vinay, 'Lettre de Busca', 50f.; Miolo, *Historia breve e vera*, p. 95. This list should be augmented by the names of Vernou and his companions, mentioned above.

[161] C. Massi, *Prosopopea e storia della città e provincia di Pinerolo* (Torino, 1833-6), III, 78f.; Caffaro, *Notizie . . . della chiesa pinerolese*, VI, 86, n. 3.

[162] Pascal, 'Ambasciere', *BSBS* XVIII, nos. 5-6 (1913), 334; 'La lotta', *BSHV* 53 (1929), 14-25; E. Ricotti, *Storia della monarchia piemontese*, (Firenze, 1861-9), II, 178f., 201.

[163] See, e.g., J. Tonsi, *Vita Emmanuelis Philiberti* (Turin, 1596), pp. 144f.; S. Guichenon, *Histoire généalogique de la royale maison de Savoye* (Lyon, 1660), pp. 680f.; G. Cambiano, *Historico discorso al serenissimo Filippo Emmanuele di Savoia*, ed. C. Saluzzo (Monumenta Historiae Patriae, Scriptorum t. I, Turin, 1840), cols. 1147 f.

by Carlo Emanuele I in 1602, with conspicuous lack of success.[164]

The events of these conflicts are best summarized quite briefly. In Piedmont the war had three phases. Its prologue was the promulgation of the Edict of Nice on 15 February 1560. This forbade, on pain of a fine and sending to the galleys, the hearing of 'Lutheran' preaching in the Valle di Luserna or elsewhere. Its first stage comprised a series of skirmishes by some local landlords, the Truchets (or Trucchietti) of the Val Germanasca, against those of that valley. Meanwhile diplomatic measures were taken to settle the matter peacefully between the Vaudois and the court of Savoy. The second stage was the disputation carried out against the ministers, among whom Scipione Lentolo was prominent, by the then only twenty-seven-year-old Jesuit, Antonio Possevino. The third stage was mostly military, and followed the commissioning of the Conte della Trinità to bring religious disobedience to heel by force. This was brought to an end, after a series of negotiations and forced abjurations, punctuated by remarkable mountain skirmishes, by the treaty of Cavour of 5 June 1561. By this treaty the failure of the armed expedition against the Vaudois was effectively acknowledged, the people of the valleys were accorded limited right to the exercise of their religion, and they were given an indemnity for their past acts of rebellion.[165]

Events were less clear-cut in the Dauphiné. The Val Pragelato probably acted as a magnet for the disaffected on the protestant side, and the Grenoble *parlement* made repeated noises about an armed expedition, to reduce what was already something of a base for the Huguenot captains de Mauvans and Montbrun. In the winter of 1560-1 an expedition was planned to attack this area; the catholic leader La Cazette was nominated as absentee chatelain for the castellany of the Val Chisone. Thanks to the uncertainty

---

[164] Armand Hugon, *Storia dei Valdesi II*, p. 52.
[165] On the War of the Edict of Nice, see Lentolo's own account in CUL MS Dd. 3. 33, fos. 1^r-2^v; Morland, *History of the Evangelical Churches*, pp. 230-5; *Storia delle persecuzioni*, ed. Balmas and Theiller, *passim; Histoire mémorable de la guerre* . . ., (*s. l.,* 1561 and 1562), and ed. E. Balmas and V. Diena (Torino, 1972), *passim*; Lentolo, pp. 116-226.

produced by the death of François II the expedition did not take place, and in January 1561 the Pragelatese met those of the Piedmontese valleys at Bòbbio and formed an agreement for mutual aid against aggression. Later in 1561 the protestants of the Val Chisone were able to spread out from the upper valley around Fenestrelle, where they had been settled, and to convert the rest of the lower valley by force.[166]

At this point it is as well briefly to sketch the history of the protestant churches of the Marquisate of Saluzzo, in so far as they relate to the themes studied here. Saluzzo was under French domination from 1548 to 1588, and so the history of its struggle for recognition is very different from that of the churches of Angrogna and thereabouts.[167] In the early years of the sixteenth century there had been Waldenses in the valley of the Po, around the villages of Paesana and Oncino; from 1509 they had been the object of a fitful persecution by the Marquise of Saluzzo and the lords of Paesana.[168] In the 1530s there was more concern shown, when a papal letter was issued on 8 November 1532 to the inquisitor in the Marquisate, referring to the spread of 'Lutheran and Waldensian heresy' and giving the inquisitor the powers to act against it.[169]

By 1559 the Reformation had made progress in Saluzzo, just as it had in the more northerly valleys. In April of that year the Piedmontese protestants reported to the German princes that their gospel was being preached in Raconigi, Valgrana, Dronero, Caraglio, Busca, and Cuneo, and also in several towns in Lombardy.[170] In 1561 the church of

[166] On the Dauphiné, see Caffaro, *Notizie . . . della chiesa pinerolese* VI, 267–70; Pazè Beda, *Riforma e cattolicesimo*, pp. 52–62; *CO*, XIX, cols. 28 f.; Bèze, *Corresp.*, III, 71, 75, note; Arnaud, *Protestants du Dauphiné*, I, 62–4.

[167] The principal work on this theme is the immense volume by A. Pascal, *Il Marchesato di Saluzzo e la riforma protestante durante il periodo della dominazione francese* (Firenze, 1960).

[168] Gilles, 1644 edn., p. 29; Morland, *History of the Evangelical Churches*, p. 223; D. Muletti, *Memorie storico-diplomatiche . . . alla città ed ai marchesi di Saluzzo* (Saluzzo, 1829–33), VI, 28 f., 381–7; Promis, 'Memoriale . . . di Saluzzo di Castellar', 492–6, 498–500, 510, 518 f., 520; A. Pascal, 'Margherita di Foix ed i Valdesi di Paesana', *Athenaeum* 4 (1916), 46–84.

[169] B. Fontana, 'Documenti Vaticani contro l'eresia luterana', *Archivio della Società Romana di Storia Patria* 15 (1892), 134–6.

[170] Vinay, 'Lettre de Busca', 53 f.

Dronero, in the Valle Màira, made efforts to gain official permission to conduct protestant worship. It secured letters to that effect from the royal *conseil* to the regional governor, Louis de Birague; shortly afterwards, however, these were revoked. Nevertheless, in 1561 Estienne Noel wrote to the ministers at Geneva commending the cause of the congregations of the Marquisate. He said they were 'thirsty and alone'; they were very pious, were meeting to discuss their religion, and wanted ministers to be sent.[171] Shortly afterwards they received two graduates of Geneva, François Guérin and François Truchi, who became ministers at Dronero. Guérin was a native of that village.[172] In 1564 pastors from their churches were amongst those represented at the Vaudois synod at Villar Pèllice.[173]

These churches took a further step in their organization at the synods of Praviglielmo and Dronero, held on 2 June and 14 October 1567 respectively. According to Pierre Gilles, these gatherings did not only involve the mountain churches, but also those in the plain. Ministers attended representing, admittedly with much pluralism, Saluzzo itself, Savigliano, Carmagnola, and Carignano, as well as places further west. Five days after the second synod the French *Lieutenant-Général*, the Duc de Nevers, issued an edict giving the protestants three days to leave the province. As a result two pastors, Soulf and Truchi, spent four years in prison. However, the ministers were released in 1571 through the intercession of the Queen of Navarre, and these congregations continued their profession into the troubles of the seventeenth century.[174]

This narrative has not made any claims to being a definitive or a complete account of all the events which shaped the

[171] *CO*, XX, col. 476.

[172] Bèze, *Corresp.*, IV, 274, n. 8; Gilles, 1881 edn., I, 411; Morland, *History of the Evangelical Churches*, p. 259; *LHG*, pp. 174, 189; *LRAG*, I, 81.

[173] Jalla, 'Synodes Vaudois', 475 f.

[174] Gilles, 1644 edn., pp. 244 f., and 1881 edn., I, 411–17; Rorengo-Lucerna, *Memorie historiche*, pp. 89–94; Pascal, *Marchesato di Saluzzo*, pp. 215–340; G. Manuel di San Giovanni, *Memorie storiche di Dronero* (Torino, 1868), II, 39 ff., 71 ff. On the sufferings of the Saluzzese after 1600 see, e.g., D. Bouteroue, *Discorsi breve*, ed. E. Balmas and G. Zardini Lana (Torino, 1978).

Waldensian church.[175] It only provides the basic framework for the social analysis which follows. Several conclusions do emerge, however. The first is that the importance of the 1530s as a time of *rapprochement* between heresy and reform has been vastly overrated and misinterpreted. Secondly, it is proper to concentrate on the gradual evolution of attitudes, rather than on the specious process of producing documents purporting to attest sudden decisions. The growth of trust between ministers and people, as strengthened by the experience of 1560-1, and of confidence amongst European protestants in the respectability of the Vaudois case, is of the utmost importance. A chronological account cannot deal adequately with such questions of attitudes, which must be dealt with by themes in the following chapters.

[175] For this see for instance Jalla, *Storia della riforma in Piemonte*, and for one year in the 1560s, A. Pascal, 'Il Piemonte riformato e la politica di Emanuele Filiberto nel 1565', *BSSS* 108 (1928), 395–453.

11. The Social Origins of Alpine Protestantism

(i) The early cliques of protestants in the Dauphiné

Evangelicalism of the type later called 'protestant' made a fairly precocious appearance in two different milieux in the Dauphiné of the 1520s. It appeared amongst some of the notarial and merchant classes of the Gapençais; it also affected a few clerical and aristocratic individuals in Grenoble and its environs. The two groups may have been in some sense connected, but for the purposes of studying their social standing we must separate them.

One of the most distinguished of the early converts to the new gospel was undoubtedly Anémond de Coct, seigneur of le Châtelard, near Theys in the Isère. He was a knight of Rhodes and probably a son of the Hugues de Coct who was *auditeur* of the Grenoble *Chambre des Comptes* in 1477. He travelled to Wittenberg, and is traditionally supposed to have persuaded Luther to write to Carlo III of Savoy, in the hope of winning him over. In the mid-1520s he was established at Baden, and was to die at Schaffhausen.[1]

One of Coct's early converts was the Franciscan Pierre de Sébiville. On Coct's instigation Zwingli wrote him a long letter of support in December 1523; Oecolampadius did the same early in 1524. Sébiville set about the conversion of the *avocat-général* of the Grenoble *parlement*. One of Sébiville's associates at this stage was Amédée or Aimé Meigret, a Dominican and bachelor of theology. Meigret preached reformed ideas in his native Lyon, then at Grenoble on 25 April 1524. Shortly after these demonstrations Meigret had to flee back to Lyon; he was then hauled before the

---

[1] Arnaud, *Protestants du Dauphiné*, I, 7–10; Herminjard, I, 128, 151, 203; for modifications to the traditional story, see J. J. Hemardinquer, 'Les Protestants de Grenoble au xvie siècle d'après des études récentes', *BSHPF* 111 (1965), 15 f.

Sorbonne and fined. Sébiville was also arrested and was only set free, it was alleged, thanks to 'the support of the powerful'. The two both planned to preach Lutheranism again at Lyon in Lent 1525, but were forestalled; Sébiville may have been burnt at Grenoble.[2]

These individuals were mostly from the clergy; they also appealed to the higher classes, trying to convert the *noblesse* of either kind. They were also distinct from traditional heretics in their learning. Sébiville's correspondence was conducted in Latin. Coct had Luther's letter, claimed to be for Carlo III, and Zwingli's to Sébiville, issued in printed form. Meigret printed his sermon of 1524, and Sébiville issued some lost works.[3]

Meigret's sermon preached at Grenoble shows his learning very clearly, despite the fact that it is a vernacular harangue, and deals with the fairly down-to-earth theme of the evils of clerical celibacy. On the one hand Meigret trounced the ban on priestly marriage as 'inique, diabolique, . . . pernicieux, detestable, erroné', and said it was the work of 'Faulx Semblant', a character of the *Roman de Renard*; on the other he cited the practice of the Greek Church, as described by the Latin doctors, the opinion of Paphnutius versus the decrees of the council of Nicea, and the sentiments of Augustine and Ambrose regarding commandments added to the word of God. Meigret was not afraid to introduce a Latin tag into the text of a public sermon.[4] In the years before his conversion, moreover, Meigret had published two works of *Quaestiones* on Aristotelian physics.[5]

Guillaume Farel is undoubtedly the most famous of the early protestants in the Dauphiné. However, he is significant here in the context of his family and relatives. Guillaume

[2]   Arnaud, *Protestants du Dauphiné*, I, 10–16, Herminjard, I, 173, 184, 193, 203, 280, 308, 313; P. France, 'Les Protestants à Grenoble au xvie siècle', *Cahiers d'histoire*, 7 (1962), 319 ff.

[3]   Arnaud, *Protestants du Dauphiné*, I, 8, 10; *Le Dauphiné, receuil de textes historiques*, ed. H. Blet, E. Esmonin, and G. Letonnelier (Paris and Grenoble, 1938), p. 104.

[4]   *Le Dauphiné . . . textes historiques*, pp. 105–7.

[5]   A. Meigret, *Quaestiones . . . in libros de Celo et mundo Aristotelis (s. l., 1514); Quaestiones . . . in libros de Generatione et corruptione Aristotelis* (Paris, 1519).

himself dabbled in the ideas of the Meaux circle, studying at Paris between 1510 and 1522. He has traditionally been supposed to have preached heresy after his return to Gap in 1522, and to have been warned about this by the bishop's vicar-general in 1523, although this rests on speculation.[6]

In 1532 Farel seems to have converted the rest of his family, with dramatic results. Gauchier Farel gave up his post as secretary to the cathedral chapter of Gap, and was to enter the service of a protestant German mercenary captain and work to alleviate the troubles of the Piedmontese Vaudois. When a relative, Antoine Aloat, came to Gap to enquire about purchasing Gauchier's position in November 1532, he was subjected to an intensive instruction in heresy from another brother, Jean-Jacques Farel. Aloat's public spreading of protestantism thereafter led to Jean-Jacques being imprisoned by the bishop of Gap. About 1536 he escaped and on 14 February 1537 the brothers Guillaume, Claude, and Jean-Jacques Farel were made *bourgeois* of Geneva.[7]

The Farel and Aloat families were closely related. Antoine Aloat, a notary from Manosque, was the son of Sauveur Aloat and Louise Aymin, his noble wife by a second marriage. Aloat himself married 'noble et honnête Toinon Riquette', daughter of 'noble Honorat Riquet', *coseigneur* of Sieyes, near Digne. Honorat's wife and Toinon's mother was Philippe Farel, daughter of Antoine Farel and Anastasie d'Orcières.[8]

The Farel family derived its status from the first of that name to live in Gap, the notary François Farel. He was born about 1427–8, moved to the town in mid-century, and was a notary to the Empire and the Dauphiné from 1462. One of his sons, Sébastien, married a noble lady in 1505 and made claims to nobility for himself, which the consuls of Gap rejected. Antoine, Sébastien's elder brother, married into the d'Orcières family. This latter family was not only noble; it also had strong links with the Church. It included Chérubin

[6] Arnaud, *Protestants du Dauphiné*, I, 3–6; G. de Manteyer, 'Les Farel, les Aloat et les Riquet', *BSEHA* (1908), 51–2; *Les Farel, les Aloat et les Riquet* (Gap, 1912), p. 108; Hermardinquer, op. cit., 17.

[7] Manteyer, 'Les Farel, les Aloat et les Riquet', 53–9; C. Charronnet, *Les Guerres de religion et la société protestante dans les Hautes-Alpes* (Gap, 1861), pp. 9–12, 16–18; Arnaud, *Protestants du Dauphiné*, I, 19–21.

[8] Manteyer, 'Les Farel, les Aloat et les Riquet', 36–9.

d'Orcières, prior of Jarjayes, canon of Gap and of Sisteron, bishop elect of Sisteron, and ultimately bishop of Digne.[9] Presumably it also included André d'Orcières, prior of Chorges in 1501.[10]

The sons of Antoine Farel seemed likely to follow the clerical traditions of their connections. The eldest, François, became a priest and was ultimately prior of Notre-Dame de Puy-Servier at Valserres. Jean-Gabriel studied at the della Rovere college at Avignon, and became rector of a chaplaincy in the cathedral of Gap. Gauchier and Claude were both notaries, the former for the chapter, as we have seen. Both married daughters of *noble* Gaspard de Beauvois, nieces of the sacristan of Gap. Jean-Jacques was a canon of Gap for a while. Guillaume studied theology, and related in later life how he had once been passionately devoted to the cult of the cross.[11]

A letter of Antoine Saunier's shows his connection with this clique. After meeting the Vaudois in autumn 1533, Saunier travelled to Provence. At Villeneuve, north-east of Manosque, he met Guillaume's sister and her husband, Honorat Riquet; with them were Antoine Aloat and his wife, to whom Saunier passed on Farel's best wishes and delivered his letters. When Gauchier Farel wrote pseudonymously to Guillaume on 24 July 1535, and related his journey with Saunier to visit 'les frères', he told how he himself had used the name of Anthoyne Munyer, and Saunier passed himself off as 'Bonti Riquet'; both said they were merchants from Digne.[12] Although a native of Moirans, near Grenoble, rather than the Gapençais, Saunier was clearly very much involved with this set of families.

It will now perhaps be clear that the first protestants of the Dauphiné were, like the obscure individuals who spoke to the Vaudois colloquy in August 1532, 'grands clercz et docteurs', 'religieux', and 'gentilz hommes'.[13] That is to say, they came from those very classes of which no members whatever appear amongst the later medieval Waldenses.[14]

[9] Ibid., 39–41, 43, 47 f.   [10] *BP*, II, fo. 20ʳ.
[11] Manteyer, 'Les Farel, Les Aloat et les Riquet', 48–51; Arnaud, *Protestants du Dauphiné*, I, 4 f.
[12] Herminjard, III, 83, 321 ff.
[13] Audisio, *Barbe et l'inquisiteur*, pp. 56 f., 107 f.   [14] See above, ch. 1 (iii).

It is very surprising, therefore, that some of them should take such pains and risks to evangelize a group so far removed from their own sympathies and social origins. These differences were to present all sorts of problems for the evangelizers and their hearers.

(ii) The settled pastors

An important change in the relations of Waldenses and reformers took place when the latter first began to send several pastors as more or less permanent ministers to specific areas in the Alps from the mid-1550s. The uncertainty produced by occasional visits from a few men like Saunier and Olivétan ceased. It is therefore important to establish how well matched this new class of ministers was to the social types found amongst its new charges.

The first question is whether at this stage all the pastors of the valleys were in fact foreigners sent by the reformers. At his trial Giafredo Varaglia related how he had been at a congregation of the valley parishes at Combe de Villar in the autumn of 1557. There were twenty-four ministers present, of which he said 'the greater part' had been sent by Calvin and other ministers of Geneva, at the request of the churches of the valleys.[15] Augusto Armand Hugon remarked that at this period no pastor originated from the valleys, unless he were, like Gilles des Gilles, a surviving *barbe*.[16] This implies that there were a few who were not new arrivals. Jalla identified those former *barbes* who participated in the synod of 1564 as being Gilles des Gilles and François Laurens.[17]

The Val Chisone affords some further examples of pastors who may not have been imported. Laurent Pinatel (Laurenzo Pignatello) and Philippe and Hugues Pastre were all three ministers in 1564;[18] both families were deeply involved in

[15] Crespin, 1565 edn., pp. 895 f.; Jalla, 'Synodes vaudois', 471 ff.; V. Vinay, *Facoltà Valdese di Teologia (1855-1955)* (Torre Pèllice, 1955), p. 15.

[16] A. Armand Hugon, 'Popolo e chiesa alle valli dal 1532 al 1561', *BSSV* 110 (1961), 17; also his *Storia dei Valdesi II*, p. 15.

[17] Jalla, 'Synodes vaudois', 475, n. 16.

[18] Morland, *History of the Evangelical Churches*, p. 186; Miolo, *Historia breve e vera*, ed. Balmas, pp. 112 f.; CUL MS Dd. 3. 35, fo. 41^r; Jalla, 'Synodes vaudois', 475, 481; Pazè Beda, *Riforma e cattolicesimo*, pp. 30, n. 68, 31, 45 f., 49.

Alpine heresy early in the 1500s.[19] Some cases fall into both categories: for instance, Daniel Bermont was enrolled at Geneva in 1559, and became a minister, but was a native of Pragelas;[20] Melchior (or Merchiot) di Dio came originally from Torre Pèllice, and was made minister at Villar, although he had apparently been a priest before his conversion.[21]

In the Dauphiné likewise, one André Ripert of Fressinières, of a traditionally Vaudois family, enrolled in the Genevan academy in 1559, and later became minister to his home parish.[22] The Genevan *Livre du Recteur* also lists several students at Geneva about 1559-64, who came from towns and valleys in Saluzzo with a heretical tradition: François Guérin and Laurent Pellot from Dronero; Jean-Pierre Buschet from Chieri; Michel Berton of Praviglielmo; and Jean-François Galatée, later minister at Saluzzo.[23] Later in the century more Piedmontese became students in Geneva; in 1578 one Antoine Bonjour of Angrogna; in 1583 Daniel Chanforan, also of Angrogna; in 1597 Pierre Gilles of Torre Pèllice and Jacques Gay, a Piedmontese.[24]

In spite of these exceptions or qualifications, however, the main point still stands. For at least a generation after 1555, what Giorgio Peyrot called 'a new Waldensian ruling class' was raised up by the structures of Genevan church-government.[25] These new ministers were, for the most part, like the early protestants in the Dauphiné, men of learning, and in some cases probably of high birth as well.

Estienne Noel is a case in point. He came originally from Troyes, and was pastor in Montbéliard from 1540 until his

---

[19] *BP*, I, fos. 253ᵛ, 258ʳ, 263ʳ, and II, fos. 396ʳ-8ʳ, 404ᵛ.

[20] *LHG*, p. 163; *LRAG*, I, 81, and II, 183; Jalla, *Storia della riforma in Piemonte*, p. 186; Pazè Beda, *Riforma e cattolicesimo*, p. 48; Miolo, *Historia breve*, pp. 113f.

[21] S. Foà, 'Valli del Piemonte', *BSHV* 24 (1907), 8; *LHG*, p. 36; Jalla, 'Synodes vaudois', 476; Miolo, *Historia breve*, p. 114; see also Gilles, 1644 edn., p. 70.

[22] *LHG*, p. 166; *LRAG*, I, 82; Miolo, loc. cit.; T. Gay, 'Esquisse d'histoire vaudoise', *BSHV* 24 (1907), 26.

[23] *LHG*, pp. 79, 189; *LRAG*, I, 81, 83f., 85, 88; Gilles, 1881 edn., I, 410f.; Arnaud, *Protestants du Dauphiné*, I, 522-4.

[24] Vinay, *Facoltà valdese*, p. 17, based on Jalla, *Storia della riforma in Piemonte*, pp. 381ff.

[25] G. Peyrot, 'Influenze franco-ginevrine', in *Ginevra e l'Italia* (Firenze, 1959), p. 223.

expulsion in 1555; in that year he met Gilles des Gilles and went to the valleys. He was pastor at Grenoble from 1562 to 1565 and was evidently in great demand from his congregations. In 1563 he wrote in some perplexity to Théodore de Bèze several times, pointing out how he was being pulled two ways, with the consuls and consistory of Grenoble trying to keep him from the clutches of those of Angrogna, and telling the church of Angrogna to be content with such pastors as it had.[26] Noel wrote of the Piedmontese valleys with a thinly disguised shudder, pointing out how he bore great affection to those of Angrogna, but that his age made him unfit for the mountains; he had lost all his books; the members of his family still at Angrogna were in great distress because of their separation from him; Angrogna and its people should feel that they had had enough out of him.[27] He did return, nevertheless, between 1565 and 1574, but later went back to Grenoble, and ended his career at Gap. The *Histoire Ecclésiastique* gave a glowing account of his work in restoring the morale of the Grenoble protestants, when they were under attack in autumn 1562.[28] Noel also stood high in the esteem of Marguerite de France, duchess of Savoy.[29]

Scipione Lentolo (1525-99), perhaps a less popular figure than Noel, was highly educated. Born in Naples, he studied at Venice and became a doctor of Theology in 1549. In 1555 he turned to the reform and married; shortly afterwards he was imprisoned for two years. In 1558 he reached Geneva and was trained for the ministry. Elected to be pastor at Carignano, he turned down the task, and went instead to Angrogna in November 1559.[30] He was expelled from the valleys of Piedmont in 1566, and spent the last years of his life in the region of the Valtelline, where he combined his ministry at

---

[26] Jalla, 'Synodes vaudois', 474, n. 1; Bèze, *Corresp.*, II, 42, n. 6, and IV, 149, 272-4; E. Comba, 'Lettres ecclésiastiques à la vén. compagnie . . . '. *BSHV* 16 (1898), 25-30.

[27] Comba, 'Lettres ecclésiastiques à la vén. compagnie', 24f.; Bèze, *Corresp.*, IV, 272f.

[28] *HE*, III, 284f.

[29] Jalla, 'Synodes vaudois', loc. cit.; Bèze, *Corresp.*, IV, 149, n.1, based on a letter in *BSHPF* 28 (1879).

[30] Lentolo, pp. 4f.; J. A. Tedeschi, 'An addition to the correspondence of Theodore Beza', 440, n. 5.

Chiavenna with forming the canons of Italian grammar[31] and taking part in the dogmatic disputes which disrupted the churches of the Grisons.[32]

Lentolo's first letter to Calvin after his arrival in Angrogna shows very clearly how ill his preparation had fitted him for a mountain pastorate. He began his letter with a florid paragraph of humanist Latin, apologizing for not having met Calvin before leaving Geneva, but pleading that the 'brute monkish barbarity' of his education had made his spoken Latin so bad that he could not speak with Calvin face to face at all easily. He told how, when he arrived in Angrogna, the brethren had doubts about him, because he did not carry any letter of recommendation. At this he took offence, as his guide to the valleys was the Vaudois' own messenger. Only when one of their number was ready to testify that Lentolo had Calvin's and Viret's recommendation was he accepted fully. He reported this dispute in still more ornamented Latin.[33] In a letter sent in October 1561, he was still anxious to show off; writing of the peace after the treaty of Cavour, he remarked how the 'leader' (he used the Greek word ἀρχος) 'still has a wolf by both ears, and will, I think, try nothing on his own; although he wishes nothing more than to destroy good people'.[34]

We know less about other ministers; but they seem to have been of the same type. Dominique Vignaux, the translator of Miolo's short history of the Waldenses, was also described by Perrin and Gilles as the 'Sieur de Vignaux'.[35] Humbert Rémond (or Artus) came to the valleys late in 1555

---

[31]　S. Lentulus, *Italicae Grammatices praecepta ac ratio* (Geneva, 1567, wrongly dated 1557), and subsequent editions in 1580, and as *Praxis Grammaticae Italicae* (1598).

[32]　Jalla, 'Synodes vaudois', 475, n.13; Lentulus, *Responsio orthodoxa pro edicto illustriss. D. D. trium foederum Rhaetiae ... adversus haereticos promulgata* (*s. l.*, 1592); *Bullingers Korrespondenz mit den Graubündern*, ed. by T. Schiess (Basel, 1904–6), esp. vol. III; T. Gay, 'Scipione Lentolo', *BSHV* 23 (1906), 104–7.

[33]　*CO*, XVII, cols. 668f.

[34]　*CO*, XIX, cols. 68f. The classical proverb 'to have a wolf by the ears' derives from Terence's *Phormio*, and means that it is equally dangerous to keep one's grip on a problem or to let go; it is found in Erasmus's *Adages*. The 'leader' to whom Lentolo referred may have been the duke himself, or a local provincial governor.

[35]　Perrin, *Vaudois*, pp. 48, 55f.; Gilles, 1644 edn., p. 55.

or early in 1556, and became minister at Bòbbio Pèllice. Gilles related how, when at Artus's arrival some monks and magistrates came to dispute with him, he said he was willing, provided due forms were observed, to dispute with them in Latin, Greek, or Hebrew, according to their choice, on any topic they cared to propose to him; hearing this, 'they retired in confusion and left him in peace'.[36]

Other pastors were at least graduates or university-trained. During Noel's absence at Grenoble he was replaced at Angrogna by François Guérin and François Truchi. Guérin, although a native of Dronero, had studied at Turin and matriculated in Geneva in 1559. François Truchi had spent the years 1559-63 at Geneva.[37] Varaglia, as we have already seen, was a high-ranking Italian churchman of the *spirituali* type.[38] Girolamo Miolo, designated as minister for Chiomonte in 1564, came from a bourgeois family of Pinerolo which had contacts in Geneva by this time.[39]

While a few ministers, in this early period, were probably slightly familiar with the ways of the valleys, for the most part those who were sent from Geneva, whether French or Italian, must have been quite out of keeping with the level of education, and indeed the language, of most of their flocks. In being thus of comparatively elevated social origins and education, they were quite typical of the products of the Genevan academy at its early stage.[40] The most successful of them, like Noel, were accomplished leaders whose services might soon be needed elsewhere. Martin Tachard, the most militant of the first ministers in the Pragelato, was moved to Montauban after 1561.[41] For such men to acquire a following amongst the introverted and self-righteous communities of the Vaudois, great strength of character and leadership would be required. The reception which they received from the Vaudois, moreover, could be very equivocal.

[36] Jalla, 'Correspondance ecclésiastique vaudoise', 75-7; Gilles, 1881 edn., I, 88 f.; Jalla, 'Synodes vaudois', 476, n. 6.
[37] *LHG*, pp. 174, 189; *LRAG*, I, 81; Bèze, *Corresp.*, IV, 274, n. 8.
[38] Above, ch. 10 (vi).
[39] Miolo, *Historia breve*, pp. 35 f.; *LHG*, p. 42; *LRAG*, I, 85; Jalla, 'Synodes vaudois', 476, n. 9.
[40] See on this Kingdon, *Geneva and the Coming of the Wars of Religion*, pp. 5-12.   [41] *CO*, XX, cols. 186 f.

12. The Attitudes of the Waldenses to the Reform

We have very little information indeed about the way in which the Waldensian people or their native pastors responded to the new arrivals in their midst. This chapter therefore can only offer an impression. This impression is that the coming of the Reformation was not particularly welcomed by the Waldenses; and that their reluctance or slowness to take the new forms of worship into their culture may explain why it took several decades for protestantism in this area to take on authentically popular forms.

(i) The sect *en masse*

Pierre Griot, speaking of the congregation of late August 1532, provided the clearest evidence of general hostility to the reformed message amongst the Waldenses.[1] He recalled how the *religieux*, Augustin and Thomas, had asserted justification by faith in the face of doubts from the 'gentlemen' Charles and Adam. These *religieux* made a tirade against good works as 'superstitious', and blamed the Vaudois for a preoccupation with ceremonial exceeding that of the catholics.[2] According to Griot, their message left the *barbes* 'scandalized';[3] this was for several rather odd reasons. The *barbes* were offended by the instruction to ignore works and ceremonies, because they said they had always taught their people to pray to God before they ate or drank anything.[4] They were offended at the precept that worship should be made only with the interior mind; and they were outraged

---

[1] His testimony is in Paris, Archives Nationales MS J 851, fos. 183ᵛ-6ᵛ, as published by Audisio, *Barbe et l'inquisiteur*, pp. 103-9.

[2] Audisio, *Barbe et l'inquisiteur*, pp. 108 f.; compare below, ch. 14 (i), where Bucer advised against too much care over regulations on conduct.

[3] 'Escandalisés'.   [4] On this, see *CUL G*, fo. 67ʳ⁻ᵛ, and above, ch. 6 (iv).

when their celibacy was condemned, because they said it was against their custom to marry, and some of them were already old.[5] Jean de Roma did not ask Griot about this meeting at any other stage; at no point, therefore, did Griot suggest that the message of these reformers was heard with anything but hostility and surprise.

Likewise, in the Angrogna propositions of 12 September 1532, we see the signs of disputation rather than concord or assimilation. Besides the reference to theses being 'disputed', several of the short clauses in the text contain riders which suggest there was argument. After six clauses there is a phrase introduced by 'the conclusion is', or 'it is concluded', implying that the issue had been controversial. After eight other clauses there is a sentence which appends a demonstration of a point by a text of scripture, implying that some proof was called for.[6]

Furthermore, nothing could be less like a coherent and agreed declaration of faith than these propositions: two of them appear to be missing; the seventh and the ninth have been scored through with diagonal lines; the only part which is unequivocally protestant in theology[7] is written in a hand altogether dissimilar to the rest of the manuscript; this last section contains the only, not very clear, statement that the previous statements are grounds for union on which all the participants were agreed; and that statement of unity may only refer to a clause on the sacraments.[8]

Although Antoine Saunier supplied some contrary indications, his claims that the people were on his side are heavily qualified. He noted that 'false brethren' had been persuading the people to be hostile to him, and that the 'council' which he had hoped would settle the issue of public preaching had not yet come about.[9] In 1533, Saunier was again in trouble

---

[5] Audisio, *Barbe et l'inquisiteur*, p. 109. On the celibacy of the *barbes* see TCD MS 259, pp. 15 f.; and Vinay, *Confessioni de fede . . . riformati*, pp. 38 f.

[6] Vinay, *Confessioni de fede . . . riformati*, pp. 139-43.

[7] See below, ch. 14 (ii).

[8] The disorderly character of the propositions in the Dublin MS has led to suggestions that the tidied-up version published by Perrin in *Vaudois*, pp. 157-61, was the definitive one and that the manuscript was simply 'notes de séance'; the tidy version was Perrin's work alone, and no alternative manuscript version exists.

[9] Herminjard, II, 452-4.

with the Vaudois because of the delay in the printing venture, when he described how

> J'ai heu des reproches, à cause de l'imprimerie, car ilz disent que je suys le promoteur de l'affaire, et qu'il y a ung an passé que les deniers sont deslivrés, et qu'il n'ya rien de faict . . .[10]

By the late seventeenth century it was accepted that the contacts between the Waldenses and the early reformers had produced dissension in the ranks of the former. The Jesuit author of the seventeenth-century *Histoire Véritable* pointed out how some *barbes* had been to Bohemia after 1532, and had received instructions from the heretics there not to change their faith. He then rather spoilt the point by claiming that these *barbes* were called Georges Morel and Pierre Masson.[11] It was, of course, undisputed that late in 1532 or early in 1533 two conservative *barbes*, Daniel de Valence and Jean de Molines, went to consult with the Bohemian brethren, and that as a result the brethren wrote their reproachful letter of 25 June 1533 to the Alpine Vaudois.[12] This letter presumably conserved some of the tone of Daniel's and Jean's report. It remarked how some 'meddlers or corrupters of Christian doctrine from Switzerland'[13] had been mingling with the Vaudois; they had caused a grievous schism, which had led to a persecution. The brethren expressed surprise that the Waldenses had allowed themselves to be imposed upon by those of whose good faith they had little or no experience.[14] According to the Bohemian theologian Matej Cervenka, Jean de Molines met Calvin some time between 1538 and 1540; as a result of this interview Calvin came to feel quite at odds with these Waldenses, because he felt they laid far too much emphasis on merit as a factor in justification.[15] Daniel and Jean were evidently irreconcilable.

At a much later date, Jehan Vernou, entrusted with a mission similar to Saunier's, came back with roughly similar

---

[10]   Ibid., II, 81.

[11]   Provana di Collegno, 'Rapports de Guillaume Farel', 260–2.

[12]   Herminjard, III, 63–9; Vinay, *Confessioni di fede . . . riformati*, pp. 144–51.

[13]   'Sacrarum scripturarum doctrinaeque christianae lusores dicamus an corruptores, nescimus, ab Helveciis . . . .'

[14]   Vinay, *Confessioni di fede . . . riformati*, pp. 144–6.

[15]   Gonnet and Molnár, *Vaudois an moyen âge*, pp. 317 f.

impressions. In Balboutet he and Lauversat had been able to preach openly to the faithful; to others they had announced the word 'par devis privés'. At Fenestrelle they required protection, because two or three of the chief men of the village were reluctant to receive them, as they were itinerant preachers. When they came nevertheless, some of these 'bonnes gens furent bien faschés'. At Angrogna the ministers had to urge the people to do something about finding more pastors.[16]

Scipione Lentolo had a cool and cautious reception when he first came to Angrogna in 1559.[17] When he recollected his experience as a pastor, he saw this coolness as part of a quite general sinful disobedience of the Waldenses towards their ministers, which he expected would in due course bring down on the former the punishment of God. In the first place, the people were very reluctant to come to hear his sermons; they would come on a Sunday, but mostly not on any other days. Although the people said they were poor, and needed to work instead, Lentolo thought it was usually the poor who came to Church more often than the rich. 'What', he asked, 'if the minister were to give to everyone one *écu* when he preached? Would you come? To be sure you would, and in such a crowd that you would fill the roads like ants in summer! . . . So how can you deny . . . that you are despising the word of God, since you rate it at less than one *écu*?'[18]

In other ways Lentolo found the Vaudois' behaviour towards their ministers disrespectful and deficient in loyalty. He would urge his flock not to go to law before the 'unfaithful'; instead he found that some would sue ministers who threatened to deprive them of the sacraments. When a minister preached against some vice, avarice for example, the people might react violently. Lentolo described their response thus: 'Tell me, I pray you, what kind of a rage and passion do you fly into? What hatred do you conceive against your pastor? . . . What would you do, if God did not restrain you through the good people who uphold him?'[19]

Lentolo's congregation had been impatient of the moral

---

[16] Vernou in *BSHPF* 17 (1868), 16-19; *CO*, XV, cols. 575-8; see above, ch. 10 (vi).
[17] Above, ch. 11 (ii).
[18] *Lentolo MS*, pp. 493-4.   [19] Ibid., pp. 497 f.

discipline of the Calvinist church. Its members went to great lengths to conceal their faults from judges and to avoid punishment, and allowed their valleys to be a sanctuary for swindlers and counterfeiters. When a minister had preached in favour of the execution of a swindler, the people had murmured against him. Finally, and perhaps most fatally of all, when Lentolo lost his temper after the people refused to elect those he recommended for the posts of syndics and *conseillers*, some people accused him of wishing to make everything go his way, of wanting all affairs to be in his hands, and to 'play the signore'.[20]

Some of this evidence is perhaps not enough to prove great reluctance to accept the Reformation amongst the Waldenses, since they ran such risks by receiving Calvinist preachers at all, as Lentolo acknowledged.[21] However, a few were certainly hostile, and most were probably lukewarm; their new ministers resembled more the old priests than the *barbes* who had reaffirmed the Waldenses' traditional morality. No wonder, in this case, that the reformers spoke of Piedmont as 'the most perilous of all the Lord's harvests'.[22]

(ii)   Some special cases

Since there clearly was some faction amongst the Waldenses in the 1530s which was in favour of inviting the reformers, we must try to establish who were its members, what were their origins and their attitudes in the early stages of the talks. Here it will be suggested that there was amongst the *barbes*, especially in Provence, a fairly definable type of 'protestantizing' heretic. One may even detect a clique.

(a)   *Georges Morel*

Most of the traditional stories of the meetings of the *barbes* with the reformers make Morel a central figure. His name is widely mentioned, sometimes in the Embrunais form 'Maurel'.[23] Most of the sources add that he was a Waldensian

---

[20]   Ibid., pp. 500-3, and 580-1.   [21]   Ibid., pp. 483, 493.
[22]   Fortunatus Andronicus to Bucer, 29 April 1533, in Herminjard, III, 44.
[23]   Crespin, 1565 edn., p. 189; Camerarius, *Historica Narratio*, p. 305; *HE*, I, 36; Perrin, *Vaudois*, pp. 157, 210; Morland, *History of the Evangelical Churches*, pp. 185, 224; Fromment, *Actes et gestes*, pp. 2f.

barbe, and that he came from Fressinières in the Dauphiné.
Equally, most associate him with the history of the Waldensian
communities in Provence. He is credited with the compilation
of the dossier on the talks with Oecolampadius and Bucer
in 1530, and is mentioned in that document twice.[24] His
scrupulous questioning has led to suggestions that he was
more cautious and less enthusiastic than the *barbe* of
Angrogna, Martin Gonin.[25]

If Morel indeed came from Fressinières and the Vaudois
families there, one would expect his family name to appear in
the records of the crusades in the 1480s. In fact, there is no
evidence whatever that a Vaudois called Morel ever lived in
Fressinières, l'Argentière, or Vallouise. On the other hand,
there were many catholic Morels around Embrun at the end
of the Middle Ages. A Georges Morel of Embrun represented
Archbishop Baile at Vienne on 5 October 1487, and witnessed
a privilege given by Cattaneo to the archbishop's brother in
1488.[26] The *coseigneur* of Fressinières, Fazy de Rame, dealt
with many Morels, some of them educated men who kept
accounts or were in orders; none of them lived in the higher
valleys.[27] On 16 May 1499 an André Maurel of Crots received
institution to a chaplaincy at Baratier, near Embrun.[28] When
the bishop of Angoulême carried out his assault on heretics
near Bardonècchia in 1514 he was helped by two local landlords, Gabriel and Claude Morel.[29] Pierre Morel, canon of
Valence, left a bequest for scholars at the Collège Royal
from which Embrun benefited; Jean Morel of Embrun was
a noted poet and humanist, and a friend of Erasmus and
Joachim du Bellay.[30]

If Morel was probably not a conventional Vaudois peasant
from the uplands of Fressinières, then what was he? If the
documents attributed to him, and the confession of the

---

[24] TCD MS 259, pp. 7, 116.

[25] Gonnet and Molnár, *Vaudois au moyen âge*, p. 307.

[26] *BP*, II, fo. 223^r; Marx, p. 156; P. Guillaume, 'Notes et documents', *BCTHS*,
Ann. 1913 (1914), 421, based on ADH-A MS G 2763, fo. 140^v.

[27] *Fazy*, II, sects. 141-2, 223, 364, 385, 1186, 1266, 1273, 1286, 1290.

[28] ADH-A MS G 2767, fos. 185^v-6^r.

[29] Chorier, *Histoire générale du Dauphiné*, II, 512.

[30] A. Sauret, *Essai historique sur la ville d'Embrun* (Gap, 1860), pp. 287-90.

Vaudois of Cabrières from 1533,[31] are indeed by him, he could write fluently in French, Latin, and Provençal. In the dossier of the talks in 1530 he cited the classical proverb about Homer sometimes nodding;[32] when he asked Oecolampadius and Bucer about usury, he referred to the *Opus imperfectum in Matthaeum*, which he ascribed to Chrysostom, only to be told that it was an Arian work.[33] The sources called Morel an 'homme bien instruict, lequel ils avoyent entretenu aux escoles', and this surely proves the fact.[34] Possibly Morel was also the learned *barbe* 'Georges' from Cabrièrette whom Pierre Griot said he had met.[35]

It is surely impossible to maintain that Morel was born and brought up within the context of rural dissent of the type we have studied hitherto. He probably came from origins which were clerical and widely literate, even though, by some means, he came to be versed in the ways of the heretics as well. When he approached the reformers Morel already knew the controversial questions to ask, for instance regarding the conflict on free will between Erasmus and Luther.[36] Although, by 1530, Morel was a *barbe* in Provence, he had entered the sect from an unusual background. He would have been especially keen, therefore, to meet the more intellectual reformers.

(b) *Anthoine Guérin*

It is chiefly in the record of Pierre Griot's trial that Guérin emerges as an important figure amongst the Waldenses. Griot travelled from Avignon into Provence early in 1532 in the company of this 'bonnetier d'Avignon'. Later Guérin told him how he had been a Dominican friar, but had laid aside his habit in Italy, had married at Rouen, and had taken to preaching in secret in Paris, Meaux, and Rouen.[37] It is just possible that this Guérin was the same as Guérin Muète.

---

[31]   As suggested below, ch. 14 (iii).

[32]   TCD MS 259, p. 5; Vinay, *Confessioni di fede . . . riformati*, pp. 72 f.

[33]   TCD MS 259, p. 104; Vinay, *Confessioni di fede . . . riformati*, pp. 46 f., 108 f.   [34]   Crespin, 1565 edn., p. 189; *HE*, I, 36.

[35]   Audisio, *Barbe et l'inquisiteur*, p. 102.

[36]   TCD MS 259, p. 111; Vinay, *Confessioni di fede . . . riformati*, p. 46.

[37]   Audisio, *Barbe et l'inquisiteur*, pp. 72-5, 104.

Muète was also known as 'le bonnetier', and was prominent
in early reformed assemblies in Geneva. He might have come
from Dauphiné or Provence originally.[38] A servant of his was
involved in a trial at Geneva early in 1533.[39]

'Guérin Muète', at least, was closely involved with Farel
and his friends. On 18 November 1532 Farel wrote to Muète
at Geneva, asking anxiously if he had any news of 'Georges'
or of Farel's brothers. He also asked for news about Pierre de
Vingle, the printer of the 1535 Bible, and said that he had
letters for Muète to pass on to 'Martin'.[40] An 'Anthoenne
Guérin de Provence' was formally admitted to Geneva in the
autumn of 1551, which may strengthen the identification.[41]

The Guérin portrayed by Griot was a former friar, a married
protestant ex-cleric; as such he was quite unlike any normal
barbe. However, he was deep in the counsels of the Waldenses.
In late August 1532 he reported to their congregation on the
persecutions of Jean de Roma. Guérin announced to the
assembly that he would take charge of the matter; he was to
sort out his business affairs and see to the needs of his wife
and children, and go to Provence himself to find a solution.[42]

(c) *Martin Gonin*

Gonin's biography has been both amplified and hindered by
hypothesis and speculation. In one authoritative account he
is portrayed as the zealous follower of Farel, contrasted with
the studious and scrupulous Morel.[43] We have little sound
basis for such judgments. No credible source refers unequivocally to a 'Martin Gonin of Angrogna' until a report on Piedmontese heretics dating from 1535;[44] the earliest printed
sources are the martyrologies, which speak only of his capture
and martyrdom in 1536.[45] Before that date we depend on
ambiguous references to a 'Martin'.

---

[38] As suggested by Herminjard, II, 459, n. 1.
[39] H. Delarue, 'Olivétan et Pierre de Vingle à Genève, 1532-3', *Bulletin d'humanisme et renaissance*, 8 (1946), 112.
[40] Herminjard, II, 460. Herminjard suggested that 'Georges' might be Morel and 'Martin' might be Martin Gonin.
[41] *LHG*, p. 21.
[42] Audisio, *Barbe et l'inquisiteur*, pp. 103 f.
[43] Gonnet and Molnár, *Vaudois au moyen âge*, p. 307, as above.
[44] Gilles, 1644 edn., p. 37.   [45] Above, ch. 10 (iv), n. 76.

Martin Gonin was perhaps born about 1500. He may have been the *barbe* 'Martin' who came back to Piedmont from Switzerland in 1526 bringing books of protestant theology.[46] In November 1532 500 *écus* had just been given by a 'Martin' to pay for printing costs, presumably for the Bible. In December 1532 a 'Thomas Italus' wrote to Farel about a 'Lodovicus' who was studying with Viret, and was waiting for money from 'Martin'. In 1535 Pantaleone Bersatore discovered that 'Martin Gounin d'Angrogne' had been teaching the heretics of Provence.[47]

In April 1536 Gonin visited Farel at Geneva, and was returning to Angrogna with letters from Farel and Saunier when he was captured in the Champsaur (perhaps on the Col de Freissinières) by the Sieur de Champoléon. At first he was only suspected of being a spy for the Emperor, and he claimed to be a printer at Geneva. By accident, however, he was discovered to be carrying heretical material, and was interrogated by inquisitors. He admitted his heresy openly and argued with the inquisitors at length. On 16 April 1536 he was drowned by night in the Isère.[48]

Gonin's connection with printing allows some further speculation. His companion in 1536 was one Jehan Girard, who was also a printer. The edition of Olivétan's *Instruction des enfans* published at Geneva in 1533 bore a dedication not from Olivétan (who had to leave Geneva before the work was finished) but from 'M.' to 'son bon frère Ant. Son.', presumably Antoine Saunier. This edition was printed by Pierre de Vingle on a press set up in the house of one Jehan Chautemps, for whom Olivétan claimed to be a 'tutor'. Pierre de Vingle, of course, was to produce a New Testament in Geneva early in 1533, and the complete Bible at Neuchâtel two years later. The 'M.' of the dedication might be none other than Gonin, the printer; the text of the preface apparently does not contradict this hypothesis.[49]

These *barbes* are better known than the others; they are also most likely to be those closest to the reformers. However,

[46]   Gilles, 1644 edn., p. 29.
[47]   Ibid., p. 37 and 1881 edn., I, 58–61; Herminjard, II, 452f., 463.
[48]   Crespin, 1565 edn., pp. 138–40; Gilles, 1644 edn., p. 43.
[49]   Delarue, 'Olivétan et Pierre de Vingle', 115–18.

these people are far too closely involved with Farel and his friends; they cannot but be special cases. We noted that one letter of Farel to Guérin referred to other members of the clique, 'Georges', 'Martin', and Pierre de Vingle. These cases show that the reformers had made some friends amongst the Waldenses, not that the sect as a whole had received them. Moreover, of these 'protestantizing' Waldenses, Guérin was certainly not from traditional Vaudois origins; Morel almost certainly was not; and Gonin, who travelled hither and thither with Saunier and Olivétan, must have grown apart from the rest of the sect. Because a group straddled the two forms of dissent, that does not mean that those two forms had coalesced. The reformers, moreover, took for the most part a very long time to accommodate themselves to the ways and reputation of the Waldenses, as we shall now see.

13. The Waldenses in the Eyes of the Protestant Reformers

It is a little easier to discover the attitudes of the reformers to the Waldenses than vice versa. Printed books from Reformation presses tell us a little; letters tell us far more. In their letters the protestants described their missions to the Vaudois; they mentioned the sufferings of the latter to their colleagues; and they wrote to ask secular powers to show sympathy with the heretics. However, there is a long gap in the series of such letters. Between the end of the Mérindol affair and the mission of Vernou and Lauversat the Waldenses were hardly mentioned, save in a brief exchange between Sleidan and Calvin regarding material for the former's *Commentaries*.[1] We shall therefore consider the periods before and after this gap in turn.

(i) The early correspondence

Nearly forty letters from the period 1530–45 survive to tell us anything about the affairs of the Waldenses, excluding those dating from the mission of Morel and Masson. The vast majority are either from, to, or between a group of five men: Farel, Viret, Calvin, Saunier, and Olivétan. These had all either been involved in the discussions in 1532, or became interested shortly afterwards in the project for the French Bible of 1535. Especially in the late 1530s and early 1540s, moreover, nearly all the references to the Vaudois occur in letters between Calvin and Farel. The Waldenses were at this stage a minority interest amongst the reformers of French-speaking Switzerland.

Even within this small group the mission to the Waldenses seems to have been regarded as a delicate and dangerous

---

[1] This was in 1553–4; see *CO*, XIV, cols. 719–20; XV, cols. 111–14, 231f.

business. Normally reformers on missions or ministers being trained were only described by Christian names or pseudo-nyms.[2] Fortunatus Andronicus mentioned that Olivétan's mission was especially perilous.[3] Such fears, of course, were amply justified by the fate of Martin Gonin when protestant papers were found in his luggage.

Concern for safety, however, cannot completely explain another kind of delicacy shown by the reformers. Even where secrecy was not needed or was unattainable, very few protestant writers referred explicitly to 'Waldenses' or 'Vaudois'; usually they used a circumlocution, like 'the brethren', 'the pious ones', 'our friends'; or they described them by location, as 'the people of the Alps', 'the Piedmontese', or 'the Provençals'. The exceptions to this rule reinforce the impression that the title of the old heretics was a matter for embarrassment. When Farel and Viret in one letter, and Jean Montaigne in another, spoke openly of the 'Waldenses', they took care to link them immediately with the 'Lutherans'.[4] Apart from these instances there is only one occasion each on which Farel, Calvin, and Viret used the term without expla-nation; Christophe Fabri used it twice; Bullinger used it when writing to Ambrose Blaurer, and Sleidan employed it in a letter to Calvin.[5]

With the sole exception of Christophe Fabri, the French speakers were shy about the title of 'Waldenses' where the German speakers were less so. The term meant, in fact, different things to the two groups. Oecolampadius assumed in 1530, for example, that Morel and Masson held the same faith as the descendants of the Bohemians who had presented a confession to the King of Hungary in the 1500s.[6] Several printed books in the sixteenth century used the title of 'Waldenses' to denote the Bohemian brethren;[7] the *Consensus*

---

[2] See esp. Herminjard, II, 460, 464, 466, and III, 321.

[3] Herminjard, III, 44; see above, ch. 12, n. 22.

[4] Herminjard, III, 45, 329.

[5] Ibid., V, 237, 267–71, 281, 306; VII, 16 f.; *CO*, XII, cols. 78 f.; XIV, cols. 719 f.; XV, cols. 111–14.

[6] TCD MS 259, p. 23; Vinay, *Confessioni di fede . . . riformati*, pp. 54–6 and notes.

[7] See for example *Apologia verae doctrinae eorum qui vulgo appellantur Waldenses vel Picardi* (Wittenberg, 1538); *Confessio Waldensium de plerisque nunc controversis dogmatibus . . . scripta*, ed. Matthias Flacius Illyricus (Basel, 1568); B. Lydius, *Waldensia* (Rotterdam, Dordrecht, 1616–17).

Sendomirensis of 1570 was even to call them by that title
when declaring solidarity with orthodox protestants against
anti-Trinitarian heretics.[8] To French speakers, on the other
hand, the name 'Vaudois' could not escape association
with the witch trials held at Arras in the 1460s,[9] and with
suspicions of witchcraft in general; it was bound to make
respectable dissenters uneasy.

Some such worry probably caused impediment to the
attempts made to arrange intercession on the Vaudois' behalf
with the King of France; it is illustrated by some special
pleading in the letters. Farel and Viret sent a manifesto of
protestant solidarity to the sympathetic cantons of Switzerland on 4 August 1535. They described and lamented the
persecution of the 'pious brethren', especially in Provence.
They said the brethren there were 'a great number, but quite
simple and resolute followers of true and Christian religion;
although thus far defamed with many names, because they
preferred to keep to a purer Christianity, than to bind themselves to the damnable rites of the Papacy and to received
custom and superstition'. Their persecutors had forced them
to admit heresies they never held.[10] The reformers added
that 'it is a common cause for all of us who are joined in the
one spirit and bond of charity, and in the one Christ'.[11]

At about the same time as Farel and Viret wrote their
manifesto, the Provençal Vaudois sent a formal plea to
the 'brethren in Germany' in which they expounded their
plight. They said they were 'formerly invidiously known as
Waldenses'; and that they had 'in the general blindness of
the world never so far declined from the true religion that
they did not retain some spark of a better light; they were
defamed with that name[12] in the common speech of the
French, but by the ignorant, who thought that they practised
some acts of sorcery[13] amongst themselves, because they did

---

[8]   Kidd, *Documents*, pp. 658 f.; *Consensus in Fide et Religione* (Heidelberg, 1605), p. 10.

[9]   Above, ch. 8, n. 53.

[10]   This refers to some of the methods used by Jehan de Roma.

[11]   Herminjard, III, 327–32; C. Schmidt, 'Aktenstücke besonders zur Geschichte der Waldenser', *Zeitschrift für die historische Theologie*, 22 (1852), 252–6; T. Balma, 'La Ville de Strasbourg et les Vaudois', *BSSV* 67 (1937), 92–5.

[12]   i.e. Waldenses.   [13]   'Maleficia quaepiam'.

not dare to profess their faith in public'. Now, they said, they had learned more, and their churches had grown to several thousands; they were as defamed as ever, but now called Lutherans instead.[14]

They described the attacks of some inquisitors on them, and an armed raid directed by the Court of Aix at the Vaudois on 19 July 1535. They asked the Germans to intercede for them with the King of France, to see if they might be left in peace, or at least allowed to leave the realm with some of their goods. They asked if the Germans had any vacant land where they might settle. Finally, they insisted that they 'differed in not one doctrine from your churches, in which the Gospel of Christ reigns'.[15]

Wolfgang Capito of Strasbourg, who had possibly met Morel and Masson in 1530,[16] replied to the reformers' letter with sympathy tinged with caution. He said he would ask the German princes and the Swiss towns to send letters in favour of the Vaudois. Nevertheless, he added a remark which seems to indicate that he suspected the protestantism of the Waldenses of being no more than superficial:

> However, I advised the brothers to take care, that nothing be done untimely, beyond their calling, and more than they altogether believe in. Further, that he should instil the living Christ vigorously into the farmers, from an understanding of whom the response against papist abominations may come, constant and firm.[17]

In 1538 Antoine Saunier, who had spoken well of the work of Berne and Basel in interceding late in 1536, was hoping for similar results as he pressed the case of the Piedmontese Vaudois whom Montjehan had attacked. While trying to secure support at Strasbourg, Saunier ran into difficulties when the church of the city asked for evidence that the Vaudois' faith was the same as their own. Saunier objected to this, thinking that it should have been enough for him to say that he himself had taught the Vaudois, and

---

[14]   Schmidt, 'Aktenstücke', 250.

[15]   Ibid., 251 f.; Balma, 'Strasbourg et les Vaudois', 89–92.

[16]   See Vinay, *Confessioni di fede . . . riformati*, pp. 70 f.; Oecolampadius and Zuinglius, *Epistolae*, fo. 199ᵛ.

[17]   Herminjard, III, 337.

that they believed what he did.[18]

Farel faced similar problems when he tried to gain the support of the *conseil* of Berne shortly after the publication of the decree against the people of Mérindol in December 1540. On 14 December the *conseil* told Farel to discuss the matter first with the German protestants at Worms, and see whether they were prepared to send an embassy; if they were not, the Bernese felt their solitary intervention would be worthless, since François had previously written to them in a similar case saying that he would not tolerate that anyone should speak to him on these matters.[19]

The disappointment of the advocates of the Waldenses amongst the protestants was even more acute after the massacres in 1545. The reformers had kept their colleagues informed of events in previous years; as soon as the news of Meynier's attack spread, Farel reported to Calvin on the reaction of François I and the Queen of Navarre. On 24 July Calvin wrote round to Bullinger at Zürich, to Myconius at Basel, to Vadian, and to the ministers at Schaffhausen. Calvin pointed out that the Cardinal de Tournon was the stumbling-block, and how essential it was to arrange an embassy to François. Evil rumours were being spread about the Vaudois, for example that they had been punished for refusing to pay tithes; Calvin asked his correspondents to scotch these.[20]

François I had, however, already pre-empted the reformers. In answer to a letter from the council of Strasbourg complaining about 'the tyrannical, cruel execution', he wrote on 27 June 1545 to tell the people of Strasbourg to mind their own business; but he also suggested that the Vaudois held ideas so outrageous that the protestants would not wish to take their side.[21] In mid-August Viret reported these diplomatic manœuvres to Calvin, who replied that now the Bernese were becoming much cooler in their enthusiasm for the cause. By late August Calvin was urging Farel not to

---

[18]   Ibid., IV, 93 f.; V, 149, n.1, 170-1 and notes; Pascal, 'Ambasciere', *BSBS* XVIII, nos. 1-3 (1913), 87.

[19]   Herminjard, VI, 397, n. 8.

[20]   *CO*, XI, cols. 391 f.; XII, cols. 55 f., 58 f., 62-4, 79-81, 110-18.

[21]   Schmidt, 'Aktenstücke', 258 f.; Balma, 'Strasbourg et les Vaudois', 82 f.

waste his time on a Latin, as opposed to a German, translation of the Mérindol story; in September there were disagreements over messengers, and with a final despairing exchange between Viret and Calvin the matter rested. The Swiss were reluctant to involve themselves in François's disfavour; it was only opinion within France which brought Meynier and Polin to trial in the next reign.[22]

It has been suggested that Calvin's attitude to the Waldenses changed significantly in the late 1530s, after his confrontation with some recalcitrant allies of the Bohemian brethren had estranged him from them.[23] On the basis of the correspondence there seems little evidence for such a change. In the 1540s Calvin was the most active promoter of the Vaudois cause amongst other protestants, and in the 1550s he organized their evangelization. His attitude was consistent, and consistently patronizing. He would take the heretics' side as long as they followed him in doctrine. In 1557, during a later row, Calvin reported how in 1541 he had been sent two Vaudois confessions; he approved the first, but disliked the second.[24] In 1545, he remarked to Farel shortly before the massacre:

It grieved me that they presented a quite different form of confession from that which I gave to Peter . . . I do not know what came into his mind to think it would please everyone . . . I do not marvel at the King's being irritated by the head on the Eucharist. Certainly the Germans will not be pleased with what they say . . .[25]

Any 'solidarity' Calvin showed with the Waldenses, as Waldenses, was bound to be moral rather than doctrinal until ministers had made doctrinal unity established fact. This attitude was probably typical of educated protestants at the time.

(ii) Education, obedience, and advocacy

For the history of protestant attitudes in the period 1555–65

---

[22] *CO*, XII, cols. 133–6, 138–40, 144–7, 155–8, 161f., 164–7, and above, ch. 10 (v).

[23] Gonnet and Molnár, *Vaudois au moyen âge*, p. 318.

[24] *CO*, XVI, cols, 500–2.   [25] Ibid., XII, cols. 62–4.

we rely first of all upon some fifty or more letters. These stressed the need to send ministers to teach the Waldenses; the need to see that the ministers behaved in the approved manner; the importance of the patronage of established protestant powers; and the desire of Calvin and the pastors of Geneva to hear news regularly. From the end of this period Scipione Lentolo's reminiscences supplement the letters in a unique way.

The earliest letters were concerned simply with the anxiety to introduce protestant ministers, beginning with Vernou's first letter.[26] Vernou seems to have felt he was starting from scratch; at his trial he said he was asked if he had met '*barbe* Paul', just as he would have been twenty or eighty years before.[27] From later 1555 to mid-1556 the chief concern of the Genevans was to find suitable ministers to send.[28] One thing mattered above all to the ministers of Geneva: the missionary pastors had to follow the lead of Geneva wherever they were. Viret reported to Calvin that he had interviewed Pierre Guérin to discover his attitude to an Alpine pastorate; he had said 'that in all things he would follow the advice and directions of the brethren'. Of an 'Estienne', either Noel or Fago, Viret wrote to Calvin 'you will advise and direct him in everything'. Viret also said he had met Fago to find out about him; in another letter he reported that 'he will not refuse the charge if he is called, but will obey our advice completely'.[29]

Once they were sent, the ministers were still to be at the disposal of the reformers and the Company of Pastors. Calvin and Farel expressed their concern to hear news of their missions regularly.[30] When making arrangements for Estienne Noel's wife to go to join her husband, Viret referred the matter to Calvin to give orders, adding that Noel's mother-in-law was going as well, which Noel did not wish.[31] When Noel was being torn between the charges of Angrogna and Grenoble, he undertook not to make any move other than as

[26] Vernou in *BSHPF* 17 (1868), 18; *CO*, XV, cols. 577 f.

[27] *CO*, XV, col. 696; Crespin, 1619 edn., fo. 353ᵛ.

[28] *CO*, XVI, col. 189; Bèze, *Corresp.*, I, 184.

[29] *CO*, XVI, cols. 189, 222 f., 523 f.; *Lettres inédites de Pierre Viret*, ed. Barnaud, p. 103.

[30] Jalla, 'Correspondance ecclésiastique vaudoise', 74 f.

[31] *CO*, XVI, cols. 532 f.

directed by Geneva.[32]

The desire of the Genevan church to supervise the Pied-montese could extend to the behaviour of flocks as well as of pastors. When Noel told Calvin in April 1556 that the Vaudois, under threat from the *parlements*, were preparing to fight back, Calvin commented to Viret and Bèze,

This is a new anxiety. As soon as a messenger is ready, I shall try to make their attitudes more gentle. But they have resolved to try any-thing, rather than to give themselves up freely. They think it absurd to flee to the mountains, since hunger and want will draw them out again very quickly.[33]

The fear of sedition was still in the air when Bèze reported to Calvin in November 1557 that Steiger had heard that the Vaudois were rebels, and that the German princes ought not to intercede for them. Bèze said he would write to contradict this impression, but added 'I think the brethren should be warned about this; in fact I wish they had long ago sent their thanks to the four cities'.[34]

Once the ministers were in the valleys, they were expected to be teachers and rulers of their congregations. In theory, therefore, the moral headship of the *barbe*, and the practical leadership of the syndics of heretic villages, should alike have passed to the minister. His duty, as far as Calvin was concerned, was to rule, and to censure if need be. This task was undertaken by Scipione Lentolo, and probably by others, with magisterial zeal.

In his recollections, he felt it was necessary to prove that the Waldenses needed a teaching ministry. If they had had an agreement to 'purge doctrine, and maintain discipline amongst you', there would not have been the scandals and dissensions there were otherwise. St Paul said that he was sent not to baptize, but to preach; so ministers must preach. Moreover, the Waldenses were so ignorant that they needed

---

[32] Bèze, *Corresp.*, IV, 149, 272-4; Kingdon, *Geneva and the Coming of the Wars of Religion*, pp. 43-51.

[33] *CO*, XVI, cols. 102-4; Bèze, *Corresp.*, II, 41 f.

[34] *CO*, XVI, cols. 719 f.; Bèze, *Corresp.*, II, 141 f. The 'four cities' in the last sentence formed the confederation of Berne, Basel, Zürich, and Schaffhausen, the first body to send an embassy to intercede for the Vaudois.

to be taught; they were mostly illiterate, so they could not use the Bible properly; even those articles of religion which they knew by heart, like the Apostles' Creed, had to be explained by the pastor for them to understand them properly. Few of them knew what it meant to say Christ was the Son of God, let alone who Pontius Pilate was. Lentolo brought home this point with a long discourse against those who believed that it was enough to know only so much of religion and no more; one who said such things showed he was one of those destined for damnation.[35]

Fortunately for us, Lentolo broke off his harangue to the people to give some account of his own preaching and catechizing technique, for the benefit of future ministers. The centre of his teaching was of course the sermon. However, since the people were illiterate, he did not expound scriptural texts, which would have been of little use; instead he preached on the Creed, and repeated his sermons many times to drive the points home. Here preaching served the same role as catechizing, since Lentolo felt country people would not tolerate two different forms of instruction.[36]

The sermon took the form of an exposition of a few clauses of the Creed at a time. At the end of the sermon Lentolo devised five or six questions and answers on the text; these were short and simple, to be easily memorized. He provided an example of this method:

Question: What do you mean by this word, 'I believe'?
Answer: That I am certain of everything which is contained in this
             confession of faith.
Q.   Why do you call God Father?
A.   Because he is the father of Our Lord Jesus Christ.
Q.   And for what other reason?
A.   Because he is also Our Father.
Q.   And by what intermediary is he Our Father?
A.   By the intermediary of Our Lord Jesus Christ.

'And that', Lentolo remarked, 'is enough for one Sunday.'[37]

---

[35] *Lentolo MS*, pp. 506-12.   [36] Ibid., pp. 513f.
[37] Ibid., pp. 518, 520. Lentolo's pedagogic method resembles very closely that used by the Thuringian pastor Johann Langepeter: see G. Strauss, 'The Mental World of a Saxon Pastor', in *Reformation Principle and Practice: Essays in honour of Arthur Geoffrey Dickens*, ed. P. N. Brooks (London, 1980), pp. 161-5.

For the rest of the week Lentolo would try to ask every-one about this same set of questions, in the course of up to four gatherings. As he delivered the same sermon twice each Sunday, he expected everyone in the parish to have heard it at least once. Before asking each parishioner about these questions he would repeat the set over again, so that they would have a chance to refresh their memory. Although he acknowledged this method was tedious, he insisted that it was necessary.[38] It does seem possible that Lentolo some-times went to meet his flock, rather than always waiting for them to come to him. Certainly he later remarked that he had had to leave the first parish to which he went after Prali, that of Sondrio in the Valtelline, because by 1567 his arthritis was so bad, and the parts of his parish were so scattered, that the continual travelling around was ruining his health. Later still he told Bullinger how at Angrogna his time was so taken up that he could not read the scriptures or write anything.[39]

Lentolo's condemnation of moral faults in his congregation seems to have been much more controversial than his doctrinal instruction. He was prepared to criticize particular examples of wrongs, and blamed avarice especially. He might act as the conscience of the community, as when he con-demned a rich landowner who cheated a poor widow out of the crops from a piece of land he had bought from her. In other cases he showed an urban intellectual's intolerance of country ways. He quoted in anger the example of a young couple for whose marriage all the arrangements had been made, when suddenly the parents put off the wedding for three months while they wrangled over the precise size of the portions;[40] yet such dealings must have been essential to the structure of rural life.

In other cases Lentolo took the 'culture of the godly' to the mountains and tried to suppress some harmless activities.[41]

---

[38] *Lentolo MS*, pp. 518f.

[39] *Bullingers Korrespondenz mit den Graubündern*, ed. Schiess: Lentolo to Bullinger, 8 Sept. 1567, III, 28f.; Lentolo to Bullinger, 6 April 1575, III, 510f. Lentolo also suffered from gout; see ibid., III, 470.

[40] *Lentolo MS*, p. 525, 523f.

[41] On this issue see P. Burke, *Popular Culture in Early Modern Europe* (London, 1978), pp. 207–34.

When some young men of one village dressed up as women and rampaged through a house, rolling its occupant in the snow, the minister thundered that by Deuteronomy 22:5 such transvestism was an abomination before the Lord; the guilty parties pleaded that it was 'just in play',[42] and it may in fact have been some sort of carnival ritual connected with the calendar. Even more oddly, Lentolo preached against those who took diviners and cunning folk up into the mountains, to show them where mineral ores were to be found, citing a passage in Leviticus 19:31 against conversing with those with familiar spirits.[43] Lentolo here showed himself stricter than Rome; for although the ore-bearing hills of Savoy had been officially declared to be abodes of evil spirits, by a papal benediction of 12 August 1560 they had been pronounced safe for good catholics to work.[44]

The ministers, then, tried to make the Waldenses respectable; for the latter, the reward was to be that powerful and respected protestants would plead their case. The Waldenses were to be sheltered under the protestants' wings on the latter's own terms. In the mid-1550s the inquiries of St-Julien and della Chiesa were reported to the Suisse Romande almost at once, in an anonymous letter early in 1556.[45] Early in 1557, when the threat was more serious, an embassy was planned. The first letter from Bèze and Farel to Bullinger at the start of the moves for the legation, in late April 1557, gave detailed accounts of their instructions. The ambassadors were to see that the King read the confessions[46] but were to give no account of where they found them, so that the Vaudois should not be exposed to the King's anger at those who had stirred up the Swiss against him. If the King asserted that much that was claimed in the accounts of the 1545 massacres was false, the legates were not to insist on the point.[47] The ambassadors themselves were told to use the Mérindol case discreetly; Bullinger was even more cautious,

---

[42] 'Per giuoco'.   [43] *Lentolo MS*, pp. 521, 524f.
[44] B. Fontana, 'Documenti Vaticani contro l'eresia Luterana', 457f.
[45] A. Dufour, 'Un document sur les vallées vaudoises en 1556', *BSSV* 128 (1970), 57–63.
[46] These were the eirenic pieces first produced in 1556; see below, ch. 14 (iii).
[47] Bèze, *Corresp.*, II, 62ff.; *CO*, XVI, cols. 459–61.

apparently advising his delegates to say that the Vaudois of Provence were essentially different from those of Piedmont about whom the protestants were now concerned.[48]

Farel and Bèze used their own doctrine as proof of the doctrine of the Waldenses; they felt, like Saunier in 1538, that they could act as surety for their beliefs. At a diet of the German protestant princes at Frankfurt they presented a document entitled 'The doctrine held by the people falsely defamed with the name of Waldenses, who live in Provence, Dauphiné, and the Alpine valleys'.[49] This listed their beliefs under the heads of their reception of the canon of scripture, their 'reverence and obedience to the ministers', their rejection of heresies condemned by the early Church, their belief in original sin, sanctification and justification by faith, and in regeneration by the Holy Spirit, their rejection of the place of good works, and their use of two sacraments as 'signs and tokens'.[50] The only mention of traditional suspicions attaching to Waldensianism was a final clause which stated that they accepted oaths sanctioned by God for civil purposes, and rejected blasphemous ones.[51]

Farel and Bèze made their attitude to Vaudois ideas even clearer when they presented a statement about the beliefs of the Vaudois on the Eucharist to Duke Christoph of Württemberg at Göppingen on 14 May 1557. Duke Christoph was anxious in case the Waldenses turned out to be 'sacramentarian' heretics.[52] The title made claims for a general solidarity, asserting that 'This is what is taught about the Lord's supper in the churches of Switzerland and Savoy.' In fact, the text was devised by Farel and Bèze on the spur of the moment; its language was that of intricate school Latin, and its passages on contested issues, like the real presence, were so verbose as to be quite unclear and to please nobody.[53]

---

[48]   Pascal, 'Ambasciere', *BSBS* XIX, nos. 1-3 (1914), 27-30; Bèze, *Corresp.*, II, 238-42.

[49]   The use of the term 'Waldenses' without pejorative implications became more common after this date. See for instance [J. Crespin], *Histoire mémorable de la persécution ... du peuple ... appelez Vaudois* (s. l., 1556).

[50]   'Testimonia et tessera'.

[51]   Pascal, 'Ambasciere', *BSBS* XVIII, nos. 1-3 (1913), 104; XIX, nos. 1-3 (1914), 30f.

[52]   Ibid., *BSBS* XVIII, nos. 1-3 (1913), 105f.; Bèze, *Corresp.*, II, 71, n. 3.

[53]   *CO*, XVI, cols. 470f.; Pascal, 'Ambasciere', *BSBS* XIX, nos. 1-3 (1914), 33f.

When Bullinger heard of this confession submitted on his behalf, he wrote a rasping letter to the Genevans on 16 July 1557, blaming the confession for his problems with the senates of Berne and Zürich.[54] He said that such confessions should be clear and straightforward, and that he would never have written or signed such a document.[55] The row stirred up over this issue lasted most of the summer and involved Piermartire Vermigli and Calvin before it was smoothed over.[56] The interesting fact about it is that the reformers were so proprietorial about the Vaudois churches and their ideas that they could indulge in such irrelevant wrangling.

Things went very differently when Guillaume Farel and the Vaudois minister Claude Berge visited Basel, Mulhouse, and Strasbourg in August 1561, to instigate an appeal to the Duke of Savoy on the Vaudois' behalf. No major disagreements disrupted this venture, and Estienne Noel sent the fulsome thanks of the churches after Berge's return in December.[57] In 1566 the Elector Palatine was recruited as intercessor on behalf of some other Savoyard protestants, especially some conventiclers captured at Bourg-en-Bresse. Thanks to some astute negotiation the protestants seem to have been able to isolate the Duke of Savoy from the sympathies of the German princes.[58] The techniques of diplomacy which were in the first instance developed to help the Vaudois had by this time been made to work fairly well. Intercession had been difficult before the 1550s, because the Waldenses were still not yet credible as protestants. After 1555 they were in the fold, and embassies could be arranged; but after 1561, especially, the ministers and people understood their respective needs, and diplomacy could operate without set-backs.

What is more, by the 1550s and 1560s the Genevan

[54]   *CO*, XVI, cols. 538 f.; Bèze, *Corresp.*, II, 75.
[55]   *CO*, XVI, cols. 472-81.
[56]   *CO*, XVI, cols. 539-41, 545f., 554-6, 567-8, 571, 586-7, 590-6, 609-17; Bèze, *Corresp.*, II, 73f., 75, 82f., 86-94, 238-42, 251; Balma, 'Strasbourg et les Vaudois', 84-7; P.F. Geisendorf, *Théodore de Bèze* (Genève, 1949), pp. 82-8.
[57]   *CO*, XVII, cols. 600-2; Bèze, *Corresp.*, III, 125f., 130f.; Jalla, 'Correspondance ecclésiastique vaudoise', 84f.
[58]   Bèze, *Corresp.*, VI, 186; VII, 66, 126, n.7, 141-6; Gilles, 1881 edn., I, 353-94.

protestants were taking even greater care to be informed of the state of the Piedmontese churches. Their writings abound with sympathetic references, intended both for those within their circle and for those outside. This concern could take strange forms. Viret reported to Calvin on 6 August 1556 that he had heard that a physician of the King of Poland had approached Calvin, promising to the Vaudois (then under threat from a *parlement*) safety and protection, and a livelihood, if they cared to emigrate to Poland.[59] Other very frequent references to the persecutions were more conventional, and expressed commonplace sympathy for those in difficulties.

(iii) Some early protestant literature

As we saw above, the reformers approached the Waldenses in order to educate them, and because they admired their tradition of dissent, not because they wished to assimilate Waldensian ideas or modify their own. Protestant writers were therefore very cautious about suggesting that Waldensian theology was one of unsullied purity. Such caution, moreover, lasted until the development of an apocalyptic tradition in the early seventeenth century, which used the Waldenses as a stage in the history of the 'true church' which was supposed always to have resisted the Roman Antichrist.[60]

The clearest reservations about the reputation of the Waldenses appeared first amongst the martyrologists. While describing Martin Gonin's motives for dealing with the reformers, Crespin noted how the Vaudois

delibererent à la façon d'icelles réformer leurs églises. Car estans fort affectionez à la parole de Dieu, avoyent de long temps eu ce desir: et cognoissoyent assez que leurs dites églises estoyent mal reiglées en plusieurs choses, et comme enrouillées par l'ignorance et les tenèbres du temps précedent.[61]

In the early stages of the stories of the massacres at Mérindol, both the Latin and the French versions of Crespin were

[59] *CO*, XVI, cols. 252f.
[60] See below, ch. 16 (iii).
[61] Crespin, 1565 edn., p. 138.

distinctly patronizing. The Latin remarked how amongst the Waldenses 'God always wished to preserve some seed of piety, although they were scattered and removed from the society of men'.[62] The account went on to say 'si peu de la vraye lumière qu'ils avoyent, ils taschoyent de l'allumer davantage de jour en jour...', describing their efforts to obtain Biblical texts and some basic instruction.[63]

The various anonymous accounts of the War of the edict of Nice published in the early 1560s served the same purpose as the stories of the massacres in Provence. They showed the same attitude, therefore. For instance, the *Histoire des Persecutions* pointed out that in the flood of ignorance spread over the whole world it was no surprise that the Vaudois' *barbes* 'did not instruct them wyth such puritie as was requisite'.[64]

Although Théodore de Bèze went to such lengths to urge the Vaudois cause, in his writings he shared the same misgivings about the beliefs the Waldenses held before the Reformation. In the *Icones* he noted how 'little by little purity of doctrine had died out amongst them, but they were still no less zealous for true piety. Therefore, when they had learned about a purer Christianity in Switzerland and the lands around . . . .'.[65] In the *Histoire Ecclésiastique* the attitudes of Crespin, the source for the details about Gonin and the massacres, were adopted altogether. Of the Piedmontese Vaudois the work said 'les fideles des valees de Piemont...de tout temps ont eu en horreur le siege Romain, et toutesfois par succession de temps avoient aucunement decliné de pieté, et de la doctrine . . .'. Of the Provençal heretics it said similarly that 'in religion, they have never adhered to papal superstitions, but through a long passage of time purity of doctrine had been greatly corrupted amongst their ministers . . .'.[66]

Amongst those outside the Genevan tradition the same feelings appeared. Sleidan described the Waldenses thus: 'by

---

[62] Camerarius, *Historica Narratio*, pp. 303 f.; Crespin-Baduel, fo. 88[r-v].

[63] Crespin, 1565 edn., pp. 189 f.

[64] *Storia delle persecuzioni*, ed. Balmas and Theiller, pp. 70, 231; and as translated by Foxe, *Actes and Monuments* (1583 edn.), p. 954.

[65] Bèze, *Icones*, sig. Cc. i.   [66] *HE*, I, 23, 35 f.

old-established custom they do not acknowledge the Roman pontiff, and have always held to a somewhat purer doctrine; when Luther became known, they avidly gained a fuller understanding . . .'.[67] The passage containing this measured judgement was incorporated by Matthias Flacius Illyricus into his *Catalogus* of 1556, in spite of the fact that Flacius was to be one of the founders of the 'true church' school.[68]

The martyrologists and Reformation historians wrote to glorify their own movement, so it is hardly surprising that they should have felt that previous reform movements had become inadequate. Nevertheless, once the Vaudois were raised to a pedestal this attitude was to be superseded. In the early years of the Reformation, however, the attitude of Crespin and Bèze was the only tenable one; ironically, J.-B. Bossuet was to try to obtain a rhetorical victory over the 'true church' school in the 1680s, by quoting these very same passages to disprove protestant claims.[69]

[67] J. Sleidanus, *De Statu Religionis* . . . *Commentarii* (Strasbourg, 1556), fo. 217ᵛ.

[68] Flacius Illyricus, *Catalogus*, 1556 edn., p. 712; 1608 edn., col. 1502.

[69] J.-B. Bossuet, *Œuvres* (Versailles, 1816–17), XX, 176–8.

14. The Transformation of the Creeds

At a number of critical stages in the *rapprochement* of the two dissenting sects, the ideas of protestants and Vaudois were set down in concrete form, as creeds and confessions of faith. No attempt will be made here to construct a single strand of theological development out of the different stages revealed by these documents. However, the creeds are useful, since they demonstrate a series of disconnected contacts and conflicts, each with its own message for the historian of popular religion.

(i) The talks in 1530, and their relevance

As we observed earlier, the complex relationship which exists between the various records of these talks[1] makes it impossible, on textual evidence alone, to set them in any chronological order. There is a little, but only a little, which is in the Latin texts but not in the dialect versions; there is much in the dialect MS which is not in any surviving Latin text; yet parts of the dialect text must have been translated directly from the Latin (not least because Provençal did not afford suitable words for many theological concepts).[2]

The reformers had a few simple messages to communicate to the heretics represented by the unusual *barbes* Morel and Masson. Some of these ideas were rather hard to swallow. In the first place, both Oecolampadius and Bucer were horrified to find that the Waldenses practised their faith only in secret, and that they took part in the services of the catholic church. Oecolampadius would have preferred them to face martyrdom rather than betrayal, and added 'I know your weakness;

[1] TCD MS 259; Scultetus, *Annales Evangelii*, II, 295–306; Oecolampadius and Zuinglius, *Epistolae*, fos. 2ʳ–3ᵛ; J.J. Herzog, 'Ein wichtiges Document', *Zeitschrift für die historische Theologie*, 3 (1866), 311–38.
[2] See above, ch. 10 (ii); also V. Vinay, 'Mémoires de Georges Morel', *BSSV* 132 (1972), 35–48, where the same conclusion is reached.

but those who know themselves to be redeemed by the blood of Christ should be stronger.'[3] Bucer was almost as unfavourable; he called this taking of catholic sacraments 'great infirmity, which we pray God will not hold against you'. He directed the Vaudois to pray, as Elisha did for Naaman in similar circumstances, that they might be forgiven. At the earliest suitable moment, they should make their confession public.[4] This so-called 'Nicodemism' was the aspect of the medieval Waldenses which most obviously distinguished them from the protestants, and as such protestant historians seized on it.[5] However, Bucer was later to moderate his injunctions in this respect.

Martin Bucer emphasized a second major theme in his replies to the *barbes*. The Vaudois, he said, should not seek a strictly regulated method or rule to guide rigidly every aspect of their religious observance and organization. This opinion, unhelpful as it clearly was for the categories of Morel's thought, was expressed on a wide range of issues. It was Bucer's answer when confronted with the respect for rank and seniority shown by the *barbes*;[6] it underlay his doubts about their itinerancy;[7] it affected several issues regarding the morality of married couples' relations;[8] finally, it inspired Oecolampadius's answer to the *barbes* when they asked about ways of teaching the people.[9] In each case the *barbes* were told not to follow a rigorous and legalist stance, and to govern everything according to charity and the inspiration of the Spirit.

This was probably not what the *barbes* wanted or expected as a response. The reformers must have said at once too little and too much; they were vague on technical points, and full in criticizing what the *barbes* did not wish to doubt. This trait

---

[3]   TCD MS 259, pp. 2–5; Vinay, *Confessioni di fede . . . riformati*, pp. 52–4.
[4]   TCD MS 259, pp. 52 f.
[5]   Perrin, *Vaudois*, pp. 157, 214–16; Gilles, 1881 edn., I, 47–9. C. Ginzburg, *Il Nicodemismo. Simulazione e dissimulazione religiosa nell' Europa del '500* (Torino, 1970), pp. 106–8, discusses the implications of Bucer's attitude in the context of disputes at Strasbourg at the time.
[6]   TCD MS 259, pp. 10 f., 56; Vinay, *Confessioni di fede . . . riformati*, pp. 78, 106.
[7]   TCD MS 259, pp. 11 f.; Vinay, op. cit., pp. 56, 82.
[8]   TCD MS 259, pp. 69–71.   [9]   Vinay, op. cit., pp. 60 f., 64 f.

was shown still more when Bucer considered the medieval ways in which Morel repeatedly asked whether some point of conduct was 'profitable' or 'meritorious' for the believer. Bucer objected, for instance, to creating an order of priorities in which one considered one's own soul's health above all.[10] Asked about the distinction between mortal and venial sins, Bucer said that to the believer all sins were venial, save rejection of God; to the unbeliever all sins were mortal, because they deprived the sinner of God and of eternal life.[11] Morel asked if the passion of Christ was 'profitable' to those persevering in sin, and if any good they did was profitable to them. Bucer replied, first, that the passion of Christ profited the elect in the way God had ordained; secondly, that good works, of themselves, did not harm the doer; and finally pointed out at length that man's salvation depended entirely on the gift of God; and it was impossible to be at all pleasing to God without faith.[12]

The reason for Bucer's refusal to endorse a legalistic, ritualistic religion, then, was a thoroughly protestant one; such ritualism contradicted the fundamental assumptions of the doctrine of justification by faith. It is therefore astonishing to note that almost nothing on justification by faith is included in the Latin texts. Only a long passage in the dialect version fills in the gap. In this text, Morel opened by quoting an arsenal of texts where the Bible appeared to attribute some importance to good works. Bucer replied first with a point a priori, that salvation, as the knowledge of God, was a gift of the Spirit which could only be received through faith. Bucer answered Morel's texts, then pointed out that good works were the activity of God in the believer; good works were only good if they proceeded from faith. He ended with an exposition of the fundamental paradox, that all good within men came from God, yet men, living in evil, were justly condemned by God.[13]

---

[10]   TCD MS 259, pp. 46-8; Vinay, op. cit., pp. 40, 104-6.
[11]   TCD MS 259, pp. 104 f.; Vinay, op. cit., pp. 108-10, 46.
[12]   TCD MS 259, pp. 106 f.
[13]   TCD MS 259, pp. 81-96; V. Vinay, 'Barba Morel e Bucero sulla giustificazione per fede', *BSSV* 133 (1973), 29-36; *Confessioni di fede . . . riformati*, pp. 118-37.

The last series of recommendations which the reformers made to Morel and Masson related to small details of conduct. These were probably the aspects of their advice which were most useful to the *barbes*. Their content, however, may have been unwelcome. Both reformers condemned in the most uncompromising way the celibacy which Morel reported was expected of the *barbes*.[14] Bucer advised against Waldenses entering into litigation before catholic judges, and suggested the ministers might take on the task of arbitrators, although it would be a distraction.[15] Bucer advised against arranged marriages, but said that these matters should be decided with respect to circumstances.[16] He justified the judicial oath at some length.[17] He advised moderation in accepting the gifts of the dying, and rejected utterly the practice of killing betrayers to prevent the detection of the sect.[18]

One of the longest passages of specific advice, however, told the Vaudois how to behave in their 'captivity'; in other words, how to continue to participate in catholic worship. This contradicted Bucer's first reply, although even in that he had been more moderate than Oecolampadius.[19] In this later passage, Bucer first repeated his injunction to the Vaudois to pray for liberation. He then said that the heretics' ministers should admonish the people, when they communicated with the catholics, to consider only the ordinance of Christ, and receive the elements as from the hands of the Lord, giving thanks to him. He drew a distinction between sacrifice to idols (as in the story of Naaman) and the papist Eucharist, since the former was solely in the service of demons, while the latter was an institution of Christ, depraved by the ministers of Antichrist. The people should ideally take communion from their ministers, but a popish Eucharist was better than none at all. No second baptism should be given by the *barbes*. The passage ended 'but we pray that, as in the

[14] TCD MS 259, pp. 15–21, 59–61; Vinay, op. cit., pp. 38, 40, 46, 58–60, 76–80, 81, 112.

[15] TCD MS 259, pp. 50f., 99f.; Vinay, op. cit., pp. 42, 46, 106, 110.

[16] TCD MS 259, pp. 66f.

[17] TCD MS 259, pp. 76–9; Vinay, op. cit., pp. 46, 102–4.

[18] TCD MS 259, pp. 109f.; Vinay, op. cit., pp. 44, 108.

[19] TCD MS 259, pp. 53f.; Vinay, op. cit., p. 84; Ginzburg, *Nicodemismo*, p. 108.

other matters, you should not separate yourselves altogether from those papists, and should use only those ministers who teach Christ impurely; but that is captivity . . .'.[20]

The reformers' position clearly underwent an important change in the course of the discussions, perhaps as Bucer came to realize more accurately the kind of dissent which the *barbes* represented. If, then, at the start of the talks the reformers may have misunderstood the Waldensian position, one must consider whether large parts of their advice may not have been directed at inappropriate targets, and have been actually irrelevant to the Waldensian case. In the first place, some specific items of advice were unnecessary. Bucer set out a very long tirade against the Anabaptists and those who challenged infant baptism.[21] There is no sign that the medieval Waldenses rejected the practice;[22] although Taborite teaching on this issue has been attributed to some Waldenses, the trial evidence from the Dauphiné does not bear out the suggestion.[23] Again, the long debate between *barbes* and reformers on free will and predestination does not seem to have percolated to the valleys until the time of protestant ministers like Girolamo Miolo.[24]

There was a larger problem. Oecolampadius and Bucer made extensive suggestions for changes in the social as well as the doctrinal position of the *barbes*. If implemented, such changes would, in fact, have turned them into protestant ministers. There is no sign whatever that such a change took place save by gradual infiltration and education. By an irony, however, the manuscript containing the debate was in the late sixteenth century owned by perhaps the only two *barbes* who did become ministers under the new dispensation, Gilles des Gilles, of the Val Pèllice, and François Laurens (Francesco Laurenzo) of the Val Germanasca.[25] By the time Bucer's wishes for the *barbes* were realized, a new organization had taken over.

[20] TCD MS 259, pp. 72-5.
[21] TCD MS 259, pp. 25-46; Vinay, op. cit., pp. 86-102.
[22] See above, ch. 6 (ii).
[23] See Gonnet and Molnár, *Vaudois au moyen âge*, pp. 434 f.
[24] TCD MS 259, pp. 111, 113-15; Vinay, op. cit., pp. 46-8, 62; Miolo, *Historia breve*, ed. Balmas, pp. 99 f.   [25] TCD MS 259, p. 128.

(ii)   The conflict of systems, 1532

As we saw above, 1532 was a year which saw contacts of a striking kind between the two groups of dissenters, but which led to no very significant outcome. In terms of the ideas discussed, the talks in that year did not so much presage eventual unity, as harden the lines of dissent between Vaudois and protestant. In the documents left behind it is the attack on Waldensian tradition, rather than any union with protestantism, which emerges most prominently.

The ideological content of the talks in August 1532 described by Pierre Griot was quite slight. The 'religious' proposed a rather burlesque form of justification by faith; they condemned the Waldenses for keeping external religious ceremonies and a separate clerical caste; they denounced the celibacy of the *barbes* in terms even more inflammatory than those used by Martin Bucer.[26]

Whoever proposed the theses of the September disputation in Angrogna repeated this largely negative approach. A lawful oath was to be permitted; the only works which could be called 'good' were those commanded by God, and others were indifferent. Auricular confession, the sacrament most cherished by the Waldenses, was not commanded by God, nor was the observance of Sundays. Special words or rites for prayer, the imposition of hands, fasting at fixed times, were all declared superfluous. Revenge, and the forbidding of marriage to anyone, were condemned. Participation in magistracy and in usury could be permitted.[27]

Clearly only a protestant, and a radical one at that, could have demolished so many taboos shared by catholics and Waldenses alike. However, for the most part the Angrogna propositions affirmed almost nothing which was positive as an alternative theology. At the end of the text, on the other hand, some further propositions were added in a quite

---

[26]   Audisio, *Barbe et l'inquisiteur*, pp. 107–9.
[27]   Vinay, op. cit., pp. 139–42.

different hand.[28] These went a little further: they asserted predestination, and denied free will in very crude terms; they denounced the mobility of ministers from place to place; they said that ministers might have property to maintain their families. They asserted only two sacraments, to be used as 'demonstrations of the perseverence in the faith which we have promised as children in baptism, and in memory of the goodness of Christ in dying for our redemption'.[29] The affirmation that the participants were agreed on these points, which has been used to prove that these propositions are synodal conclusions, is found only in the interpolation, and related in all probability only to the sacraments.[30] Whatever the circumstances in which this document, so untidy, so full of erasures and incoherent phrasing, was produced, the role of pure high protestantism in it was fairly limited, and mostly confined to the later passage.

Very few indications about talks on beliefs can be gleaned from the reports of Saunier and his friends on their early contacts with the Vaudois. They did, however, set about having a new translation of the Bible printed, and their reasons for that project do not suggest that they felt the Vaudois already had the scriptures well under their belts.[31] It seems fairly certain that the Waldenses did provide a great deal of money for the printing projects, although reliable estimates vary from 500 to 800 *écus*.[32] The Vaudois wanted value for money: they pestered Saunier in 1533; in 1549

[28] J. H. Todd and V. Vinay have alleged that this second hand is a cursive version of the hand used in the rest of the manuscript, and was written by the same scribe. See Todd, 'The Waldensian manuscripts', *British Magazine*, XIX (1841), 401; Vinay, op. cit., p. 142, n. 24. This supposition is not endorsed by the present Keeper of Manuscripts at Trinity College, Dublin, Mr. W. O'Sullivan, for whose advice regarding the MS I am indebted.

[29] Vinay, op. cit., p. 142: 'He stato concluso per la scriptura che noy non havemo sinon doy segni sacramentali che Christo ne ha lasati luno he il baptismo laltro sie la heucarestia laquale noy usemo en demostramento la perseveracion nostra nela fede la quale havemo promesso nelo baptismo essendo filholi. Et ancora alamemora dequello grande beneficio che Jesu Cristo ha facto anoy morendo per la redentione nostra . . .'.

[30] Ibid.: 'siamo venuti aprender dichiaration dela presente conclusione [*sic*] en tuti siamo stati uniti et duno medmesimo spirito . . .'.

[31] Herminjard, II, 453, n. 19: 'tant de sectes et hérésies . . . sordoient en ce temps au monde, et que tout cela venoit par ignorance de la parole de Dieu.'

[32] J. Jalla, 'La Bible d'Olivétan', *BSHV* 58 (1932), 88.

they had some of the printer Pierre de Vingle's property sequestrated at Neuchâtel to make sure they were not cheated.[33] However, once the Bible was printed there is less evidence that the Vaudois were keen to buy individual copies of the immense and no doubt costly folio volume. Scipione Lentolo found on this issue yet another grievance with his former congregation:

Also, how many are there amongst you, who take pleasure in having the Bible in your home? And if some of your pastors wish to compel the better-off to buy one, what a violence they think this is against them! How tyrannically they say they are being treated! Also, how keen are you to send your sons to school, so that they may at least learn to read the Holy Scriptures?[34]

Finally, the whole project ran out of steam. On 12 September 1561 Christophe Fabri reported to Viret that Claude Berge would be speaking to him about the books of the deceased printer Pierre de Vingle; it was agreed that the books would be sold and the money used to repay the remainder of the 800 *écus* which the 'good people' had provided to have the Bible printed.[35] In fact Olivétan's product was probably too massive and splendid a volume to fulfil the needs of the Waldenses for a compact volume to read more or less in secret. One surviving copy bears the ex-libris not of any Vaudois, but of Ysabeau Panthuyesse, daughter of an *échevin* of Limburg.[36]

Alongside the insistence on a better text of the Bible at this period went a use of the theological writings of Martin Bucer. Saunier had apparently worked on a translation of the *Unio dissidentium* published under the name of Hermannus Bodius; in his letter of November 1532 he asked for a copy of this to be sent to him.[37] Bodius was Bucer's pseudonym; the work itself was a small-format summary of the essentials

[33] Herminjard, III, 81; Jalla, 'La Bible d'Olivétan', 87.
[34] *Lentolo MS*, p. 495.
[35] *CO*, XVIII, col. 712; Jalla, 'La Bible d'Olivétan', 87.
[36] As shown by contemporary marginalia to the copy in the Bodleian Library, Oxford, Bib. Fr. 1535 c. 1.
[37] Herminjard, II, 453, n. 20.

of protestant doctrine, with texts to support.[38] It was also one of the books found in the possession of the minister Giafredo Varaglia when he was captured.[39]

(iii) The eirenic confessions, 1488-1556

We have seen that the most important personal and social changes in the Waldensian heresy took place in the later 1550s, not in the 1530s. This conclusion is further supported by the curious fact that from the late Middle Ages until the mid-sixteenth century Waldensian thought continued to be expressed in very similar forms. This was because 'confessions of faith', as instruments setting down beliefs in concrete form, served a different purpose amongst the Vaudois from that which they served for the reformers. For the protestant churches a confession was normally used to define a faith in distinction, either from catholicism, or from another protestant creed. The Waldenses used a confession to show, for the benefit of persecutors or possible allies, that they were respectable and credible Christians, not disreputable heretics with scandalous ideas. Their confessions were eirenicons rather than rallying-points. Their character was expressed perfectly in the preamble to a declaration by the Provençal Vaudois of 3 February 1533:

> . . . à celle fin que vous et tous aultres cognoissez et sçaichez que nous sommes bons fidèles et vraiz crestiens, contre les faulx rapports de nos ennemys, . . . nous vous faisons assavoir par ces présentes, selon Dieu et conscience, . . . la foy et créance que nous tenons et croyons . . .[40]

The conditions of challenge and threat under which such confessions were produced were many and various. One was produced for Alberto Cattaneo during the negotiations between the crusaders and the heretics of the Val Chisone early in 1488.[41] A second formed the brief declaration of

---

[38] H. Bodius, *Unio dissidentium in sacris literis locorum* (Coloniae, 1531; Lyon, 1532; Basel, 1557, and subsequently)); P. Chaix, *Recherches sur l'imprimerie à Genève de 1550 à 1564* (Genève, 1954), p. 90.

[39] Crespin, 1565 edn., p. 895. Varaglia's other books were the *De fatti dei veri successori di Jesu Christi* (a translation by Gianluigi Pascale of a tract by Viret) and the pasquil *Alcoranum Franciscanorum*.

[40] Herminjard, VII, 466.

[41] Fornier, II, 426.

Vaudois doctrine submitted by Morel to Oecolampadius and Bucer, which faced a different kind of challenge.[42] A third was the confession presented by the Vaudois of Cabrières to Jehan de Roma on 3 February 1533, just quoted.[43] A similar pattern was followed in the series of confessions presented by the Vaudois of the villages in the Luberon at the time of the decree against Mérindol between 1541 and 1544.[44] One of the most interesting of these confessions was offered to the commissioners of the *parlement* of Turin in reply to the edict issued against them on 23 March 1556.[45] Its tone was echoed by the articles produced for the Cardinal de Lorraine by the German princes' ambassadors in August 1557.[46] The *Histoire Mémorable* published by an anonymous protestant in 1561 even described the confession submitted to the Duke of Savoy in 1560 in the same terms.[47]

It is not that these confessions put forward exactly the same doctrine, or that nothing changed between the late 1480s and the mid-1550s. It is rather that they all show a similar approach, and a comparable desire to appear both catholic and reasonable, which was to distinguish them from protestant confessions properly so called. In the first place, many of these confessions placed more emphasis on the creeds, especially the Apostles' creed, than was found in pure protestant formulae. The creed was paraphrased in the 1488 declaration;[48] it was the first statement Morel made about his ideas in his submission to Oecolampadius.[49] The Provençal Vaudois included the creed in their statement in 1533, and paraphrased it in 1541;[50] the three creeds, of the Apostles, Nicea, and

---

[42] TCD MS 259, pp. 21f.; Vinay, *Confessioni di fede . . . riformati*, pp. 40–2.

[43] Herminjard, VII, 466–8.

[44] Crespin-Baduel, fos. 104ʳ–110ʳ (1541 confession); summary in *HE*, I, 39–41; Schmidt, 'Aktenstücke', 256–8 (1543–4 confession); see below, ch. 16 (iii).

[45] *Storia delle persecuzioni*, ed. Balmas and Theiller, pp. 80–5, 236–40; summary in Vinay, *Confessioni di fede . . . riformati*, pp. 153f.

[46] Pascal, 'Ambasciere', *BSBS* XVIII, nos. 5–6 (1913), 322.

[47] *Histoire mémorable*, ed. Balmas and Diena, pp. 78f.

[48] Fornier, II, 426.

[49] TCD MS 259, p. 21: 'Nos predit ministres cresen e fermament tenen eiosta nostra poysancza ensegnen lo nostre poble tot quant se conten en li 12 article del cinbollo, lo qual es dit de li apostol . . .'.

[50] Herminjard, VII, 467; Camerarius, *Historica Narratio*, pp. 366–75; Lentolo, pp. 46–53.

Athanasius, were explicitly mentioned in 1556 and 1557.[51]

Secondly, these confessions emphasized the role of the Ten Commandments as an uncontroversial element in religion. The 'Law of God', whether expounded in full, as in Lentolo's version of the Provençal confession of 1541,[52] or referred to only, as in 1533 and 1556,[53] seemed to offer another path to respectability for the Waldenses.

Care was also taken to point out that the Vaudois were quite orthodox in their ideas about the nature of the Trinity. In the creed of 1543-4 the Trinity and the position of Christ were emphasized first of all.[54] The exposition of the creed early in the 1541 version offered a rendering of the doctrine of the Trinity.[55] In other documents this item was implied when the creeds themselves were mentioned. Again, especially from the 1540s, the confessions referred explicitly to the Vaudois' readiness to obey secular magistrates.[56] Finally, several of these sets of articles stated that their subscribers were prepared to submit to correction, if they could be shown to be wrong by teaching and by scriptural texts.[57] This last affirmation might even accompany points, such as the Mass and auricular confession in the 1556 affirmation, in which the dissenters were quite frank about their own opinions.

Although not every point listed above is found in all of these statements, the general drift is the same in each. This form was forced on the Waldenses by their peculiar situation, as heretics living within a hostile state, trying to become respected as protestants without wishing to appear a threat to fundamental beliefs. A very similar approach was taken by the small protestant community of Locarno before its expulsion in 1555.[58] Only when the legal position of these dissenting

---

[51] Pascal, 'Ambasciere', loc. cit.; *Storia delle persecuzioni*, ed. Balmas and Theiller, p. 236; Vinay, op. cit., p. 153.

[52] Lentolo, pp. 53-8.

[53] Herminjard, VII, 467; Vinay, op. cit., p. 153.

[54] Schmidt, 'Aktenstücke', 256f.

[55] Camerarius, *Historica Narratio*, pp. 366f.

[56] Camerarius, *Historica Narratio*, p. 383; Pascal, 'Ambasciere', *BSBS* XVIII, nos. 5-6 (1913), 323.

[57] Fornier, loc. cit.; Herminjard, loc. cit.; Vinay, op. cit., pp. 153f.

[58] TCD MS 1149, fos. 10ᵛ-12ᵛ; J. G. Altmann, *Tempe Helvetica, dissertationes . . .* (Zürich, 1736-43), IV, 162f.; F. Meyer, *Die evangelische Gemeinde in Locarno* (Zürich, 1836), I, 499f.; below, ch. 17 (ii).

communities was changed could their forms of collective expression fall more consistently into line with protestant norms. That change of legal status took place between 1559 and 1561; and as we shall see, it was during and after those years that a Calvinist hegemony in the valleys was definitively established.

(iv) The orthodox line, 1558-66

In these few years, and against the threat of armed attack, the solidarity of the new ministers and their flocks was strengthened by the acceptance in the Piedmontese valleys of a distinctively Calvinist set of articles of faith and church discipline. At a synod on 13 July 1558, certain articles of ecclesiastical discipline were decreed; these reflected essentially Genevan assumptions about church government. They provided for synods and colloquies at regular intervals; they planned for excommunication to be imposed by consent of the consistory; they foresaw the establishment of orders of deacons, elders, and 'superintendents'; and regarding issues such as marriage and the prohibited degrees of affinity, they referred to the *Ordonnances* of the Genevan church.[59]

A more fundamental step was taken in May 1560. In that month the Waldenses of the domains of Savoy presented their 'Apology and Confession of faith' as part of the negotiations to avert the threat imposed by the Edict of Nice. Scipione Lentolo prepared these documents in his native Italian. His preface to the 'Apology' was a historical discourse which tried to encourage Emanuele Filiberto to protect the reformed gospel; nearly all the rest, however, was translated more or less exactly from articles 7 to 40 of the *Confessio Gallicana* drawn up by the French churches the year before.[60] Given Calvin's reservations about the latter document, Lentolo might appear to have been separating himself from Calvin by using the French confession.[61] However, he used only the second draft as approved by Calvin, in which the first two

[59] Jalla, 'Synodes Vaudois', 476-8.
[60] Lentolo, pp. 126-45; Vinay, *Confessioni di fede . . . riformati*, pp. 29f., 155-78.
[61] Delumeau, *Naissance et affirmation de la réforme*, p. 151.

articles had been rewritten, and mention of the creeds had been omitted.[62]

By the time of the peace of Cavour the Calvinist ministers had shown their devotion and their usefulness to the Waldensian cause. Two ministers, including Claude Berge of Tagliaretto, were amongst the negotiators and signatories of the peace.[63] Testimony to the effect of the war on local politics was given by one 'Bovenne' (perhaps the minister Cosme Brevin) in a report to the Genevan ministers on 6 October 1561. He described how the ministers had attempted earlier to remedy the ignorance of their flocks, but until the persecutions of the previous year had 'brought them to think more soundly about the matter' they had had little success. Now he asked for a regent to be sent for the schools which were to be set up in the Val Chisone, where he ministered. He also reported on the increased success the reform was enjoying in the lower Val Chisone.[64]

A further synod of the ministers of the Piedmontese churches was held in Angrogna in September 1563, at which the 'articles, faits et arrêtés' of the synod of 1558 were ratified. A third meeting at Villar Pèllice, held on 18 April 1564, enunciated the general principle that 'the ordinances established at Geneva shall be followed by us as closely as possible'.[65] By 1566 the churches 'of Savoy', presumably including the Piedmontese, were included in the list of subscribers to the Second Helvetic Confession.[66]

The importance of these events has been evident even to those historians who have exalted the role of the discussions in the 1530s.[67] It may be felt that the ideological development of the reformed Vaudois churches lost its individuality, and therefore much of its interest, from that point. However that may be, the synods and their decrees only showed that

---

[62]   Vinay, op. cit., pp. 166f. and n. 17.

[63]   *Storia delle persecuzioni*, ed. Balmas and Theiller, p. 200; Lentolo, p. 224.

[64]   *CO*, XIX, cols. 28f.; Pazè Beda, *Riforma e cattolicesimo*, pp. 60f.

[65]   Jalla, 'Synodes Vaudois', 476; the original decrees of the synod of 1564, on which Jalla's study of all these synods was based, have been lost.

[66]   *A Harmony of the Confessions of Faith of the Christian and Reformed Churches* (Cambridge, 1586), prefatory material.

[67]   J. Jalla, 'Notice historique sur le S. Ministère', *BSHV* 16 (1898), 20; G. Peyrot, 'Influenze franco-ginevrine', 225.

part of the absorption of the reform which was most theoretical and precarious.[68] A study of the practical limitations imposed by local customs and behaviour is much more rewarding.

[68] Much detail on the theoretical aspect is provided by Peyrot, op. cit., pp. 238-59.

15. Disobedience and Violence: the Limits to Reformation

(i) The assimilation of protestant doctrines

A study which is confined to the formal creeds as sources for the beliefs of the Waldenses as they moved towards the Reformation tends to impose a rigidity foreign to the character of the dissent portrayed in contemporary testimonies. Old habits of expression and even old ideas died very hard indeed; when ministers tried to teach a formalized, logical gospel, their hearers might revert to the loose, proverbial wisdom of past decades.

Certainly it seems that the Waldenses continued to express their faith in short, pithy sayings; and since consistency was not an issue, they might express either traditional or new-fangled ideas in the same way. This syncretism was shown especially well in Provence in the 1530s. When Jehan de Roma gathered information against Catherine Castagne, of Apt, one witness said that he had heard her say 'You other people go to pray to God in church, but it would be as good to pray to God at home. When the priest lifts Our Lord, it would be as well to see someone lift a crust of bread'—a statement which combined the two heresies neatly. Thomas Dauphin was supposed to have said that indulgences were a waste of money and that 'the Pope was giving paradise for three sous . . .'; he also said that 'there were Popes of evil life, and they had no power to absolve', but based this rejection on his reading of sermons written in French, and on quotations from Erasmus. A tailor of Roussillon who looked forward to the arrival of Luther, who would make all the priests marry, also denied purgatory, hell, and heaven, and rejected the saying of the Ave Maria. Great confusion existed over even important issues in these statements; one Jean Roux said that there was no purgatory, and one must do all the good

one could in this world; while another called 'Eustache'
doubted whether the Pope had the power to deliver souls
from a purgatory in which he seems to have believed.[1]

In Provence, before there was any ordered protestant
hierachy, old and new ideas became mingled, and new radical
doctrines, including extreme doubts about the real presence,
were added to the heap in a disorderly fashion. Each set of
ideas would be expressed by ordinary people in the same
way. One deposition reported the proverbs 'as well to pray at
home as elsewhere', and 'keep the days of the Apostles, Our
Lady, and Sundays, go ploughing the other days'; but also
included the newer sayings such as 'in Germany, they collect
the tithes but they give some to the ministers and some to
the poor', and 'better for priests to marry, than to go after
other men's wives.'[2]

This confusion and lack of coherence is less surprising
when one realizes that the leading protestants were just as
confused. Antoine Aloat, who had been instructed in protestantism by Jean-Jacques Farel, confessed his heresies in the
diocese of Sisteron about Easter 1533.[3] Farel had taught him
that the Mass was a recent invention, and one should receive
it only in memory of Christ's body and blood; he said that
the souls of the dead went to sleep until the last judgement;[4]
he said that holy bread and water had no special power,
although one might still keep the reserved sacrament. He had
rejected the church hierarchy, auricular confession, and the
distinction of special buildings and special days, as well as
the paying of tithes.[5] Of indulgences, Farel had warned that
one 'poet ben garir l'argent de la bourse, non pas les peccats
de la conscience'.[6] Not only did Aloat either forget or never
learn the fundamental logical prop for protestant religion, the
belief in justification by faith; he also went further than
normal in some directions (like the Eucharist or the 'soul-

---

[1]   R. Aubenas, 'Un registre d'enquêtes de l'inquisiteur Jean de Rome (1532)',
Etudes d'histoire du droit canonique dédiées à Gabriel le Bras (Paris, 1965), I, 6–8.
[2]   These statements occur in the trial of Jehan Serre in 1539; see M. Venard,
'Jacques Sadolet, évêque de Carpentras, et les Vaudois', *BSSV* 143 (1978), 44.
[3]   Manteyer, 'Les Farel, les Aloat et les Riquet', 55–7.
[4]   This is the heresy denounced by Calvin in his tract *Psychopannychia* of 1534.
[5]   Manteyer, *Les Farel, les Aloat et les Riquet* (Gap, 1912), pp. 127–71.
[6]   Arnaud, *Protestants du Dauphiné*, I, 19.

sleeping') and less far than normal in others (such as the use
of the reserved host). He did not link his new beliefs into
anything other than a list of unconnected, mostly negative
statements. Perhaps this traditional character of his dissent
explains why his inquisitors referred to his ideas as 'la loy et
secte valdeyse et luthérienne'.[7]

After 1561 ordinary believers among the Waldenses did not
reveal their beliefs to inquisitors so readily. However, many
probably expressed their faith in the same unconnected way.
According to Rorengo, Guillaume Brunet, of Molines-en-
Queyras, had begun to spread 'the new heresies about purgatory, the intercession of saints, and the worship of images';
he abjured at Embrun in 1559 in these rather conventional
terms.[8] In the Alpes-Maritimes, Antoine Planca of Tende
confessed in Ventimiglia on 4 February 1574 to believing

> that there is no purgatory; that one must not invoke saints and that the
> popes have no power; I have denied the confession made to a priest,
> rejecting the sacrament of ordination, claiming that we are all priests
> and that it is enough to tell our sins to God; that one should not keep
> fasts but eat everything each day; that one should not keep Holy days
> except Sunday; and that our works have no merit . . .[9]

These assertions are not, of course, Waldensian; it may have
been the churchmen as much as the people who preserved
this habit of listing ideas rather than expounding them. Yet
when the people of the Alps were as wary of doctrinal
instruction as Lentolo found them, it would not be surprising
if they had reverted to old patterns of thought.

The rule of the pure Calvinist ideal could break down
for other reasons. In 1563 one Cosme Brevin was deposed
from the parish of Fenestrelle after quarrels with the other
ministers. He had preached in a way which was all too
popular, as Dominique Vignaux reported on 23 July 1563:[10]

[7] Charronnet, *Guerres de religion*, p. 9.

[8] Rorengo-Lucerna, *Memorie historiche*, p. 82; Gioffredo, *Storia delle Alpi marittime*, cols. 1516 f.

[9] Biau, *Protestants . . . dans les Alpes maritimes*, pp. 62 f.

[10] *CO*, XX, cols. 79 f.; Jalla, 'Synodes vaudois', 474; Pazè Beda, *Riforma e cattolicesimo*, pp. 85 and 87. It is my conjecture that the 'Diguaulx' who signed the letter was 'D. Vignaux'.

He cracked jokes; he used affected language; he made gestures and exclamations quite out of proportion; in such a way, that one saw the people collapsing in laughter and foolery over this man. Many, returning from the sermon to their homes, remembered rather these amusements . . . than any good point; they made jokes of things, and made fun of each other after the example of their pastor.

After a warning, Brevin went from bad to worse, as he began to endanger the ministers' position by lampooning secular rulers:

When he mentioned in his sermons or prayers King François II, he called him *François cucuc*; Phillip, King of Spain, he called *Phillipin coquin* . . . When he meant Bourdillon, he was not ashamed to say *brouillon merdillon*, or if he meant Monbrun, he would patter *monvert, monbrun, monrouge*.

When he spoke of the syndic of Fenestrelle with whom he had quarrelled, Brevin apparently said 'Robin Robinet, feed your piglet well, so that he fattens up . . .', referring to the syndic's son, whom Brevin had refused to baptize because his family was excommunicate.[11]

From the report it is clear that Brevin carried on in this manner for some time; after his deposition he went down to Pinasca in the Val Perosa, and preached there without authority, drawing the protestants there away from their official pastor.[12] Later he returned to Geneva, from where he was sent to cool his heels in the Channel Islands; he ended up as minister of Sark, and kept his independence by playing the *colloques* of Jersey and Guernsey off against each other.[13]

It was perhaps as well for Scipione Lentolo that he never had to cope with competition of this order for the attention of his congregation. Probably there was far more of this sort of breakdown in order than we have evidence of. It is a symptom, not only of the pressures laid on the Calvinist system by operating where it had little or no support from the civil power, but also of the tendency of popular habits, of lampooning and verbal entertainment, to break into the routine of earnest instruction which was expected of a

[11] *CO*, XX, cols. 80 ff.   [12] Ibid., XX, col. 84.
[13] A. H. Ewen and A. R. de Carteret, *The Fief of Sark* (Guernsey, 1969), pp. 42, 46, 57 f.

protestant preacher. The attitudes of the valleys were beginning to transform the protestantism which had set out to transform them. In several other ways this process was probably continued for some time.

(ii) The habits of the *barbes* die hard?

Bucer, we saw, wanted to make the *barbes* into ministers; Calvin ended up by simply supplanting them. However, if the *barbes* were largely replaced by the new pastors, it does not follow that all their habits of behaviour lapsed at once. Two habits probably lasted into the Calvinist supremacy: the readiness of pastors to move around from parish to parish, alternating their charges with those of other ministers; and the willingness of protestants to take up arms in defence of religion.

According to Georges Morel, the *barbes* were appointed to districts for two or three years only, until they reached an age where excessive mobility would have been a burden.[14] Oecolampadius objected to this practice on grounds of principle, and Bucer because it went against Christian liberty.[15] It is curious, therefore, that many of the ministers about whom we know anything occupied more than one parish in a few years. In no more than seven years Scipione Lentolo ministered first at Angrogna, then at the church of Ciabàs near San Giovanni, and finally at Prali.[16] Gilles des Gilles (admittedly an ex-*barbe*) was from 1555 first at Villar Pèllice, then at Pinasca in the Val Perosa, then finally at Tagliaretto, close to Torre Pèllice.[17] François Soulf, one of the first ministers of Praviglielmo in the 1560s, had moved to Rorà, in the Valle di Luserna, by the 1570s.[18] Antoine Falc is listed in one record as pastor at Angrogna, in another as at

---

[14] TCD MS 259, pp. 11f.; Vinay, *Confessioni di fede . . . riformati*, pp. 40 f.

[15] Vinay, op. cit., pp. 58, 82.

[16] *CO*, XVII, cols. 668f.; XIX, col. 69; Jalla, 'Synodes vaudois', 475, n. 13; Armand Hugon, *Storia dei Valdesi II*, p. 23.

[17] Gilles, 1644 edn., pp. 53, 55, 69f.; Morland, *History of the Evangelical Churches*, p. 186; Jalla, 'Synodes vaudois', 475, n. 12; S. Foà, 'Valli del Piemonte, soggette all' Alt^za di Savoia, infette d'heresia', *BSHV* 24 (1907), 8; TCD MS 259, p. 128.

[18] Gilles, 1881 edn., I, 411; Foà, loc. cit.

Rorà; likewise, Melchior di Dio was minister at Rorà in 1558, but at Combe de Villar from 1564 at least.[19] Humbert Artus started as minister at Bòbbio Pèllice, but was in 1561 writing to Geneva from Cesana Torinese; he reappeared at Bòbbio in 1564.[20] Other ministers were moved between entirely different provinces of the Calvinist sphere of influence.. In 1556 one Thomas Bertran, who had been minister in Jersey under Edward VI, reached Geneva and was sent to Piedmont, where he may have ministered in Perosa; in 1564 Jersey informed the Company of Pastors that they wanted him back.[21] Other examples of the same phenomenon could be cited.

Some ministers, like Claude Rodigues of the Val Chisone, appear to have had a general brief extending to a number of parishes.[22] According to a catholic source from after 1573, the ministers of Prali, Riclaretto, Massello, Maniglia, and San Martino in the Val Germanasca 'did not stay in one fixed place of their own, but moved around changing from place to place'.[23] Such instability may have been the result of problems in providing men suited in language and temperament to the regions. On the other hand, it is tempting to speculate as to how far the people's expectations influenced the behaviour of the local synods.

In the case of armed resistance there is a clear and continuous tradition of the defence of dissent by force, although that tradition is apt to be disguised by the fact that protestants in France began to behave in the same way from the 1560s. Victims of the crusade in the 1480s had said that *barbes* had hidden in the caves in the Val Chisone along with other Waldenses; they had exhorted the people to remain loyal and promised them victory if they endured.[24]

The threat of violent resistance provided the impetus for the excessive violence used in the execution of the decrees against Mérindol in Provence. Letters patent issued in 1538 and 1539 had referred to royal fears about Waldensian

---

[19] Gilles, 1644 edn., p. 70; Jalla, 'Synodes vaudois', 476, notes 4–5; Foà, loc. cit.

[20] Jalla, 'Correspondance ecclésiastique vaudoise', 75–7, 83f.; Gilles, 1881 edn., I, 88f.

[21] *LHG*, p. 71; *RCPG*, II, 105f.; Jalla, 'Synodes vaudois', 475.

[22] Jalla, 'Synodes vaudois', 475, n. 11.

[23] Foà, op. cit., 9.   [24] *BP*, I, fos. 279^v, 284^v-5^r.

resistance. In 1539 one heretic confessed that the Waldenses were gathering arms and powder in the Luberon, and that they were planning a stronghold in Liguria. Two other witnesses also spoke of plans for resistance, and in September 1540 the *huissier* of the *parlement* of Aix claimed that the people of Mérindol were holding a fort at St-Phalles where they stored their arms.[25] The armed expeditions led by the heretics' leader Eustache Marron in 1532-5 and 1543 lent substance to the fears aroused by such evidence.[26]

As early as 1556 Calvin had been worried about the Piedmontese heretics' readiness to use force.[27] Following Calvin's wishes, in the early stages of the War of the Edict of Nice the ministers told the people to escape with their possessions to the mountains and to avoid violence.[28] However, this intention did not last long, since 'this article of not defendyng themselves, seemed very strange to the people, being driven to such an extremity, and the cause being so just'. A few days later,

Certeyne other ministers hearyng what they of Angrogne and Luserne had concluded, wrote unto them, that this resolution seemed very straunge to some, that they ought not to defend themselves against the violence of their enemies, alleadging many reasons, that in such an extremitie and necessitie, it was lawful for them so to do; especially, the quarrell being so just, that is, for the defence of true Religion, and for the preservation of theyr owne lives, and the lives of theyr wives and children: knowing that it was the Pope and hys ministers which were the cause of all these troubles and cruell warres, and not the Duke.[29]

Within a short while the ministers had become the patrons of armed resistance, as their predecessors were in the 1480s. In one of the battles for Pradeltorno, a stronghold in the Val d'Angrogna, early in 1561 there appeared the so-called 'light company', consisting of 'a hundred harquebushes, with one of their ministers, according to their manner, which are wont

[25] Aubéry, *Histoire de l'exécution*, pp. 21-3, 25 f., 30-2.

[26] Arnaud, *Protestants de Provence*, I, 9 ff., 50 ff.

[27] *CO*, XV, cols. 102-4.

[28] *Storia delle persecuzioni*, ed. Balmas and Theiller, pp. 121, 258; Lentolo, pp. 178 ff.; Armand Hugon, *Storia dei Valdesi II*, p. 24.

[29] *Storia delle persecuzioni*, pp. 121-3, 258 f., as translated by Foxe, *Actes and Monuments*, 1583 edn., p. 960.

to sende out a minister withall, as well for prayer and exhortation, as to kepe the people in order, that they excede not measure'.[30] In due course the divine sanction thus given to armed warfare was incorporated into protestant propaganda. A pamphlet of 1561 recalled how a soldier had talked with some Vaudois after the war, and had asked about the prayers which they said before battle, saying that when the soldiers heard these prayers they thought the Waldenses were conjuring devils, and were terrified.[31] Such propaganda, issued months before the massacre at Vassy, must have done much, not only to make the Waldenses' behaviour acceptable, but also to prepare minds in France for the breakdown in order which occurred.

This armed resistance was not confined either to the war of 1560-1 or to those ministers with links with the heresy before the Reformation. By March 1560 the Grenoble *parlement* was complaining about how the minister in the Val Chisone, Martin Tachard, had invaded and despoiled the catholic churches of Fenestrelle, Pragelas, and Usseaux; his forces had smashed the ornaments to turn the buildings to protestant use. In April Tachard led an armed band of perhaps 150 men from the area of Pragelas into the Val Germanasca to help the people of Riclaretto, who were under attack from their local landlords.[32] So notorious did the minister of Pragelas become that the sixteenth clause of the treaty of Cavour excluded him alone from being re-elected as a Waldensian minister; it has been suggested that the duke was still afraid of his influence.[33]

On other occasions the protestants of the Waldensian valleys took up arms again. In April 1569 it was reported that the protestants of Angrogna had been persuaded by their ministers to go to the help of the Huguenots who were besieged in the fort of Exilles, in the Valle di Susa, recently captured by the captain Colombin of Grenoble and the

[30] Foxe, *Actes and Monuments*, p. 966; *Storia delle persecuzioni*, pp. 168, 288; also Lentolo, in Morland, *History of the Evangelical Churches*, p. 234.

[31] *Histoire Mémorable*, ed. Balmas and Diena, pp. 100-2.

[32] *Storia delle persecuzioni*, pp. 103-5, 248f.; J. Jalla, 'Le Pasteur Martin Tachard à Riclaret', *BSHPF* 41 (1892), 272-4; Hemardinquer, 'Les Vaudois du Dauphiné', 62f.

[33] *Storia delle persecuzioni*, p. 198; Pazè Beda, *Riforma e cattolicesimo*, p. 59.

minister Giusto Blanc. The fort fell to the catholics at the end of the month; but thereafter the ministers of the Val Chisone, Philippe Pastre and Claude Perron, made arrangements to secure the military support of those of Angrogna on a regular basis.[34] In July 1573, when the catholic leader Carlo Birago threatened violence against the protestants of San Germano Chisone, the ministers and people from the surrounding valleys descended in force and routed the catholics. Only their leaders, especially the minister François Guérin (Francesco Guarino) prevented the people from hanging their catholic prisoners.[35]

As one might expect, Scipione Lentolo was very much opposed to this violent trait in the Vaudois character, which he felt was endemic:

Although yours is the true religion . . . nevertheless, as far as you are concerned, it might be just superstition. For if in haste, and in the frenzy of a mob, you take up arms, and put men to death for religion; all the same few or none of you of the valleys make a good confession of that religion, and seal it with your blood . . .[36]

The protestant ideal, that of Crespin and Foxe, was of the believer who admitted his beliefs openly before his judges, and faced punishment bravely; the medieval custom was to deny heresy as far as possible to save one's skin, if one had not first succeeded in escaping capture. In the late sixteenth century, defence and not martyrdom was still the norm for the Waldenses.[37]

It hardly matters whether in these patterns of conduct the ministers consciously adopted the standards of their people, or whether they responded to the exigencies of their surroundings. It is clear that, one way or another, they followed the logic of their situation rather than anything Calvin or Geneva expected of them. This breakdown of the synods' control, when they were in theory so all-powerful, becomes even clearer when one looks at the protestants of the Queyras.

[34] A. Pascal, 'La lotta', *BSHV* 53 (1929), 77–80; Pazè Beda, *Riforma e cattolicesimo*, pp. 71f.
[35] A. Pascal, 'Le lettere del . . . Castrocaro', *BSHV* 26 (1909), 28–36; 'La lotta', *BSHV* 55 (1930), 43f.
[36] *Lentolo MS*, p. 492.   [37] Compare above, ch. 5 (iv).

(iii) Protestant extremism in the Queyras

The region of the Queyras comprises a group of valleys from which the Guil and its tributaries flow west through the defile of the Combe de Queyras to join the Durance near Guillestre. On its extreme eastern end this enclave abuts on to the Val Pèllice; a path leads from Ristolas over the Col de la Croix to Villanova, west of Bòbbio. There is no firm evidence of the presence or absence of heresy in this area before the Reformation. The Reformation made small inroads in the 1560s: a carpenter obtained a copy of a Geneva Bible and read from it, and in 1565 two men of Château-Queyras opposed edicts against hearing protestant ministers.[38]

At the end of March 1574 the minister François Guérin, usually called Guarino or Garin in the sources, invaded the valleys of the Queyras with 200 armed men from Angrogna and converted the region forcibly to the protestant faith. According to one account, Guérin made the village of Ristolas pay a composition of 200 ducats, and took over all the payments which were due to the King of France in order to pay for the ministers which he imposed on the communities.[39] On 20 June 1574 it was reported that another captain of 200 protestant 'banditti', Pietro Fraschia, had invaded the Queyras.[40] In July a further detachment came over the Col Vieux from Angrogna and invaded Molines, where the Huguenot forces had their stronghold.[41] In the same year the *parlement* at Grenoble issued an edict forbidding La Cazette and other catholic captains to harass these protestants.[42]

These protestant soldiers came to be called 'Chapeaux-blancs'. The title had some pedigree. A 'barba' who had preached at Manosque in 1533 had been distinguished by an impressive plumed hat.[43] Cosme Brevin had made jokes about some protestant gentry who heard his sermons at

---

[38] Gioffredo, *Storia delle Alpi marittime*, col. 1517.
[39] Gioffredo, loc. cit.; Pascal, 'Le lettere del ... Castrocaro', *BSHV* 26 (1909), 37 f.; 'La lotta', *BSHV* 55 (1930), 70.
[40] Pascal, 'La lotta', *BSHV* 55 (1930), 79.
[41] Blet and Letonnelier, *Le Dauphiné ... textes historiques*, p. 107.
[42] Chabrand, *Vaudois et protestants*, p.119; Arnaud, *Protestants du Dauphiné*, I, 296, based on ADI B 2035.
[43] Manteyer, 'Les Farel, les Aloat et les Riquet', 54 f.

Fenestrelle, calling them 'couchons blancs' after the white felt hats they wore.[44]

Whatever their origins, the protestant rulers of the Queyras behaved with violence and tyranny. They demanded that the catholics convert; they put a notary of Villevieille in a well and kept him there for ransom. They raised taxes on the catholic population to support their army, and tried to uncover conspiracies against themselves which would justify confiscating property. Atrocity stories spread, for example that they had placed a priest in a barrel, driven knives through it, and rolled it down a hill.[45] They turned the church tower of Molines into a fort, where they took their plunder and stored it.[46]

The events of 1574 were not isolated. About ten years later the catholics Mures and La Cazette tried to retake the valleys. The protestants of the Queyras promptly sent for help to the other side of the Alps; some 'banditti' of the Piedmontese valleys under Giacomo Pellenco and Pietro Fraschia were sent, each commanding 100 crossbowmen. After the capture of the upper reaches of the Durance by Lesdiguières in 1585, they were made secure in their stronghold.[47]

Even the catholic accounts admit that there was more to the reformation of the Queyras than mere violence, however. According to one source, when Guérin took control of these protestants, he gave a messianic character to his apostolate: 'Il luy fit dire, qu'il estoit Christ, ou pour le moins envoye de Christ.'[48] He chose twelve followers who were called his evangelists and apostles. Guérin preached around the valleys, on horseback and with his weapon in hand, trying to convert by force of personality and threats. Some of his group behaved in carnival fashion. Having terrified the priests, they then thought how best to abolish the mass; they decided to bury it. They dressed up one of their number as a priest, then carried

---

[44]   *CO*, XX, col. 81.

[45]   Gioffredo, op. cit., col. 1511; *Le Dauphiné . . . textes historiques*, p. 107.

[46]   Gioffredo, op. cit., cols. 1517-23; Chabrand, *Vaudois et protestants*, pp. 116-34; Pascal, 'Le lettere del . . . Castrocaro', *BSHV* 26 (1909), 37; Rorengo-Lucerna, *Memorie historiche*, pp. 81-9.

[47]   Jalla, 'La Riforma in Piemonte durante il regno di Carlo Emanuele I', *BSHV* 42 (1920), 28f.

[48]   Gioffredo, op. cit., col. 1518.

the crucifix of one of the churches in a mock procession for the dead, and buried it in the village square. Apparently they made their procession 'singing filthy songs and abominations of their devising'.[49]

Even allowing for the exaggeration natural to religious propaganda, one has difficulty in fitting in the reformation described in these sources with the rest of the story so far. However, the 'Francesco Guarino of Dronero or thereabouts, an infantry soldier and a man resolved on every kind of ploy', was a Waldensian minister like anyone else.[50] He had studied at Geneva before beginning his ministry. In 1565 he had been entrusted with a letter from Théodore de Bèze to the Duchess of Savoy; in 1596 he, or perhaps one of his descendants, was to represent the Queyras at the synod of Aspres.[51]

As we saw, Guérin had been at the head of those who routed Birago's troops at San Germano in 1573. In that year he also brought about the dramatic and sudden coup of the conversion of the village of Pramollo, in the foothills of the Pinerolese, when he drove the priest away and converted the village at a stroke.[52] In the summer of 1575 he was using the valleys of the Queyras for amassing his troops; in the late autumn he led a raid on his native Dronero in what proved an abortive attempt at its capture.[53] Nor was Guérin unique amongst the heretic leaders of the Alps; the letters of the Savoyard governor Castrocaro are full of reports and complaints in the mid-1570s about the depredations of other 'banditti', for example Pietro Fraschia, Martino Bonetto, and Claude Perron, the minister of Fenestrelle. What little we know of their activities suggests they were men of similar ferocity.[54]

[49] Gioffredo, op. cit., col. 1522; Rorengo-Lucerna, op. cit., p. 85, quotes the cry on this occasion: 'Nous aven enterrà la Messo, che iamais retornerà en à quest pais.'

[50] Gioffredo, op. cit., cols. 1518, 1619, and Rorengo-Lucerna, op. cit., p. 83.

[51] Jalla, 'Synodes vaudois', 489; *LHG*, p. 189; *LRAG*, I, 81; Bèze, *Corresp.*, IV, 274, n. 8; VI, 26, n. 2.

[52] Gilles, 1881 edn., I, 428–30; E. Balmas, *Pramollo* (Torre Pèllice, 1975), pp. 16–23.

[53] Pascal, 'Le lettere del . . . Castrocaro', *BSHV* 28 (1910), 21–30; 'La lotta', *BSHV* 55 (1930), 86f.

[54] See esp. Pascal, 'Le lettere . . .', *BSHV* 28 (1910), 17; 'La lotta', *BSHV* 53 (1929), 8f.

By this time the ministers installed in the Waldensian valleys were clearly no longer estranged from their congregations as they had been. However, they probably went much further than any of the leaders of dissent before the Reformation. The authority of the *barbe* had been combined, at least in men like Guérin, with the authority wielded over dissenting communities by the syndics in the past; if that leadership were used in favour of an aggressive protestant policy, the results would be more dramatic than ever before.

(iv) The social base of the new churches

For most of this study we have depended upon protestant witnesses, and upon accounts relating to the ministers. We have a little glimpse of the Waldensian laity after the Reformation in the records of catholic pastoral visitations; these were made, in 1583 in the Val Chisone by the vicar-general of Oulx, Hugues Peralda, and in 1584-5 and 1594-6 by Angelo Peruzzi and Archbishop Broglia in the Piedmontese valleys.[55]

All these visitations showed how complete had been the success of the reform in insinuating itself into the structures of village society. The commissaries reported a series of church lands alienated and church buildings demolished or converted to other uses. The only priest left in the Val Chisone was the prior of Mentoulles, who could not reside;[56] in the Broglia visitation it emerged that the priest of Torre Pèllice had fled because of threats to his life.[57]

Peralda and his company made contact with the heads of various communities, the consuls of Pragelas, Usseaux, Fenestrelle, and Mentoulles. They dealt with Jehan Guiot, *dict* Papon, consul of Pragelas, and with Martin Flot, *conseiller* to the community; they also met several others of the names of Guiot or Ponsat.[58] All of these names figured in the trial records of the 1480s; there is no evidence that the

[55] Caffaro, *Notizie . . . della chiesa pinerolese*, VI, 287-96, 477 ff.; Pazè Beda, *Riforma e cattolicesimo*, pp. 84 f.; A. Pascal, 'Communità eretiche', *BSHV* 30 (1912), 61-73.

[56] Pazè Beda, *Riforma e cattolicesimo*, pp. 60 f.

[57] Pascal, 'Communità eretiche', 69, 72.

[58] Caffaro, *Notizie . . . della chiesa pinerolese*, VI, 288 f., 291, 294 f.

composition of village society had changed in the mean time.[59] Moreover, when the community met the catholic visitors, it was represented by its lay leaders, as had always been the case. Some ministers might acquire the prestige formerly held by syndics; but as Lentolo found out to his cost, they could not supplant them. The Waldensian communities were also unusual in the completeness with which their ordinary people had converted to protestantism in the face of a hostile state; in other supposedly 'protestant' regions the position was more equivocal.[60]

---

[59] *BP*, I, fo. 244ᵛ; II, fos. 379ʳ, 414ʳ, 416ᵛ, 418ʳ, 424ʳ; *ADI A*, fos. 55ᵛ-8ʳ, 262ᵛ, 275ʳ, 282ʳ, 330ᵛ.

[60] See below, ch. 17 (ii).

16. The Historians and the Waldenses

The heirs of the first protestant ministers of the Piedmontese valleys have founded a tradition of 'Waldensian' historiography, which has written the history of the sect from the inside. However, the solidarity maintained by that small but self-conscious church has tempted historians to push 'Waldensian' history further back into the past than it will really reach. The history of the Waldenses, in the early modern period, was history written by those within a literate, protestant, urban cultural tradition, regardless of whether or not it was in fact the work of ministers in the valleys. That historical tradition will be studied here as a final chapter in the relationship between protestantism and rural dissent.

(i) Reformed pastors: Lentolo, Miolo, Vignaux

It is appropriate to begin this survey with those authors who have already figured as protagonists in the story. It is not very clear when Scipione Lentolo wrote the largest of these indigenous treatises, his *Historia delle Grandi e Crudeli Persecutioni*. The earliest date to be suggested is 1562, and the latest possible is 1595; from the internal evidence of the eighth book it seems probable that most of the text was compiled shortly after Lentolo's expulsion from Piedmont in 1566.[1]

Lentolo's only editor so far[2] suggested that the book was entirely original and written from first hand; and that it was written in Italian because Italian was spoken in the valleys before the plague of 1630.[3] Both these claims were mistaken.

---

[1] Lentolo, pp. 4f., 11-16. See also E. Comba, 'La Storia inedita dei Valdesi narrata da Scipione Lentolo', *BSHV* 14 (1897), 45-61.

[2] Teofilo Gay, in the 1906 edition.   [3] Lentolo, pp. 7f.

Lentolo wrote Italian because he came from Naples, had trained at Venice, and was sufficiently interested in the language to write a grammar of it.[4] It was as natural for him to use Italian as it was for Estienne Noel to use French. Secondly, the first seven of the eight books of the *Historia* are almost entirely derivative. Lentolo began the work with an account of Peter Waldo's first break with the catholic church; he then listed a series of articles of faith associated with the Waldenses.[5] All of this was taken, with the most minor variations, from the articles on the Waldenses in the *Catalogus Testium Veritatis* of Matthias Flacius Illyricus.[6]

The remainder of the first book presented an account of the massacres in Provence, derived from the Latin version of Crespin's martyrology issued by Baduel.[7] Lentolo only diverged from the Latin original when he inserted (after the confession of faith of 1541) an exposition of the Ten Commandments,[8] and near the end of the narrative, where he turned to follow a different text, closer to the French editions.[9]

Most of books two to six of the *Historia* was taken up with accounts of the persecutions from 1555 to 1561 in the valleys of Piedmont. For events up to 1559 (before his own arrival) Lentolo used the Crespin corpus, which in turn used sources such as the anonymous *Histoire des Persécutions*, sometimes mistakenly attributed to Lentolo himself.[10] This was especially true of his account of the trial of Giafredo Varaglia.[11]

Lentolo was only original, in fact, when he described what he had himself done or seen: his preaching at Carignano and Villanova d'Asti; his confession of faith of 1560; a letter to Racconigi, and materials on events in the plain of Piedmont; and his own dispute with Possevino.[12] Even his long seventh

---

[4] See above, ch. 11 (ii).   [5] Lentolo, pp. 19-22.

[6] Flacius Illyricus, *Catalogus*, 1608 edn., cols. 1498-1501.

[7] Lentolo, pp. 22-76; Crespin-Baduel, fos. 88ʳ-117ʳ.

[8] Lentolo, pp. 53-8.

[9] Compare Crespin, 1565 edn., pp. 212ff.; Lentolo, pp. 70-6.

[10] See *Storia delle persecuzioni*, ed. Balmas and Theiller, esp. pp. 26f.; Lentolo, pp. 77-87; Crespin, 1619 edn., fos. 583ᵛ-6ᵛ; P. Chaix, A. Dufour, and G. Moeckli, *Les Livres imprimés à Genéve de 1550 à 1600* (Genève, 1959), pp. 272, 315; Bèze, *Corresp.*, III, 103, n. 5.

[11] Lentolo, pp. 87-115; compare Crespin, 1619 edn., fos. 457ʳ-60ᵛ.

[12] Lentolo, pp. 117-18, 126-45, 147-51, 153-70, 171-5.

book on the martyrdom of Gianluigi Pascale, the pastor in Calabria executed in 1560, contained many overlaps with Crespin.[13]

The true purpose behind the book was only made clear in the eighth and final book, which is not a piece of historical writing at all. Using the previous books as exempla, Lentolo set out to show why the Waldenses had suffered so much. Their persecutions were a punishment for their five principal sins: their despising the word of God; their lack of fear of God; their lack of zeal for his honour; their lack of respect for pastors; and their excessive avarice and dedication to the things of this world. Lentolo would accept no excuses, and warned the Waldenses that God would punish them if they did not change.[14] He then turned to a lengthy description and justification of his pastoral technique. Only at the very end did he reveal the chief scandal which had prompted this outpouring of invective. As pastor in the valleys he had preached before the local elections and pointed out the people's duty to them. The previous syndics had nominated two candidates with Lentolo's approval, but in a stormy and tempestuous election two others 'of little or no value' were elected.

If after all these things the poor pastor is transported with an excessive rage, and calls them devils, . . . saying that he would rather he and all his own children were in the fires than amongst those who, under pretence of being the people of God, dishonour him so manifestly, taking no account of the admonitions made to them according to the word of God . . . and show they have no respect either for God, or for men, and are the most profane and impious one could ever find; whom would anyone think was to blame?[15]

Lentolo's history was plagiarized because he did not set out to be a historian. His intention was immediate and political; he wished to teach his former flock a lesson through his account. The title of a lost manuscript suggests he may have done the same thing at Chiavenna, where he also ran into trouble with dissidents.[16]

---

[13] Ibid., pp. 257–80, 290–7, 304–15; compare Crespin, 1619 edn., fos. 556r–v, 559v–65v.

[14] *Lentolo MS*, pp. 473–5, 482f., 491–511.   [15] Ibid., pp. 580f.

[16] T. Gay, 'Scipione Lentolo', *BSHV* 23 (1906), 106; the title of the MS was 'Della Chiesa di Chiavenna da notarsi le cose che alla giornata si risolvono'.

Many of the points just made regarding Lentolo have already been established in the modern edition of the *Historia breve e vera* for the minister Girolamo Miolo.[17] Miolo came from a bourgeois Pinerolese family; he left the Dominican order to become a protestant and studied at Geneva from the end of 1563. He was a minister in the Val Pragelato about 1579, and according to his own preface wrote his history about 1587.[18] When the Dauphinois protestant Daniel Chamier was collecting manuscripts for a study on Waldensian history proposed by the synod of Embrun in 1603, a translation of Miolo's work was made by Dominique Vignaux for Chamier's use. This French version, now lost, was used by Perrin under the title of the 'Mémoires de Vignaux'; it was suggested that Vignaux might have added some material to Miolo's text as well as translating it.[19]

Although much shorter than Lentolo's work, Miolo's pamphlet still used some of the same sources. When discussing the history of the ancient Waldenses and their ideas, Miolo quoted Flacius Illyricus, with only minor alterations explicable on theological grounds.[20] This excerpt from Flacius, thus given a spurious historical basis, was copied by Perrin from Vignaux's translation and printed in his *Histoire*.[21]

Some small sections of Miolo's work were original: he provided a colourful (if historically vague) description of some persecutions in the Val Chisone and the Val d'Angrogna in the late Middle Ages, and a list of *barbes* and of ministers to Waldensian parishes which had no written antecedents. Nevertheless, these items do not add very much to the rather diffuse information, mostly from protestant sources, found in the book.[22]

Unlike Lentolo, on the other hand, Miolo began the

[17] *Historia breve*, ed. Balmas.

[18] A. Pascal, 'Un episodio ignoto nella vita di Girolamo Miolo', *BSHV* 25 (1908), 41-56; Miolo, *Historia breve*, ed. Balmas, pp. 19-43, 81; *LRAG*, I, 85.

[19] Miolo, *Historia breve*, ed. Balmas, pp. 7-10. The only extract from Vignaux's work which is known and is not a translation of Miolo's history is a paragraph quoted by Perrin, *Vaudois*, p. 48.

[20] Miolo, *Historia breve*, ed. Balmas, pp. 45 f., 55-7, 59 f., 81-4, 98 f.; Flacius Illyricus, *Catalogus*, 1608 edn., cols. 1498-1501.

[21] Miolo, *Historia breve*, ed. Balmas, p. 61; Perrin, *Vaudois*, pp. 48-50.

[22] Miolo, *Historia breve*, ed. Balmas, pp. 65, 70, 90-2, 94-6, 107-15.

process of special pleading on the Waldenses' behalf. When he discussed their 'Nicodemism' or their attitude to dancing and revelry, he acted as a conscious advocate, trying to present the Vaudois as the upright, respectable protestants whose origins were lost in the past.[23] This trend was to be developed further, first of all by the small clique who had ready access to the debris of the Embrun archive, and later on in ever greater detail by seventeenth-century theologians.

(ii)   Apologetics, apocalyptic, and Gallicanism

With two authors from the Dauphiné, Jean-Paul Perrin and Marc Vulson, the history of the late medieval heretics in the Dauphiné comes full circle; for it was through their hands that the records of the inquisitions made in the 1480s first passed into print. During the siege of Embrun by the Huguenot leader Lesdiguières in November 1585, the catholic defenders had retired from the archbishop's palace to the Tour Brune, a fortress which was linked to the palace by a wooden gallery. The defenders cut down the gallery to try to stop the assault; the records of the inquisition, which had been stored there, were spilt in the street. They were later collected by two of the besiegers, the chancellor of Navarre, Soffrey de Calignon, and Marc Vulson. Perrin made this episode an excuse for the lavish praise he heaped on Lesdiguières in the preface to his *Histoire des Vaudois*.[24]

Perrin did not acquire the records directly. Daniel Chamier was the first choice of the synod of Embrun in 1603 to be the author of a work on the Waldenses; however, after he had examined the texts he decided the task was not for him.[25] It was reported to a synod at Grenoble in 1605 that the minister Cresson had been appointed in his place, and that he had been referred for documents to Chamier, Perrot, Anastaze, de Rotier, Videl, and others. Cresson also turned down the task, protesting that he did not understand the dialect of the texts. In 1605 Jean-Paul Perrin of Lyon, minister at Nyons, was appointed in turn; the ministers

---

[23]   Ibid., pp. 47–53, 97, 101, 104.

[24]   Perrin, *Vaudois*, preface and p. 128.

[25]   Miolo, *Historia breve*, ed. Balmas, pp. 7 f.; Fornier, II, 195.

Perron and the younger Ripert were assigned to help him with the material in dialect. The work was three times presented to various synods, finally to that of Vitré in 1617; the Dauphiné province of the protestant church paid for its printing, and it was issued in 1618 and 1619.[26]

Manuscript sources in fact played a rather secondary role in Perrin's work; he was offered the text of Lentolo's history, but never used it.[27] He sought first to vindicate the reputation of the medieval Waldenses from the aspersions of unnatural vice and outrageous error which had lain upon them, and to establish them as protestants *avant la lettre*. To this end he amassed a great list of quotations from other authors out of context, and from translations of the Taborite texts in Provençal, which he deployed so that the protestants might find, in Fornier's words, 'la resemblance de leurs professions dans les siècles passez'.[28]

The second book of the *Histoire* sat rather uneasily on top of this detailed and sophistical argument. While Perrin clearly read the records of the Embrun inquisitions and the Morel-Bucer dossier, he used them only to draw the descriptions of the persecutions, or as a quarry, for example for the more orthodox of Morel's remarks. Perhaps advisedly, he made no clear attempt to forge any link between the profession of the late medieval Waldenses, as his history revealed them, and the reformers. On the contrary, as he claimed the two sects held the same beliefs anyway, he played down the talks in 1530 and thereafter as far as possible.[29] His companion volume on the Albigenses showed the same diffuseness; the histories of persecution and of belief were not related one to another, and many of the documents adduced as 'Albigensian' were transcriptions of the pseudo-Waldensian Taborite tracts.[30]

The Marc Vulson who rescued the Embrun registers may have been the same man who was the author of the tract *De la puissance du Pape, et des Libertés de l'Église Gallicane*

[26] Miolo, *Historia breve*, ed. Balmas, pp. 8f.; J. Jalla, 'Synodes Vaudois', *BSHV* 21 (1904), 62f.; E. and E. Haag, *La France protestante* (Paris and Genève, 1846-59), art. Perrin.

[27] Comba, 'Storia inedita dei Valdesi', 46-9.

[28] Perrin, *Vaudois*, Book I, chs. 3-14; Fornier, II, 177.

[29] Perrin, *Vaudois*, Book II, ch. 3, at pp. 109-49.

[30] J. P. Perrin, *Histoire des chrestiens albigeois* (Genève, 1618).

published in 1635.[31] If not, he must have been a relative of this later Marc Vulson, and left him some of his papers. This tract sought to achieve the more limited historical aim of showing that the Papacy only possessed its authority in France as a result of usurpations. Vulson claimed that one of the worst of these usurpations took place in the thirteenth century, under pretext of a crusade against the Albigenses.[32]

Although not explicitly a protestant work, Vulson's tract used many protestant arguments. It asserted that the Waldenses and Albigenses held the same doctrine down to the time of the Hussites and Lutherans, chiefly in their rejection of the power of the Pope. It referred to the proof of this claim as being in the 'livres et procés qui sont riere moy, . . . et a esté verifié par plusieurs mesmes en dernier lieu par le Sieur Perrin . . .'; it rejected explicitly the suggestion that these heretics held extreme ideas, such as dualism, or that they committed 'des sorceleries, et des incestes abominables, les chandeles esteintes . . .'. Vulson resurrected Perrin's suggestion that the inquisitors wrote up the registers of the trials in much fuller form than the first evidence warranted; he cited the case of Pietro di Jacopo (referring to a piece of trial summary which still exists) and referred in support to a protest made against Nicholas Paris in 1483 (he said 1493) and to the decree of the *Grand Conseil* of 27 May 1502 in the Waldenses' favour.[33]

In his few pages Vulson made, entirely *hors de propos*, a rather more coherent contribution to the thesis of the Waldenses as antecedents of the Reformation than Perrin had done in several hundred. However, such arguments were not confined, either to authors native the Dauphiné, or to those with a particular polemical interest in the Waldenses. The Waldenses earned inclusion, if only in passing, in the works of nearly all the major religious writers of the early Reformation era; a brief study of the role played by the Waldenses in protestant apologetics is indispensable.

---

[31] M. Vulson, *De la puissance du Pape* (Genève, 1635); *BV*, no. 1011.
[32] Vulson, op. cit., pp. 204–12.   [33] Ibid., pp. 205, 207.

(iii) The martyrologists and their heirs

The term 'Waldenses' became a respectable one for protestants to use from the mid-1550s onwards. From that point the name referred to two distinct entities: first, the real people who had suffered persecution in the fifteenth and sixteenth centuries in the Alps; and secondly, some idealized hypothetical antecedents of the reformed church, usually dated to the mid-twelfth century, who were little more than a bundle of doctrines in the works of most writers. Usually, but not always, the martyrologists were concerned with the historical Vaudois, and the theologians with the theoretical Waldenses; the former are considered here, and the latter in the next section.

Naturally enough, the most comprehensive, and often most diffuse, coverage of the sufferings of the Vaudois people and their associates was provided by the French protestant martyrologies. Crespin's treatment of the Vaudois may be divided into two classes of material. He listed with increasing fullness individual martyrdoms: Martin Gonin and Estève Brun before the 1550s; after that period, Jehan Vernou and his companions, Barthélemi Hector, Nicholas Sartoire (a protestant from the plain of Piedmont), Giafredo Varaglia, and Gianluigi Pascale.[34] Secondly, he provided occasional reports of the experience of whole peoples, whether the Waldenses of Provence,[35] or those of Piedmont.[36] Most of the individual victims were in fact protestants, so their confessions were suitably edifying; the people of Provence might have been corrupt in beliefs, but their moral tone and sufferings provided the value of the propaganda.[37]

Crespin's approach to the problem of the Waldenses was immensely influential. Even before the *Actes des martyrs* had established itself as the main source, the same method was being used by other authors. Ludovicus Rabus, a native of Memmingen who had trained at Tübingen, then succeeded Caspar Hedio at Strasbourg, and had become the leading

---

[34] Crespin, 1619 edn., fos. 118^r-19^r, 124^{r-v}, 345^r-60^v, 428^v-30^v, 446^r, 457^r-60^v, 555^r-66^r.

[35] Ibid., fos. 141^r-55^v, 195^v-7^v, 678^r.

[36] Ibid., fos. 445^v-6^r, 583^v-600^r, 839^r-41^v.

[37] See above, ch. 13 (iii).

pastor of the protestants at Ulm,[38] published between 1554
and 1557 a martyrology in which he included a German
version of Crespin's account of Martin Gonin's sufferings.[39]
Johann Sleidan (1506-56), the historian of the Schmalkaldic
league, used Genevan sources for his short notice of the
persecution of the Waldenses of Provence.[40] At the end of his
abrupt narrative of Meynier's brutality, Sleidan appended a
description of a confession of faith which the Waldenses of
Provence were supposed to have submitted in 1544: this set
out articles of faith on the Trinity, the Church, magistracy,
the sacraments, marriage, good works, false doctrine, and
the role of the creeds as the rule of faith.[41] This confession
had a curious history. Independently of Sleidan, Charles du
Moulin, in his treatise *On the Monarchy of France*, claimed
that the persecution of Mérindol had begun under Louis XII,
who halted the course of events until he had heard of their
morals from Fumée; he then quoted in full a confession of
faith, dated 1544, clearly identical in substance to that
described by Sleidan.[42] Du Moulin's entire passage was
reprinted in 1605 by Joachim Camerarius of Bamberg in
his collection of pieces on the Vaudois of Provence; the
confession on its own was included in the specialist histories
of Perrin and Morland.[43] Sleidan's own version of events was
copied by Flacius Illyricus and by his Calvinist editor and
plagiarist, Simon Goulart.[44]

Meanwhile other writers were using the Crespin material
more directly, with the same simple hagiographic intent.
Heinrich Pantaleon (1522-95) was an early ecumenist and at
different times a deacon at Basel and a Count Palatine of the

---

[38] H. Pantaleon, *Prosopographiae Heroum . . . totius Germaniae* (Basel,
1565), p. 509.

[39] L. Rabus, *Historien der . . . Martyren* (Strasbourg, 1554-7), VI, 121^{V}ff.

[40] J. Sleidanus, *De Statu Religionis et reipublicae, Carolo Quinto Caesare,
Commentarii* (Strasbourg, 1556), fos. 217^r-19^r.

[41] For the French original of this confession in full, see C. Schmidt, 'Aktenstücke', 256-8.

[42] C. Molinaeus, *Tractatus de origine, progressu et excellentia Regni et
Monarchiae Francorum et coronae Franciae* (Lugduni, 1564), pp. 96-101.

[43] Camerarius, *Historica Narratio*, pp. 443-8; Perrin, *Vaudois*, pp. 87 ff.;
Morland, *History of the Evangelical Churches*, pp. 37-9.

[44] Flacius Illyricus, *Catalogus*, 1556 edn., pp. 712-20; 1608 edn., cols.
1502-5.

Empire.[45] He published during one of his more protestant phases in 1563 a martyrology, used by Foxe, in which he called energetically for Christian unity, but also rendered into Latin the articles in Crespin on Martin Gonin, Jehan Vernou, Giafredo Varaglia, and the Vaudois of Provence and Piedmont.[46] The *Commentaires de l'estat et de la religion* of Pierre de la Place took their title from Sleidan, but also included a brief discussion of the War of the Edict of Nice, possibly deriving some material from Lentolo's account in his letter of 1561 via the *Histoire mémorable*, and printing the text of the edict of Cavour.[47] John Foxe's *Actes and Monuments*, at least from the edition of 1583, included translations of the later articles in Crespin on the massacres in Provence and the War of the Edict of Nice.[48] Théodore be Bèze dedicated a special section of his *Icones* to the Waldenses, in which he abridged the material transmitted by Crespin; he also provided a separate tribute to the minister of the Waldenses in Calabria, Gianluigi Pascale.[49] The *Histoire ecclésiastique* renounced even this attempt to bring all the Waldensian material under one umbrella, as it provided separate articles on the familiar material of Martin Gonin, Estienne Brun, the Vaudois of Provence, Jehan Vernou, Barthélemi Hector, the attacks on the Piedmontese in the 1550s, and Giafredo Varaglia, in strict chronological order.[50]

Neither the content nor the approach of the martyrologists to their material is in any way surprising; they saw the Waldensian people as examples of suffering for religion borne with fortitude, and their pastors as models for the protestant missionary. It is more surprising that some of the same language and an identical approach to the heretics were used by historians writing from a different ideological standpoint. Henri-Lancelot Voisin de la Popelinière (1540-1608), in spite of serving as a captain in the Huguenot army, adopted a

[45] L.-G. Michaud, *Biographie universelle* (Paris, 1842-65), art. Pantaleon.
[46] Pantaleon, *Martyrum Historia*, pp. 73-6, 111-45, 310-28, 334f., 340ff.
[47] P. de la Place, *Commentaires de l'estat et de la religion et république sous les rois Henry et François seconds, et Charles neufième* (s. l., 1565), fos. 199ᵣ-207ᵛ; *Histoire mémorable*, ed. Balmas and Diena, p. 16.
[48] Foxe, *Actes and Monuments*, 1583 edn., pp. 942-72.
[49] Bèze, *Icones*, sigg. Cc i-ii, Hh iv.
[50] *HE*, I, 23, 26, 35-47, 97, 111, 137f., 158.

neutralist stance in his *Histoire de la France* of 1581, which consciously eschewed religious polemic. He held an exalted view of the task of the historian as seeker after truth;[51] he adopted an even-handed approach to his narratives of the most atrocious episodes of the Wars of Religion, apparently anxious to write a work which catholics and protestants might both believe.[52] Notwithstanding these high-minded aims La Popelinière fell foul of the protestant authorities and his work was censored.[53] This aspect of his history did not imply any different approach to the Waldenses, however, since he described the massacres in Provence and the war in Piedmont in conventional terms.[54] Théodore-Agrippa d'Aubigné (1550-1630) also tried to show, in his *Histoire universelle* of 1618-20, some fairness to both parties in the religious wars.[55] Yet he gave the Vaudois a pedigree in the line of Albigenses, Hussites, Wycliffites, and Lollards; he admired the self-defence of the Piedmontese Vaudois in 1560-1, and listed them amongst the martyrs.[56]

Jacques-Auguste de Thou (1553-1617), perhaps the most distinguished of these historians, stood for the *politique* stance against fanatics of either creed, and so far tempered his catholicism as to have his history placed on the Index in 1609.[57] His account of the early Waldenses resembled that of Flacius Illyricus in its description of Waldo's protest and its similarities to other heresies; his version of the massacres in Provence improved on the Latin of Claude Baduel, but left the content unchanged; he rejoiced in the terrible disease which destroyed Meynier after his acquittal.[58] In describing

[51] C.-G. Dubois, *La Conception de l'histoire en France au XVIᵉ siècle (1560-1610)* (Paris, 1977), pp. 124-53; M. Yardeni, 'La Conception de l'histoire dans l'œuvre de La Popelinière', *Revue d'histoire moderne et contemporaine*, 11 (1964), 112-16.

[52] G. W. Sypher, 'La Popelinière's *Histoire de France*', *Journal of the History of Ideas*, 24 (1963), 47-52.

[53] Sypher, op. cit., 43-5; Yardeni, op. cit., 110-11.

[54] H.-L. Voisin de la Popelinière, *L'Histoire de France* (La Rochelle, 1581), fos. 24ʳ-9ᵛ, 245ʳ-54ᵛ.

[55] A. Garnier, *Agrippa d'Aubigné et le parti protestant* (Paris, 1928), III, 71-85; Dubois, *Conception de l'histoire*, pp. 185-95.

[56] T. Agrippa d'Aubigné, *Histoire universelle* (Maillé, 1616-20, actually 1618-20), I, 66-81.   [57] Dubois, *Conception de l'histoire*, pp. 172-85.

[58] J. A. de Thou, *Historiarum sui Temporis* (Paris, 1604-8), I, 455-73.

the War of the Edict of Nice he only deviated from the traditional accounts by describing the Vaudois as the 'Convallenses', a neutral term without religious purport.[59] De Thou was not unique amongst Catholic lawyers; Thomas Cormier of Alençon, in his history of the reign of Henri II, reported all the details of the massacres in Provence, albeit without moral commentaries.[60] The reason for this consensus among writers who were not protestant propagandists must be that, while moderate catholics did not draw theological conclusions from Waldensian history, they were so shocked by the way the heretics were treated that they could report their experiences in a way which was at variance with their attitude to other forms of protestantism.

In the second half of the seventeenth century the martyrological tradition was given further impetus by the atrocities perpetrated against the Waldenses in the so-called *Pasque Piemontesi* of 1655.[61] These events incited the publication of numerous tracts relating mostly to events just past.[62] The anonymous author of the *Waldenser Chronick* of 1655, probably D. Sudermann,[63] took the occasion of the massacre to compile and publish an exhaustive *Jahrbuch* of all the miscellaneous persecutions of the Waldenses which had come to his notice; set out in a strict chronological order, with no attempt at historical narration, far less interpretation, this work ran to over 500 duodecimo pages.[64]

Samuel Morland's *History of the Evangelical Churches* of 1658 was partly in the same genre as these tracts. This work was published when its author (1625-95) was thirty-three and newly returned from an embassy to the court of Savoy to protest about the massacres and persecuting edicts. The

[59]   Ibid., III, 19–50.

[60]   T. Cormerius, Alenconius, *Rerun Gestarum Henrici II regis Galliae* (Paris, 1584), fos. 48ʳ–53ʳ.

[61]   Armand Hugon, *Storia dei Valdesi II*, pp. 73–102.

[62]   See for example *Matchless Crueltie, declared at large in the History of the Waldenses* (London, 1655); *Relation véritable de ce qui s'est passé dans les persecutions et massacres faits cette année aux églises réformées de Piémont* (*s. l.*, 1655); and numerous translations into other European languages.

[63]   *BV*, no. 88.

[64]   *Waldenser Chronick, das ist von dem harkommen Lehr und Leben wie auch Vervolgingen der Waldenser 1160 bis in das 1655* (*s. l.*, 1655), esp. pp. 35 ff.

part which related solely to the recent massacres seems to have been written at the suggestion of the Secretary, John Thurloe. However, Archbishop Ussher had also met Morland before he set about his embassy, and had urged him to gather materials for the history of the earlier Waldenses. In his travels Morland collected numerous manuscripts, some describing the events of 1655, some, like the surviving registers of the Embrun inquisition, probably collected from the Lesdiguières family at Geneva. All these found their way to the University Library at Cambridge. Morland's *History*, therefore, drew on a wider documentary base than almost any other similar tract. It included a description of the Waldensian valleys and their churches; it repeated the apocalyptic arguments used by Perrin, Flacius, and Ussher to prove the antiquity of the Waldenses; most importantly, it printed excerpts from numerous manuscripts, including the dialect tracts of catechisms and moral instruction, the poem 'Nobla Leyczon' of uncertain date, the Taborite treatises on Antichrist, purgatory, and the sacraments, extracts from Miolo's and Lentolo's writings, and pieces from the Embrun archive (Morland repeatedly translated 'Ebredunum' as 'Evreux'). Very little of this material was used with sufficient dexterity to make a coherent or original argument; Morland did not help his own reputation with later historians by appending the date of 1120 to numerous transcribed documents dating from the early modern period. Nevertheless, the value of the *History* as propaganda was immense; Morland was able to report the collection of no less than £38,241 10s. 6d. in England to relieve the sufferings of the victims of the massacre. The *History* was translated into French and reprinted with very little significant variation by the Vaudois pastor Jean Léger in his *Histoire Générale* of 1669.[65]

Similarly, in 1686, just after the revocation of the Edict of

[65] *DNB*, art. Morland, Sir Samuel; Morland, *History of the Evangelical Churches, passim*; of this book, pp. 29–41, 72–92, and 142–87 are copies and translations of materials either discussed or already printed by Perrin; much of the rest up to this point came either from printed sources or the Cambridge MSS; pp. 196–242 contain materials from the Embrun inquisition and from the war of 1560–1; materials relating to events in 1655 and after occupy pp. 287–709. See also Léger, *Histoire générale, passim*; and for the influence of the 1655 massacre in England, John Milton's sonnet 'On the late massacre in Piemont'.

Nantes, Vittorio Amedeo II, duke of Savoy, expelled the Waldenses from the Piedmontese valleys by force. After three years of exile in Genevan territory the Vaudois fought their way back to their valleys.[66] This feat of arms unleashed another torrent of pamphlets, not least the account written by the leader of the 'glorious return', Henri Arnaud.[67] Some historians, like Pierre Boyer, took advantage of the occasion to reissue the general accounts of the Waldenses derived from Perrin, with much additional material relating to recent persecutions.[68]

The martyrologies of the Waldenses evolved somewhat in 150 years. At first individuals commanded attention rather than whole communities, and patient suffering was held up as the supreme protestant virtue. Later on, however, these mountain communities were seen as a whole, and their histories were written as collective rather than individual biography. Vigorous resistance to persecution, which had always been typical heretic behaviour, was now exalted into an antitype of the warfare of the Old Testament.

(iv) The slaughtered saints and the true church

It was mentioned previously that the term 'Waldenses' referred to two separate entities in the early modern period: some real dissenters and sufferers in the Alps at the time of the Reformation, and some hypothetical heretics of the late twelfth century, of interest only for their beliefs, schematically reported. We have just seen how the martyrologists treated the real dissenters, concentrating on their sufferings and fortitude, and ultimately their victory. Now we must see how the theologians treated the hypothetical followers of Waldo. This style of propaganda started at about the same time as the martyrologies, but reached its full flowering in

[66] A. Pascal, *Le Valli valdesi durante la prigionia dei Valdesi* (Torre Pèllice, 1966); *Le Valli durante la guerra di rimpatrio dei Valdesi* (Torre Pèllice, 1967–8); Armand Hugon, *Storia dei Valdesi II*, pp. 119–95.

[67] Anon., *Histoire de la persécution des valées de Piemont* (Rotterdam, 1688), and translations; H. Arnaud, *Histoire de la glorieuse rentrée des Vaudois dans leurs vallées* (*s. l.*, but Cassel, 1710); see Armand Hugon, op. cit., p. 182.

[68] P. Boyer, *Abrégé de l'histoire des Vaudois* (La Haye, 1691).

the works of seventeenth-century authors such as James Ussher. It followed a totally separate course, although sometimes the techniques of martyrologists and theological disputants overlapped in the same book. The basic protestant claim was that the existence and survival of the Waldenses, along with that of other heretics such as the Albigenses, the Lollards, and the Hussites, proved that the 'true church', as foretold by prophecy, had not always existed in the Church of Rome, which had been taken over by Antichrist. This sanctified tradition of dissent showed that the reformers were continuing and amplifying the work of those who had kept the true church alive for centuries, not breaking away to form something new.[69]

The first and simplest way of making this claim was used by Matthias Flacius Illyricus (1520-75), conservator of arch-Lutheran orthodoxy and leader of the Magdeburg centuriators. The Waldenses figured as one of an enormous number of entries in Flacius's *Catalogue of Witnesses to the truth, who have cried out against the Pope before our time*. Their entry combined several kinds of material. A short account was given of how Waldo was suddenly converted into a pious ascetic at Lyon around 1160; then Flacius described how Waldo fell out with the Church, and was expelled from the city with his followers. Then, without any explanation or reference, a list of supposedly 'Waldensian' articles of faith was appended. These asserted the sole sufficiency of scripture; the sole mediation of Christ; the non-existence of purgatory; two sacraments; the rejection of the Mass, human traditions, and the primacy of the Pope; they also urged that communion be taken in both kinds, claimed the church of Rome was Babylon, rejected indulgences and clerical celibacy, and said the church of God resided in the hearers of His word. These articles were immensely influential; but their origin is unknown, and their correspondence to the belief of the Waldenses studied above is fairly remote.[70]

[69] See the prefaces to Flacius Illyricus, *Catalogus*, 1608 edn., sig. ** 4ʳ; and to Foxe, *Actes and Monuments*, in the same sense.

[70] M. Flacius Illyricus, *Catalogus Testium Veritatis qui ante nostram aetatem reclamarunt papae* (Basel, 1556), pp. 704-12; compare the use of the articles by Lentolo, Miolo, and Vignaux in (i) above; and the beliefs of the Waldenses as set out above, chs. 4-9.

Thereafter Flacius quoted Sleidan on the persecutions in Provence. More original, however, was the first introduction of a device which was to shape the rest of the debate: argument around medieval texts. Flacius quoted a long excerpt from the so-called 'Pseudo-Reinerius treatise', an influential medieval summary of the beliefs and morals of the Eastern German Waldenses.[71] Some parts of this text were welcome, as when pseudo-Reinerius praised the humility, simplicity, and chastity of the heretics; other parts where he criticized their doctrine required an antidote. For instance, when the medieval text claimed the Waldenses had a vow of poverty, Flacius commented in the margin that only persecutions taught them to be poor. To the allegations that the Waldenses condemned excommunication, oath-taking, or marriage, the marginalia asserted that the heretics condemned the abuse of the thing, not the thing itself.[72] At other times, Flacius tried to discredit his text by claiming that another author, for example Pius II, had not made such allegations.[73]

This attempt to identify antecedents of protestantism in heresy was brought a little further forward in other works. The *Magdeburg Centuries* included an account of Waldo's first schism, based on Flacius's *Catalogus*; the 'articles' were cited with some reorganization, and some new ones were added: these were more fierce, asserting that vows were human inventions which promoted sodomy; that orders were signs of the beast; that monasticism was a 'stinking carcase'; and that many Roman ceremonies were devilish inventions.[74] These new claims about Waldensian belief appear to have been taken from a short entry in the *Catalogue of famous writers of Great Britain* published in 1557 by John Bale, later bishop of Ossory (1495-1563); this entry had referred to some 'Waldenses' who had begun to teach in England in 1164.[75]

---

[71] Flacius Illyricus, *Catalogus*, 1556 edn., pp. 723-57; compare Nickson, '"Pseudo-Reinerius" Treatise'.

[72] Flacius Illyricus, *Catalogus*, 1556 edn., pp. 724, 732, 735, 743.

[73] Ibid., pp. 739, 746.

[74] *Duodecima Centuria Ecclesiasticae Historiae* . . . (Basel, 1569), cols. 1204-8.

[75] J. Baleus, *Scriptorum Illustrium maioris Brytanniae . . . Catalogus* (Basel, 1559), p. 207; *DNB*, art. Bale; compare the use of these same claims in de Thou, *Historiarum*, I, 455 ff.

John Foxe, in a quite separate part of his *Actes and Monuments* from that in which he described the sixteenth-century Waldenses, quoted in translation large sections of the article on the Waldenses by Flacius; however, he rearranged and abridged many of the Lutheran's authorities, and purged the 'articles' of several elements (for instance the reference to only two sacraments) which were unacceptable to the Church of England.[76]

The influence of the Flacian approach, finally, was shown towards the end of the sixteenth century in two short works which were otherwise closer to the martyrological tradition: the *Oration on the Christian Waldenses and Albigenses* of Peter Wesenbec (1546-1603), published at Jena in 1585;[77] and the *History of the Albigenses* of Jean Chassanion, published in 1595.[78] Wesenbec took care, when narrating the persecution of the Waldenses of Provence, to explain that they were persecuted for no other reason than because they stood up against the errors of Rome, and quoted Pius II for the essence of their beliefs.[79] Most of Chassanion's work consisted of a narrative of the Albigensian crusade; but in his first nine chapters he set out to show that the Albigenses were like any other medieval heretics, including the Waldenses; and that many of the opinions they were supposed to have held either were falsely ascribed to them, or were not in themselves heretical.[80]

Up to the end of the sixteenth century, most of the use made of the Waldensian example was not integrated into a closely argued case for the antiquity of the principles of the reformed church. The rhetoric was there, and the evidence was there; but the rigid logic which could bind the two into a coherent argument was not. Under pressure from a host of Jesuit polemics, but most of all from Robert Bellarmine (1542-1621) and Jacob Gretser (1561-1625) the early seventeenth century saw a new tradition of protestant

[76] Foxe, *Actes and Monuments*, 1583 edn., pp. 230-3.
[77] P. Wesenbecius, *Oratio de Waldensibus et Albigensibus Christianis* (Jena, 1585); P. Freher, *Theatrum Virorum eruditione clarorum* (Nuremberg, 1688), II, 962.
[78] J. Chassanion, *Histoire des Albigeois* (Genève, 1595).
[79] Camerarius, *Historica Narratio*, pp. 427-9.
[80] Chassanion, *Albigeois*, pp. 23-63.

propaganda establish itself.

The *Historical exposition of the unbroken Succession and State of the Christian Church*, published by James Ussher (1581–1656) when professor of theology at Trinity College, Dublin, was not the first of these theological works to use the Waldenses as a counter in argument.[81] However, it stands alone as the fullest treatment of the case by an established academic at this period. Its publication fell between Ussher's second visit to England and his work on the Irish articles of religion, and it was its author's first major work.[82] The extensive and scholarly use which Ussher made of material relating to the Waldenses foreshadowed the interest he was later to show in collecting manuscripts from Perrin's library; however, at this stage he depended almost entirely on printed sources which were freely available.

The aim of Ussher's work, according to his prefaces, was the same as that of Flacius or Foxe; he wished to prove that the 'True Church', which was bound to suffer persecution, but was always destined to survive, had survived within dissenting movements from the Dark Ages up to the time of Luther's first schism.[83] However, to further his argument against the English Jesuits, Ussher incorporated his chronology of dissent into a pattern of the ages of the binding and releasing of Satan, as foretold in Revelation 20.[84] The appearance of the Waldenses coincided with the loosening of Satan, and the rule of Antichrist in the Roman Church.[85] In his sixth chapter Ussher dealt with the morals and the beliefs of the Waldenses. For their morals, he quoted pseudo-Reinerius on their modesty and chastity, commenting that it was a wretched age in which modesty in morality was taken as a sign of heresy.[86]

For the belief of the Waldenses, Ussher relied on the

[81] J. Usserius, *Gravissimae Quaestionis, de Christianarum Ecclesiarum . . . continua successione et statu, Historica Explicatio* (London, 1613).
[82] *DNB*, art. Ussher.   [83] Ussher, op. cit., preface, sigg. A1ᵛ–2ʳ.
[84] Ussher's contribution to this form of literature is largely overlooked by K. R. Firth, *The Apocalyptic Tradition in Reformation Britain 1530–1645* (Oxford, 1979).   [85] Ussher, op. cit., pp. 142–9.
[86] Ibid., pp. 151–4, with reference to M. Freher, *Rerum Bohemicarum antiqui Scriptores* (Hanoviae, 1602), p. 231, and to J. Lilienstayn, *Tractatus contra Waldenses fratres* (?1505).

reports of the Bohemian brethren found in Pius II's and others' works; he quoted the *Magdeburg Centuries*; he quoted without disapproval a long passage of Bohemian inspiration from William Rainolds's *Calvino Turcismus*.[87] By far the greater part of this chapter, however, was occupied by a long piece-by-piece refutation of errors which the Waldenses were supposed to have held, and which Ussher blamed Sanders's *Visible Monarchy of the Church* for introducing into the debate.[88] These included the charges of libertinage; the rejection of all oaths; the rejection of capital punishment; despising the Apostles' Creed; and so forth. Ussher's technique was to quote an immense number of authorities to show that the catholic claims were either inherently contradictory, or were confuted by other witnesses. Once Ussher had found a text contradictory to Sanders's, he simply left the argument at that point; he did not try to establish what orthodoxy on the contested issue actually was.

In his eighth chapter Ussher dealt with the age of the Waldenses (by which he really meant all medieval heretics) and their various names. He insisted that their origins were in remote antiquity, as against the catholic claim that they were no older than the time of Waldo. He explained, with copious references, the origins of the names Patarene, Cathar, Bulgar, and Paulician, and outlined the careers of Peter of Bruis and Henry of Lausanne, pointing out the various stages at which these groups or men had been condemned. At the same time he took care to argue against some of the charges made against the Cathars. Most of the tenth chapter consisted of a narrative of the Albigensian crusade, although it was preceded by more argument about beliefs, in the course of which Ussher quoted the Provençal confession of 1544 (from du Moulin's work) in full.[89]

Ussher's work was undoubtedly full of a great deal of gratuitous and repellent pedantry; the task of organizing all the texts describing heresies before the Reformation seems to have been nearly too much for him. However, in this attempt

---

[87] Ussher, op. cit., pp. 154–8, with reference to G. Rainoldus, *Calvino Turcismus, id est, Calvinisticae perfidiae cum Mahumetana Collatio* (Antwerp, 1597).

[88] N. Sanderus, *De visibili monarchia ecclesiae* (Louvain, 1571).

[89] Ussher, op. cit., pp. 158–74, 209–55, 301–72.

to marshal the authorities for a protestant interpretation of the Waldensian past he not only anticipated Perrin; he was more thorough, more scholarly, and at least no more lacking in a sense of history than the minister of Nyons. Seen in a European context, the work of one Huguenot minister appears much less remarkable.

Both before and after the publication of Ussher's work a similar vindication and exploitation of the Waldenses was attempted by others on a smaller scale. Philippe de Marnix, Seigneur of Ste-Aldegonde (1538–98), one of the protagonists of the early stage of the revolt of the Netherlands, used the Waldensian case in his argument against Bellarmine in his *Tableau des Differens de la Religion*, first published in 1599. He described Waldo's schism briefly, offered a simple account of his followers and their beliefs, and described the Waldenses and Albigenses as 'the two olives or the two lamps, of which St John spoke, whose oil and light spread to the ends of the earth'. He made an explicit link between the Albigenses and the Waldenses in Provence and Piedmont, and was one of the first to refer to the dialect poems ascribed to the Waldenses, including the 'Payre Eternal'.[90] Nicholas Vignier, similarly, presented the Waldenses as the true Christians persecuted by Antichrist in a brief entry in his *Théâtre de l'Antechrist* of 1610.[91] As we saw above, the Dauphinois theologian Daniel Chamier (d. 1621) decided not to undertake a full history of the Vaudois. However, in his *Panstratiae Catholicae*, first published in 1610, he used the example of the persecutions of the Vaudois of Provence and the Alps (drawn from de Thou) as proof of the cruelty characteristic of Antichrist.[92]

The Aberdeen theologian John Forbes of Corse (1593–1648) found the Waldenses useful to his case at several points. To prove the cruelty of the Popes, he cited the Albigensian crusade; as proof of the beliefs of the Albigenses he cited the ideas ascribed to the Waldenses by de Thou, which derived in turn from Bale. He cited them also as having opposed

---

[90] P. de Marnix, *Le Tableau des differens de la religion* (Leiden, 1603–5), I, fos. 149r–53r.

[91] N. Vignier, *Théâtre de l'antechrist* (*s. l.*, 1610), pp. 235–8; on Vignier see Dubois, *Conception de l'histoire*, pp. 533–51.

[92] D. Chamier, *Panstratiae Catholicae* (Genevae, 1626), II, 682–4.

idolatry and transubstantiation.[93] Much later, the Huguenot
theologian Jacques Basnage de Beauval (1653–1723) used the
history of the Waldenses as a fundamental part of his explanation of the development and growth of the Reformation;
in this he found a new antagonist, the J.-B. Bossuet who, in
his *Histoire des variations des églises protestantes*, had done
so much to discredit the 'true church' school of thought.
Basnage continued to confound the Waldenses and the
Albigenses, using the beliefs of the former as proof of the
orthodoxy of the latter. He was also able to take full advantage
of the new materials on the fifteenth-century persecutions
then published by Perrin and Allix. In this context the
Waldenses were seen as part of a greater tradition, including
the Wycliffites and Hussites, which had preceded the Reformation. He was also able to use the Waldenses of Piedmont to
prove that the protestants disliked violent resistance; he
referred to La Popelinière's and de Thou's accounts of the
War of the Edict of Nice, which reported that the Waldenses
had decided first of all to flee rather than resist.[94]

In all the works considered in this section so far, the
Waldenses have been only a part, if an important one, of a
greater polemical design. In a few cases, however, they could
justify equally arid theological theses which concentrated on
the heretics for their own sake. The pattern followed by
these works was similar to that established by Ussher and
Perrin, and they need not be studied in detail. The Sedan
theologian Jacques Cappel, seigneur du Tilloy (1570–1624),
took issue with two catholic attackers of the Waldenses,
Claude de Seyssel and Claude Coussord, in a long and minute
debate over Waldensian belief published in 1618.[95] Caspar
Waser (1565–1625), a professor at Zürich, seems to have
published a very rare tract with a similar intent in 1621.[96]

---

[93] J. Forbesius, *Instructiones Historico-Theologicae* (Amsterdam, 1645),
pp. 216 ff., 371 f., 609.

[94] J. Basnage, *Histoire de l'église* (Rotterdam, 1699), II, 1433–48, 1499; see
also above, ch. 15 (ii).

[95] J. Cappel, *La Doctrine des Vaudois representée par Cl. Seissel archevesque
de Turin, et Cl. Coussord* (Sedan, 1618).

[96] C. Waser, *Assertio theologica: Deum omnibus seculis excitasse homines
pios . . . conprobatos Waldensium exemplo* (Zürich, 1621, not seen); see *BV*,
no. 1621.

The theme was taken up in Lutheran Wittenberg by Johann Frisch, in a disquisition published in 1663;[97] and by Elias Weihenmaier, in a work which appeared in the same place in 1690.[98] A similar dissertation has been attributed to Samuel Desmarets (1599-1673), a Picard Huguenot who had become minister to protestant Groningen.[99] Although the two tracts written by the exiled Huguenot Pierre Allix, treasurer of Sarum (1641-1717), have become more useful to scholars than the rest, thanks to their inclusion of the only editions of some of the Cambridge MSS, they were strictly within the theological school, as polemical and unhistorical as the rest; Allix's volume on the Albigenses included a long *discursus* on the English Lollards, taking it for granted that the two sects held the same beliefs.[100]

After the explosion of religious polemic in the seventeenth century, the debate rested in the eighteenth;[101] it was taken up again by evangelical Anglicans like William Jones and George Faber in the early nineteenth, eventually to perish in the face of a more critical approach to religious history.[102] From that time the history of the Waldenses became more and more the preserve of those within that church; and early modern Waldensian history has been seen as the succession of the authors closest to the sect, Lentolo, Miolo, Perrin, Gilles, Morland (and his shameless plagiarist Jean Léger), and Allix.

[97] J. Frischius, *De Waldensibus, Historico-Theologicam Disquisitionem* (Wittenberg, 1663).

[98] E. Weihenmajerus, *Vicissitudines et Fata Waldensium* (Wittenberg, 1690).

[99] S. Maresius, *Dissertatiuncula historico-theologica de Waldensibus* (Groningen, 1660, not seen); *BV*, no. 828; Nicéron, *Mémoires pour servir à l'histoire des hommes illustres* (Paris, 1727-45), XXVIII, 83.

[100] P. Allix, *Some Remarks upon the Ecclesiastical History of the Ancient Churches of Piedmont* (London, 1690); *Remarks upon the Ecclesiastical History of the Ancient Churches of the Albigenses* (London, 1692).

[101] Very few works were published relating to the Waldenses in this century; but see T. Bray, *Papal Usurpation and Persecution* (London, 1711-12), II, and T. Taylor, *The History of the Waldenses and Albigenses* (Bolton, 1793), both of which reprinted or abridged Perrin's history.

[102] See for example W. Jones, *The History of the Waldenses* (London, 1816); G. S. Faber, *An inquiry into the history and theology of the ancient Vallenses and Albigenses* (London, 1838); A. Blair, *History of the Waldenses* (Edinburgh, 1833). This traditional approach was strongly contradicted by S. R. Maitland, *Facts and Documents illustrative of the ancient Albigenses and Waldenses* (London, 1832).

However, we have seen that for a century and a half the Waldenses occupied a much more prominent place on the European literary stage. They were a symptom of the social upheaval inherent in a Reformation which appealed for spiritual as well as physical support in an intellectual quarrel to a tradition of popular dissent. As martyrs, they had an appeal which almost transcended confessional barriers; as primitive dissenters they authenticated the protestants' most extreme claims. If writers in either of these schools did not always see them as they were, their misunderstanding was at least shared by nearly all the intellectuals with whom the Waldenses ever came into contact.

17. Conclusions and Comparisons

It is not the aim of this study to conduct an iconoclastic revision of Waldensian history for its own sake. No service would be done to the cause, either of the surviving 'Waldensian Evangelical Church', or of history itself, if the myths of a previous generation of confessional historians were perpetuated. For several centuries the Vaudois were used as counters in theological arguments conducted far from their native valleys. In recent decades their history has been studied as a parallel to the history of European protestantism; hence we have seen emphasis placed on synods, on confessions of faith, on theological debates conducted by learned ministers, to the point where the highly individual identity of these Alpine communities almost ceases to figure in their history. More recently still, historians have come to treat 'popular culture' with more respect. Through such respect, and by a comparison between features of 'popular' religion with the religious practice of those more given to a rationalized form of worship, we may identify the most important lessons of this study. First, the more unexpected elements in previous chapters will be summarized; then a very brief comparison will be attempted between the protestantism of Piedmont and of the Alps around the Valtelline; finally, we shall attempt to draw from the whole some points which help to define features of protestant dissent itself.

(i) Results

The first striking feature of Waldensian heresy to emerge from this examination is its lay character. By this we do not mean simply that the beliefs and practices of the sect were carried on by those not in holy orders. The first 'Waldenses' were ordered to desist from preaching because they were 'private people and laymen';[1] a similar suspicion attached

---

[1] *Thesaurus Novus Anecdotorum*, V, col. 1778: 'Idiotae et laïci.'

itself to beghards and their kind, because they sought sanctification by immediate access to God without the mediation of the church.[2] In each case the 'heresy' lay in the usurping of the role of priests and friars, where laymen acted like churchmen. The Alpine Waldenses were not, by and large, a group of mystic enthusiasts imitating the stricter orders. The *barbes*, as far as we can see, played a rather subordinate part. The leaders of Waldensian dissent were those who led appeals, summoned meetings, appointed proctors, and levied taxes; they were also those who summoned *barbes* to dispute on their behalf. These were laymen who acted like laymen, although their dissent had spiritual as well as cultural overtones.[3]

Equally, the most distinctive features of heretical practice were those which were on the fringes of religious behaviour. They were: a preference for intermarriage and the maintenance of a close community; a conscious avoidance of casual blasphemy, to the point of seeming sanctimonious; the use of separate rituals in burial; and the cultivation of special emblems, like the *barbes'* needles.[4] In contrast to these signs, the worship and beliefs of the Waldenses were distinguished by irregularity and conventionality. Their confession was made to a *barbe* infrequently, and at intervals which varied immensely. Their statements on minor issues of faith, like the keeping of fasts and feasts, differed greatly from one witness to another.[5] The conventional nature of Waldensianism was shown in its prayers and penances, which closely resembled those of the church; in the lack of 'radicalism', or even of consistency, in the repudiation of purgatory; and in morality, where the grosser charges made against the Waldenses were almost certainly unfounded.[6] The popular nature of this dissent, finally, is most important. Its popular character lay most visibly in its failure to use logic to sort out the implications of its beliefs. For instance, although the saints were reduced in importance, this did not mean that prayers to them or feast-days for them were rejected out of hand; doubts about purgatory did not prevent some heretics from

---

[2] See R. E. Lerner, *The Heresy of the Free Spirit in the Later Middle Ages* (Berkeley, 1972), pp. 44–54; Kieckhefer, *Repression of Heresy*, pp. 19–21.

[3] See above, ch. 1 (iii).   [4] Ch. 8 (ii, iv–vi).

[5] Chs. 6 (iii), 7 (ii).   [6] Chs. 6 (iv), 4 (ii), 8 (iii).

saying prayers for the dead; above all, uncertainty about the value of priestly orders did not lead to a total neglect of Catholic worship.[7] Proverbial sayings can contradict one another, and yet each may be conserved with equal firmness; such sayings seem to have been the purest form of heretical creed.

A whole area of unexpected results surrounds the relations between Waldenses and churchmen. Before crusades disrupted life in the Alpine valleys, Vaudois and churchmen got on, or failed to get on, according to the play of personalities and local politics.[8] As far as the inquisitors' articles show us anything, they suggest that churchmen did not even adopt a very empirical approach to finding out about their local heretics.[9] It may be easy enough to explain persecution in theory, and the trends in modern writing seem to favour an approach which takes account of religious, social, and cultural factors. Here such factors must account for the *support* for persecution, since no class stood to gain from it.[10] Crusading, however, had almost no social dimension; those individuals who *initiated* such activity appear to have had little but self-aggrandizement and greed to inspire them.[11] Perhaps the worst problem is that social factors, which must somehow explain why local people acquiesced in the persecution of heretics, must also explain why heretics were also tolerated, when persecution revealed itself as a worse evil.[12] Heresy had turned out to be a social illness whose medicine was not only worse than the disease; it was also ineffective.

The consequences of a detailed inquiry into the contacts between Waldenses and protestants are in retrospect perhaps less surprising. Clearly, the sort of strict chronology which is appropriate to institutional history is out of place in the world of ideas and beliefs. The changes which have been suggested in the usual pattern have the effect of placing the conversion of the Waldenses in a later era of protestantism; not the first decades of optimism and intellectual discovery, but the time of intense organization, self-defence, and religious war.[13]

[7] Chs. 4 (i–ii), 5 (i), 7 (ii).
[9] Ch. 9.
[11] Ch. 2 (iv).
[13] Ch. 10.

[8] Ch. 5 (i).
[10] Above, ch. 2 (iii).
[12] Ch. 3 (iii).

In the context of the conflict of attitudes and social assumptions, however, it seems more surprising that protestants and Waldenses ever joined forces at all. In their doctrines we have seen little evidence to place the Waldenses amongst the precursors of the reformers. In terms of their education and backgrounds, the ministers had more in common with priests (from whom many, for instance in Germany, were converted)[14] than with popular heretics. Since the heretics had traditionally rejected the tutelage of priests and learned religious figures, we are forced to conclude that only their hostility to Rome made the Vaudois suitable subjects for conversion to Calvinism. In other respects they must have been, if anything, more intractable than rural catholics, and certainly more so than the urban artisan and professional classes which formed the bulk of French protestants.[15] Protestantism, ultimately, set out to rationalize religion; Lentolo's questionnaires and Calvin's *Catechisms* were alike designed to show the believer the logical reasons for his belief.[16] The attack on superstition, one of the most prominent results of Reformation thought,[17] was only a part of a message profoundly inimical to the popular, proverbial belief which has just been described, in its 'catholic' and 'heretical' aspects alike.

The final result of the study so far has been to show two unresolved problems of the process of protestant infiltration. First, the protestant church could barely come to terms with the Waldenses in fact; severely as candidates for Vaudois parishes were vetted, they might still turn out to be more violent leaders of dissent than the *barbes* ever were. Secondly, protestant theology did not understand Waldensianism any the better for a close association. Thirteenth-century churchmen had extrapolated the consequences of Waldensian beliefs to make them more radical and coherent than they were in fact; protestants welcomed such extrapolations, because they

---

[14]   See R. W. Scribner, 'Practice and Principle in the German Towns: Preachers and People', in *Reformation Principle and Practice: Essays in honour of Arthur Geoffrey Dickens*, ed. P. N. Brooks (London, 1980), pp. 99–103.

[15]   See J. Garrisson-Estèbe, *Protestants du Midi 1559–1598* (Toulouse, 1980), pp. 13–56.

[16]   Above, ch. 13 (ii).

[17]   Compare Thomas, *Religion and the Decline of Magic*, pp. 58–89.

seemed to vindicate their own radicalism. Literary students of heresy were no more respectful of the subtleties of popular thought than were ministers in the parishes.

(ii) Comparisons

Features of the Waldensian experience which seem strange to the modern historian may not have appeared so in their own period. Perhaps the most useful way to check one's assumptions is to compare protestantism in the western Alps with the same faith as practised in another, quite specific, region. The valleys of the Grisons and the Valtelline, where Scipione Lentolo preached after his expulsion from Piedmont,[18] provide a useful case for comparison. In both regions protestantism was a minority creed; in both areas the distribution of the population was overwhelmingly rural;[19] the Valtelline and its environs, on the other hand, had not known medieval heresy.

The experience of ministers in dealing with secular authority was no different in Piedmont from the Valtelline: they had to face catholic representatives in disputation;[20] they ran the risk of capture and execution.[21] The case of Piedmont was unusual in that a monarchy, albeit a weak one, was prepared ultimately to tolerate a religious minority; in the Valtelline, plurality of religions was a result of the complex play of forces within the Swiss confederation.[22] Equally unheard-of in the Valtelline or northern Lombardy was violent resistance to persecution, still less resistance which succeeded; for example, when the small protestant community of Locarno fell foul of the catholic cantons of Switzerland, it was simply

---

[18] Above, ch. 11 (ii).

[19] K. J. Beloch, *Bevölkerungsgeschichte Italiens* (Berlin, 1937-61), III, 235-42, 250-6.

[20] T. McCrie, *History of the Progress and Suppression of the Reformation in Italy*, 2nd edn. (Edinburgh and London, 1833), pp. 380f.; *Bullingers Korrespondenz*, ed. Schiess, I, 280, 445.

[21] See above, ch. 10 (vi); McCrie, *Reformation in Italy*, pp. 401f.; F. Ninguarda, *Atti della visita pastorale diocesana* (Como, Società Storica Comense, 1892-4), I, 251.

[22] McCrie, op. cit., pp. 361-8, 385f., 393f.; see also O. Vasella, 'Zur Entstehungsgeschichte des 1. Ilanzer Artikelbriefs', *Zeitschrift für schweizerische Kirchengeschichte*, 34 (1940), 182-91.

told to convert or leave; and many of its members went and settled in Zürich.[23]

The most remarkable difference, however, is not between these two different forms of rural protestantism, but between the course of the Reformation in the countryside and the towns. In the countryside protestant and catholic could mix, and in the case of the Valtelline even share places of worship.[24] Disputations were real contests, where the outcome was not determined in advance. Such a state of unresolved tension was almost unknown in the cities of Germany, where protestant infiltration would nearly always provoke a crisis.[25]

We have seen that the ministers of the Piedmontese valleys were men of learning, apt to be estranged in sympathies from their congregations.[26] Those of the Valtelline, like Vergerio the younger, Mainardi, Zanchi, and Lentolo himself, were likewise distinguished churchmen; many less well-known figures came from clerical backgrounds.[27] However, the Piedmontese congregations were unusual in their almost uniformly peasant origins. The Valtelline protestants were often from a few distinguished families, and 'rustic heretics' were the exception rather than the rule.[28] In spite of this difference, some of the same problems arose. As Lentolo complained of the grudging way he was paid at Prali,[29] so did the leaders of the Grisons churches.[30] The problem of language was even more acute in the lands of Romansch and Ladin than in those of the Piedmontese dialect called 'Provenzale'.[31]

[23] TCD MS 1149, *passim*; Altmann, *Tempe Helvetica*, IV, 131-202; McCrie, op. cit., pp. 272-84 and refs.; Meyer, *Evangelische Gemeinde, passim*; F. C. Church, *The Italian Reformers 1534-1564* (New York, 1932), pp. 224 ff.

[24] Ninguarda, *Atti*, I, 245, 289, 358.

[25] Compare the stereotype of German urban reformation discussed by Ozment, *Reformation in the Cities*, pp. 121-31.

[26] Above, ch. 11 (ii).

[27] Ninguarda, *Atti*, I, 249, 270, 280, 349.

[28] Ibid., I, 281 ff., 330 ff., 340 ff., for the families of the Malacrida, the Paravicini, the Cattanei, and the Capelli; for 'rustic heretics' see ibid., I, 285 f., 300, 306, 311, 334.

[29] *Lentolo MS*, p. 498.

[30] McCrie, op. cit., pp. 373-5; P. D. Rosius de Porta, *Historia Reformationis Ecclesiarum Raeticarum* (Chur, 1771-7), I, pt. 2, 178-98; *Bullingers Korrespondenz*, ed. Schiess, I, 230, II, 107, 108 f., 128 f., 154 ff.

[31] Rosius de Porta, *Hist. Ref. Raeticarum*, I, pt. 1, 186 f.; McCrie, op. cit., pp. 372 f., *Bullingers Korrespondenz*, ed. Schiess, I, 406 ff.

The Piedmontese valleys were, by contrast with the Valtelline, exceptional in their lack of serious dissension amongst the ministers. Valtelline ministers quarrelled for many reasons, some because of cultural antagonism between German- and Italian-speakers,[32] some over administrative or doctrinal issues.[33] There was nothing similar to these disputes in Piedmont, save in exceptional cases like that of Cosme Brevin.[34] There were at least three reasons for this discrepancy. First, the company of pastors at Geneva exercised a more stringent control over candidates for parishes than the churches at Zürich and Chur.[35] Secondly, Piedmont was not turned into a refugee camp for all kinds of unorthodox spirits fleeing from the Roman inquisition, as were the Alps north of Milan. Even in the late 1580s Morbegno, in the Valtelline, sheltered a group of refugee Italian protestants with their own minister.[36] Finally, since the ministers sent to Piedmont were apt to be at odds with their congregations, they had to keep solidarity amongst themselves; had they quarrelled with each other as well, their isolation would have been even worse. The Waldensian parishes, therefore, were a rather specialized kind of protestant community. Their ministers were not the *primi inter pares* of a group sharing a common heritage; they were foreigners called in to lead a body of people which had existed before them, and with whose ways they had come to terms.

Finally, the protestants in the valleys of Piedmont were, for a rural heterodox community, unusual in being concentrated in one small area. Most of the Waldensian villages were reckoned by about 1580 to be totally heretic, and only a few on the fringes of the Vaudois ghetto were of mixed faith: Luserna, Torre Pèllice, Perosa and its hamlets, and the parish of San Bartolomeo. Even in these parishes the protestants tended to gather in one hamlet.[37] On the other hand, in the Valtelline even the strongholds of protestantism, like

---

[32] *Bullingers Korrespondenz*, ed. Schiess, I, 238, 247, 286; II, 542, 544, 552.

[33] For documents of some of these disputes see Rosius de Porta, *Hist. Ref. Raeticarum*, I, pt. 2, 62 ff., 81 ff., 180–230; *Bullingers Korrespondenz*, ed. Schiess, I, 106 f., 131 ff., 144, 243, 421; Church, *Italian Reformers*, pp. 192 f.

[34] Above, ch. 15 (i).   [35] See above, ch. 13 (ii).

[36] Ninguarda, *Atti*, I, 269 f.   [37] Foà, 'Valli del Piemonte', 8 f.

Caspano, Sondrio, or Poschiavo, were only partially converted to the new faith, protestant 'hearths' rarely exceeding a quarter of the total. Most cells of heresy were far smaller.[38] Equally, the old heretic communities, with their tradition of endogamy, were much less prone to dividing families over religion, whereas mixed marriages were frequent and common in the Valtelline.[39]

In so far as this comparison shows differences between a rural protestant community with and without a heretical past, it is safe to say that most, if not all of those differences were caused by the continued influence of heretical traditions in the Waldensian valleys. Violent resistance to authority, and the readiness to dissent without official approval, had been the way of medieval dissidents. The Vaudois protestants were mostly peasant farmers, as their Vaudois forebears had been; probably there were few actual 'converts' from catholicism in these valleys. Because the heretics were traditionally intractable, their ministers had to band together more tightly and teach them more consistently. A long tradition of dissidence had created heretic villages and heretic households in a way in which piecemeal conversions failed to do. As a social, rather than as a religious phenomenon, Waldensianism shaped the character of its protestant future very profoundly.

(iii) Conclusions

Any attempt to write a history of such an introverted and self-conscious form of popular belief as Waldensianism must find itself entangled in a disabling paradox. Truly popular belief and behaviour in this period tends not to leave written records of its own; we have seen that even those sources supposed to be 'Waldensian' are very suspect.[40] Therefore this study has had recourse again and again to the records and activities of the literate and the clergy, whether sympathetic to the Waldenses or not: to the behaviour and attitudes of inquisitors, and the records they created; to the reactions

---

[38] Ninguarda, *Atti*, I, 280, 299–306, 350f.
[39] Above, ch. 8 (ii); compare Ninguarda, *Atti*, I, 247, 251f., 268f., 286.
[40] Above, ch. 4 (introduction), and ch. 14 (i).

of early and later protestants to meeting the Vaudois; and to the way they were used by theologians.

However, this irony has a lesson of its own; for the experience of the Vaudois is perhaps even more important for what it teaches us about protestantism than for what it teaches us about heresy. The Waldenses reveal themselves simply as a group of people dedicated to their distinct, communal vision of their own importance and their own holiness, a group which refused to be bullied or distracted by outsiders unless for the most pressing of reasons. This result is hardly surprising in retrospect. However, it does reinforce the lesson which the late medieval clergy could not learn, that heretics were not like another kind of public church, mirroring the official institution in every detail. It also gives us a stern warning against being too confident of the absolute truth of the conclusions just reached. These conclusions are answers to questions which the Waldenses would almost certainly never have asked.

The results of our comparison between 'Waldensian protestantism' and the protestantism of the Valtelline are, on the face of it, a little discouraging. The Waldensian experience was, after all, unique, and the atmosphere of Angrogna cannot be transported lock, stock, and barrel to another part of protestant Europe. However, the outcome is not wholly negative. The uniqueness of the protestantism of the south-western Alps lay in certain features—violent self-defence, a close-knit community at odds with its pastor, predominantly peasant congregations—which had nothing to do with the purely spiritual aspects of 'Waldensianism'. These features were prominent because the rural proletariat was Waldensian first, and only later protestant by adoption; the pattern by which scattered middle-class groups were the first to become protestant, as in the Valtelline, did not hold. Therefore, we should look for the parallels to Lentolo's complaints about impiety, insubordination, and ignorance in those rural areas where protestantism was imposed from higher up the social scale—England, Scandinavia, or some of the German states. The Waldenses' attitudes to the practice of religion and the imposition of a highly trained pastorate may be just better publicized examples of the reaction of the majority of

European country folk when suddenly subjected to a severely rational religion; they were special only because propagandists paid so much attention to them. To test this suspicion we need many more studies of rural protestant communities than have so far been written; the most one can say is that the reaction of the Waldenses to protestantism has nothing psychologically improbable about it.

The behaviour of the protestant ministers, on the other hand, is very unexpected. They chose to unite themselves to a pre-existent popular heretical group, and that choice, even if it meant becoming the senior partner in the union, was not one which any intellectual leaders of dissent could possibly have made before the sixteenth century. It was a breaking of ranks with the social and intellectual élites within which all normal religious disagreement had hitherto been conducted. Popular heresy had always either been exclusively popular from the start, or had become popular through the debasement of a conflict which had started in the schools. To take up the cudgels on behalf of a group which had no spiritual or intellectual respectability was very nearly class treason; it was also a sign that the Reformation split had become irrevocable. It implied, moreover, that the protestant church now explicitly supported a revolt of ordinary people against their superiors, if there were compelling religious reasons for such revolt. It was perhaps not accidental that several editions of propaganda about the Savoyard war of 1560-1 were circulating in French about the time that the first Wars of Religion broke out in France.[41] We are a long way from the spirit of the Lutheran or English Reformations, where access to the traditional sources of power and influence was the natural way to bring about religious change.

Not unnaturally, such a drastic reinterpretation of the history of popular heresy as that which the protestants made required a theoretical justification. The admission of the Waldenses to the protestant communion was justified, retrospectively, by an attempt to turn the real Waldenses into model protestants; it was justified in Reformation propaganda, ironically and with little regard for consistency, by producing

[41] On this propaganda see above, ch. 10, n. 165, and ch. 15, nn. 29-31.

massive arguments to prove that the heretics had always been model protestants anyway. Johann Eck intended to insult Luther when he accused him of Hussitism, just as Alfonso de Castro intended to vilify the protestants by accusing them of Waldensianism. The reformers turned the flank of their opponents by accepting the charge of old-fashioned heresy and turning it into a title of honour. Protestants had nothing to lose by such a stratagem, once they had decided that the break with Rome was irreparable, and especially since they had resolved to condemn the whole history of medieval catholicism, not just for intellectual error, but as the embodiment of Antichrist's rule in the Church. Rarely can such a small group of people, neglected and despised for more than a century, have been so suddenly raised to prominence in helping to justify such a sweeping process of change; rarely can there have been such a slender basis for those claims in fact.

Appendix
Chanforan: the making of a myth

It proved necessary earlier[1] to restate the history of the Piedmontese Vaudois in 1532 without dismantling the story of the 'Synod of Chanforan' piece by piece. However, the historiography of this particular myth is not without its own lessons. A brief survey of the authorities on this point helps to explain both why the story was first accepted, and more importantly, why it is perpetuated although the evidence against it is so strong.

None of the protestant martyrologists, whether from protestant countries or from the Waldensian valleys, explicitly described a synod held in September 1532, still less did they call it the Synod of Chanforan.[2] Perrin's chapter on the Piedmontese Vaudois described a synod held in 'Angrogna' on 12 September 1535 (*sic*), at which he said the letters of Oecolampadius and Bucer were read out, and a confession of faith was adopted. Perrin was careful to suggest that this confession contained nothing alien to the ancient Waldensian beliefs.[3] The confession which he printed was a reorganized form of the manuscript Angrogna propositions of 1532; the latter's clauses of protestant theology, from the end of the text, were moved to the beginning, and those about Waldensian beliefs were relegated to a position further back.[4]

Pierre Gilles established 12 September 1532 as the date of the gathering, in his work of 1644; he also added that some proposals on conducting public worship were adopted. He

---

[1] Above, ch. 10 (iii).

[2] This excluding, of course, the Genevan chroniclers such as Fromment, who did not write about the Vaudois for their own sake.

[3] Perrin, *Vaudois*, pp. 157–61. It will be remembered that Perrin's chief aim was to represent the Waldenses as proto-reformers; so it was impossible for him to admit that events in 1532 changed anything of substance.

[4] Compare Vinay, *Confessioni di fede . . . riformati*, pp. 139–43.

followed Perrin for the reordered version of the propositions.[5] Several authors took these articles at face value, and there the matter rested for two centuries.[6] Jacques Brézé's *Histoire des Vaudois*, published in 1796, spoke of an assembly at Angrogna, in terms identical to those used by Gilles.[7] Alexis Muston, in the first of his many works, spoke of the doctrines of the 'Synod of Angrogna' as 'a necessary condescension made to the religious movement of the time, and a result of the *barbes*' modesty. . . .'[8] C. U. Hahn, writing in 1847, followed the same line.[9]

The 'Synod of Chanforan' had to wait until the publication of the *Histoire des Vaudois* written by Antoine Monastier, a reformed pastor like Pierre Gilles, which appeared in 1847.[10] Monastier cited Gilles's history, p. 40, as evidence that the synod took place at Chanforan, and that one called Farel, with a red beard, had been there on a white horse.[11] Alexis Muston's *Israel of the Alps*, first published in 1851, took up the story of Chanforan, as did J. J. Herzog's work of 1853.[12] These authors were followed by Emilio Comba, who settled the orthodoxy from that point on.[13]

However, the point was not taken up everywhere. The histories of Ferdinand Bender and Wilhelm Dieckhoff, written respectively in 1850 and 1851, both ignored Monastier's 'discovery', as did Aléxandre Bérard's *Les Vaudois* of 1892.[14] Doubts really began to be felt after the publication of

---

[5] Gilles, 1644 edn., pp. 30-3.

[6] Morland, *History of the Evangelical Churches*, pp. 39-41; Léger, *Histoire générale*, I, 95 f.

[7] J. de Brézé, *Histoire des Vaudois* (Paris, 1796), II, 44.

[8] A. Muston, *Histoire des Vaudois des vallées du Piémont* (Paris, 1834), p. 372.

[9] C. U. Hahn, *Geschichte der Ketzer im Mittelalter* (Stuttgart, 1847), II, 158-61.

[10] A. Monastier, *Histoire de l'église vaudoise depuis son origine jusqu'à nos jours* (Toulouse, 1847).

[11] A. Monastier, *A History of the Vaudois Church* (London, 1848), p. 146.

[12] A. Muston, *L'Israël des Alpes* (Paris, 1851), I, 181-7; J.J. Herzog, *Die Romanischen Waldenser* (Halle, 1853), pp. 377-80.

[13] Comba, 'Sinodo di Chanforan', and 'L'Introduction de la réforme dans les vallées du Piémont', *BSHPF* 43 (1894), 7 ff., where Comba postulated not one synod of Chanforan, but three.

[14] F. Bender, *Geschichte der Waldenser* (Ulm, 1850), pp. 133-8; A.W. Dieckhoff, *Die Waldenser im Mittelalter* (Göttingen, 1851), pp. 129-33; A. Bérard, *Les Vaudois, leur histoire sur les deux versants . . .* (Lyon, 1892), p. 167.

Herminjard's *Correspondance des Réformateurs*, which contained many marginal strictures about points of Waldensian history. It was noticed that what Pierre Gilles reported on p. 40 of his history had nothing to do with events in 1532. His account was this:

Jean Peiret d'Angrogne, l'un des surpris par Bersour faisant la garde, déposa le 22 de September [1535] qu'ils faisoyent la garde pour les ministres qui enseignent la bonne loy, qui estoyent assemblez en la bourgade des Chanforans au milieu d'Angrogne, et dit qu'entre autres il y en avoit un qui s'appeloit M. Farel,[15] qui avoit la barbe rouge, et un beau cheval blanc, et deux autres en sa compagnie, desquels l'un avoit un cheval quasi noir, et l'autre estoit de grande stature, un peu boiteux. C'estoyent des Pasteurs qui continuoyent de venir des quartiers de Suisse, pour les causes susdites. Il nomma aussi des Barbes des Valées, et tesmoigna que tous les habitants d'Angrogne adhéroyent à leur doctrine. Un autre prisonnier confessa que les Barbes avoyent tenu alors leur synode qui avoit duré six jours. Le procez latin dit Capitulum.[16]

This entire episode dates from Bersatore's campaign of 1535. The witness would have had no reason to make statements about events three years before; Gilles did not tie in this testimony with his story of the 1532 assembly. It is not even clear from the text that the 'chapter' of the *barbes* was the same gathering to which the protestant ministers, as Gilles called them, had come.

Yet, on this basis, it has been insisted that the Waldenses met at Chanforan, on the date mentioned in the Dublin MS propositions, 12 September 1532, and that their conference lasted six days, or in some versions to 18 September (which is in fact seven days, counting inclusively). Jean Jalla found other reasons, grounded in the supposed etymology of 'Foran' from the Latin 'forum', for saying that any large meeting would have taken place at the traditional location, marked in 1932 by a great stone monument.[17] This suggestion is accepted as a hypothesis by Molnár.[18] It is, however, curious to see a

---

[15]   According to Herminjard, this was Gauchier Farel and not Guillaume; see Herminjard, III, 352, note.

[16]   Gilles, 1644 edn., pp. 40 f. See also Provana, 'Rapports', 276-8.

[17]   J. Jalla, 'Le Synode de Chanforan', *BSHV* 58 (1932), 42.

[18]   Gonnet and Molnár, *Vaudois au moyen âge*, p. 308.

very modern author, confronted with evidence which gives the lie to this farrago of misreading, still choosing to adhere to the traditional account.[19]

[19]   Audisio, *Barbe et l'inquisiteur*, pp. 55-60, 103.

Select Bibliography

Manuscript Sources

This section lists only those documents consulted either directly or in photographic copies.

Cambridge, University Library

Dd. 3. 25 — Materials from the inquisition at Embrun, 1483–1502, chiefly collected by the notary Nicholas Paris. Classed as G in the list of the Cambridge collection prepared by Morland, *History of the Evangelical Churches*, sigg. g2^v–h3^v.

Dd. 3. 26 — Further materials relating both to the inquisition and rehabilitation at Embrun. Classed as H by Morland.

Dd. 3. 33, fos. 1^r–2^v — The letter of Scipione Lentolo describing the early stages of the 1560–1 war. Classed as P by Morland.

Dd. 3. 35, fos. 30^r–41^v — The manuscript of the *Historia breve e vera* of Girolamo Miolo. Classed as R by Morland.

Dublin, Trinity College Library

259 — The dossier on the talks between Morel and Masson and Oecolampadius and Bucer in 1530, and the text of the propositions of 12 September 1532.

260 — A collection of texts of moral treatises in a dialect of Provençal, preceded by an ecclesiastical calendar, dating from the early sixteenth century.

263 — As for 260. These volumes contain material of catholic and Taborite origins.

265 — Materials from the Embrun inquisition, translated into Latin in the early seventeenth century. Derived from 266.

266	Materials from the Embrun inquisition, in copies of the sixteenth or early seventeenth century. Some appear to be taken from the manuscripts at Cambridge; others are original.
267	As for 260 and 263, except that only catholic material is included in this volume.
1149	Daniel Orell, *Locarnensis Persecutio*.

Gap, Archives départmentales des Hautes-Alpes

G 2761–4, 2766–7	The 'Registres d'Insinuation' of the archbishopric of Embrun, covering the period 1463–1513. Most of the material here relating to this topic was discovered by the Abbé P. Guillaume.

Grenoble, Archives départmentales de l'Isère

B 4350	Registers of the inquisition of Alberto Cattaneo, including interrogations taken in the Val Chisone from 19 September 1487 to 2 March 1488. Much damaged by damp and wear.
B 4351	The registers of the Cattaneo inquisition in Fressinières and l'Argentière, taken mostly in April 1488.

Oxford, Bodleian Library

Barlow 8	Scipione Lentolo, *Historia delle Grandi e Crudeli Persecutioni*. This MS is a copy of MS no. 716 of the Municipal Library of Berne, checked and edited by the author's nephew. It contains material not found in the 1906 printed edition of the Berne MS edited by T. Gay.

Paris, Bibliothèque Nationale

Fonds Latin, 3375, I–II	Material from the process of rehabilitation of the people of Fressinières, l'Argentière, and Vallouise, 1501–7. This manuscript also contains extensive transcriptions of earlier material submitted as evidence in the case.

Works printed before 1700

The conventional distinction between primary and secondary material cannot be applied to the literature on this subject. Many 'secondary' articles consist chiefly of editions of original source material, and many early narratives are both the objects and the instruments of study in the course of this work. This section and the following have therefore been arranged alphabetically within a simple chronological division.

Allix, P., *Some remarks upon the Ecclesiastical History of the Ancient Churches of Piedmont* (London, 1690).
—— *Remarks upon the Ecclesiastical History of the Ancient churches of the Albigenses* (London, 1692).
Aubéry, J., *V. C. Jacobi Auberii pro Merindoliis ac Caprariensibus Actio*, ed. D. Heinsius (Leiden, 1619).
—— *Histoire de l'exécution de Cabrières et de Mérindol* (Paris, 1645).
Aubigné, T.-A. d', *Histoire universelle*, 3 vols. (Maillé, 1616–20).
Baduellus, C., *Actiones et Monumenta Martyrum*, (*s. l.*, 1560). The first edition of this work appeared in 1556.
Baleus, J., *Scriptorum Illustrium maioris Brytanniae . . . Catalogus* (Basel, 1559).
Basnage de Beauval, J., *Histoire de l'église, depuis Jesus-Christ jusqu'à présent*, 2 vols. (Rotterdam, 1699).
Bellarminus, R., *Disputationes de controversis Christianae fidei, adversus huius temporis haereticos*, 4 vols. (Ingolstadt, 1601).
Belvedere, T., *Relatione all' Eminentiss: congregatione de propaganda fide de i luoghi di alcuni valli di Piemonte . . . dove sono state e sono gl'eretici* (Torino, 1636).
Benoist, J., *Histoire des Albigeois et des Vaudois, ou barbets*, 2 vols. (Paris, 1691).
Bèze, T. de, *Icones, id est, Verae Imagines . . . (s. l.*, 1580).
—— attr., *Histoire ecclésiastique des églises réformées au royaume de France*, 3 vols. ('Anvers', i.e. Geneva, 1580).
La Bible, qui est toute la Saincte Escripture . . . (Neuchâtel, 1535).
Boyer, P., *Abrégé de l'histoire des Vaudois* (La Haye, 1691). An English translation appeared in London in 1692.
Bucer, Martin, *Unio dissidentium in sacris literis locorum, per Hermannum Bodium* (Coloniae, 1531).
Camerarius, J., *Historica Narratio . . . de fratrum orthodoxorum ecclesiis* (Heidelberg, 1605).
Cappel, J., *La Doctrine des Vaudois representée par Cl. Seissel archevesque de Turin, et Cl. Coussord . . .* (Sedan, 1618).
Castro, A. de, *Adversus omnes hereses* (Coloniae, 1539).
Catalogi Librorum MSS. Angliae et Hiberniae (Oxoniae, 1697).
Chamier, D., *Panstratiae Catholicae*, 4 vols. (Genevae, 1626).
Chassanion, J., *Histoire des Albigeois* (Genève, 1595).
Comander, J., and J. Blasius, *Una cuorta et Christiauna forma da intra-*

guider la giuventüna (Puschcleef, i.e. Poschiavo, 1571).

Cormerius, T., *Rerum Gestarum Henrici II regis Galliae* (Paris, 1584).

Coussord, C., *Valdensium ac quorundam aliorum errores praecipui* (Paris, 1548).

Crespin, J., *Actes des martyrs*, later *Histoire des martyrs* (*s.l.*, 1565 and 1619). The first edition appeared in 1554.

—— *Histoire mémorable de la persécution et saccagement du peuple de Mérindol et Cabrières et autres circonvoisins, appelez Vaudois* (*s.l.*, 1556).

Dinothus, R., *De Bello Civili Gallico* (Basel, 1582).

Eymericus, N., *Directorium Inquisitorum*, ed. F. Pegna (Rome, 1578).

Ferrerius, M., *Rationarium Chronographicum missionis evangelice ab Apostolicis operariis, presertim Capuccinis* (Turin, 1659).

Flacius Illyricus, M., *Catalogus Testium Veritatis qui ante nostram aetatem reclamarunt papae* (Basel, 1556); this work was also edited in a Calvinist direction by S. Goulart (Geneva, 1608).

—— *Duodecima Centuria Ecclesiasticae Historiae* (Basel, 1569).

Forbesius, J., *Instructiones Historico-Theologicae* (Amsterdam, 1645).

Foxe, J., *Actes and Monuments of matters most speciall and memorable, happenyng in the Church* (London, 1583).

Freherus, M., *Rerum Bohemicarum antiqui Scriptores* (Hanoviae, 1602).

Frischius, J., *De Waldensibus, Historico-Theologicam Disquisitionem* (Wittenberg, 1663).

Gaufridi, J. F. de, *Histoire de Provence*, 2 vols. (Aix-en-Provence, 1694).

Gilles, P., *Histoire ecclésiastique des églises réformées receuillies en quelques valées de Piedmont et circonvoisins, autresfois appellées églises vaudoises* (Genève, 1644); also ed. P. Lantaret, 2 vols. (Pinerolo, 1881).

Giovio, P., *Historiarum sui temporis*, 2 vols. (Paris, 1558).

Godefroy, D., *Histoire de Charles VIII* (Paris, 1684).

Grassern, J. J., *Waldenser Chronik . . .* (Basel, 1623).

Guichenon, S., *Histoire généalogique de la royale maison de Savoye*, 2 vols. (Lyon, 1660).

Henricus, de Bartholomaeis, de Segusio, alias Ostiensis, *Aurea Summa* (Venice, 1605).

La Place, P. de, *Commentaires de l'estat de la religion et république sous les rois Henry et François seconds, et Charles neufième* (*s.l.*, 1565).

La Popelinière, H.-L. Voisin de, *L'Histoire de France* (*s.l.*, but La Rochelle, 1581).

Léger, J., *Histoire générale des églises évangéliques des vallées de Piémont*, 2 vols. (Leiden, 1669).

Lentulus, S., *Italicae Grammatices praecepta ac ratio* (Geneva, dated 1557 but actually 1567).

—— *Responsio orthodoxa pro edicto illustriss: D. D. trium foederum Rhaetiae . . . adversus haereticos promulgata* (*s.l.*, 1592).

Lutzenbürgo, B. de, *Catalogus Hereticorum* (Coloniae, 1522).

Lydius, B., *Waldensia*, 2 vols. (Rotterdam and Dordrecht, 1616–17).

Maresius, S., *Dissertatiuncula Historico-Theologica de Waldensibus* (Groningen, 1660).

Marnix, P. de, *Tableau des differens de la religion*, 2 vols. (Leiden, 1603–5).

Martin, G., *Inscription en faux . . . contre le livre intitulé 'De la puissance du Pape', par le sieur Marc Vulson* (Grenoble, 1640).

— *La Religion enseignée par les démons aux Vaudois sorciers* (Paris, 1641).

Meigret, A., *Quaestiones . . . in libros de celo et mundo (s. l.,* 1514).

— *Quaestiones . . . in libros de Generatione et Corruptione* (Paris, 1519).

Molinaeus, C., *Tractatus de origine, progressu et excellentia regni et monarchiae Francorum* (Lyon, 1564).

Morland, S., *History of the Evangelical Churches of the valleys of Piemont* (London, 1658).

Nostradamus, C., *L'Histoire et chronicque de Provence* (Lyon, 1614).

Oecolampadius, J., and H. Zuinglius, *Epistolarum libri quatúor* (Basel, dated 1536, actually 1548).

Pantaleon, H., *Martyrum Historia* (Basel, 1563).

— *Prosopographiae Heroum* (Basel, 1565).

Perrin, J. P., *Histoire des Vaudois, divisée en trois parties* (Genève, 1618 and 1619).

— *Histoire des chrestiens albigeois* (Genève, 1618).

— *The bloudy rage of that great Antichrist of Rome . . . declared . . . in the historie of the Waldenses*, trans. S. Lennard (London, 1624).

Piccolomini, E. S., *Opera Omnia* (Basel, 1551).

Rabus, L., *Historien der . . . Martyren*, 8 vols. (Strasbourg, 1554–7).

Richardus, C., *Memorabilis Historia persecutionum . . . ab anno 1555 ad 1561 religionis ergo gestorum* (Geneva, 1581).

Rorengo-Lucerna, M. A., *Breve narratione dell'introduttione degli heretici nelle valli di Piemonte* (Torino, 1632).

— *Memorie historiche dell'introduttione dell'heresie nelle valli di Lucerna, marchesato di Saluzzo, e altre di Piemonte* (Torino, 1649).

Rubys, C. de, *Histoire véritable de la ville de Lyon* (Lyon, 1604).

Scultetus, A., *Annalium Evangelii passim per Europam . . . renovati decades duae*, 2 vols. (Heidelberg, 1618–20).

Seyssel, C. de, *Adversus errores et sectam Valdensium disputationes* (Paris, 1520).

Sleidanus, J., *De Statu Religionis et reipublicae, Carolo Quinto Caesare, Commentarii* (Strasbourg, 1556).

Spanheim, F., *Geneva Restituta, Oratio* (Geneva, 1635).

Sudermann, D., attr., *Waldenser Chronick (s. l.,* 1655).

Thou, J.-A. de, *Historiarum sui temporis*, 5 vols. (Paris, 1604–8).

Tonsi, J., *Vita Emmanuelis Philiberti* (Torino, 1596).

Turrecremata, J. de, *Summa de ecclesia* (Lyon, 1496).

Ussher, J., *Gravissimae Quaestionis de Christianarum Ecclesiarum . . . continua successione et statu, Historica Explicatio* (London, 1613).

Vignier, N., *Théâtre de l'antechrist* (*s. l.*, 1610).

Vulson, M. de., *De la puissance du Pape, et des libertés de l'église gallicane* (Genève, 1635).

Waser, C., *Assertio Theologica: Deum omnibus seculis excitasse homines pios . . . conprobatos Waldensium exemplo* (Zürich, 1621).

Weihenmajerus, E., *Vicissitudines et Fata Waldensium* (Wittenberg, 1690).

Wesenbecius, P., *Oratio de Waldensibus et Albigensibus Christianis* (Jena, 1585).

Works printed after 1700

Abbot, T. K., 'On a volume of Waldensian tracts', *Hermathena*, xviii (1892), 204-6.

Albanès, J.-H., 'Premières années du protestantisme en Provence', *BCTHS*, Ann. 1884 (1884), 25-41.

Alessio, F., 'Luserna e l'interdetto di Giacomo Buronzo', *BSBS* VIII, no. 6 (1903), 409-24.

Allard, G., *La Vie de Jean Rabot, conseiller au parlement de Grenoble*, ed. H. Gariel (*Delphinalia*, pt. 2, Grenoble, 1852).

Amati, G., 'Processus contra Valdenses in Lombardia superiori . . . anno 1387', *Archivio Storico Italiano*, series 3 (1865), I, pt. 2, 3-52, and II, pt. 1, 3-61.

Armand Hugon, A., 'Popolo e chiesa alle valli dal 1532 al 1561', *BSSV* 110 (1961), 5-34.

— *Storia dei Valdesi II: dal sinodo di Chanforan all' emancipazione* (Torino, 1974).

Arnaud, E., *Histoire des protestants du Dauphiné*, 3 vols. (Paris, 1875-6).

— *Histoire des protestants de Provence, du Comtat Venaissin et de la Principauté d'Orange*, 2 vols. (Paris, 1884).

— 'Histoire des premières persécutions des Vaudois Luthériens du Comtat Venaissin et de la Provence, d'après de nouveaux documents', *BSHV* 8 (1891), 43-58, and 9 (1892), 3-14.

— 'Histoire des persécutions endurées par les Vaudois du Dauphiné aux xiii, xiv et xv siècles', *BSHV* 12 (1895), 17-140.

— 'Louis XI et les Vaudois du Dauphiné', *BCTHS*, Ann. 1895 (1896), 513-18.

— 'Récit historique de la conversion au protestantisme des Vaudois des Alpes', *Revue de théologie et des questions religeuses* (1895), 1-70.

— *Mémoire historique sur l'origine, les moeurs, les souffrances et la conversion au protestantisme des Vaudois du Dauphiné* (Crest en Dauphiné, 1896).

Aston, M., 'Lollardy and the Reformation: survival or revival', *History*, 49 (1964), 149-70.

Aubenas, R., *La Sorcière et l'inquisiteur* (Aix-en-Provence, 1945).

— 'Un registre d'enquêtes de l'inquisiteur Jean de Rome (1532)',

Études d'histoire du droit canonique dédiées à Gabriel Le Bras, 2 vols. (Paris, 1965), I, 3–9.

Audisio, G., 'Un aspect des relations entre le Piémont et la Provence aux xve et xvie siècles . . . les Vaudois', *BSHPF* 121 (1975), 484–515.

—— 'Les Barbes vaudois aux xve et xvie siècles', *BSSV* 139 (1976), 65–75.

—— 'Le Procès de Pierre Griot par l'inquisiteur Jean de Roma (Apt 1532)', *BSSV* 143 (1978), 15–26.

—— *Le Barbe et l'inquisiteur: procès du barbe vaudois Pierre Griot par l'inquisiteur Jean de Roma (Apt, 1532)* (Aix-en-Provence, 1979).

—— 'Il sentimento religioso dei valdesi della Provenza attraverso gli atti notarili, 1460–1520', *Quaderni Storici*, 41 (1979), 451–69.

—— 'Une organisation ecclésiale clandestine: les barbes vaudois', *Histoire et Clandestinité*, ed. Tilloy, Chiffoleau, and Audisio, q.v. (Albi, 1979), pp. 75–88.

—— 'Une mutation: les Vaudois passent à la Réforme (1530–1532)', *BSHPF* 126 (1980), 153–65.

Baird, R., *Sketches of protestantism in Italy past and present, including a notice . . . of the Vaudois* (Glasgow, 1847).

Balma, T., 'La ville de Strasbourg et les Vaudois', *BSSV* 67 (1937), 63–95.

Balmas, E., *Pramollo* (Torre Pèllice, 1975).

—— *Manoscritti valdesi di Ginevra* (Torino, 1977).

Barjavel, C. F. H., *Histoire des guerres excitées dans le Comté Venaissin . . . par les Calvinistes du xvie siècle* (Carpentras, 1859).

Barnaud, J., *Pierre Viret, sa vie et son œuvre 1511–1571* (Saint-Amans, 1911).

—— *Quelques lettres inédites de P. Viret* (Saint-Amans, 1911).

Bautier, R.-H., and J. Sornay, *Les Sources de l'histoire économique et sociale du moyen âge: Provence, Comtat Venaissin, Dauphiné, états de la maison de Savoye*, 3 vols. (Paris, 1968–74).

Beloch, K.J., *Bevölkerungsgeschichte Italiens*, 3 vols. (Berlin, 1937–61).

Bender, F., *Geschichte der Waldenser* (Ulm, 1850).

Benoît, F., *La Tragédie du sac de Cabrières* (Marseille, 1927).

Bérard, A., *Les Vaudois, leur histoire sur les deux versants des Alpes* (Lyon, 1892).

Berruto, G., *Profilo dei dialetti Italiani: I, Piemonte e Valle d'Aosta* (Pisa, 1974).

Bèze, T. de, *Correspondance de Théodore de Bèze* collected and ed. H. Aubert and others (Genève, 1960–   ).

Biau, K., *Essai sur les protestants du xvie siècle dans les Alpes-Maritimes* (Cahors, 1903).

Blair, A., *History of the Waldenses*, 2 vols. (Edinburgh, 1833).

Blet, H., E. Esmonin, and G. Letonnelier, eds., *Le Dauphiné, recueil de textes historiques* (Paris and Grenoble, 1938).

Boffito, G., 'Eretici in Piemonte al tempo del Gran Scisma', *Studi e Documenti di storia e Diritto*, 18 (1897), 381–431.

Bollea, L. C., 'Alcuni documenti di storia valdese (1354–1573)', *BSHV*

44 (1922), 71–87, and 45 (1923), 5–14.

Bossuet, J.-B., *Histoire des variations des églises protestantes*, in *Œuvres*, vols. 19–20 (Versailles, 1816–17).

Bourquelot, F., 'Les Vaudois au xve siècle', *Bibliothèque de l'école des chartes*, 2nd series, 3 (1846), 81–109.

Bourrilly, V. L., *Guillaume du Bellay, Seigneur de Langey 1491–1543* (Paris, 1905).

Bray, T., *Papal Usurpation and Persecution*, 2 vols. (London, 1711–12).

Brézé, J. de, *Histoire des Vaudois*, 2 vols. (Paris, 1796).

Brown, G. K., *Italy and the Reformation to 1550* (Oxford, 1933).

Brunel, L., *Les Vaudois des Alpes françaises et de Freissinières en particulier* (Paris, 1888).

Caffaro, P., *Notizie e documenti della chiesa pinerolese*, 6 vols. (Pinerolo, 1891–1903).

Calvin, J., *Joannis Calvini Opera quae supersunt omnia*, ed. G. Baum, E. Cunitz, and E. Reuss, 59 vols. (Corpus Reformatorum, vols. 29–87, Braunschweig, Berlin, 1864–1900).

Cambiano, G., *Historico Discorso al Serenissimo Filippo Emmanuele di Savoia* (Monumenta Historiae Patriae, Scriptorum t. I, Turin, 1840).

Camenisch, E., *Geschichte der Reformation und Gegenreformation in der italienischen südtälern Graubundens und die ehemaligen Unteranenlanden Chiavenna, Veltlin und Bormio* (Chur, 1950).

Campell, J. U., *Ulrici Campelli Historia Raetica*, ed. P. Plattner, 2 vols. (Quellen zur schweizer Geschichte, vols. 8–9, Basel, 1887–90).

Cantimori, D., *Eretici Italiani del '500* (Firenze, 1939).

—— 'Studi di storia della riforma e dell'eresia in Italia, e studi sulla storia della vita religiosa nella prima metà del '500 (Rapporti fra i due tipi di ricerche)', *BSSV* 102 (1957), 29–38.

—— *Prospettive di storia ereticale del xvi* (Bari, 1960).

—— 'The problem of heresy', in Cochrane, ed., *The Late Italian Renaissance*, q.v., pp. 211–25.

Carutti, D., *La Crociata valdese del 1488 e la maschera di ferro, con alcune appendici alla storia di Pinerolo* (Pinerolo, 1894).

Chabrand, J. A., *Vaudois et protestants des Alpes. Recherches historiques contenant un grand nombre de documents inédits* (Grenoble, 1886).

Chaix, P., *Recherches sur l'imprimerie à Genève de 1550 à 1564* (Genève, 1954).

——, A. Dufour, and G. Moeckli, *Les Livres imprimés à Genève de 1550 à 1600* (Genève, 1959).

Charronnet, C., *Les Guerres de religion et la société protestante dans les Hautes-Alpes (1560–1789)* (Gap, 1861).

Chevalier, J. A., *Mémoire historique sur les hérésies en Dauphiné avant le xvie siècle* (Valence, 1890).

Chianéa, G., *La Condition juridique des terres en Dauphiné au 18e siècle* (Paris, 1969).

Chorier, N., *Histoire générale du Dauphiné*, 2 vols. (Valence, 1878–9,

repr. Grenoble, 1971). This work first appeared in 1661.

Church, F. C., *The Italian Reformers, 1534-1564* (New York, 1932).

Cochrane, E., ed., *The Late Italian Renaissance 1525-1630* (London, 1970).

Cohn, N., *Europe's inner demons* (London, 1975).

Comba, Emilio, *History of the Waldenses of Italy, from their origin to the Reformation*, trans. T. E. Comba (London, 1889).

—— 'L'Introduction de la réforme dans les vallées du Piémont', *BSHPF* 43 (1894), 7-35.

—— 'La Storia inedita dei Valdesi narrata da Scipione Lentolo', *BSHV* 14 (1897), 45-61.

—— 'Lettres ecclésiastiques à la vén. compagnie des pasteurs de Genève aux 16e et 17e siècles . . .', *BSHV* 16 (1898), 22-31.

—— 'La Campagna del Conte della Trinità narrata da lui medesimo', *BSHV* 21 (1904), 3-32, and 22 (1905), 7-27.

Comba, Ernesto, 'I Valdesi prima del sinodo di Cianforan', *BSHV* 58 (1932), 7-33.

—— *Breve Storia dei Valdesi*, 4th edn. (Torino, 1961).

Conti da Foligno, S. dei, *Le Storie de' suoi tempi dal 1475 al 1510*, ed. and trans. D. Zanelli and F. Calabro, 2 vols. (Rome 1883).

Crivelli, C., 'La Disputa di A. Possevino con i Valdesi', *Archivum Historicum Societatis Jesu*, 8 (1938), 7-41.

Dainotti, V., 'Roghi a Carignano', *BSBS* XXXIV (1932), 283-7.

Davis, N. Z., *Society and Culture in Early Modern France* (London, 1975).

Degiovanni, P., 'Gli Eretici di Tenda, Briga e Sospello', *Rivista Cristiana* 9 (1881), 256-69.

Delaborde, H.-F., *L'Expédition de Charles VIII en Italie* (Paris, 1888).

Delarue, H., 'Olivétan et Pierre de Vingle à Genève, 1532-33', *Bulletin d'humanisme et renaissance*, 8 (1946), 105-18.

Delumeau, J., *Le Catholicisme entre Luther et Voltaire* (Paris, 1971).

—— *Naissance et affirmation de la réforme* (Paris, 1973).

De Simone, R., 'Tre anni decisivi di storia Valdese: Missioni, repressione e tolleranza', *Analecta Gregoriana*, Ser. Fac. Hist. Eccles., 97 (1958), 1-327.

—— 'La pace di Cavour e l'editto I^o di San Germano nella storia della tolleranza religiosa', *BSSV* 110 (1961), 35-50.

Dieckhoff, A. W., *Die Waldenser im Mittelalter* (Göttingen, 1851).

Döllinger, I. von, *Beiträge zur Sektengeschichte des Mittelalters*, 2 vols. (Munich, 1890).

Doucet, R., *Les Institutions de la France au xvie siècle*, 2 vols. (Paris, 1948).

Douglas, R. M., *Jacopo Sadoleto 1477-1547* (Cambridge, Mass., 1959).

Douie, D. L., *The nature and effect of the heresy of the Fraticelli* (Manchester, 1932).

Dufour, A., 'Un document sur les vallées vaudoises en 1556', *BSSV* 128 (1970), 57-63.

Duvernoy, J., *Le Catharisme: la religion des cathares* (Paris, Toulouse, 1976).

Egidi, P., and A. Segre, eds., *Emmanuele Filiberto* (Torino, 1928).

Erk, W., *Waldenser Geschichte und Gegenwart* (Frankfurt, 1971).

Esposito, M., 'Sur quelques MSS. de l'ancienne littérature religieuse des Vaudois du Piémont', *Revue d'histoire ecclésiastique*, 46 (1951), 127-39.

Faber, G. S., *An inquiry into the history and theology of the ancient Vallenses and Albigenses; as exhibiting . . . the perpetuity of the sincere Church of Christ* (London, 1838).

Fabre, A.-L., *Recherches historiques sur le pélerinage des rois de France à Notre-Dame d'Embrun* (Grenoble, 1860).

Guillaume Farel, biographie nouvelle (Paris, Neuchâtel, 1930).

Fauché-Prunelle, A.-A., *Essai sur les anciennes institutions autonomes ou populaires des Alpes cottiennes-briançonnaises* 2 vols. (Paris, Grenoble, 1856-7).

Firth, K. R., *The Apocalyptic tradition in Reformation Britain 1530-1645* (Oxford, 1979).

Foà, S., 'Valli del Piemonte soggette all'Alt^{za} di Savoia, infette d'heresia et suoi luoghi', *BSHV* 24 (1907), 8-9.

Fontana, B., 'Documenti Vaticani contro l'eresia luterana in Italia', *Archivio della Società Romana di Storia Patria*, 15 (1892), fasc. I-II, 71-165, and III-IV, 365-474.

Fornier, M., *Histoire générale des Alpes maritimes ou cottiennes et . . . de leur métropolitain Embrun*, ed. J. Guillaume, 3 vols. (Paris, 1890-2).

Fournier, J., *Le Registre d'inquisition de Jacques Fournier* ed. J. Duvernoy, 3 vols. (Toulouse, 1965).

France, P., 'Les Protestants à Grenoble au xvie siècle', *Cahiers d'Histoire*, 7 (1962), 319-31.

François, M., *Le Cardinal François de Tournon* (Paris, 1951).

Fromment, A., *Les Actes et gestes merveilleux de la cité de Genève . . .*, ed. G. Revilliod (Genève, 1854).

Frossard, L., *Les Vaudois de Provence* (Avignon, 1848).

Gabotto, F., *Roghi e vendette. Contributo alla storia della dissidenza religiosa in Piemonte prima della riforma* (Pinerolo, 1898).

—— 'Valdesi, catari e streghe in Piemonte dal secolo xiv al xvi secondo nuovi documenti', *BSHV* 18 (1900), 3-20.

Gaffarel, P., 'Les Massacres de Cabrières et de Mérindol en 1545', *Revue Historique*, 107 (1911), 241-71.

Gay, T., 'Scipione Lentolo', *BSHV* 23 (1906), 104-7.

—— 'Esquisse d'histoire vaudoise', *BSHV* 24 (1907), 10-53.

Geisendorf, P. F., *Les Annalistes genevoises du début du dix-septième siècle, Savion, Piaget, Perrin: Études et textes* (Genève, 1942).

—— *Théodore de Bèze* (Genève, 1949).

—— *Le Livre des habitants de Genève*, vol. 1 (Genève, 1957).

Gerdesius, D., *Historia Reformationis, sive annales evangelii*, 4 vols. (Groningen, 1744-52).

—— *Specimen Italiae Reformatae* (Leiden, 1765).

Gilmont, J.-F., 'Le Pseudo-Martyre du Vaudois P. Masson (1530)',

BSSV 133 (1973), 43-8.

Ginevra e l'Italia, collected essays (Firenze, 1959).

Ginzburg, C., *I Benandanti* (Torino, 1966).

— *Il Nicodemismo. Simulazione e dissimulazione religiosa nell'Europa del '500* (Torino, 1970).

— *Il Formaggio e i vermi* (Torino, 1976).

Gioffredo, P., *Storia delle Alpi marittime*, ed. C. Gazzera (Monumenta Historiae Patriae, Scriptorum t. II, Turin, 1839).

Gonnet, G., 'Le Premier Synode de Chanforan de 1532 avec une note sur les itinéraires Vaudois', *BSHPF* 90 (1953), 201-21.

— 'Olivétan e il primo sinodo di Chanforan. Itinerari Alpini Valdesi', *Ricerche di Storia Religiosa*, 1 (1954), 120-32.

— 'I Rapporti tra i valdesi franco-italiani e i riformatori d'Oltralpe prima di Calvino', *Ginevra e l'Italia*, q.v., pp. 1-63.

— 'Casi di sincretismo ereticale in Piemonte nei secoli xiv e xv', *BSSV* 108 (1960), 3-36.

— 'Les Relations des Vaudois des Alpes avec les réformateurs en 1532', *Bulletin d'humanisme et renaissance*, 23 (1961), 34-52.

— 'Le Confessioni di fede valdesi prima della riforma', *BSSV* 117 (1965), 61-95.

— 'Waldensia', *Rivista di Storia e Letteratura Religiosa* 2 (1966), 461-84.

— *Le Confessioni di fede valdesi prima della riforma* (Torino, 1967).

— 'Remarques sur l'historiographie vaudoise des xvie et xviie siècles', *BSHPF* 120 (1974), 323-65.

— and A. Armand Hugon, *Bibliografia Valdese* (Torre Pèllice, 1953); also issued as a separate number of *BSSV* for that year.

— and A. Molnár, *Les Vaudois au moyen âge* (Turin, 1974).

Gretserus, J., *Opera Omnia*, 17 vols. (Ratisbon, 1734-41).

Grosso, M., and M. F. Mellano, *La Controriforma nella arcidiocesi di Torino (1558-1610)* (Rome, 1957).

Gui, B., *Manuel de l'inquisiteur*, ed. G. Mollat and G. Drioux, 2 vols. (Paris, 1926-7).

Guillaume, P. P. M., 'Sentence de réhabilitation des Vaudois des Alpes françaises', *BCTHS*, Ann. 1891 (1891), 248-65.

— 'Notes et documents relatifs aux Vaudois des Alpes à la fin du xve siècle', *BCTHS*, Ann. 1913 (1914), 416-26.

Haag, Eugène, and Emile Haag, *La France protestante*, 1st edn., 10 vols. (Paris and Genève, 1846-59), and 2nd edn. (A-G), 6 vols. (Paris, 1877-88).

Hahn, C. U., *Geschichte der Ketzer im Mittelalter*, 3 vols. (Stuttgart, 1847).

Haton, C., *Mémoires*, ed. F. Bourquelot, 2 vols. (Paris, 1857).

Haupt, H., 'Un traité complètement oublié de Jean Cochlée contre les Vaudois', *BSHV* 20 (1903), 133-6.

Hemardinquer, J. J., 'Pour le 403e anniversaire de la prédication publique à Fenestrelles: Les Vaudois du Dauphiné et la résistance à l'insurrection d'après des documents inédits', *BSSV* 103 (1958), 53-63.

—— 'Les Protestants de Grenoble au xvie siècle d'après des études récentes', *BSHPF* 111 (1965), 15–22.

Herminjard, A.-L., *Correspondance des réformateurs dans les pays de la langue Française*, 9 vols. (Genève and Paris, 1866–97).

Herzog, J. J., *Die Romanischen Waldenser* (Halle, 1853).

—— 'Ein wichtiges Document betreffend die Einführung der Reformation bei den Waldensern', *Zeitschrift für die historische Theologie*, 3 (1866), 311–38.

Histoire mémorable de la guerre faite par le duc de Savoye contre ses subjectz des vallées, ed. E. Balmas and V. Diena (Torino, 1972); the original text was first published in 1561.

Histoire des persécutions et guerres faites despuis l'an 1555 jusques en l'an 1561 contre le peuple appelé Vaudois, ed. E. Balmas and C. A. Theiller (Torino, 1975); the original text was first published in 1562.

Hollaender, A., 'Eine schweizer Gesandtschaftsreise an den französischen Hof im Jahre 1557', *Historische Zeitschrift*, N. S. 33 (1892), 385–410.

Imbart de la Tour, P. G. J. M., *Les Origines de la réforme* (Paris and Melun, various edns., 1914–48).

Jalla, J., 'Le Pasteur Martin Tachard à Riclaret', *BSHPF* 41 (1892), 272–4.

—— 'Notice historique sur le S. Ministère et sur l'organisation ecclésiastique au sein des églises vaudoises', *BSHV* 14 (1897), 3–22, and 16 (1898), 3–22.

—— 'La più antica storia dei Valdesi', *BSHV* 17 (1899), 93–110.

—— 'Synodes vaudois de la réformation à l'exil, 1536–1686', *BSHPF* 50 (1901), 471–89; also in *BSHV* 20 (1903), 93–133, 21 (1904), 62–86, and subsequently.

—— *Storia della riforma in Piemonte fino alla morte di Emmanuele Filiberto 1517–1580* (Firenze, 1914).

—— 'Correspondance ecclésiastique vaudoise du seizième siècle', *BSHV* 33 (1914), 72–92.

—— 'La Riforma in Piemonte durante il regno di Carlo Emanuele I fino alla occupazione del Marchesato di Saluzzo', *BSHV* 42 (1920), 5–49.

—— 'Le Synode de Chanforan', *BSHV* 58 (1932), 34–48.

—— 'La Bible d'Olivétan', *BSHV* 58 (1932), 76–92.

—— 'Le Refuge français dans les vallées vaudoises et les relations entre la France protestante et le Piémont', *BSHPF* 83 (1934), 561–92.

Jochnowitz, G., *Dialect Boundaries and the question of Franco-Provençal* (The Hague and Paris, 1973).

Jones, W., *The History of the Waldenses*, 3rd edn., 2 vols. (London, 1818).

Kaepelli, T., 'Un processo contro i valdesi di Piemonte (Giaveno, Coazze, Valgioie)', *Rivista di Storia della Chiesa in Italia*, 1 (1947), 285–91.

Kidd, B. J., ed., *Documents Illustrative of the Continental Reformation* (Oxford, 1911).

Kieckhefer, R., *Repression of Heresy in medieval Germany* (Liverpool, 1979).

Kingdon, R. M., *Geneva and the Coming of the Wars of Religion in France 1555–63* (Geneva, 1956).

—— and others, eds., *Registres de la compagnie des pasteurs de Genève au temps de Calvin* (Genève, 1962–).

Knecht, R. J., *Francis I* (Cambridge, 1982).

Labande-Mailfert, Y., *Charles VIII et son milieu (1470–1498)* (Paris, 1975).

Ladoucette, J.C. F., Baron de, *Histoire, topographie, antiquités, usages, dialects des Hautes-Alpes* (Paris, 1834).

Lea, H. C., *History of the Inquisition of the Middle Ages*, 3 vols. (London, 1888).

Leff, G., *Heresy in the later middle ages*, 2 vols. (Manchester, 1967).

Le Goff, J., ed., *Hérésies et sociétés* (Paris and the Hague, 1968).

Lentolo, S., *Historia delle grandi e crudeli persecutioni fatti ai tempi nostri . . . contro il popolo che chiamano valdese*, ed. T. Gay (Torre Pèllice, 1906).

Léonard, E. G., *Histoire générale du protestantisme*, 3 vols. (Paris, 1961–4).

Lerner, R. E., *The heresy of the Free Spirit in the Later Middle Ages* (Berkeley, 1972).

Little, L. K., *Religious poverty and the profit economy in Medieval Europe* (London, 1978).

Lortsch, D., *Histoire de la Bible en France* (Genève and Paris, 1910).

McCrie, T., *History of the Progress and Suppression of the Reformation in Italy*, 2nd edn. (Edinburgh and London, 1833).

McNair, P., *Peter Martyr in Italy* (Oxford, 1967).

Maitland, S. R., *Facts and Documents illustrative of the ancient Albigenses and Waldenses* (London, 1832).

Major, J. R., *Representative Government in Early Modern France* (New Haven and London, 1980).

Manteyer, G. B. M. P. de, 'Les Farel, les Aloat et les Riquet', *BSEHA* (1908), 33–89.

—— *Les Farel, les Aloat et les Riquet* (Gap, 1912).

—— ed., *Le Livre-Journal tenu par Fazy de Rame en langage embrunais (1471–1504)*, 2 vols. (Gap, 1932).

Manuel di San Giovanni, G., *Memorie storiche di Dronero e della valle di Maira*, 3 vols. (Torino, 1868).

Martène, E., and U. Durand, eds., *Thesaurus Novus Anecdotorum*, 5 vols. (Paris, 1717).

Martin, P. E., 'Une Lettre inédite de Guillaume Farel relative aux Vaudois du Piémont', *BSHPF* 61 (1912), 204–13.

Marx, J., *L'Inquisition en Dauphiné: Étude sur le développement et la répression de l'hérésie et de la sorcellerie du xive siècle au début du règne de François Ier* (Bibliothèque de l'École des Hautes Études, Sciences Historiques et Philologiques, 206e fasc., Paris, 1914).

Massi, C., *Prosopopea e storia della città e provincia di Pinerolo*, 4 vols. (Torino, 1833-6).

Merlo, G. G., *Eretici e inquisitori nella società piemontese del trecento* (Torino, 1977).

— 'I Registri inquisitoriali come fonti per la storia dei gruppi ereticali ... il caso del Piemonte basso medievale', Tilloy, Chiffoleau, and Audisio, eds., *Histoire et clandestinité*, q.v., pp. 59-74.

Meyer, F., *Die evangelische Gemeinde in Locarno*, 2 vols. (Zürich, 1836).

Miolo, G., *Historia breve e vera de gl'affari de i valdesi delle valli*, ed. E. Balmas (Torino, 1971).

Monastier, A., *A history of the Vaudois church from its origin, and of the Vaudois of Piedmont to the present day* (London, 1848).

Montet, E., *Histoire littéraire des Vaudois du Piémont* (Paris, 1885).

Moore, R. I., *The origins of European dissent* (London, 1977).

Muletti, D., *Memorie storico-diplomatiche appartinenti alla città ed ai Marchesi di Saluzzo*, 6 vols. (Saluzzo, 1829-33).

Muston, Alexis, *Histoire des Vaudois des vallées du Piémont* (Paris, 1834).

— *L'Israël des Alpes*, 4 vols. (Paris, 1851); also as translated by W. Hazlitt (London, 1852, 1853).

Muston, Arturo, 'I Valdesi dopo il sinodo di Cianforan', *BSHV* 58 (1932), 49-75.

Nickson, M., 'The "Pseudo-Reinerius" treatise; the final stage of a thirteenth-century work on heresy from the diocese of Passau', *Archives d'histoire doctrinale et littéraire du moyen âge*, 42 (1967/8), 255-314.

Nicolas, J., and R. Nicolas, *La Vie quotidienne en Savoie aux xviie et xviiie siècles* (Hachette, 1979).

Ninguarda, F., *Atti della visita pastorale diocesana*, 2 vols. (Como, Società Storica Comense, 1892-4).

Ozment, S. E., *The Reformation in the Cities* (New Haven and London, 1975).

Pascal, A., 'Un episodio ignoto nella vita di Girolamo Miolo', *BSHV* 25 (1908), 41-56.

— 'Le lettere del governatore delle valli Sebastiano Graziolo Castrocaro', *BSHV* 26 (1909), 15-38, and 28 (1910), 17-49.

— 'Communità eretiche e chiese cattoliche nelle valli valdesi secondo le relazioni delle visite pastorali del Peruzzi e della Broglia (secolo xvi)', *BSHV* 30 (1912), 61-73.

— *I Valdesi e il parlamento francese di Torino* (Pinerolo, 1912).

— 'Le Ambasciere dei cantoni e dei principi protestanti di Svizzera e Germania al Re di Francia in favore dei Valdesi durante il periodo della dominazione francese in Piemonte (1535-59); contributi ad una storia diplomatica dei Valdesi di Piemonte', *BSBS* XVIII, nos. 1-3, 80-119, and 5-6, 316-36 (1913); and XIX, nos. 1-3 (1914), 26-38.

— 'Valdesi ed ugonotti a Pinerolo sul principio del 1595', *BSHV* 34 (1915), 73-8.

—— 'Margherita di Foix ed i Valdesi di Paesana', *Athenaeum*, 4 (1916), 46-84.

—— 'Il Piemonte riformato e la politica di E. Filiberto nel 1565', *BSSS* 108 (1928), 395-453.

—— 'L'inquisizione a Chieri e a Carignano nell'anno 1567', *BSHV* 51 (1928), 88-114.

—— 'La lotta contro la riforma in Piemonte al tempo di Emmanuele Filiberto, studiata nelle relazioni diplomatiche tra la Corte Sabauda e la Santa Sede (1559-1580)', *BSHV* 53 (1929), 5-88, and 55 (1930), 5-108.

—— 'La riforma nei domini Sabaudi delle Alpe Marittime Occidentali', *BSBS* 48 (1950), 5-52.

—— 'La colonia piemontese a Ginevra nel secolo xvi', *Ginevra e l'Italia*, q.v., pp. 64-110.

—— 'Postille a la "Controriforma . . ." di Grosso-Mellano', *BSSV* 105 (1959), 83-98.

—— *Il Marchesato di Saluzzo e la riforma protestante durante il periodo della dominazione francese (1548-1588)* (Firenze, 1960).

—— 'Fonti e documenti per la storia della compagna militare contro i Valdesi negli anni 1560-1561', *BSSV* 110 (1961), 51-125.

Patrucco, C., 'La lotta contro i Valdesi . . .', Egidi and Segre, eds., *Emmanuele Filiberto*, q.v., pp. 427-62.

Pazè Beda, B., and P. Pazè, *Riforma e cattolicesimo in val pragelato 1555-1685* (Pinerolo, 1975).

Pécout, H., *Études sur le droit privé des hautes vallées alpines de Provence et de Dauphiné au moyen âge* (Paris, 1907).

Pétavel-Olliff, E., *La Bible en France, ou les traductions françaises des Saintes Escritures* (Paris, 1864).

Peter, R., 'Le Comte Guillaume de Furstenberg et les Vaudois', *BSSV* 143 (1978), 27-36.

Peyrot, G., 'Influenze franco-ginevrine nella formazione delle discipline ecclesiastiche valdesi alla metà del xvi secolo', *Ginevra e l'Italia*, q.v., pp. 215-86.

Pons, T. G., 'I nostri proverbi', *BSHV/BSSV* 57 (1931), 98-130; 58 (1932), 98-133; 59 (1933), 70-106; 64 (1935), 87-114; 70 (1938), 39-63; 116 (1964), 71-89.

—— 'Sulla pace di Cavour del 1561 e sui suoi storici', *BSSV* 110 (1961), 127-55.

—— 'Barba, barbi e barbetti nel tempo e nello spazio', *BSSV* 122 (1967), 47-76.

Promis, V., 'Memoriale di Gio. Andrea Saluzzo di Castellar dal 1482 al 1528', *Miscellanea di storia italiana*, 8 (1869), 409-625.

Provana di Collegno, F.-X., 'Rapports de Guillaume Farel avec les Vaudois du Piémont', *BSEHA* (1891), 257-78.

Ricotti, E., *Storia della monarchia piemontese*, 6 vols. (Firenze, 1861-9).

Rivoire, P., 'Alcuni documenti relative alle persecuzioni del 1560-1561', *BSHV* 10 (1893), 3-10.

—— 'Storia dei signori di Luserna', *BSHV* 11 (1894), 3-86; 13 (1896),

38-112; 14 (1897), 23-44; 17 (1899), 3-93; 20 (1903), 38-85.

— 'Les Colonies provençales et vaudoises de la Pouille', *BSHV* 19 (1902), 48-62.

Rodolfo, G., 'Documenti del secolo xvi e xvii riguardanti i valdesi', *BSHV* 50 (1927), 5-37; 55 (1930), 116-31; 58 (1932), 153-60.

Rol, C., 'Valdesi e cattolici in Val Pragelato', *Rivista di Storia della Chiesa in Italia*, 23 (1969), 135-43.

Romier, L., 'Les Vaudois et le parlement français de Turin', *Mélanges d'archaeologie et d'histoire*, 30 (1910), 193-221.

— 'Les Institutions françaises en Piémont sous Henri II', *Revue historique*, 106 (1911), 1-26.

Roset, M., *Les Chronicques de Genève*, ed. H. Fazy (Genève, 1894).

Rosius de Porta, P. D., *Historia Reformationis Ecclesiarum Raeticarum*, 2 vols. (Chur, 1771-7).

Ruchat, A., *Histoire de la réformation de la Suisse*, 6 vols. (Genève, 1740).

Saint-Genis, V. de, *Histoire de Savoie*, 3 vols. (Chambéry and Paris, 1868-75).

Sambuc, J., 'Documents sur le procès de Jean de Roma inquisiteur', *BSHPF* 109 (1963), 180-95.

— 'Le Procès de Jean de Roma inquisiteur, Apt 1532', *BSSV* 139 (1976), 7-17.

Sauret, A., *Essai historique sur la ville d'Embrun* (Gap, 1860).

Schiess, T., ed., *Bullingers Korrespondenz mit den Graubündern*, 3 vols. (Quellen zur schweizer Geschichte, vols. 23-5, Basel, 1904-6).

Schmidt, C., 'Aktenstücke besonders zur Geschichte der Waldenser', *Zeitschrift für die historische Theologie*, 22 (1852), 238-62.

Scuderi, G., 'Il Sacramento del battesimo nella fede, nella pietà, e nella teologia del valdismo medioevale (dalle origini a Chanforan) 1173-1532', *BSSV* 124 (1968), 3-16.

— 'I Fondamenti teologici della non violenza nel valdismo anteriore al xvi secolo', *BSSV* 129 (1971), 3-14.

Stelling-Michaud, Sven, and Suzanne Stelling-Michaud, eds., *Le Livre du recteur de l'académie de Genève*, 2 vols. (Genève, 1959-66).

Taulier, J., *Histoire du Dauphiné* (Grenoble, 1855).

Taylor, T., *The History of the Waldenses and Albigenses* (Bolton, 1793).

Tedeschi, J. A., ed., *Italian Reformation Studies in honour of Laelius Socinus* (Firenze, 1965).

— 'An addition to the correspondence of Theodore Beza: Lentolo's lettere ad un signore di Geneva', *Il Pensiero Politico*, 1 (1968), 439-48.

— *The Literature of the Italian Reformation, an exhibition catalogue* (Chicago, 1971).

Thomas, K., *Religion and the Decline of Magic* (London, 1971).

Tilloy, M., G. Audisio, and J. Chiffoleau, eds., *Histoire et clandestinité du moyen âge à la première guerre mondiale: Colloque de Privas, Mai 1977* (Albi, 1979).

Todd, J. H., 'The Waldensian Manuscripts in the Library of Trinity College, Dublin', *British Magazine*, 19 (1841), 393–402, 502–11, 632–7; 20 (1842), 21–5, 185–93.

—— *The Books of the Vaudois* (London, Cambridge, and Dublin, 1865).

Tron, E., 'La strage di Pragelato', *BSHV* 20 (1903), 85–93.

Vaillant, P., *Les Libertés des communautés dauphinoises (des origines au 5 janvier 1355)* (Paris, 1951).

—— 'Les Origines d'une libre confédération de vallées: les habitants des communautés briançonnaises au xiiie siècle', *Bibliothèque de l'école des chartes*, 125 (1967), 301–48.

Vasella, O., 'Zur Entstehungsgeschichte des 1. Ilanzer Artikelbriefs vom 4 April 1524 und des Eidgenössischen Glaubenskonkordates von 1525', *Zeitschrift für schweizerische Kirchengeschichte*, 34 (1940), 182–91.

Venard, M., 'Jacques Sadolet, évêque de Carpentras, et les Vaudois', *BSSV* 143 (1978), 37–49.

Vernou, J., 'Une mission en Piémont' (the text of Vernou's letter of April 1555), *BSHPF* 17 (1868), 16–19.

Veyret, P., and G. Veyret, *Atlas et géographie des Alpes françaises* (Genève, 1979).

Villard, M., 'Vaudois d'Apt au xvie siècle', *BCTHS*, Ann. 1965 (1966), 641–53.

Vinay, A., 'Lettre de Busca (Ides d'avril 1559)', *BSHV* 7 (1890), 43–60.

Vinay, G., 'Roghi e forche nella Savoia del secolo xv', *BSSV* 62 (1934), 82–5.

—— 'Il Valdismo alla viglia della riforma', *BSSV* 63 (1935), 65–9.

Vinay, V., 'Mémoires de Georges Morel', *BSSV* 132 (1972), 35–48.

—— 'Barba Morel e Bucero sulla giustificazione per fede', *BSSV* 133 (1973), 29–36.

—— 'La Dichiarazione del sinodo di Chanforan 1532', *BSSV* 133 (1973), 37–42.

—— 'Il Breve Dialogo fra prima e seconda riforma', *BSSV* 136 (1974), 99–115.

—— *Le Confessioni di fede dei Valdesi riformati* (Torino, 1975).

Viora, M., 'Le Persecuzioni contro i valdesi nel secolo xv^o; la crociata di Filippo II', *BSHV* 47 (1925), 5–19.

Weitzecker, G., 'Processo di un Valdese nell'anno 1451', *Rivista Cristiana*, 9 (1881), 363–7.

Wendel, F., *Calvin* (London, 1963).

Williams, G. H., *The Radical Reformation* (London, 1962).

—— 'Camillo Renato (c. 1500–?1575)', Tedeschi, ed., *Italian Reformation Studies*, q.v., pp. 103–83.

Index